RODERICK BEATON

Greece

Biography of a Modern Nation

PENGUIN BOOKS

PENGUIN BOOKS

UK | USA | Canada | Ireland | Australia
India | New Zealand | South Africa

Penguin Books is part of the Penguin Random House group of companies
whose addresses can be found at global.penguinrandomhouse.com

First published by Allen Lane 2019
Published in Penguin Books 2020

002

Copyright © Roderick Beaton, 2019

The moral right of the author has been asserted

Typeset by Jouve (UK), Milton Keynes
Printed and bound in Great Britain by Clays Ltd, Elcograf S.p.A.

A CIP catalogue record for this book is available from the British Library

ISBN: 978-0-141-98652-4

In loving memory of my parents, who first introduced me to Greece, and supported me as I went on to discover more and more wonders of the Greek world

Janet Mary Beaton
24 July 1922–15 April 2018

Duncan MacGillivray Beaton
13 September 1922–7 April 2018

Αἰωνία ἡ μνήμη

Τα μάτια μου δεν είδαν τόπον ενδοξότερον από τούτο το αλωνάκι.

My eyes have seen no land more glorious than this small threshing-floor.

Dionysios Solomos, *The Free Besieged* (1826–9)

Those principles which are now in action in Greece will gradually produce their effect, both here and in other countries . . . I cannot . . . calculate to what a height Greece may rise. Hitherto it has been a subject for the hymns and elegies of fanatics and enthusiasts; but now it will draw the attention of the politician.

Lord Byron, speaking at Missolonghi, Greece (1824)

A nation? says Bloom. A nation is the same people living in the same place . . . Or also living in different places.

James Joyce, *Ulysses* (1922)

A people that has within it a spirit, when it reaches the final depth of despair, finds the strength to react against itself. It reacts suddenly without any warning and without at all preparing the ground . . . The time is ripe for bold pioneers.

Giorgos Theotokas, *Free Spirit* (1929)

Contents

List of Illustrations and
Photographic Acknowledgements

Every effort has been made to contact all copyright holders. The publishers will be happy to correct any errors or omissions brought to their attention in future editions of this book.

1. Ali Tepedelenli, Pasha of Yanya [Ioannina], known as Ali Pasha. Illustration from Thomas Smart Hughes, *Travels in Sicily, Greece & Albania* (London, 1820). (*Getty Research Institute*)
2. Rigas Velestinlis, also called Pheraios. (*National Historical Museum, Athens*)
3. The tricolour banner of Rigas's Hellenic Republic, 1807. (*Library of the Romanian Academy of Sciences (Ms. Gr. 928, f.275v))*
4. Adamantios Korais (Coray). (*National Historical Museum, Athens*)
5. *Karaiskakis' trophy from Arachova.* Watercolour by Athanasios Iatridis, 1827. Benaki Museum, Athens. (*Bridgeman Images*)
6. Theodoros Kolokotronis. Pencil sketch by Karl Krazeisen, 14 May 1827. (*National Gallery-Alexandros Soutzos Museum, Department of Prints and Drawings, Athens*)
7. Count Ioannis Kapodistrias. Oil painting by Sir Thomas Lawrence, 1818–19. Royal Collection Trust. (*Copyright © Her Majesty Queen Elizabeth II, 2018/Bridgeman Images*)
8. *Entry of King Otto of Greece into Nauplia on 6 February 1833* (detail). Oil painting by Peter von Hess, 1835. Neue Pinakothek, Munich. (*Copyright © Blauel Gnamm/Artothek*)

List of Maps

Names, Dates and Titles

Greek names can be difficult for non-Greeks to pronounce. The problem is compounded because there is no agreed system for representing the sounds of the modern Greek language in the Latin alphabet. Letter-for-letter equivalence worked in antiquity. But since then the pronunciation of Greek has changed, over a period of time when English did not even exist. Rather than trying to reproduce roughly the sounds of the language on the page, I have tried so far as practicable to stay close to the Greek spelling, while avoiding forms that look excessively strange in English.

By applying a few simple rules, you can usually recreate the correct pronunciation of Greek names as they appear in this book:

'ai', 'e' = 'e' (as in 'yet')
'ch' (as in 'loch')
'd' = 'th' (as in 'that' not 'thatch')
'ei', 'i', 'oi', 'y' = 'ee' (as in 'meet')
'g' before 'a', 'o' or 'ou' = 'gh' (like the hard 'g' in Spanish or Dutch)
'g' before 'e' or 'i' = 'y' (as in 'yield')

Position of the stress accent is important too. This is often not predictable, and in written Greek is indicated by an acute accent. To avoid a cluttered appearance I have added these only in the Index, to which the reader may refer for guidance.

Obvious exceptions are those Greek names that have long-established equivalents in English: 'Athens' (not 'Athina'), 'Salonica' (not 'Thessaloniki'), 'Pericles' (not 'Periklis'). Another long-standing convention, followed here, is to represent Greek royal names by their English equivalents: 'George' and 'Constantine', not 'Georgios' and

'Konstantinos'. Older histories often anglicize other given names too: 'John Metaxas', 'George Papandreou'. All these, following more recent custom, I have restored to their Greek forms: 'Ioannis' and 'Georgios' respectively.

Until 1 March 1923 the Orthodox Church and the Greek state continued to use the older, Julian calendar (named after Julius Caesar) while most Western states had adopted the Gregorian calendar (named after Pope Gregory XIII, who introduced it in 1582). Julian dates, commonly referred to as 'Old Style', in the nineteenth century fell twelve days earlier than the equivalent Gregorian ('New Style') dates, and thirteen days earlier in the twentieth century. So in Athens, Christmas Day in the nineteenth century would be celebrated on the equivalent of 6 January. In the twentieth century, up to and including 1922, the equivalent date would be 7 January. Histories written in Greek still regularly use 'Old Style' dates for the period when these were in use, a potential source of confusion. In this book, all dates in the main text are given according to the Western, Gregorian, or 'New Style' calendar. (In the notes, dates of documents follow the source cited, and if in Greek they can be assumed to be 'Old Style'.) Where the 'Old Style' date is significant, or frequently cited, I have alerted the reader to the difference – as in the conventional date for the start of the Greek Revolution in 1821: 25 March, which in western Europe fell on 6 April.

No small part in this story is played by diplomats, particularly British ones. Before the Second World War, only the most illustrious foreign missions were granted the title 'embassies' by the Foreign Office, headed by 'ambassadors'. Until then, Great Britain was represented in Athens by a 'Legation' headed by a 'Minister', strictly speaking a 'Minister Plenipotentiary'. In the text and notes that follow I use the terminology of the period. There is no difference in role between a 'Minister', in this sense, and an 'ambassador'.

To *the* Reader

I started work on this book in August 2015. Only a month before, Greece had for the third time narrowly avoided a chaotic exit from the Eurozone, with potentially incalculable knock-on effects elsewhere. By the time I had finished it, my own country had embarked on its own exit from the European Union. 'Grexit' had been all but forgotten, while during 2016 'Brexit' was reported to have become the most frequently used new word in British English. But 'Grexit' came first. The Greeks had been the first to face that existential choice. And they had come through to the other side. Greeks in modern times have often been the pioneers – that is one of the arguments of this book.

Writing it, I was always conscious of doing so at a particular historical moment – little more than the blink of an eye between a 'Grexit' that didn't happen and a 'Brexit' whose consequences remain to be seen. That moment is the 'now', or 'today', that often features in the pages that follow. But the genesis and the real heart of this book go back much further.

I have been engaging with Greece and the Greek-speaking world all my adult life – from student days in the shadow of military dictatorship, running the gauntlet of tanks and rooftop snipers in the streets of Athens in the 1970s, all the way to the lecture halls and seminar rooms of King's College London, where I served as Koraes Professor of Modern Greek and Byzantine History, Language and Literature for exactly three decades until the summer of 2018. As a teacher no less than as a student, I have constantly been learning – from peers, colleagues, and particularly from cohorts of students, many of them Greeks themselves. From them I have learned to appreciate a multitude of different perspectives that have contributed to my own changing and deepening understanding of Greece, and of what it means to be Greek in the modern world.

What has fascinated me so deeply and for so long is not so much the story of the Greek *state* – dramatic and sometimes heart-rending as that story can be – but rather the interplay between the solid historical facts of state-building and the more nebulous complex of ideas, attitudes and aspirations that go to make up the shared consciousness of a *nation*. In order to discover what makes a nation, we have to look farther than to the headline facts of history, beyond the actions and words of leaders, or the graphs and statistics that can capture human activity across groups and populations. The story of a nation must also be the story of how people have thought about themselves, and the world, and their place in it.

This is why I have chosen to call the story told in this book a 'biography' rather than a 'history'. A biography requires long and deep acquaintance with the subject, but also a certain distance. Usually, you don't write the biography of someone you are close to, or a member of your own family. I have no family connection to Greece or Greeks. I write as an outsider, and the distance that that implies has helped to shape this particular way of telling the story. But I do not claim to write dispassionately. I believe – indeed with passion – that Greece and the modern history of the Greek nation *matter*, far beyond the bounds of the worldwide Greek community. If I have done my work at all adequately, by the time you have finished this book you will understand why, and will decide for yourself whether I am right.

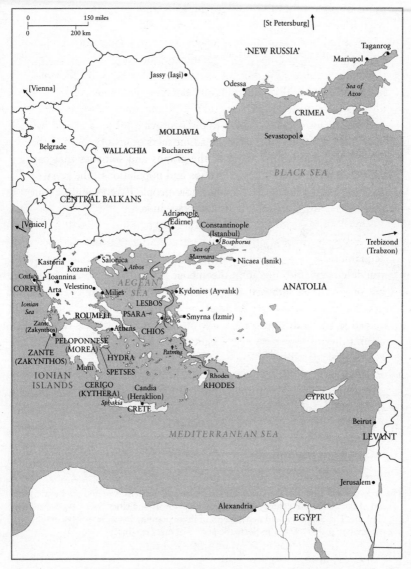

The 'Orthodox commonwealth' in the late eighteenth century, showing centres of Greek population and education, with present-day national frontiers superimposed

The geographical extent of the Greek nation in Europe, western Asia and the Levant at the end of the nineteenth century, showing regions, towns and cities with Greek-speaking populations. The definition and percentages of these populations were highly contentious at the time (see p. 161). Dates indicate the period of mass exodus.

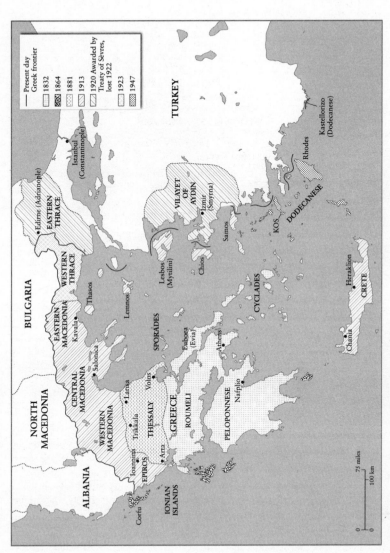

The expansion of the Greek state (1832–1947)

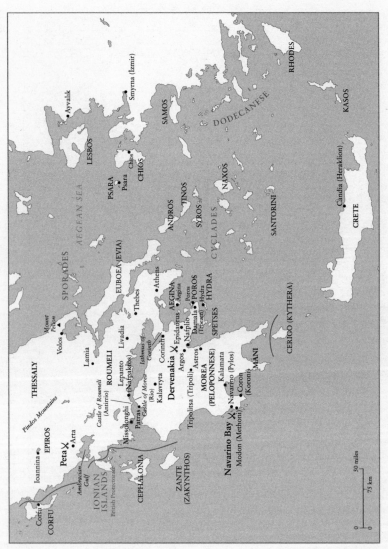

Main sites involved in the Greek Revolution of the 1820s

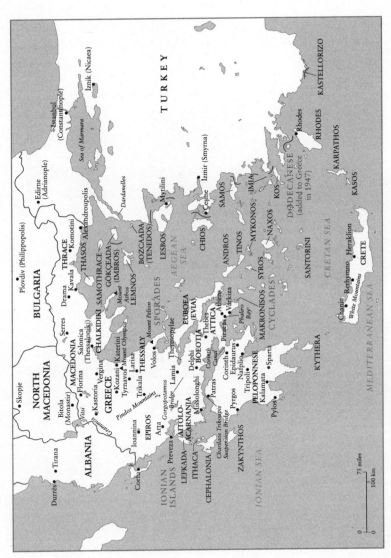

Greece and immediate neighbours since 1923

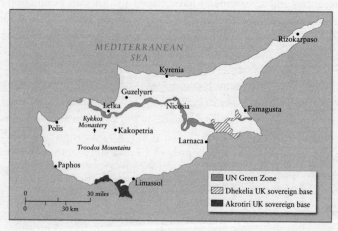

Cyprus, divided since 1974

Introduction

The Nation and its Ancestors

Who are the Greeks? What shared experiences, collective memories, aspirations and achievements have shaped a worldwide population of some fifteen million people today? Most of these live in the southeast corner of Europe in two member states of the European Union, Greece and Cyprus, while communities can also be found in all the earth's inhabited continents and are known as the 'Greek diaspora'.

There have been many books asking the question, who *were* the Greeks? That is a question that has preoccupied western European thinkers ever since the Renaissance, when scholars and travellers began to rediscover the literary, philosophical, political and scientific achievements of the civilization that had flourished in the same corner of Europe between three thousand and two thousand years ago. It is an important question, because just about everything that defines 'European' or 'Western' culture today, in the arts, sciences, social sciences and politics, has been built upon foundations laid down by the makers of that ancient civilization, whom we also know as 'Greeks'.

Those long-dead Greeks play a part in this story too, but it is not *their* story. This book begins and ends with the Greek people of today. It explores the ways in which today's Greeks have become who they are, the dilemmas they and generations before them have faced, and the choices that have shaped them subsequently. Above all, this book is about the evolving process of collective *identity*. In the case of Greeks over the last two centuries, it makes sense to call that identity a *national* one, since this has been the period that witnessed the creation and consolidation of the Greek nation state. So let us begin with the nation.

Opinions are divided on just what constitutes a nation. Since the late twentieth century an influential trend in historical thinking has redefined the nation as by definition a modern phenomenon, a product of the eighteenth-century Enlightenment and the Industrial Revolution. According to this view, you cannot have a nation without modern ideas of the self-governing state in which most of its citizens voluntarily participate. Others have revived the older counter-argument: that communities based upon more or less 'ethnic' lines have always existed in human society – in which case, why should not these, too, be called nations?

The case of the Greek nation polarizes opinion even more than most. According to the first definition, the Greek nation as we know it today, based upon a geographical homeland, shared institutions and participatory democracy, was brought into being by a revolution against the rule of the Ottoman Turks in the 1820s. On the other hand, the Greek language enjoys a continuous recorded history that can be traced back in the geographical area of today's Greece for more than three thousand years. Is not the story of the Greek nation, then, every bit as old?

Either perspective is valid. But the story I have set out to tell in this book is the story of Greece as a *modern* nation. I have chosen, there-fore, to understand the term in its narrower, more rigorous sense, and so to begin the narrative with the century that led up to that nation's birth.

Another choice has been to imagine this modern nation as though it were a living person, the subject of a biography. The life of a nation and the lives of individuals present fascinating, perhaps even illumin-ating, analogies – notably the ideas that bind a nation together are more often than not themselves based on organic metaphors. Let us then suspend disbelief and concede – hypothetically, experimentally – that the Greek nation 'born' out of revolution in the 1820s shares some of the characteristics of a human subject. We can trace the his-tory of that subject just as a biography teases out the life and career of an individual.

A nation, just like an individual, has distant ancestors and a more immediately traceable genealogy, or family tree. In the life of nations, Greece, born in this sense in the early nineteenth century, must be considered still a youngster. And there is one characteristic of biography, as a genre, that in this case we can happily escape. A nation in the fullness of time may evolve into something else, but there is no reason to expect the story to end in death. All will surely agree on this in the case of Greece. No obituary is to be expected. The biographer is spared the dubious benefit of looking back on a life complete and ended. Think of this book, in this respect at least, as more like a 'celebrity' biography that leaves its subject still in the prime of life and fame. The story does not end with the end of the book.

But first, we need to begin at the beginning, with ancestors, and the complex inheritance that issues from them.

ANCESTORS: ANCIENT HELLENES AND MEDIEVAL ROMANS

None of us knows who our most distant ancestors were. If all modern humans are descended from groups that began to migrate out of Africa more than fifty thousand years ago, then the Greeks must be no exception. Future advances in genetics may reveal to what extent those who speak the Greek language today share genetic material with the builders of the 'classical' civilization of antiquity. In terms of understanding the history of the Greeks in modern times, it really doesn't matter. History on the scale of a few millennia is shaped by such things as environment, actions, events and ideas, not evolutionary biology. What is at stake here is not the literal, biological ancestry of the individuals who make up a population – even if those are the terms in which it is most often expressed – but rather the 'ancestry', in a partly metaphorical sense, of a nation, a state or that complex phenomenon that we call a culture. It is doubtful whether ancient Greek civilization can properly be called a nation, and it certainly was never a state. Nevertheless, Greeks experience a *sense* of kinship with those they call 'our ancient ancestors'. The phrase has become something of a cliché in recent decades, and is widely acknowledged as such. Even so, it sums up a great deal of what continues to define the Greek nation in the modern world.

This sense of kinship was articulated in its most nuanced form by the poet George Seferis, in his speech accepting the Nobel Prize for

Literature in 1963: 'I do not say that we are of the same blood [as the ancient Greeks] – because I have a horror of racial theories – but we still live in the same country and we see the same mountains ending in the sea.'[1] Seferis also laid stress on the continuity of language: the words for 'light of the sun', he pointed out, are almost unchanged from the equivalent words used by Homer almost three thousand years ago. Like most of his generation, Seferis had experienced the horrors unleashed upon the world by the racist dogma of the Nazis in the 1930s and 1940s. It is an *affinity* that he asserts, based upon landscape and the language in which humans have engaged with it over time – an affinity deeply felt, but not a dogma, and not built upon genetic assumptions.

It is not only Greeks who share this perception. How often in the years following the financial crisis that began in 2010 have the cartoonists of the world's media drawn upon classical stereotypes and images in order to give visual expression to the sorry state of a once-great civilization? Images of ancient temples with their gleaming marble riven with cracks, of a euro coin as a badly thrown discus causing havoc, have gained a place in the popular imagination in countries far removed from Greece, often with an edge that is critical, if not downright hostile. Among Greeks themselves, it is the same sense of affinity that lends such passion to calls for the return of the 'Elgin Marbles', or Sculptures of the Parthenon, removed from the Acropolis of Athens by Lord Elgin in the first years of the nineteenth century and since 1817 exhibited in the British Museum in London. These creations by craftsmen of extraordinary skill and imagination who have been dead for two and a half millennia have come to be imagined in their turn, in the memorable words of the film star and popular singer, and later Minister of Culture, Melina Mercouri, as 'our pride ... our aspirations and our *name* ... the essence of Greekness'.[2]

This is not something that can be denied, or simply wished away. Some have argued that the gene pool of the ancient Greeks cannot possibly have survived successive migrations and invasions over the centuries. Others dismiss an obsession with ancestors as a way of avoiding the facts of history. But this is to miss the point. We are talking about a *sense* of kinship, a perception, not a set of facts that can be objectively verified. The sense of affinity with the ancients is itself a historical fact, to be understood and explained. How it came to exist at all, and then to exercise such an enduring hold, is an essential part of the story of how Greece became modern, which is the story of this book.

So used are we, today, to thinking of 'modern Greece' as an offshoot of ancient Greece, it can be hard to realize that for many of the centuries separating classical antiquity from ourselves no such sense of affinity existed among Greek speakers. The people we call 'ancient Greeks' did not call themselves that. The names 'Greek' and 'Greece' derive from Latin: *Graecus* and *Graecia*. It was the Romans, as they conquered most of 'Graecia' in the second century BCE, who made these names famous. Ancient Greeks called themselves 'Hellenes' – the word is almost identical in English and Greek. The lands where Hellenes lived were collectively called Hellas. The same names, in their modern form, are standard in Greek today: the people are *Ellines* (with the stress on the first syllable), the country is either *Ellas* (the older form) or *Ellada*. So what has changed?

The answer is: a great deal. By the fourth century CE, those populations of the eastern Mediterranean hinterlands that spoke and wrote in Greek had been living for hundreds of years under the rule of Rome. When Christianity was adopted as the official religion of the Roman Empire during that century, the use of the term 'Hellenes' in Greek came to be reserved for those Greeks who had died too soon to benefit from the new religion, and could therefore not help being pagans. Before long, and by extension, 'Hellene' came to mean just 'pagan', that is, anyone who was not a Christian. Throughout the Christian Middle Ages, that remained the primary meaning of the word in Greek. With the spread of secular ideas in the eighteenth century, 'Hellene' became predominantly an antiquarian term: the 'Hellenes' were the *ancient* Greeks, whereas living speakers of the Greek language had centuries ago found a different name for themselves. It was a conscious choice, taken during the First National Assembly of the Provisional Greek Government in January 1822, to revive the ancient names: 'Hellenes' for the citizens of the new state that was then fighting for its independence, 'Hellas' for the state itself.[3]

In the same way, the drachma, to which it is often supposed that Greece would return if the country were to leave the Eurozone, is often called 'the world's oldest currency'. The name is as old as you could wish for – but for approximately seventeen centuries before its re-introduction in 1833, not a single drachma had ever been minted. To take another example, Athens in antiquity had fought its way to pre-eminence among the rival Greek city states; the ruined classical temples on the Acropolis at its centre have for long been iconically synonymous with Greece itself. It is an easy assumption to suppose that Athens has always been the capital city. In fact, it became the capital for the first time on 13 December 1834.

Names, too – place names and personal names – often seem to imply a closer kinship than historically exists. Look at any map of Greece, and at least half the names of towns and geographical features can also be found in ancient sources. But many of these were deliberately revived, after independence, to replace the customary names that had been in use for centuries, and which still appear on older maps and in travellers' accounts. On the Gulf of Corinth, for instance, the hard-to-pronounce 'Aigio' has replaced 'Vostitsa' that Lord Byron visited and where a famous conclave of revolutionary leaders took place in 1821. 'Troezene', the birthplace of Theseus in mythology, returned in the 1820s to oust the long-familiar 'Damala', where a medieval French barony had once had its seat. *Old* names have been replaced by *ancient* ones, replacing one history with another. Or take personal names. For a millennium and a half all children of Greek Orthodox parents had been baptized with the names of saints in the Church calendar. It was not until the 1790s that these names came to be paired, or replaced altogether, with the names of famous pagans from antiquity. A Greek today can be called Odysseus or Socrates or Euclid, Penelope or Calliope, and one might suppose these names had run in families ever since ancient times. Not so. This is something else about ancestors: you can pick and choose.

To acknowledge these facts is not, of course, to diminish the immense significance that these ancestors have come to assume in defining Greek collective identity over the last two centuries. Only when you realize the full extent of the choices made by hundreds and thousands of Greeks during those years does the scale of the achievement become apparent. It was a conscious and, it would seem, a little-contested policy choice, beginning around 1800, to *reassert* kinship with the lost civilization of classical antiquity. It has also been a highly selective one. Think of all those ancient practices that have been entirely airbrushed out: nudity, pederasty, slavery, submission of women, infanticide, paganism, animal sacrifice.

And, as a policy, it has been overwhelmingly successful – as those cartoons of discus-euros and cracked marble columns sadly testify all too well.

It can be difficult enough to live with one famous ancestor. The Greek nation has not one, but two. The second of these has never enjoyed the prestige of the first, at least in western Europe. On the other hand, it is less remote, both in time and perhaps also in the affections of many Greeks. This is the civilization that has been known since the nineteenth century by the label 'Byzantine' – yet another problematic term, since the 'Byzantines' never called themselves that, and among English speakers there is not even agreement on how the word should be pronounced. The Byzantine Empire is usually said to have begun when the Roman emperor Constantine renamed the city of Byzantium, on the European side of the Bosphorus facing Asia, after himself: Constantinople (today's Istanbul, the largest city in Turkey). This was in the year 330 and coincides with the adoption of Christianity. For more than a thousand years after that, Constantine's successors ruled, from the capital city that he had founded, over a Christian empire whose official language and sole medium of education soon became Greek. This is how Greek speakers came to lose their attachment to the old name of 'Hellenes', preferring instead to define themselves simply as 'Romans' (*Romaioi*, later *Romioi*, pronounced *Romyí*) – because politically the empire to which they belonged was the continuation of the Roman Empire in the east. They kept this name even after their empire came to an end in 1453 and Constantinople became, instead, the capital of the Ottoman Turks. For the same reason the modern Greek language was until the early nineteenth century known not as 'Greek' but as 'Romaic'. For a millennium and a half, those whom westerners called 'Greeks' were accustomed to define themselves as 'Romans'.

Throughout much of that time Constantinople was the largest and most prosperous city in Europe, if not the entire world. At its greatest extent the empire reached from North Africa and Italy in the west to the borders of Persia in the east. With the brief exception of Alexander the Great in the fourth century BCE, no Greek speaker had ever ruled over such wide dominions or so many subjects, or would again. Byzantine civilization is often portrayed as intensely spiritual, even ascetic. It is true that its surviving literature, architecture and art are overwhelmingly religious in purpose. But the Byzantines, or at least their elite, enjoyed high standards of literacy and secular education. They were meticulous scholars and sophisticated readers of ancient Greek drama, poetry, philosophy and history. Indeed, it was thanks to Byzantine librarians, copyists and men (and some women) of learning that all of the literature and much of the science of Greek antiquity that we know today came to be preserved, and in due course transmitted to western Europe from the fourteenth century onwards. The Byzantines gloried in the possession of wealth and power such as few who spoke Greek had ever possessed before or have since.

These were all good reasons for Byzantium to exert a strong pull of attraction for the Greek imagination during the centuries after the empire's final destruction in 1453. Another is the institutional continuity of the Orthodox Church, which continued to function without a break through the centuries of Ottoman Turkish rule that followed. By contrast, no *institution* that began in classical times has a similarly continuous existence. The modern supreme court perpetuates the name of the court of justice in ancient Athens, the Areopagus – but only since 1844. Drama, one of the greatest cultural legacies of the ancient Greeks, has never been more alive than it is today, and revivals of Greek tragedies and comedies thrill audiences in London and other major cities. But there is no continuous history of performance, neither in Greece nor anywhere else.

When national institutions were being set up, beginning in the 1820s and 1830s, the models could perfectly well have been drawn from the eastern Roman Empire, and backed by a religious tradition shared by most Greek speakers at the time. Instead, it was only later that Byzantium began to emerge as a role model for the modern nation state to emulate. That was another choice that had defining consequences. Byzantium had to wait until the second half of the nineteenth century to come into its own, as the second most illustrious ancestor after the ancients.

DESCENDANTS: WESTERN HELLENES OR EASTERN *ROMIOI*?

For at least a century and a half these two illustrious ancestors, the ancient and the Byzantine, have jostled uneasily together in the national imagining. There have been various attempts made at a precarious synthesis, sometimes called 'Helleno-Christian civilization'. But that terminology was hijacked by the military junta of the late 1960s and early 1970s and ever since has been tarnished beyond use. Ancient Greece and Byzantium were two civilizations so different from one another that it is hard even to think of them at the same time.

The consequence of looking back simultaneously towards two such different ancestors has been a remarkable doubling, or perhaps better a splitting, of identity. The modern language has not one but two words to describe a person as 'Greek': 'Hellene' and *'Romios'* (*Romioi* in the plural). When it comes to translation, both have the same meaning. But they are not interchangeable. 'Hellene' (*Ellinas*) is the standard term. Ever since 1822 it has been used in all official contexts. Indeed the official name for the Greek state in English is the 'Hellenic Republic'. *'Romios'*, on the other hand, appears on no passport or official document. Increasingly, since the early nineteenth century, it has become the *unofficial*, more intimate way for Greeks to refer to themselves – and, more often than not, *among* themselves too. 'Hellene' is the outward-facing term, it defines the Greek for the outsider. *'Romios'* carries an emotional weight. The poet Kostis Palamas, writing at the beginning of the twentieth century, detected in the very word 'something poetically and musically charged', 'something soaring, that fills us with youthful vigour, something ethereal even'.[4] This is an understanding tacitly shared and appreciated by *insiders*. It is nobody else's business. When Melina Mercouri, in the days before she became Minister of Culture in a socialist government, was stripped of her Greek citizenship by the military junta, she recorded in song her scorn for the petty bureaucrats who had dared to make out 'that I'm no longer a *Romia*'. The point of the song-lyric is that citizenship may be conferred or taken away, but one's identity as a *Romia* or *Romios* is inalienable. It exists beyond a threshold where officialdom has any right to interfere or can even reach.

It has sometimes been suggested that each of these overlapping but distinct identities, as 'Hellene' and '*Romios*', can be mapped onto cultural traits or patterns of behaviour. So when Greeks think of themselves as 'Hellenes', they are apt to have in mind elites and official culture, to identify with Western Europe in their politics and cultural preferences (admiring classical music, for example), to embrace a secular outlook and rational ways of thinking. When they think of themselves as '*Romioi*', on the other hand, they do so in order to emphasize intimacy and informality, to identify with traditional forms of culture linked more immediately to the Balkans and the Middle East (admiring *rebetika*, for example, a musical style with its roots in the traditions of the Levant), to embrace a religious outlook, spontaneity and emotional ways of thinking.[5]

It is not that individuals can be pigeon-holed as belonging to one category or the other. Rather, *both* identities are experienced by the same individual, perhaps in different but rarely in fixed proportions. It is no accident that Melina Mercouri has been mentioned twice in this Introduction: once as the charismatic champion of the return of the 'Elgin Marbles' to Greece, a quintessentially 'Hellenic' choice, and once as the gutsy proponent of a 'Romaic' identity that contemptuously defies the bureaucratic categories of the Western mindset.

As these examples have already begun to show, the duality between ancient and Byzantine ancestors encourages, or reflects, a far deeper duality of thought and perception. Does Greece (do Greeks) belong to the East or to the West? The actual geographical space in which the two ancestor civilizations flourished was not so very different. But in geopolitical terms we always think of ancient Greece as belonging to the West. No doubt this is because of its influence on Rome and then, much later, on the Renaissance. Byzantium, on the other hand, was always the *eastern* half of the Roman Empire. Constantinople was (and is) the pre-eminent centre of the *eastern* Orthodox Church, from which the western Catholic Church split off in 1054. To identify with Byzantium is to identify with an Orthodox tradition that today is shared predominantly with Russia, with most but not all of the Balkan states, as well as with Moldova, Ukraine and Georgia.

Samuel Huntington, in his influential book *The Clash of Civilizations and the Remaking of the World Order*, published in 1996, noted the paradox: 'Greece is not part of Western civilization, but it was the home of Classical civilization which was an important source of Western civilization.'[6] In fact, Greece *is* part of Western civilization, for the very simple reason that over the last two hundred years Greeks have determined that it should be. But as the double inheritance from its ancestors shows, Greece does not belong *only* to the West. It belongs also to the East. This is part of the same duality and is not reducible to a single proposition. It is not 'either/or', but 'both/and'.

It is quite true, as the author of an insightful introduction to the subject summed it up in 2015, partly in response to Huntington, that in its two-hundred-year history as a nation state, 'Greece never seriously considered abandoning the West'.[7] Every lasting political decision, just about every official action and every democratic choice made since the 1820s, has affirmed the westward alignment of Greece – and in the fullness of time also of the Republic of Cyprus. But we should not overlook the cost of this repeated affirmation. More often than not, the argument has been won only after internal conflict and by the narrowest of margins. During the 1820s and again in the 1940s, Greeks killed one another in civil wars that were fundamentally about this issue. Scars such as that are not easily healed.

During the Balkan wars of the 1990s, when the former Yugoslavia fragmented along the lines of its pre-communist religious divisions, Greek public opinion sided overwhelmingly with the Orthodox Serbs. Sometimes official government policy did too, in a rare break from solidarity with the West. Then as recently as the spring and early summer of 2015 the government of the Coalition of the Radical Left (known in Greek as SYRIZA), led by Alexis Tsipras, seriously considered an alternative alignment with Vladimir Putin's Russia, if Greece had been unable to remain within the Eurozone. If the nation has always ended up aligned (more or less) with the West, it has never done so unanimously or without tremendous cost, as these instances illustrate. The story of the ancestors reveals why this should be. When circumstances have forced a binary choice, either answer is bound to ride roughshod over a sizeable portion of the nation's deepest allegiances.

Given this history, it would be unwise to assume that the decision must always go the same way in the future.

FAMILY TREE

Distant ancestors are important as role models, points of reference against which to measure up. In addition, a nation, just like an individual, can trace its origin back through the equivalent of a family tree. There is a genealogy that can be reconstructed through the 'hidden centuries', as one recent historian has called them, separating the collapse of the Byzantine Empire from the first stirrings that would lead to the formation of the Greek nation state.[8]

Continuity through those centuries was provided by the Greek language, both in speech and as a medium of education, and by the Orthodox Church. Those two essential ingredients of a modern nation were already in place, with a long tradition behind them, before the eighteenth century. But what about the political and cultural systems under which Greek-speaking Orthodox Christians lived during those centuries? There were several different ones, and the part played by Greek speakers in each of them was different.

The Byzantine Empire continued to exist until 1453. But its collapse had begun two and a half centuries earlier. The decisive blow that shattered the political unity of the Greek-speaking Christian world of Byzantium came not from the East, or from Islam, but from the Catholic West. In 1204 the knights of the Fourth Crusade, strapped for the cash they needed to reach the Holy Land, turned aside from their objective and ended up attacking Constantinople instead. In the name of a holy war, the richest and most populous city of medieval Christendom was sacked by Christians. In the words of Steven Runciman, author of a classic history of the Crusades, 'There was never a greater crime against humanity than the Fourth Crusade.'[9] Eight hundred years after the event, in June 2004, Pope John

Paul II delivered a historic apology for the event to his counterpart, Patriarch Bartholomew of the Orthodox Church.

The Byzantines would regroup and recapture their capital in 1261. But what had been broken could not be mended. From 1204 onwards, Greek-speaking Orthodox Christians had to get used to living in a fragmented world, ruled over by masters who were usually in deadly competition with one another. Some Greek speakers remained the subjects of the Byzantine emperor or his local vassals, who were Orthodox for as long as they lasted. Others came under French or Italian jurisdictions, which were Roman Catholic. More and more of them, as time went on, came to be absorbed by conquest into the ever-expanding Muslim empire of the Ottoman Turks.

In Constantinople and a steadily decreasing amount of its hinterland, from 1261 to 1453, there was the 'rump' state of Byzantium itself. Isolated dependencies also existed for different periods of time: to the west the 'Despotate of Epiros' (the northwestern part of today's Greece), to the south the 'Despotate of the Morea' (the medieval and later name for the Peloponnese), and to the east the 'empire of Trebizond' on the southern shore of the Black Sea, which lasted the longest, until 1461. During the fourteenth and fifteenth centuries these last Byzantine outposts, including the capital, Constantinople, were no more than city states, and by this time less powerful or wealthy than the great Italian maritime city states of Venice and Genoa with which they had to compete.

Elsewhere, the descendants and successors of the Crusaders ruled. In the Peloponnese, until the Byzantines temporarily recaptured it, an independent state flourished for more than a hundred years in the thirteenth and early fourteenth centuries, under the sway of a colonizing French nobility. Far to the east, the island of Cyprus with its Greek-speaking Orthodox population had come into the possession of Crusaders even before 1204. There the French Lusignan dynasty ruled over the 'Kingdom of Cyprus and Jerusalem' down to 1489, when control passed to Venice for almost a century until the Ottoman conquest of 1571. The Venetians also held Crete from 1211 to 1669 and kept control of the Ionian islands, to the west of the Greek mainland, until the end of the Venetian Republic in 1797.

Crete under the Venetians, especially during the sixteenth and early seventeenth centuries, saw an extraordinary flourishing of the arts. A distinctive school of religious painting emerged. Plays and poems were written in the contemporary Cretan dialect of Greek; performances took place in the main towns. In these works the spirit of the Italian Renaissance met the local vernacular tradition – just as was happening in the plays of Shakespeare and his contemporaries in England at exactly the same time. Venetian Crete gave the world the painter Dominikos Theotokopoulos, better known in the West as El Greco. Candia (the modern Heraklion), capital of Crete, was as civilized a city as any in Europe in the early seventeenth century. Cretan aristocrats, merchants and artisans identified with their island and with its composite Greek and Italian way of life.

Lastly, there was the Ottoman Empire itself. Ottoman expansion across the Bosphorus into Europe had begun during the 1340s – ironically enough in the form of mercenaries recruited by one side against the other in a Byzantine dynastic war. By 1669 the vast majority of Greek speakers had become a subject people within the Ottoman Empire. As such they were excluded from many privileges allowed only to Muslims and liable to special taxes and prohibitions. But they were not systematically persecuted in the way that 'heretics' were in medieval and early modern Europe. The Ottomans never sought to impose uniformity on their subjects. Under the sultans, Orthodox Christians educated in the Greek language rose to become an aristocracy and an elite that would wield considerable power and influence within the Ottoman system – without thereby losing anything of their distinct religious identity.

These, then, are the political and cultural antecedents of the Greek nation state – its genealogy or 'family tree'. Just like any real family tree, this one includes its 'black sheep' – those whom later generations might rather prefer to forget. The legacy of Crusaders from the west, or of an Ottoman civilization imposed by conquest from the east, may not be much prized by most Greeks today, particularly when compared to the more distant glories of ancient Greece or Byzantium. But like it or not, these and other byways of late medieval and early modern history would play at least as large a part in the formation of the modern Greek nation. The story of how that came about begins in the early eighteenth century.

I

East Meets West?

1718–1797

The Greek nation state would be born out of a series of encounters between Christian Europe and the Ottoman Empire, from whose body it would literally be torn. These began during the period of relatively peaceful co-existence between these traditionally embattled adversaries.

Ottoman expansion into Europe had come to an end with the second siege of Vienna in 1683. However, peace did not break out immediately. The Austrians and the Venetians would each fight two more wars against the Ottomans, and the Russians one, before a relatively stable, defensible and more or less mutually agreed set of boundaries would be established to mark off Muslim Turkey from Christian Europe. These boundaries were consolidated by the Treaty of Passarowitz, signed between the Habsburgs and the Ottomans in July 1718.

To the west, the Adriatic and Ionian seas marked the limits of the Ottoman Empire. To the north, natural boundaries were formed by the river Danube, from Belgrade where its course turns eastwards, and then by the Black Sea into which it flows. On the European side of each of these three natural barriers lay three buffer zones, or borderlands. The first of these was formed by the seven Ionian islands to the west of the Greek peninsula, from Corfu in the north to Cerigo (ancient and modern Kythera) in the south. The second consisted of the principalities of Wallachia and Moldavia to the north of the Danube. The third was made up of the northern shores of the Black Sea and their hinterland. In each of these borderlands, Greek-speaking Orthodox Christians occupied elite positions and enjoyed the benefits of wealth and education. It was in these borderlands, too, that the first interactions between East and West took place.

BORDERLANDS

In the Ionian islands, Venetian rule had been established in the aftermath of the Fourth Crusade and was still continuing. In the eighteenth century, conditions there remained very much as they had been in Venetian Crete until the Ottoman conquest, completed in 1669. Indeed many Cretans of the upper classes, who had had a stake in the Renaissance-inspired culture of their native island, had since found refuge there. Almost everyone permanently settled in the islands by this time professed the Orthodox faith and spoke the local dialect of Greek in daily life. But the official language was Italian. Sons of the aristocracy were sent to be educated at schools and universities in Italy. In this way, Western ideas began to filter through to the better-off sections of society during the course of the century. This education was generally available only to the landed gentry, so it was not especially likely to lead to ideas of revolutionary change. The primary loyalties of educated Ionians during the eighteenth century were to their native island, to the Orthodox Church and to the Most Serene Republic of Venice.

The second borderland, the 'Danubian principalities' of Wallachia and Moldavia, today forms part of Romania. Here, there was no significant Greek-speaking *native* population. Most of the inhabitants were Orthodox Christians who spoke the Latin-derived language that we know today as Romanian and was then called 'Vlach' or 'Wallachian'. The Treaty of Passarowitz in 1718 confirmed Ottoman sovereignty, but not direct rule. Instead, the sultans appointed trusted proxies, 'princes' drawn from the wealthiest and most highly educated of their Orthodox Christian subjects established in Constantinople. This metropolitan elite was a kind of quasi-aristocracy that had grown up in the service of the Ecumenical Patriarchate of the Orthodox Church. For that reason its members became known collectively as 'Phanariots', from the name of the district of the city where the Patriarchate was (and indeed continues to be) housed. Irrespective of their mother tongue, all these people had been educated in the Greek language. In that sense the Phanariots could be thought of as 'Greek', even though in modern, 'ethnic' terms many were not.

Increasingly, from the late seventeenth century, this group came to be trusted with important offices of state in the Ottoman system, especially those involving a knowledge of languages and a high degree of education. In an age when expansion by military means had given way to the new art of diplomacy, there was a need for a suitably qualified corps of diplomats. Often given the title of *dragoman*, or 'interpreter', these versatile linguists who were also Orthodox Christians became increasingly embedded in the Ottoman system of governance through the course of the eighteenth century.

For a little over a hundred years, from 1711 until the outbreak of the Greek Revolution in 1821, with only brief interruptions during times of war, Moldavia and Wallachia would be ruled by a succession of Phanariot princes. Competition for these offices was intense, and reigns tended to be short. None of his successors would last as long as Nikolaos Mavrokordatos, who after a short period of office in Wallachia and another in Moldavia, settled down to eleven years of undisturbed rule in Bucharest, the capital of Wallachia, from 1719 until his death in 1730.

Just as the Greek-speaking aristocracy of the Ionian islands was continuously and unproblematically loyal to Venice, so the over-whelming majority of Phanariots throughout the eighteenth century identified with the Ottoman state. Indeed, such was the extent of their ascendancy, and so great the trust placed in them, that for Orthodox Christians the standard route to preferment within the Ottoman system, by the second half of the century, had become the Greek language and the educational institutions organized by wealthy Phanariots and the Orthodox Church.

The third borderland consisted of the Crimea and parts of today's Ukraine. This one does not enter the story until the beginning of the 1770s. From 1768 until 1774 the Russians and the Ottomans were at war. The Russians won, and as a result gained control of the coast and hinterland north of the Black Sea. The same conflict brought disruption to the Danubian principalities, which for the duration passed under Russian control, and devastation to the Peloponnese and some of the islands of the Aegean. At the end of 1769, for the first time, a Russian fleet from St Petersburg sailed via the Straits of Gibraltar into the eastern Mediterranean. A half-hearted attempt by the Russians to induce their Greek-speaking co-religionists to rise up in their support sparked rebellions in the Peloponnese and Crete. When the Russian fleet withdrew, these were easily crushed. The *Orlofika*, as these events are known in Greek (after the Russian admiral Count Orloff), are often remembered as a kind of proto-national revolution. But self-determination for the Christian inhabitants of the Peloponnese or the islands was never on the table. If the revolts had succeeded, and if the promised military support from Russia had materialized, the local populations would only have exchanged one foreign master for another.

A more significant consequence of the war was the way in which Russia, under Catherine the Great, chose to populate and administer the newly gained territories north of the Black Sea, which at this time came to be named 'New Russia'. Beginning around 1770, the Russian state embarked on an ambitious programme of resettling there the families of Orthodox Christians who had been displaced from their homes in the Ottoman Empire by the fighting. It is estimated that as many as a quarter of a million Ottoman Christians were encouraged to migrate to 'New Russia' during the last quarter of the eighteenth century.[1]

By the end of the century, a large proportion of the trade carried on in southern Russia, across the Black Sea and up the Dnieper river was in the hands of these Greek-speaking subjects of the tsars. Positions of responsibility in the Russian government and army were thrown open to talented members of this immigrant population. It was during the same period, and on Catherine's initiative, that the new towns of Mariupol and Sevastopol were established, with transparently Greek names. The port cities of Odessa on the Black Sea and Taganrog on the Sea of Azov grew up during the same period. Both had large Greek-speaking populations. Catherine and her ministers, during the 1780s, even drew up a grand plan that would have reestablished the Christian Orthodox Byzantine Empire with its capital at Constantinople. Had the plan succeeded, it would have left no room for an independent Greek nation state. But by 1792, at the end of yet another war with the Ottoman Empire, although Russian gains had been considerable, it was clear that the Ottoman capital was not for the taking. The plan was quietly abandoned.

Once again, as in the Danubian principalities, the Greek elite in the new territories of southern Russia were incomers from the Ottoman Empire. But this time they were not a *ruling* elite. Their newly acquired wealth and status derived from the entrepreneurial skills fostered by Catherine's policies. This was not an aristocracy but a middle class. In other respects, it functioned like its counterparts in the other two borderlands. This was a group that had every reason to owe its primary loyalty to the state that supported it and made its activities possible – that is to say, in this case, to Russia.

Finally, during the second half of the eighteenth century, a fourth 'borderland' would open up in which Greek-speaking Orthodox Christians could interact with western Europeans. This, unlike the previous three, was not a single space, and not literally situated near a frontier. Rather, it consisted of a series of local communities established by merchants and traders in ports and trading centres across the Christian continent: Venice, Vienna, Trieste, Livorno, Marseille, Paris, Amsterdam. (Others, further afield, would come later.) These scattered Greek-speaking communities were the pioneers of what would later become a worldwide Greek 'diaspora'.

This development, too, was very much a consequence of the Russo-Ottoman war of 1768–74, although it had begun even earlier. The treaty of Küçük Kaynarcı, which brought that war to an end, allowed new trading privileges to Ottoman Christian merchants, who were now entitled to some degree of nominal protection by Russia. But there was an important difference between the merchants newly settled in Russia and those who set up trading centres in the west. In 'New Russia' the Greek trading communities had been brought there and been helped to prosper as a result of a deliberate policy. In the west the same thing was happening quite spontaneously in many different centres. It follows that the communities in western Europe were apt to be politically more independent-minded than their counterparts in Russia – or, for that matter, than the aristocracy of the Ionian islands or the Phanariots in the Danubian principalities. Perhaps predictably, it would be among these communities of merchants in western Europe that the most active preparations for a revolution would come to be made – although not until the very last years of the century.

CROSSING BORDERS: PEOPLE, IDEAS, GOODS ON THE MOVE

These, then, were the four borderlands where interaction between Christian Europe and the Muslim empire of the Ottomans took place during the eighteenth century. In each of them, Orthodox Christians who spoke Greek occupied elite positions.

Individual members of these elites were extraordinarily mobile, and not only along the trajectories that might have been expected: Ionian islanders to and from Venice, Phanariots between the Danubian principalities and Constantinople, settlers and merchants between their new homes and their native provinces. A glance at the careers of some of the most famous of these men reveals a remarkable mobility, at a time when travel over long distances was invariably slow and uncomfortable, sometimes also hazardous. Take the case of Evgenios Voulgaris. Born into an aristocratic family in Corfu in 1716, Voulgaris went on to study, write and teach at Arta in Epiros, Venice, Ioannina, Kozani, the self-governing Orthodox monastic community of Mount Athos, Salonica, Constantinople, Jassy (capital of Moldavia) and the German city of Leipzig. From there, now under the patronage of Catherine the Great, Voulgaris went on to become one of the first Orthodox bishops to be consecrated in the 'New Russian' lands north of the Black Sea. His last years were spent at Catherine's court at St Petersburg, where he died at the age of ninety. In this way Voulgaris's restless progress encompassed in turn each of the three borderlands between Europe and the Ottoman Empire, as well as European centres such as Venice and Leipzig, the Ottoman capital itself and several of its provinces in southeast Europe.

The world through which people like Voulgaris moved in the eighteenth century has been characterized in the twenty-first century as an 'Orthodox commonwealth'.[2] That is to say, a sense of commonality was based on a shared religion and a shared education in the Greek language. This 'commonwealth' had no single geographical centre. Its heartland could be described as the southeastern corner of Europe, known today as the Balkans, but it was sustained by links deep into Russia in one direction and into Anatolia and parts of the

Middle East in the other. Under its umbrella came together a broad mix of peoples who would later go on to forge distinct and often competing national identities of their own: Serbs, Bulgarians, Romanians, Moldovans, Ukrainians and (some, but not all) Albanians, as well as Greeks. The collective identity of this 'commonwealth', loose though it was, was capable of transcending the different political loyalties of the different elites of the borderlands.

There are two transforming achievements associated with this commonwealth during the eighteenth century. One of these is the development of education, along with the circulation of printed books in modern Greek and the dissemination of secular learning adapted and translated from the West. The other is the expansion of trade. Both have been seen, from the perspective of later national history, as precursors that paved the way for the Revolution of the 1820s. But it is not as simple as that.

What has come to be known as the 'Greek Enlightenment' was essentially a process of dissemination of ideas eastwards and southwards from France, Britain and the German states, with gathering momentum during the second half of the century. Much of what was published, or circulated in manuscript, consisted of translations or adaptations, particularly of scientific and philosophical works. It is worth asking how enlightened *were* these 'enlighteners'. It is only in retrospect that they have acquired this name, since the 1940s. Most of them believed that the sun revolves around the earth, as their Church still taught. The first exposition of the physics of Galileo and Newton in Greek, ironically enough, and suitably hedged about, comes from a future bishop of the Russian new territories, Nikiphoros Theotokis, in a book published in Leipzig in 1766. It was not until very late in the century that anyone writing in Greek began to question the truth of revealed religion, or criticized the Church as an institution – and even then only rarely.[3] This was in marked contrast to the Enlightenment in France. Indeed, very many of these 'enlighteners' were themselves in some form of holy orders – unsurprisingly, since the great patron of these early advances in Greek education in the eighteenth century was the Orthodox Church itself. When it came to politics, some were reformers and many were interested in political theory. But none was in any sense a democrat, still less a revolutionary.

Exemplary, in many ways, for those who came later, was Nikolaos Mavrokordatos, whom we met earlier as one of the first, and the longest-reigning, among the Phanariot princes of Wallachia and Moldavia. His father had been educated abroad, in Italy; he himself was unusually little-travelled. Like his father, in addition to his native modern Greek, Nikolaos was proficient in ancient Greek, Latin, Italian, French, Ottoman Turkish, Arabic and Persian. To these, late in his life, he added Hebrew. As a ruler he introduced to southeast Europe the model of the 'enlightened despot', overhauling the ancient feudal system and encouraging the foundation of schools. Mavrokordatos was truly a philosopher-prince. Among his surviving works are a book of maxims, written in response to the more famous ones by the seventeenth-century French nobleman La Rochefoucauld. He was also the author of a treatise on the art of ruling. Essays by Mavrokordatos praise books and reading, and condemn the vice of smoking. A long disquisition on contemporary manners has been hailed by some as the first 'modern Greek' novel.[4]

If there was ever truly a Greek 'Enlightenment', it made no original contribution to philosophy or science. These pioneers may not have made any detectable contribution to the Europe-wide movement. But they did make one very important discovery, one that would come to make an enormous impact within their own sphere. This was the discovery of *themselves*.

It started with geography. Geographical treatises written in modern Greek, based largely on Western sources, began to appear, the first in 1716, the second in 1728. The purpose of the writers was avowedly educational, and the scope of these works was the whole world. But when they came to adapt the descriptions, which they found in their sources, of a land called '*Graecia*', they felt bound to draw on sources available to them and familiar in *their own language*: the chronicles of the Byzantine Empire.

The result was a curious hybrid of geography and history, of radically different modern Western and medieval Eastern ways of looking at the same things. By the time that Grigorios Phatzeas published his *Geographical Grammar* (freely adapted from an English work of the late seventeenth century) in Venice in 1760, the readers of his book found themselves named indiscriminately as 'Romans', 'Hellenes' and 'Greeks'. The first of these terms was what the Byzantines had called themselves, and most speakers of Greek still did. 'Hellenes' at this time normally referred only to the pre-Christian, pagan Greeks of ancient times. On the other hand 'Greeks' (the Latin-derived name) was what Phatzeas's foreign sources called both ancient and modern inhabitants of these regions, without distinction. No wonder he and his readers were confused.

During the same period Greek-speaking readers were becoming familiar with the idea that the world beyond the Ottoman Empire was peopled by loosely defined groups known as 'nations'. This was not yet the era of nationalism, still less of the self-determination of nation states. But the consciousness and articulation of differences based on language, customs and environment, rather than religious affiliation as was customary in the Ottoman Empire, were among the factors that would lead to the emergence of national thinking early in the next century. During the 1780s, writers in Greek were beginning to refer to their own people (still by a bewildering variety of names) as a *nation* – in the new sense that was then emerging in the West.

By the beginning of the next decade, historical geography was making even larger claims – though these were still well short of revolutionary. Daniel Philippidis and Grigorios Konstantas were cousins, born into an up-and-coming mercantile family in the small town of Milies on the slopes of Mount Pelion in Thessaly. Both took minor orders in the Church, then as professional teachers gravitated towards the Danubian principalities. While based there, in 1791 they published in Vienna the first volume of an ambitious treatise entitled *Modern Geography*. The long section 'Concerning Hellas' was an up-to-date topographical account of the southern Balkan peninsula and the islands of the Aegean, preceded by a hundred-page 'chronology and history of the transformations of Hellas' from ancient to modern times. For these authors the inhabitants of the regions they described were 'modern Hellenes', the descendants of an ancient 'nation'. Two things, only, held these moderns back from being as happy and as prosperous as their ancestors had supposedly been. One was the unfortunate habit of quarrelling among themselves (the downside of that illustrious heritage, as the authors saw it), the other the 'Despotic government' under which they lived.

In several passages the cousins lament the absence of the rule of law in the Ottoman Empire. Only this prevented its European provinces from being richer than France. Touchingly, though, they write loyally of the Sultan. Following a practice going back to the Ottoman conquest, they give him the Greek title *Basileus*, which had always been the official title of the Christian emperors of Byzantium. Their programme, insofar as they had one, was for reform of the empire from within. Although more outspoken than their predecessors, Philippidis and Konstantas still wrote nothing that would have encouraged their compatriots to rise up in rebellion against their masters. Their own political loyalties, like those of so many educated Greek speakers of the time, were apt to be fluid. They were Ottoman subjects and their pleas for reform are respectful. On the other hand *Modern Geography*, published at a time when the empire was at war with Russia, carried a fulsome dedication addressed to 'Prince Gregory Potemkin, commander-in-chief of Russian forces'.[5] But then again, after the Revolution, both authors would choose to spend their last years back in the Ottoman Empire, rather than in independent Greece.

The key to this process of self-discovery was language. The Greek language was an evident and indisputable common denominator linking pagan ancient Greece, Christian Byzantium, the present-day Orthodox elites of southeast Europe and a broadly dispersed series of rural communities, each with its own dialect. The notorious Greek 'language question' emerged in the mid-1760s, at a time when the elite of the 'Orthodox commonwealth' had identified themselves with this language to such an extent that they felt the need to codify it. The 'question' boiled down to this: what should be the proper, or correct, or 'official' form of the Greek language in which future generations should be taught to write? It was all about writing – there was no attempt to interfere with the diversity of speech.[6] With more and more people learning to read and write, and more and more books being published in the language with every passing year, the more urgent it became to decide what should be considered correct and acceptable in a book published in Greek. In this way, the pursuit of a national *language* began several decades before anyone seriously imagined creating a national *state*.

The debate was often ill-tempered, reflecting the rivalries and the passions of individuals more noted for the strength of their opinions than for any willingness to give ground in the common interest. They spectacularly failed to agree. Indeed it was not until as recently as 1976 that the attempt to legislate for a standard written form of Greek would gain anything approaching universal acceptance. But for our purposes what matters far more is that they asked the question. And for all their disagreements, their different backgrounds, and irrespective of whether they spoke Greek or a Slavic language or Vlach (Romanian), Albanian or even Turkish at home, it was this yet-to-be-standardized written Greek language, along with their affiliation to the Orthodox Church, that brought them together. This was the language in which the self-discovery that was the 'Greek Enlightenment' took place. It was also the medium through which the second transforming achievement of the 'Orthodox common-wealth' in the eighteenth century came to be made. This was the expansion of trade, both within the Ottoman Empire and between the empire and Christian Europe.

The second half of the eighteenth century and the first years of the nineteenth saw a huge increase in coastal shipping in the Aegean. Most of this trade was carried on in small ships that covered relatively short distances. Control of long-distance routes came to be concentrated upon three very small islands: Hydra and Spetses, both close to the northeast coast of the Peloponnese, and Psara in the eastern Aegean. Ships were locally built and owned by small businesses based on the extended family, patronage and the sharing of risk. It was a business model that, astonishingly, survives more or less intact today, and would go on to generate the vast wealth of such legendary shipping dynasties as Onassis, Niarchos and many others.

By the first years of the nineteenth century, ships of between one and two hundred tons, carrying crews of up to sixty men, were operating out of the three islands. Most of this tonnage, we now know, was *Ottoman* shipping. Owners registered their vessels and paid for the protection of the Ottoman state, and they flew the Ottoman flag. Ottoman records show that most of the owners were Orthodox Christians. Records held in western ports reveal that the captains were 'Greek'.[7] Even during times of relative peace in the Mediterranean, seaborne trade was a dangerous business and piracy was common. Routinely, merchant ships were armed (indeed, the traditional Greek expression meaning 'to equip a ship for sea' means literally to arm it). The largest Hydriot ship in 1805 is recorded as carrying '16 cannon, 60 rifles, 40 carbines, 60 knives, and 60 pistols'.[8] In precisely what sense these merchants and crews were 'Greek' at this time is debatable: most of the inhabitants of Hydra and Spetses spoke Albanian as their mother tongue, but now began to add Greek endings to their family names. Since their own language had no written form, all their records were kept in Greek, which was also the language of their Church.

In this way the three small islands grew rich, and their most successful merchants and sea captains came to acquire a knowledge of the whole Mediterranean. They were also able to amass a tonnage of shipping, and ship-mounted firepower, that would come to play a decisive part in the Revolution once hostilities broke out. But during the eighteenth century, and the first two decades of the nineteenth, there is no reason to believe that their aims were anything other than commercial.

Land trade expanded during the same period, a natural consequence of relative peace in the Balkans. Caravans of camels set out from urban centres in the north of today's Greece to cross the mountain ranges of the Balkans to Belgrade, Bucharest and Jassy, or to wind along the coast to Constantinople. Often these merchants were 'ethnic' Vlachs, speaking Romanian at home, but just like their seafaring cousins of the Aegean, they relied on Greek as a medium for conducting their business and keeping their records. When they opened schools, to enable their sons and the sons of others to expand the business, they could count upon the Orthodox Church to provide the administration and the teaching, and naturally the language of instruction was Greek. In this way the basis for Greek education came to be expanded more and more into the secular sphere, throughout the 'Orthodox commonwealth'. Exchange of goods and exchange of ideas went hand in hand, each reinforcing the other in a virtuous circle.

These developments would have far-reaching consequences. Without them, it is hard to imagine how the Greek nation state could ever have come into existence. But if these were necessary foundations, on which others would build later, they did not in themselves make revolutionary change inevitable.

TRAVELLERS IN AN ANTIQUE LAND

The movements of people and ideas were not all in the one direction. The new opportunities opened up by trade between Europe and the Ottoman Empire also brought westerners to the great coastal cities of the eastern Mediterranean, or 'Levant' as it was most often called at the time: Constantinople, Salonica, Smyrna, Beirut, Alexandria. Many, perhaps the majority, of these were only ever transitory visitors. Others put down roots: Catholic and Protestant families, originally from northern European states, established a presence in each of these cities that would last into the twentieth century. This movement was more or less symmetrical with that of Greek-speaking merchants to European trading centres, though the number of westerners in the Ottoman Empire was probably a good deal smaller. But here the symmetry ends.

What brought Greek speakers to Europe, apart from trade, was the prospect of studying in western centres of learning. The books that they wrote as a result were full of what they had learned, but have little to say about where they went and what they saw there. In the opposite direction, though, a small but growing number of travellers set out to explore the lands beyond the borders of Christian Europe. Many of them wrote up their experiences afterwards, and described in great detail the discoveries they had made. British and French travel literature about Greece and the Levant makes up a sub-genre of its own during the eighteenth century. Some of these books were much read. Even more influential than the travellers were some who never made the journey at all, but wrote about a 'Greece' that existed only in their imagination.

One of the oddest – and, with the benefit of hindsight, the saddest – things about these journeys is that the travellers rarely, if ever, encountered the similarly educated elites of the lands they visited. The reason is simple: what brought the travellers to these lands in the late seventeenth and throughout the eighteenth century was not the prospect of meeting and exchanging ideas with people like themselves. That they could do at home. Theirs, as the title of one recent study of the seventeenth century has it, was a 'quest for classical Greece'.

One of the most respected and frequently cited of these travellers was Joseph Pitton de Tournefort. Commissioned by King Louis XIV of France, from 1700 to 1702 Tournefort led a small expedition through today's Greece, Turkey, Georgia and Armenia. The account of these travels appeared in two large volumes in 1717, and was translated into English the following year. Tournefort was unusual in that he was a botanist, not an antiquarian. His mission was an official, scientific one. But even *his* brief included 'to compare the Antient Geography with the Modern'.[9] Others drew detailed architectural plans of ancient monuments, recorded ancient inscriptions and tried to identify sites recorded in ancient sources.

Exemplary in establishing the much later science of archaeology were Jacob Spon from France and Sir George Wheler from England in the 1670s, and the Anglo-Scottish duo of James Stuart and Nicholas Revett in the 1750s. It is very much thanks to their efforts that the attention of western armchair travellers came to focus as intensely as it did on the antiquities of Athens that in future would become the focal point of Greece's capital city. Less reputable, by today's standards, was the habit of bringing back works of ancient art and on occasion even whole buildings or the decorated parts of them, when resources allowed. The notorious 'Elgin Marbles', or Sculptures of the Parthenon, in the British Museum since 1817, or the 'Venus de Milo' in the Louvre, in Paris, are only the best-known examples of a practice that was taken for granted by connoisseurs of ancient art throughout the eighteenth century and beyond.

This is not to say that the travellers were indifferent to the modern inhabitants of the lands they visited. One who devoted a large amount of space to the modern Greeks was another Frenchman. Pierre Augustin Guys was a well-to-do merchant who spent many years in the Ottoman Empire. Guys evidently knew the Greeks with whom he did business on a daily basis. But the full title of his book, first published in 1771, gives the game away. The first part was rendered, in the English translation that appeared soon afterwards, as *A Sentimental Journey through Greece*, which is fair enough. The rest can be literally translated as 'or letters on the ancient and modern Greeks, with a parallel between their manners and customs'. The reader has been warned. Note, too, the order of words in the title: 'ancient' precedes 'modern'. In the minds of those travellers, it always did.

This meant that a set of stereotypes about the 'character' of the modern Greeks became established very early, through these British and French accounts. Words such as 'debased' and 'enslaved' dominate their vocabulary. Having little concept of the political realities of life in the Ottoman Empire, and conveniently forgetting that most Europeans at this time lived under governments scarcely less autocratic than that of the Sultan, the travellers judged the people whom they met according to their idea of the character of the ancient Athenians and Spartans. The condition of 'slavery' in which the Christian subjects of the 'Grand Turk' were universally said to live was rarely the object of the travellers' compassion; more often it excited their contempt. With 'slavery' went servility, a character trait repeatedly attributed to those whose apparently willing servitude the visitors found incomprehensible. Other regular attributes of the 'modern Greeks' in the travellers' accounts are deceitfulness and trickery. Not even the precedent of the epic hero Odysseus, who had excelled in just these modern 'vices', could lessen the viciousness of his modern descendants in the eyes of the travellers – though some did note the family resemblance.

Only here and there does a more positive counter-narrative peep through. Johann Hermann von Riedesel was the only notable German to make the journey to Ottoman-ruled classical lands in the entire eighteenth century (and even he wrote his account in French). Riedesel set out from Italy for Athens and Constantinople in 1767. A disciple of the Swiss philosopher Jean-Jacques Rousseau, he was prepared to see in the contemporary inhabitants of Greek lands something of the primal innocence of mankind that Rousseau believed was natural to the human condition. In the Greeks whom he met Riedesel detected a kind of antidote to the corruption he deplored in the contemporary European cities of his day. This was still a patronizing view, to be sure, and it would remain marginal until the 1940s, when the novelists Henry Miller and Lawrence Durrell would popularize their own twentieth-century version of it.[10]

More influential even than the travellers in shaping the ideas of northern European elites about Greece was one of those who never went there. Johann Joachim Winckelmann has been described as 'the first German writer of the modern era to achieve European celebrity' and a 'hero to a generation of Germans' during the half-century after his death.[11] Born in Prussia in 1717, Winckelmann spent his most productive years in Rome. There, he made his name as a historian and connoisseur of ancient art. More than once he had the opportunity to visit Greece. But he held back from going. In this, Winckelmann set the trend for much of German intellectual engagement with the idea of Greece until well into the nineteenth century. What Winckelmann did, based on his research in Italy, was to convince the art world of his time that the true origins and the true greatness of classical art were to be identified not with the Romans but with the Greeks, whom the Romans had merely copied.

Winckelmann's *History of the Art of Antiquity*, published in 1764, quickly established a set of ideas about the ancient Greeks that would become embedded in the consciousness of European elites for half a century or more. Ancient Greek art had been superior to all others because it had been born in the most perfect *climate* (you could only write this if you had never been there). Then, the ancient Greeks had valued above all *freedom*. That they had been the first to experiment with early forms of democracy, and therefore invented the concept of political liberty that was dear to Winckelmann and like-minded contemporaries, is true enough. But it is a blatant exaggeration to assert that 'Freedom always had its seat in Greece, even beside the thrones of the kings, who ruled paternally.'[12] Some of what Winckelmann writes about ancient Greek political institutions is frankly bizarre. According to him, mankind had reached an ideal state of perfection in the historical circumstances of the fifth century BCE. Cultivation of the arts, political liberty and harmony between man and nature had all come miraculously together in ancient Greece. It was an achievement at once unrepeatable and at the same time a point of reference against which any aspiring civilization in the present or future would have to be measured.

In this way, modern Europeans in the second half of the eighteenth century began more and more to think of their own 'civilization', and even to define themselves, in relation to that gold standard from the past. A preface added by the anonymous translator to the English edition of Guys' *Sentimental Journey*, in 1773, spells out the new way of thinking, as an incentive to draw readers to the book:

> It is therefore not surprising, that the civilized countries of Europe should eagerly embrace every opportunity of information, with respect to a people to whom they owe so many obligations. We hereby trace, as it were, our origin; at least, we may say, the source of our manners, and the fountain of our knowledge.[13]

The notion that the rest of the world, and Europe in particular, owes a huge cultural debt to Greece is today deeply embedded in Greek history and the Greek collective consciousness. It has gained a new resonance in the second decade of the twenty-first century, when Greece is crippled by literal debt to European institutions. We should not forget that this is a notion that originated in western Europe, in the time of Winckelmann and the travellers who set out to uncover *their own* origins in those provinces of the Ottoman Empire that they thought of as 'Greece'. Truly, as some recent studies have begun to suggest, the 'idea of Europe' in the eighteenth century is inseparable from the 'idea of Greece'.[14]

This is why it was such a missed opportunity when the western European 'quest for classical Greece' failed to meet and find common ground with the parallel project of the 'Greek Enlightenment'. In the Orthodox east, too, intellectuals were grappling at just this time with the question of their own communal identity, and looking to the example of the contemporary 'nations of Europe' for the new ideas and the new prosperity that they valued so highly.[15] Both groups were fascinated by the ancient Hellenic past. Both were trying to make meaningful connections between that past and the present in which they lived. But there was no meeting of minds. The more that western intellectuals idealized *ancient* Greece, the harder it became for them to recognize that their quest was shared by men of education and ability who had a much more direct relation to the Greek language than they did themselves. Even today, when there are excellent studies available of the 'Greek Enlightenment' and of the works of western travellers and idealists of the period, no one has yet thought to explore these two bodies of writing in parallel – so fundamentally different do they still seem.

That *failure* of understanding, right at the beginning, before Greece was even born into the world as a modern nation, would cast its shadow over much that would come later. Whenever, in later times, Greeks and westerners have misunderstood or distrusted one another – which has been often – the origin of that distrust can be traced back to these two parallel paths that never met.

PEASANTS, FISHERMEN, FARMERS, MONKS

The story so far has been about elites, whether they lived in the borderlands on the edge of the Ottoman Empire, in the empire itself or in western Europe. But what about the people whose descendants, within a few generations, would come to think of themselves as 'Hellenes' and make up the population of the new Greek nation state? Beyond the elites who had the education and the leisure to reflect on the issue, who, during the eighteenth century, *were* the 'Greeks'?

Histories written since independence usually take it for granted that there existed an identifiable Greek population under Ottoman rule too. But the Ottomans didn't divide up their subjects on the basis of language, or what we would today call 'ethnicity'. The subject peoples of the Ottoman Empire were identified by their religion. In official terminology, all Orthodox Christians were called *Rum* (the equivalent of *Romioi* in Greek) and defined as a *millet*, meaning a religious community. By no means all Orthodox Christians were native speakers of Greek. It was education, and especially the increased use of writing, that established Greek as *the* common language among the different language groups that made up the *Rum millet* – in some ways the equivalent of 'international English' today.

At the same time, those who did speak Greek as their first language were not invariably Orthodox Christians. There were communities of Roman Catholics in the islands and Romaniot Jews in the larger towns. Followers of all three faiths had the option of converting to Islam. Some did. If Greek had been their first language before their conversion, more often than not it continued to be afterwards. This was most conspicuously the case in Crete, where most of the Muslim population, some 40 per cent of the total in the nineteenth century, were 'Turcocretans' who had no other language than the Cretan dialect of Greek. Greek speakers could be Muslim, too.

Still, subject to these caveats, some broad generalizations can be made. Speakers of Greek as a first language seem to have been in the majority throughout most of the islands of the Aegean and the Ionian seas, in Crete and in Cyprus, in the Peloponnese (at this time still more commonly known as the Morea) and the southern mainland of what is now Greece, an area loosely known at the time as Roumeli. Even within that area, significant regions were primarily Albanian-speaking: the trading islands of Hydra and Spetses, for instance, and the southeast corner of Roumeli, comprising ancient (and modern) Boeotia and Attica, including Athens. Further north in the Balkans, around the Sea of Marmara and down the Aegean coast of Anatolia, there were many Greek speakers too, but here they were more evenly interspersed with speakers of other languages. There were Greek-speaking enclaves as far east as the district around Trebizond on the Black Sea, known in Greek by its ancient name of Pontos, and in Cappadocia, the Greek name for the area around Kayseri (Caesarea) in central Anatolia.

Who were these Greek speakers? Apart from their language and (for many, but not all) their religion, what did they have in common? How did they live?

Most would have been peasant farmers, herders, small-time merchants, fishermen, seafarers, monks and lower clergy. The conditions of life in most of the regions where they lived were harsh. Cultivable land is broken up and squeezed between seas and mountains. Communities have always been scattered. Until about the middle of the twentieth century, survival depended on a constant balance of risk. Local economies were based on subsistence. During the eighteenth century it began to be possible for young men to emigrate and find work abroad, and for young women to be married outside their local community. When mouths to feed exceeded the resources available, an alternative solution was brigandage in the mountain regions or piracy by sea. In Roumeli, in particular, the Ottoman authorities recruited local militias, often made up of Orthodox Christians, to keep the bandits in check. But mostly these militias were recruited from the same bandit groups they were meant to control, so that men whose only profession was arms were in the habit of moving back and forth, from enforcers to outlaws and back again. The pirates of Mani, the untamed southernmost part of the Peloponnese, had become notorious by the turn of the nineteenth century. In conditions such as these, the relative peace that gave opportunities to the elites was relative indeed. Ordinary lives were often short. Violence or the threat of violence, crop failure and starvation were never far away.

Any attempt to generalize across these different groups, spread over widely separated geographical areas, is bound to be little more than speculation, if not wishful thinking from the perspective of later times. What kinds of evidence can we draw on instead? There are several, and all have to be approached, for different reasons, with caution. We can start with the European travellers. To them we owe countless anecdotes and observations of customs, opinions and superstitions that might otherwise have gone unrecorded – among them, for instance, the first evidence for the Greek popular superstition about the living dead, or vampires, which much later would lie at the root of a worldwide subgenre of novels and horror films.

Another possible window into the lives of these communities, again through the eyes of outsiders, comes from modern anthropology. Beginning in the 1950s, British, American, French and latterly also Greek anthropologists began to study what were thought of as 'traditional' communities in Greece, and elsewhere around the Mediterranean. The classic study of a Greek community was made by John Campbell in the 1950s. Campbell chose as his subject the pastoralists of northwestern Greece called Sarakatsanoi – a proud, self-contained people who in those days still used to move with their flocks of sheep and goats from summer pastures high in the Pindos mountains to the coastal plains for the winter. Confronted by what appeared to the outside observer to be the 'anarchy of their communal life', Campbell noticed how a shared code of values, based on honour and shame, had the effect of regulating the mutual hostility of unrelated families.[16]

If you cannot trust anyone to whom you are not related either by blood or by marriage, then you can rely on them only if you can bind them to you by an equivalent obligation. The shared code ensures that to honour such an obligation is honourable, to break it shameful. Therefore, those who honour their obligations are the most respected members of the community. Anyone who does not is despised, or even risks being cast out altogether. It is a self-maintaining system. On the one side, it entails the giving of gifts, on the other the bestowal of patronage. In the context of modern, democratic and accountable institutions, this pre-modern system has come to be known as 'corruption'. In the absence of these institutions, or where they remain weak and underdeveloped, it is a mechanism for survival.

These insights from modern anthropology in turn may help explain the frustration experienced by the early travellers and many different outsiders ever since, with what has so often been called the 'dishonesty' of the Greeks. Paradoxical though it might seem, the 'corrupt' system of patrons and clients places the highest possible value on *trust*: the system can only work if all parties are playing by the same (unwritten) rules. These rules, in turn, are founded upon the traditional, deep-seated code of honour and shame. An outsider cannot be assumed to be bound by this code, and so can never be trusted to keep his word. Therefore, the unspoken, internalized logic goes, if you can't trust him, it's all right to cheat him.[17]

The anthropologist, of course, is always working with the present. Campbell himself thought that the way of life and the social values he had observed had probably remained little changed since late Byzantine times. Anthropologists today are more cautious about making such claims. But in this case we can be fairly confident in supposing that communities of Greek speakers in the eighteenth century must have operated in much the same way.

It is time, now, to turn back to evidence from the period itself. Here, we face different problems. Despite the growth of schools in towns, in the countryside throughout the Ottoman Empire very few people could read or write before the late nineteenth century. As a result, written evidence is hard to come by. A rare example of history written 'from below', from the beginning of the period, tells of what the author calls the 'disaster and enslavement' of the Peloponnese by the Ottomans in 1715. The writer, one Manthos of Ioannina, was apparently a witness to some of the events he narrates and afterwards ended up in the Greek community of Venice, where he published his history in rhyming couplets. Manthos blamed the defeated Venetians almost as much as the victorious Ottomans for the subjugation of his people. In form, his work is an elaboration of the kind of lament that had become current shortly after the fall of Constantinople in 1453. There are many references to 'Romans', that is, the Orthodox Christians who in this region would have been overwhelmingly Greek-speaking.

Manthos presents these 'Romans' as helpless victims of the actions of others. In his whole narrative there is only a single moment when any of them take the initiative: when the inhabitants of a group of villages in the remote mountains of the central Peloponnese put up a token resistance. As it happens, these insurgents included the ancestors of Theodoros Kolokotronis, who would win fame more than a century later in the Revolution. The pious Manthos, having in the meantime found refuge far away in Venice, dismisses these few defenders of their faith as 'all of them crazy; they should have known better'.[18] The idea of victimhood, which will often resurface in later years, was already thriving in the early eighteenth century.

Towards the end of the century, the revolt in Crete, which had been sparked by the campaign of Catherine the Great against the Ottoman Empire in 1770, was also commemorated in verse not long afterwards. The *Song of Daskalogiannis* was composed orally in Sphakia, the mountainous southwest of the island where the revolt had originated. According to the text itself, it was written down just sixteen years after the events it describes. Its hero is one of the richest and 'worthiest' of the Christians of Sphakia, Daskalogiannis, or 'John the Teacher'. Unusually gifted in being able to read and write, Daskalogiannis can communicate with other parts of the Greek-speaking world. When reports arrive that Russian troops have landed in the Peloponnese, he decides that this is the moment to rebel – against the advice of the head of the local Church. It all goes tragically wrong. Daskalogiannis and his associates are forced to capitulate. In captivity the hero remains defiant to the last, and is flayed alive by the Pasha of Candia (Heraklion).

It is a stirring tale, told with epic vividness and an epic love for long speeches. The hero's explanation of his motives, if these words really were fixed in writing in 1786, are revealing of the attitudes of the time. Daskalogiannis had acted, he declares:

> firstly for my native place, and second for the Faith,
> and thirdly for the other Christians who live in Crete.
> For if I am a Sphakian, I am a child of Crete,
> and to see any Cretan suffer gives me pain.

Patriotism begins at home, in Sphakia, and from there extends to the rest of the island. There is no sense of a wider 'national' identity in this account. The poet ends with a conclusion not dissimilar to that of Manthos, though his whole narrative has been couched in far more heroic terms: the priest had been right all along. The people of Sphakia had *already* enjoyed independence, in practice, from the Turks. Thanks to Daskalogiannis's rash actions, they had now thrown it away.[19]

The *Song of Daskalogiannis* is almost the only case we have of an orally composed narrative that was written down during the eighteenth century. But before long, a rich and varied repertory of narrative and lyrical songs would start to be collected from the oral tradition of just about every Greek-speaking community from the Ionian islands to Cyprus, from Crete to the foothills of the Balkan mountains. These songs reveal a remarkable world of the imagination. In that world, men are expected to be heroes. They have to prove their worth by acts of defiance and violence. Women should be beautiful and modest when young, but at any age are apt to be fickle and devious. It is women who mourn for the dead and also for those condemned to live far away, in *xenitiá*, a much-used term that may be translated either as 'exile' or 'foreign parts', and is always imagined as not much better than being dead. Love songs are bursting with richly inventive imagery, often seeming to convey half-hidden meanings. The fantastic and the irrational are never far away: birds and animals speak, thunder and lightning reflect and magnify human dramas, a dead man rides a horse among the clouds (vampires again).

Some of the most characteristic, and widely diffused, themes have to do with death. In a male world where you can only prove your valour by defying ever more potent adversaries, the ultimate test is to take on Death himself. Personified as Charos, a name deriving from the ferryman on the river Styx in the underworld of ancient mythology, Death is a gruff, curmudgeonly figure. Always dressed in black, riding a black horse, he is often depicted trailing a long line of helpless women and children behind him, no doubt like the slave-traders who could still be a threat to daily life in the eighteenth century. Charos in these songs is the opposite of the idealized male hero in every way. Goaded to envious rage by the hero's irrepressible love of life, Charos confronts him and tells him he has to die. The hero, being a hero, refuses. Instead, he offers to fight his enemy on equal terms. The struggle takes place on the threshing-floor, where in real life the chaff is separated from the edible seed through violent beating. Nine times the hero throws down his enemy. But Charos cannot bear to be beaten. Unable to win on the equal terms he has promised, he cheats: Charos grabs the hero by the hair and pulls him down.[20] So Death wins, as he must in the end – but only by violating the code of honour and shame. Death is the ultimate outsider. His behaviour proves, in extreme form, why the outsider can never be trusted: Death is a cheat. So the hero – the upholder of the code of honour and shame, the standard-bearer of the values of the insider – is morally the victor, even when he dies.

We find much the same set of attitudes in the very many songs that have been preserved from the oral tradition that are dedicated to the lives, and usually also the violent deaths, of the mountain brigands known as klefts. The word comes from the Greek *klephtis*, meaning literally a thief, which during the eighteenth century is what these people were. The later role of these warrior-bands as the most effective fighting force in the Revolution would give to the very word 'kleft' a heroic aura that it has never lost since. The songs that commemorate these men first began to be published during the Revolution, and have remained part of the national 'grand narrative' ever since.

Most of these songs refer to individuals who lived in the early nineteenth century. But a few songs date back further. The oldest of them narrates an episode that may have taken place in Roumeli around 1750. In it, Christos Milionis has been proscribed by the Ottoman authorities. A Muslim by the name of Suleiman is sent to bring him in:

[Suleiman] caught up with him at Almyros, they kissed as friends,
all night they stayed up drinking, until dawn,
and when dawn broke they went out to the bandit lairs.
And Suleiman called out to *kapetán* Milionis:
'Christos, the Sultan's after you, the Muslim nobles want you.'
'So long as Christos lives, he won't bow down to Turks.'
Musket in hand they went for one another;
fire answered fire and both of them fell dead.[21]

There is no knowing whether the specific form of defiance hurled by Milionis in the song was actually uttered in or around 1750, or may instead reflect the patriotism of a later age when the story came to be written down in this form. In any case, just as striking is the evidence the song provides for a shared code of behaviour, and even intimacy, between Christian and Muslim armed men in the mountains of Roumeli under Ottoman rule.

Finally, among the Greek-speaking Orthodox population there was in circulation a series of tales and prophecies that linked the fall of the Christian empire of Constantinople with divine providence and faith in a future restoration. Much of this material, too, is known to us only through texts that were published later. These include what is perhaps the most famous of all the Greek folk songs. Called simply 'Of St Sophia' or 'The Last Mass in St Sophia', versions of this song tell, in only a dozen or so lines, how on the eve of the Ottoman conquest the celebration of the liturgy in the great cathedral of Orthodoxy was interrupted by a voice from heaven: it is God's will that 'the City' (Constantinople) should fall to the infidel. The shock experienced by the faithful is projected onto the icons of the saints. Miraculously, all the painted likenesses begin to weep. The voice – or is it perhaps the voice of the poet and singer of the song? – soothes the distraught saints in touching, homely fashion. Addressing the icon of the Mother of God as an earthly mother would comfort a crying child, the song ends:

Hush, Lady Mother, do not cry and weep,
once more with years and ages, once more these things are yours.[22]

In the nineteenth century, and into the twentieth, these lines were read as a positive statement about the future. But in the oldest versions the tense is not future but present, and the word translated here as 'once more' can also have the force of 'still', or 'all the same'. The song of St Sophia, as it was performed shortly before the Revolution of 1821, is above all an affirmation on the part of Orthodox Christians that their faith has not been lost with the conquest, that the bond linking them with the familiar figures depicted on the icons in every church is indissoluble, come what may. If these words also implied a prophecy of redemption in the future, it concerned the Orthodox Church, not (as it would later come to be reinterpreted) the Greek nation state.

Another often-repeated story tells of the 'marble emperor', Constantine XI Palaiologos, whose body was never found after the conquest of his city by the Ottomans in 1453. Constantine did not die, the story goes, but instead had been taken by an angel to a secret place within the city walls and there turned to stone. In various versions it is prophesied that when the day comes, appointed by God, the emperor will be restored to life and at the head of a victorious army will chase the former conquerors all the way to their original homeland in central Asia.

Other prophecies can be traced through written sources going back to the late fifteenth century, or even before the fall of Constantinople itself. It is hard to tell to what extent, if at all, these build upon originally popular traditions. A set of 'oracles' attributed to a thirteenth-century mystic by the name of Agathangelos (meaning 'Good Angel') began to circulate at the beginning of the 1750s. But this pious forgery seems to have been a top-down intervention. References to a fair-haired, or fair-skinned, race from the north that would bring deliverance were seized upon, during and after the war between the Russian and Ottoman empires from 1768 to 1774. The deliverers must surely be the Russians. On the other hand, evidence for the circulation of the oracles of the supposed 'Agathangelos' comes mainly from the very end of the century and well into the next. So it is hard to be sure how widely these beliefs were shared, or how seriously they were taken, during the earlier period.

What this evidence does show is the deep devotion of Orthodox

Greek speakers to their religion, to its accumulated traditions and to some collective memory of the lost empire of Constantinople. When it comes to the *ancient* past, the enthusiasm of their own elites and the western travellers was met with puzzled wonder or disbelief. As good Christians, the Orthodox flock knew that people called 'Hellenes' had lived in these lands a long time ago and had worshipped false gods. These 'Hellenes' were therefore the exact antithesis of the decent, honourable, God-fearing *Romioi* of the eighteenth century. Oral traditions, mostly recorded later, tell how the 'Hellenes' must have been a race of giants, to have built the walls and monuments that could still be seen. Pagan temples and particularly statues were apt to possess supernatural, dangerous powers – hence, no doubt, the inspiration for the emperor turned to marble.

Even in the nineteenth century, when travellers and antiquarians came looking for the ruins of the ancient sanctuary of Delphi, the locals would apply their own logic and ingenuity to make sense of it all:

> The Mylords aren't Christians, that's why no one ever saw them make the sign of the Cross [in the Orthodox manner]. They're descended from the ancient pagans the Adelphians, who kept their treasure in a castle that they called Adelphi [Brothers], after two brother princes who built it. When the Virgin Mary and Christ came to these parts and everyone round about became Christian, the Adelphians thought they'd better make themselves scarce. So they left for Frank-land [western Europe] and took all their treasure with them. The Mylords are their descendants, and they come here now to worship those stones.[23]

It makes for a delightful story – and it serves to highlight the conceptual gap that separated the Greek villagers from not just the western antiquarians, but also from the elite of the 'Orthodox commonwealth' who shared the same language and religion. If this was the picture even after independence, we may ask ourselves how much of a meeting of minds did take place between eastern Christians and the emerging secular identity of western Europeans during the century before. These first encounters were at best partial and full of mutual misunderstandings. The new ideas that spread eastwards helped the elite of the 'Orthodox commonwealth' to begin to redefine its own identity, but left the great majority of Greek speakers untouched. Expanding commerce brought wealth to some and opportunities to many that had not known them before. But whether among the educated elites or at the level of popular culture, there is little evidence for anything that could be called revolutionary sentiment during most of the eighteenth century.

All this was about to change, as the century drew towards its close.

2

A Seed is Sown

1797–1821

On 28 June 1797 a squadron of French naval ships and troop transports arrived off the fortified port of Corfu, the administrative capital of the Ionian islands. For six hundred years the islands had been overseas possessions of the Most Serene Republic of Venice. The arrival of the French that June day was the first news anyone in the islands had that the *Serenissima* was no more. The tone of the general's first message sent ashore was friendly. The last Venetian governor, whose predecessors for centuries had been honoured by the title *Provveditore Generale*, found himself addressed by the French commanding officer as 'Citizen', and was ordered to provide quarters for the newly arrived troops. The Venetian Senate had capitulated to the superior firepower of Napoleon Bonaparte, he explained, so the French were now the legitimate rulers of the islands. The letter was dated according to the French Revolutionary calendar: *6 Messidor, Year V*. Once the troops had gone ashore, billboards appeared all over Corfu town, promising in French, Italian and Greek to bring 'liberty, equality, fraternity' to 'long-enslaved Greece'. The revolution that since 1789 had thrown the whole of western Europe into turmoil had arrived in the east.

A 'Tree of Liberty' was planted in one of the main squares two days later. Aristocratic symbols were publicly burned amid a ritual thanksgiving to the 'Supreme Being' (place-server for the Christian deity in the French Revolutionary pantheon). Not everyone was equally pleased. A French naval officer, who joined the squadron shortly afterwards, reported general satisfaction at the arrival of his compatriots, but felt obliged to add the rider: 'with the exception of the nobles, those employed by the former government, and priests'.[1]

The traditional hierarchy of the islands had been suddenly turned on its head. By autumn 1797 the French were fully established throughout the seven islands. All the indications were that they meant to stay. They even created a new administration based on three new *départements* that were added to France.

Some months later, on 20 December 1797, came a shock of a different sort. From Trieste, the Austrian port city on the Adriatic, the local governor, Baron Brigido, wrote to his superior, Count von Pergen in Vienna, to report the uncovering of a conspiracy. A tip-off from a Greek merchant in the city had led to a number of arrests. Incriminating proof had been found. The arrested men had been plotting a French-style revolution in the neighbouring Ottoman Empire. The ringleader was not himself a merchant, but belonged to the educated Greek-speaking elite of Bucharest, the capital of Wallachia. It turned out under interrogation that the conspirators had spent the past year in Vienna, printing the revolutionary tracts that had just been found in their possession. The ringleader's name was given as Rigas Velestinlis.

The documents found in Rigas's possession during the night of 19–20 December 1797 were a set of blueprints for turning the Ottoman Empire into a democratic republic on the French model. There was even a rousing 'Battle Hymn' or 'War Song', in verse, including an oath of allegiance to the newly imagined republic.

The Austrian authorities had good reason to fear anything that smacked of Revolutionary France. As recently as October, the Treaty of Campo Formio had divided the spoils of the defeated Republic of Venice between Napoleon and the Austrians, forcing the latter to give up territory to the French in northern Europe and accept Napoleon's conquests in Italy. Until then it had been thought likely that the next target for French expansion would be Vienna itself. By the end of the year, diplomatic relations had only just been restored, and remained fragile. The prospect of revolutionary activity on Austrian soil, even if aimed primarily at a different power, was bound to horrify the authorities. Their response was swift and deadly. The discovery of Rigas's conspiracy was hushed up. The accused were brought secretly to Vienna. There, they underwent a series of interrogations, but nothing so public as a trial, during the first months of

1798. Finally, eight of the accused, including Rigas, all of them Otto-man subjects, were transported down the Danube and passed in chains from Austrian into Ottoman custody. On or about the night of 24 June they were executed in prison in Belgrade and their bodies thrown into the Danube.

One of the ironies of this story is how little impact it can have made on public consciousness at the time. The interrogations of Rigas and his associates, first in Trieste and then in Vienna, were conducted in secret. The transcripts did not come to light until almost a century later. Nothing of what was happening was reported in the press. Only the last journey of the extradited men down the Danube was covered in a few Austrian and German reports. Indeed, so successful were the Austrian authorities in suppressing all trace of the conspiracy that not a single one of the three thousand copies of his revolutionary proclamation that Rigas had had printed in Vienna survives today. Only the 'Battle Hymn' would reach the public domain any time soon – naturally enough in French-controlled Corfu, within a few months of its author's death.

In another respect the Austrian interrogators were less successful. The documents in their possession were proof enough of revolution-ary intentions. But we do not to this day know how Rigas planned to implement them, or indeed whether at the time when he arrived at Trieste, to find that he and his comrades had been betrayed, he had any firm plan at all. According to one account, his next port of call was to have been Venice, and a summit meeting with Napoleon him-self. Another has Rigas and his associates heading for the southern tip of the Peloponnese, there to raise rebellion among the fierce and semi-independent warlords of Mani, whose fortified towers still form part of a wild, mountainous landscape. A third account gives their intended destination as the town of Preveza on the west coast of the Greek mainland, a dependency of the Ionian islands and there-fore under French control. The first plan would have been a waste of time, since Napoleon had already left Italy, as Rigas may or may not have known. Most probable is the third scheme, and this was what the Austrians believed. It is hard to see how else a handful of political idealists could have challenged the might of the Ottoman Empire, unless with military backing from France. Preveza was one of only a handful of toeholds on the mainland that the French had acquired with mastery of the islands. This idea would have made sense. But perhaps there was no firm plan at all. On the available evidence, Rigas was not the most practical of would-be revolutionaries.

The great majority of Greek speakers, elite or not, could have had little awareness of these events at the time when they happened. But within a few years the ripples sent out by Napoleon's campaigns in Europe had spread throughout the East. And the name of Rigas would be on the lips of every Greek as the 'protomartyr' of a movement that had not yet been born, but would soon crystallize into something that would have astonished Rigas himself: a movement for a new kind of self-determination that was fast becoming known as 'national'.

A WORLD IN TURMOIL

During the first months of 1798 nobody in Europe could tell which way Napoleon would turn next. Austria was temporarily off the hook – its turn would come in 1805. An invasion of Great Britain was on the cards. Rigas and his friends were not alone in hoping for liberation at the hands of French Revolutionary troops. It would have been only a logical extension of what had just happened in the Ionian islands. There is some evidence that Napoleon himself toyed with the idea, while he was in Italy in 1797. In the event, the forces of the French Revolution did turn eastwards towards the Ottoman Empire – but not its European provinces. On 1 July 1798 a French expeditionary force landed at Alexandria. Napoleon's three-year occupation of Egypt had begun.

For centuries Egypt had been an Ottoman possession. At this time its Mameluke rulers were all but independent of Constantinople. But the shock of an invasion from Europe went all the way to the heart of the empire. In August, while the British Royal Navy under Horatio Nelson destroyed the French fleet in Aboukir Bay (the battle of the Nile) and cut off the supply lines to Napoleon's occupation, diplomacy in the Ottoman capital brought together the unlikeliest of allies. A century of enmity between Turkey and Russia was set aside. Both empires now joined an alliance with Great Britain.

The upheavals of the next fifteen years affected every corner of the European landmass and the entire Mediterranean. Consider the fortunes of the Ionian islands. After little more than a year of incorporation into the French Republic, the seven islands were taken over by a combined Russian and Ottoman naval force during the closing months of 1798. Then in 1800 the new rulers, unable to agree on anything else to do with them, set up a 'Septinsular Republic' under the nominal protection of Russia. This was an extraordinary step. At a stroke, for the first time in modern history, it gave a Greek-speaking population control of its own administration, and that under the provocative title of 'republic'. The experiment was not a great success. While the republic lasted, British troops were briefly landed to maintain order in Corfu in 1801. Then from 1802 the Russians moved back to take effective control – though it is significant that they did so through a plenipotentiary who was himself a member of the Ionian aristocracy and therefore belonged to the 'Orthodox commonwealth' that now extended far into the Russian establishment. When in 1807 Tsar Alexander made peace with Napoleon, as a gesture of goodwill he handed the Ionian islands back to France, although strictly speaking they were not quite his to give. For the next two years the islands were absorbed into what had in the meantime become the French Empire. But then in the autumn of 1809 all except Corfu were seized by the British Royal Navy. Finally, Corfu too capitulated after the Treaty of Paris was signed in 1814. For fifty years after that, the Ionian islands would be ruled by Great Britain as a 'protectorate'.

Confused? Imagine what it must have been like for Greek speakers at the time. There were no newspapers in the islands or in the Ottoman Empire. News travelled slowly, and was often unreliable. None of these shifts was decisive; each was rapidly overtaken by the next. Most of the Great Power players in the game changed sides at least once. Whether you lived on one of the Ionian islands and experienced these upheavals directly, or heard about them long afterwards, it was bound to seem as though all political certainties had been thrown up in the air.

In the Ottoman principalities that lay to the north of the Danube, another of those borderlands in which Greek elites had come to predominate during the previous century, the situation was even worse.

A sideshow to the continent-wide story of the Napoleonic Wars, and barely noticed by historians of that conflict, yet another Russo-Turkish war raged from 1806 until 1812. This war was fought mainly in and over the principalities, and involved horrific sieges and sackings of fortified towns. For six years Wallachia and Moldavia were annexed by Russia; the traditional office of prince was abolished. Even so, most of the actual administration of the principalities continued in the hands of the same Greek Orthodox elite as previously. It was only the worsening relations between Tsar Alexander and Napoleon, in 1812, that brought this vicious and finally inconclusive war to an end. With Napoleon's fateful invasion of Russia imminent, peace was established between the Russian and Ottoman empires by the Treaty of Bucharest on 28 May 1812. Russia permanently annexed part of Moldavia. Apart from that, the status quo that had worked so well throughout the eighteenth century was restored. The Greek princes returned to the devastated principalities, under the same arrangements with the Sultan as before.

Napoleon's campaign against Russia in 1812 marked the beginning of the end for the French Empire, that vast projection of military power and certain sorts of idealism that had been born out of the Revolution of 1789. By the summer of 1814 it was all over – bar Napoleon's dramatic escape from imprisonment on the island of Elba and his 'hundred days' that ended with the battle of Waterloo on 18 June 1815. The representatives of the victorious powers that had gathered at Vienna the previous year would soon finish their work of re-establishing a deeply conservative set of regimes across Europe. After the Congress of Vienna, all traces of revolutionary rhetoric and reform were removed throughout the continent. The 'Concert of Europe', which had emerged victorious from the Napoleonic Wars, established a new watchword instead: restoration. But the spirit that had animated the revolution in France in 1789, and nostalgia for the all-conquering brilliance of Napoleon Bonaparte, lived on in many quarters in Europe. The years of 'restoration' after 1815 were also years of conspiracies and secret societies, of plots and abortive revolutions. This was the climate in which the seed that would grow into the Greek Revolution of 1821 would be nurtured.

The changes and the instability that came to the Greek-speaking

populations of the borderlands and the Ottoman Empire from outside, thanks to the French Revolutionary and Napoleonic wars, are
only one part of the story. During those years the empire was also
subject to internal challenges in which the Christian Orthodox inhabitants of several different regions found themselves caught up.

It used to be a truism in Western historical accounts that from the
second half of the eighteenth century onwards the Ottoman Empire
was in a state of terminal decline, fatally weakened by a series of wars
against the rising power of Russia. Internally, the centralized authority of the sultans was being eroded by the rise of regional and local
players at every level. It was a sure recipe for imminent collapse. So
the standard story goes. Certainly there were many European observers around the turn of the nineteenth century who believed this to be
true – including Napoleon, who might not otherwise have invaded
Egypt. In this way was born the 'Eastern Question' that would come
to dominate diplomatic and strategic attitudes to Europe's southeastern border throughout the nineteenth century. The existence of this
perception is part of the background to the Greek Revolution of the
1820s. But was it any more than a perception?

Reports of the imminent demise of the Ottoman Empire would
prove premature by more than a century. Napoleon failed in Egypt,
after all. It would take the Great War of 1914–18 and the rise of a
secular nationalist movement among the Turks of Anatolia finally to
kill off the empire – and not until 1923. The Ottoman Empire, at the
time of the Napoleonic Wars, had been undergoing complex internal
changes. But the picture as it emerges today is not one of irreversible
decline. During the last decades of the eighteenth century and the
first two of the nineteenth, the empire did indeed face very serious
internal threats. But by the early 1830s, with the single exception of
Greek independence, it had successfully seen them off. Viewed in that
context, the Greek achievement is all the more remarkable.

These threats took a variety of different forms. At the most local
level, in many regions, increasing numbers of armed brigands 'took
to the mountains', as the traditional Greek phrase has it. Rising up
the social scale, but still at a fairly local level, power was becoming
concentrated in the hands of a landowning and relatively wealthy

class – and this despite a legal framework in which officially all property belonged to the Sultan alone. During the eighteenth century the practice of 'tax farming' had become general in the provinces. Officials would subcontract the obligation to collect and deliver taxes to local notables, traditionally known in English as 'primates'. These primates, in turn, had every incentive to collect more than they were obliged to deliver, and to live handsomely on the difference.

In some areas, such as the Peloponnese, where the Muslim population was sparse, it became possible for Orthodox Christians to claim most of the prerogatives of this class. In the absence of any centralized authority, such as a police force, to maintain order in their localities, Christian primates would rely on locally recruited manpower, just as their Muslim counterparts did. In the Peloponnese, by the beginning of the nineteenth century, brigandage had become such a scourge that the landowners, Muslim and Christian, made common cause in 1806 to root it out. This policy was remarkably successful. Many brigands were killed. Others took refuge in the Ionian islands. Brigands and brigandage would not return to the Peloponnese until the outbreak of the Greek Revolution, all the more effective for the military training that had come with service in any or all of the foreign armies that had occupied the islands during the Napoleonic Wars.

Local landowners and tax farmers were in a position to make the most of the weakness of the central authority at the time, and in turn profited from it. But they were still nothing like a threat. That began to change when individual primates began to increase their power and wealth at the expense of their neighbours. This was notoriously the case with Ali Pasha, also called Ali Tepedelenli (from his birthplace now known as Tepelenë in Albania) and nicknamed the 'Lion of Ioannina'. Born into an Albanian-speaking family that had recently converted from Orthodox Christianity to Islam, Ali during a long life combined devious diplomacy with ruthless cruelty to make himself the effective ruler, by the 1790s, of a swathe of territory that today makes up the southern half of Albania and much of northern Greece. He held this enormous power nominally from the Sultan. But the title 'Pasha of Yanya [Ioannina]', like others that he had enjoyed before it, had been granted retrospectively. Everybody knew that it had been a land grab, and the Sultan had grudgingly had to acquiesce in it.

Ali Pasha, by the turn of the nineteenth century, had become powerful enough to hold his own court, wage wars and even engage in diplomacy with foreign powers on his own account, without much reference to the Sultan. He was not the only one. Further east, from his base at Vidin on the south side of the Danube, Osman Pasvanoğlu became the first of these warlords to defy the authority of the Sultan openly. His revolt, beginning in 1795, would take three years and an army estimated by one source at 200,000 men to suppress – inconclusively, as Pasvanoğlu would then be pardoned by the Sultan, to die in his bed in 1807.[2] Two decades after the revolt of Pasvanoğlu, Ali Pasha, now in his seventies, would make his own bid for full independence. The result this time was different. In 1822 Ali's severed head with its famously long white beard would be displayed outside the Topkapı palace in Istanbul. In this case, so soon after the outbreak of the Greek Revolution the year before, Ottoman central authority had successfully reasserted itself.

The internal threats posed by warlords such as Osman Pasvanoğlu and Ali Tepedelenli had nothing to do with either religious or what today we would call ethnic allegiances. Both men were Muslims. Both made war on neighbouring Christians, but they also harboured and encouraged members of the Orthodox elites at their own courts. There is a story that Pasvanoğlu once owed his life to Rigas and tried to repay the debt by marching on Belgrade to spring him from jail on the eve of his execution. The story is probably not true. But it is a fact that Rigas's 'Battle Hymn' singles out Pasvanoğlu as an example of a heroic freedom fighter to be emulated by the Greeks.

In Ioannina, Ali Pasha revelled in creating the court of an 'enlightened despot', attracting men of letters and the arts from all over the 'Orthodox commonwealth'. The teacher and educationalist Athanasios Psalidas and the poet and translator Ioannis Vilaras found employment there. The personal physician entrusted with the welfare of one of Ali's sons was the young Ioannis Kolettis, who would later emerge as one of the most effective of the political leaders during the first two decades of independent Greece. All the official correspondence of Ali's court was written in Greek. But when it came down to it, Ali was far more despot than enlightened. Like all the primates-turned-warlords, great and small, Ali Pasha was motivated by nothing other than self-aggrandizement. When he finally came to risk everything in a desperate act of defiance against his master the Sultan, Ali, like Pasvanoğlu before him, represented nothing but his own personal ambition. And this must be at least part of the reason why both men failed.

A different kind of threat to the authority of the Sultan came from within the imperial military establishment. For centuries the janissaries had been an elite corps of shock troops, charged with guarding the Sultan's person and always in the vanguard during the Ottoman wars of expansion. In those days they had been recruited from the Christian population. Young boys had been forcibly removed from their families, converted to Islam and brought up to an austere life in barracks. Janissaries had been forbidden to marry, so that they would know no other loyalty than to their sovereign. But no longer. By the late eighteenth century the janissaries had become a self-serving anachronism, a privileged caste that now enjoyed and exploited the right to recruit its own members without limit. The costs of maintaining this corps were rising in proportion to the decline in its military efficiency. For some years, Sultan Selim III had been trying to reform them. But with a near-monopoly on the use of force within the empire, the janissaries were in a strong position to resist. Indeed so powerful had they become that they were the driving force behind a rebellion in the capital that led to the murders of two reigning sultans, the would-be reformer Selim III and his successor Mustafa IV, within the space of a few months in 1808. It was out of this debacle that Sultan Mahmud II would come to power – and decisively reverse the fortunes of his office.

During the reign of Selim, the janissaries had thought nothing of taking the law into their own hands. In one distant corner of the empire their excesses sparked a local conflict that would turn out to be prophetic of things to come. The revolt of the Serbian *knezes*, or peasant leaders, in 1804, has often been seen as the first of the 'national' revolts that would lead to the creation of the modern Balkans. But that is the interpretation of hindsight. A typically vicious set of tit-for-tat killings in Belgrade province had been sparked by the janissaries asserting their own authority over that of the Sultan's representatives. In the conflict that followed, the Orthodox Christian population found itself fighting *for* the Ottoman Sultan against his internal enemies. The revolt of 1804 was eventually crushed, though it took nine years and in the meantime the situation had become further complicated by Russian involvement.

A second Serbian revolt, in 1815, succeeding in establishing, for the first time, an Orthodox Christian warlord, Miloš Obrenović, in charge of an Ottoman province. Sultan Mahmud, preoccupied with larger threats to his authority, was content to accept this state of affairs in return for the new warlord's loyalty. Compared to the Muslim Ali Pasha further south, this was no threat at all. Still, a precedent had been set. And the prolonged struggles of the Orthodox Serbs had nourished the first stirrings of what in time would grow into a strong popular movement for national self-determination. In this way a reactionary, decentralizing force (the janissaries) had set in train a series of events that would long outlast that force itself. Sultan Mahmud's annihilation of the janissaries in 1826, while the Greek Revolution was at its height, would prove to be one of the most spectacular achievements of a ruthless reign.

During the first two decades of the nineteenth century – and despite the sometimes lurid prognostications that circulated in Europe – the empire was undergoing a slow process of internal upheaval and reform. Where this might lead, nobody could tell. At all levels of society, but particularly among the elites, Muslims and Christians were capable of making common cause against perceived threats to all their livelihoods. Allegiances were unstable, shifting in response to unpredictable transfers of power from one centre or institution to another. It was, in a way, only a mirror of what was going on throughout the rest of Europe between 1789 and 1815.

In the midst of all this turmoil, ideas of national self-determination, of the rights of citizens, of *liberté, égalité, fraternité*, were beginning to circulate, and nowhere more so than in the borderlands where Greek-educated Orthodox Christians made up the elite. For the time being, though, these ideas were for the few.

REVOLUTIONARY IDEAS

First into print was Rigas Velestinlis, the doomed conspirator arrested in 1797. Of Rigas himself we know rather little. He was born in either 1757 or 1758, into a well-to-do family in the village of Velestino in Thessaly, not far from today's city of Volos. His parents could afford to give him an education, and this became his passport into the Greek-educated elite of the Ottoman Empire. Baptized as Antonios the son of Kyritsis, in adult life he chose to adopt the name 'Rigas'. This is not normally a name in Greek, but is a homely word meaning 'king' (mostly in fairy tales and card games – it is never used of real royals). In the social class that Rigas came from, no one had a surname. So, like many others before and after him, he invented one from his birthplace. Confusingly, Rigas has two such names: Velestinlis, which means 'of Velestino', and 'Pheraios', from Pherai, an ancient place name associated with the locality. Portraits show Rigas to have been bull-necked, with twirled moustaches and black curly hair, florid-faced with a paunch, and a slightly mournful expression in his jet-black eyes.

Rigas's career, to the extent that we know about it, follows a path familiar enough in the 'Orthodox commonwealth': from a rural province to the capital and from there to the Greek-speaking court of Bucharest in the Danubian principalities. From there he would pay several visits to Vienna. In keeping with the spirit and the practice of the 'Greek Enlightenment', most of his work consisted of translations and adaptations of Western originals.

Nothing else that he did was so radical as Rigas's final choice, to translate the French Revolutionary constitution of 1793. At the time, and for those contemporaries who were touched by Rigas's work, what was shocking, new and (depending on your point of view) exhilarating was the fact of importing these ideas into the Greek language and the thought-world of the Ottoman Empire at all. On the other hand, for historians of ideas and political theorists of later times, what is remarkable about Rigas's translation is not what he took from his original, but what he added to it.

The translator's individual stamp appears already in the title. What is baldly presented in French by the one word *Constitution* becomes, in Greek, *New Civil Government of the Inhabitants of European Turkey, Asia Minor and the Mediterranean Islands and Wallachia and Moldavia*.[3] Rigas's blueprint is not for any narrowly defined homeland but for a 'Hellenic Republic' that is to encompass all the

Ottoman provinces in Europe and the whole of Anatolia, including today's Greece, Turkey and most of the Balkans. Rigas's most startling achievement was drastically to adapt the prototype hammered out during the 'Terror' in Paris to the multi-cultural, multi-faith reality of the Ottoman Empire.

His vision is astonishingly inclusive, and not just in terms of territory. Article 7 of the section that lays down constitutional principles reads:

> The sovereign people consists of all the inhabitants of this kingdom without exception for religion or language: Hellenes, Bulgarians, Albanians, Vlachs, Armenians, Turks and every other kind of race.

Elsewhere the 'sovereign people' are named as 'Hellenic' and as 'the descendants of the Hellenes' (that is, of the ancient Greeks).[4] Clearly this population will not be defined by any unified genetic inheritance, but rather by a shared culture and a shared geographical space, as well as the voluntary commitment, on the part of all these disparate language groups and different religious communities, to identify themselves with it.

Rigas's ideas have often been termed utopian, and in some ways they are; but not necessarily in this respect. Rigas's 'Hellenic Republic' was an attempt to capitalize on something that did actually exist, in the form of the 'Orthodox commonwealth'. The prestige of Greek as the common language of education had been thoroughly established by this time throughout the empire's European provinces and large parts of Anatolia. And although Rigas's ideas were entirely secular (he removed from the French original even the reference to the 'Supreme Being'),[5] it is the existing role and reach of the Orthodox hierarchy and Greek-educated Phanariot networks that tacitly underpin the whole enterprise.

Article 4 is more inclusive still. Almost anyone can *become* Hellenic, in Rigas's understanding of the term, if his (or seemingly even her) services can be useful to the state. It is in this sense, for the first time in Greek, that Rigas uses the word *ethnos*. Residence, religion or language will count too: 'Someone who speaks either modern or ancient Greek, and aids Greece, even if he lives in the Antipodes (because the Hellenic yeast has spread into both hemispheres), is a

Hellene and a citizen.' Religious tolerance is fundamental. So is equality, which Rigas takes further than in the French original to extend to women as well as men. Women are even expected to serve in the army, 'carrying spears, in case they cannot handle a musket'.[6]

There is a certain magnificence about all this. In some ways Rigas is far ahead of his time (it was not until 2016 that full combat roles were opened to women in the UK or the US military). The multi-culturalism that since the late twentieth century has often been nostalgically attributed to the Ottoman Empire, in the pages of Rigas's *New Civil Government* becomes harnessed to a modernizing programme that might have turned the cities of the eastern Mediterranean into pluralist, democratic, law-governed communities long before London, Paris or New York. Rigas's 'Hellenic Republic' is 'Greek' in the way that the English poet Shelley would soon declare that the whole of Europe was: as the *cultural* inheritor of the ancient legacy. At a time when American and French republicans were fashioning their own identities and institutions after the models of classical Athens and Rome, and when disparate groups of European immigrants on the other side of the Atlantic were finding a common identity as US citizens, it was not necessarily unrealistic to imagine something similar happening in the Balkans and Anatolia. Or was it?

The French constitution of 1793 was the product of very particular conditions that followed the Revolution. Within two years it had been replaced by another, less radical. Even in France the provisions that Rigas was attempting to transplant into the very different conditions of the Ottoman Empire had been found to be unworkable. We know that Rigas knew this, because he drew on some of the later provisions in his own version. What chance did such wholly foreign ideas have in what was essentially a feudal, theocratic society? How was the new system to be brought into existence?

This is where there really is something utopian about Rigas's blueprint. There is scarcely a hint of a practical programme anywhere in his document, such as might lead to the new state of affairs it sets out. Where there is, it seems either pettifogging or overblown. An added paragraph about the military organization of an insurgency tells us only that in charge of every ten men there should be a decurion, of every hundred a centurion, and so on. Soldiers are to sport the black, white and red colours of the Republic, respectively in their under-wear, their tunics and their boots. Red boots – really? It was hardly Rigas's fault that his choice of colours, which were also to feature on the Republic's tricolour flag, would later be adopted by Hitler's Nazis for their own emblem, the swastika. Every soldier, writes Rigas, is to wear a helmet and every citizen a cap, on which will be emblazoned the symbol of the Republic: the club of Hercules with three small crosses planted on the upper side of its bulbous tip.[7]

Much else that Rigas added to his French original was clearly designed to *persuade* – something that was unnecessary in Paris in 1793, where the revolution had already happened and enforcement took the form of the guillotine. A floridly written preface elaborates on the evils of tyranny experienced in the Ottoman Empire. Still more emotive and still more aspirational is the entirely original 'Battle Hymn' or 'War Song' with which the *New Civil Government* ends – a rousing call to revolution of a sort that the French legal text had no need for.[8] Also entirely original to Rigas's project was the accompanying map of southeast Europe and western Anatolia, printed on twelve separate large sheets, in which ancient place names and images of historical events were superimposed on the contem-porary geography of those regions. Here Rigas was attempting to mobilize the new historical geography that had been gathering momentum in Greek throughout the preceding century, to underpin a political project that was vastly more ambitious. These visual accompaniments, no less than the stirring 'Hymn', have a clearly per-suasive function, and may have been aimed at a wider public than could easily have read and understood the main text.

Rigas's constitution for an imagined 'Hellenic Republic' would remain a dead letter, his revolution a paper exercise, a stillbirth. But the idea of Greek emancipation along the lines of Revolutionary France did not go away. Beginning at the very time of Rigas's execu-tion in the summer of 1798, this idea would be taken up again, and elaborated in a quite different direction.

In 1798, Adamantios Korais was already fifty years old, and living in Paris. His career as a public intellectual had not yet begun. Korais knew of the arrest and extradition of Rigas and his companions, though not yet their ultimate fate. He cannot have known much of what was in Rigas's ill-fated *New Civil Government*. But what he knew was enough to make him salute 'those brave martyrs for liberty'.[9] On his desk before him, Korais had a pamphlet in Greek, issued by the newly established printing press of the Ecumenical Patriarchate in Constantinople, the highest authority in the Orthodox Church. The pamphlet reminded the faithful that it was God himself who had 'raised up out of nothing the mighty empire of the Ottomans' to rule over them, for the ultimate good of the Orthodox faith and to guarantee the 'salvation of the chosen peoples'. Nothing remarkable about that: it had been the official position of the Church since the fifteenth century. What was new was what followed: the faithful were warned of the latest ruse thought up by the Devil to damn them in this world and the next. This was none other than 'the much-vaunted political programme of liberty'.[10] The *Paternal Instruction*, as this pamphlet was titled, was not the first, but it was the strongest reaction by the Orthodox hierarchy to the dangerous new secular ideas spreading from France. Its timing may well have been a response to news of Rigas's thwarted conspiracy.

Adamantios Korais – former merchant in silks, trained doctor of medicine, self-educated classical scholar, and close observer of every phase of the French Revolution in his adopted city – took up his pen to strike back. He chose to do so anonymously. Parodying the title of his target, he called his rebuttal *Fraternal Instruction*. The third component of the French Revolutionary trinity, *Fraternité*, had arrived in Greek. On Korais's side he had a devout and erudite knowledge of the Scriptures. But he also mobilized principles he had learnt from Dutch Protestant masters, first in his native Smyrna and then in Amsterdam. Obedience to God, Korais thundered:

> means nothing other than that we must obey the laws because the laws are nothing other than the unanimous and common opinion of a people, and the voice of a people is the voice of God.

Therefore, he concluded, far from owing obedience to the Ottomans, 'Those ruled by tyrants have the inalienable right to seek every sort of means in order to throw off the yoke of tyranny and to enjoy once more the precious gift of self-government.'[11]

So began the thirty-five-year career of the foremost intellectual architect of Greek independence, often hailed subsequently as the 'father of the Greek nation'.

In this way, Korais seems to slot naturally into the story as Rigas's intellectual heir, continuing the work that Rigas had begun. But it was not really like that. Korais, born in 1748, was older by ten years. The two men were as different in intellectual outlook as they were in background, appearance and temperament. Korais had started out as a city boy, brought up in cosmopolitan Smyrna, one of the great cities of the Ottoman Empire, while Rigas's background was provincial. Rigas had acquired his learning within the empire, Korais in Europe. Rigas in his portraits looks as though he must have enjoyed the good things of life. Korais, dressed in the Western manner, is austerely portrayed in high collars. He appears hollow-chested with thin, tapering shoulders (he may have suffered from tuberculosis in his youth). He is clean-shaven with a severe expression that seems to owe something to classical Roman portraiture. Rigas may have dreamed of putting his ideas into practice in person, placing himself at the head of a band of revolutionaries. Korais's entire life was dedicated to books – to reading and writing. The few other things that he ever did, such as running his father's business in Amsterdam or qualifying as a medical doctor in Montpellier, according to his own testimony he did only in order to assuage his 'thirst for learning'.[12] There was never any question, for Korais, of taking an active part in political affairs. Having settled in Paris a year before the French Revolution, he never again travelled far from the city. Indeed, so far as is known, Korais never at any time set foot in any part of today's Greece. His was a life of the mind.

Where Rigas had leapt ahead to legislate for an imagined republic, Korais never made concrete proposals for how an independent Greece ought to be run – until much later, when the Revolution of 1821 forced his hand. To begin with, while the French Army of the Orient remained in Egypt, and for a little while after, Korais was one of those who saw French arms as the way to the liberation of Greece. In that case, he would have been content to see the government of the French Republic extended to his fellow citizens, as had briefly happened in the Ionian islands in 1797 and 1798. There would be no need to legislate further. But even during this earliest phase of Korais's political thinking, certain new features stand out. These mark a decisive shift away from the approach of Rigas.

Where Rigas's constitution translates the French word *nation* in contexts where it means primarily the *state*, Korais uses the same Greek word, *ethnos*, to translate the then-emerging, more nebulous concept of what today we would call an 'ethnic group'.[13] Where Rigas had allowed for all the religious and linguistic identities of the Balkans to buy into a new 'Hellenic' identity, the logic of Korais's position obliged him to exclude all those who were not Greek from his understanding of the 'nation'.

Korais followed Edward Gibbon and other Western historians of the ancient world during the eighteenth and early nineteenth centuries, in placing the demise of the ancient Greek world very early. The Greeks had already become a subject people under the Roman Empire, he insisted. They had continued in subjection throughout the millennium when Greek-speaking emperors ruled from Constantinople. In another polemical tract, written in 1801, also published under a pseudonym, Korais deplored the legacy of Byzantium to the Greeks of his own day:

> many times the [Byzantine] army would raise up to the imperial throne not genuine Romans, but Thracians, Bulgars, Illyrians, Triballi, Armenians, and other such thrice-barbarous despots, whose yoke became the heavier, as one by one the lights of [ancient] Greece went out . . .[14]

Liberty now became attached to the bloodline of the nation. Rigas's political vision had been founded upon what today we would call civic, or voluntarist, nationalism: individuals and groups choose to give up some element of their sovereignty for the good of all. This was what Rousseau had proposed in *The Social Contract* four decades before. For Korais, instead, the nation is defined by its inheritance – which incidentally explains why so much of his intellectual energy was directed towards what he called 'one of the most inalienable possessions of the nation', namely the Greek language.[15] Already, in Korais's writings from the very beginning of the nineteenth century, the idea of the Greek nation is being defined in terms that today we would call 'ethnic'.

Korais addressed his fullest early statement of these ideas not to his fellow Greeks, but to a learned society in Paris, the 'Society of the Observers of Mankind'. These men were forerunners of modern anthropologists. All of them, except Korais himself, were French by birth. Their society had been formed during the Revolution. On 6 January 1803, Korais read to them a paper entitled 'Dissertation on the present state of civilization in Greece'.[16] Here, the extent of the shift from Rigas's ideas becomes apparent. Rigas's 'Hellenic Republic' was to have been something *new*. The 'sovereign people' might be the 'descendants of the Hellenes' of antiquity, but their political system was to be unlike any that had ever existed, unless perhaps the fledgling United States of America. By contrast, Korais seems to have been the first to envisage a future independent Greece in terms of a revival of the past. Writing in French, in the opening paragraph of this essay he introduced the terms that would define his later political trajectory: 'nation', 'regeneration', 'civilization'. The last was a concept beloved of the Enlightenment. Although the ancient Greeks were generally credited with having invented it, there was no equivalent word in the Greek language. It was Korais himself who first coined one, and it remains standard today. The Greek 'nation', Korais conceded, echoing the terms of eighteenth-century French and British travellers, had 'degenerated from the virtues of its ancestors' and was at present 'stagnating' in a kind of 'barbarism'.[17] But this deplorable state had begun to change around the middle of the previous century.

The greater part of the essay is then devoted to the advances in education and commerce made in 'Greece' during the previous decades. Taken together, Korais declares, they amount to nothing less than a 'revolution' – but a 'moral' one.[18] The process has lately been fuelled by the actual revolution in France. But the essay makes no mention of violent action. Instead, Korais describes the 'awakening' of the Greeks to the responsibility of trying to live up to the ancient ancestors whose name they bear. (This could more easily be said in French than in Greek, at a time when contemporary Greek speakers were still known as *Romioi* or, in Korais's own preferred term, *Graikoi*, not by the ancient name of 'Hellenes'.) The 'regeneration' of the 'fatherland' has begun. Finally, addressing the personification of that fatherland, Korais concludes that what gives purpose to his own life is 'the hope of seeing you take up once again your proper rank among the nations'.[19]

For almost twenty years after that, Korais would devote his energies to promulgating this view among Greek speakers, particularly those in the Ottoman Empire. To this end he devised a series of editions of ancient texts, which he called the *Hellenic Library*. Produced to the highest standards of classical scholarship, these were prefaced by long essays in the modern language in which Korais elaborated his ideas for linguistic, educational and moral reform that would bring about the revival he so desired. Throughout these essays, Korais eschewed the language of violence and revolution that had characterized his early, unsigned polemics. Instead, he went to great lengths to flesh out the concept of 'regeneration' that he had first proposed in French. He did not expect to live to see the result. Indeed, near the end of his life he confessed that he had not expected the Greeks to be ready for their independence until 1851 – thirty years after the Revolution actually broke out.[20]

Not everyone who shared these ideas was prepared to be so patient. *Hellenic Nomarchy, or Discourse on Liberty* is an impassioned, at times an intemperate, work. Published anonymously in 1806, probably in the Italian port city of Livorno, it runs to just over 250 closely printed pages of modern Greek, without division into chapters or even paragraphs. Its author has never been convincingly identified.[21]

The book is dedicated to the memory of Rigas, whom it describes as a 'great Hellene', a 'Hero', 'philhellene and patriot' and the 'liberator of Hellas' – if only it hadn't been for the 'baseness and cowardice of his vile comrade, the most worthless traitor' who had denounced Rigas to the Austrians. These phrases give something of the flavour of the work. But for all his admiration for Rigas, there is no sign that the anonymous author, any more than Korais before him, could have had access to the detail of Rigas's political ideas. What the author of *Hellenic Nomarchy* knows and admires is the revolutionary 'War Song', which had been published in French-ruled Corfu shortly after its author's death, and the story, which by this time had been well circulated, of Rigas's betrayal and execution.[22] The thrust of his argument, on the other hand, is far closer to that of Korais, whom he mentions with respect, than of Rigas, whom he venerates.

The essential premise of the work is that the only guarantor of human happiness and human advancement is the rule of law. The word *nomarchy* is the author's own invention, a play on the word 'monarchy' that works the same in Greek as it does in English. By changing round two consonants, he neatly inverts the meaning: rule not of 'one man' (*monos*) but of 'law' (*nomos*). The whole book is a plea for liberation – for humankind in general, but more particularly for that population which the author has no hesitation in calling 'Hellenes'. This was the term still usually reserved, in Greek, for the ancients. Even Korais, at this time, referred to his own contemporaries by the Latin-derived name *Graikoi*. But now, in *Hellenic Nomarchy*, the moderns were no longer simply the *descendants* of the Hellenes, as they had been for Korais and Rigas. They were not even the 'new' or 'modern' Hellenes that they had become in the 1791 *Modern Geography* of Philippidis and Konstantas. They *were* Hellenes. It can be hard for us, today, to appreciate what a radical step this was in 1806. In effect it translated into Greek a usage that had long been standard in the languages of the rest of Europe, in which the same words ('Greece' and 'Greek') did duty for a historic civilization, a geographical region and its present-day inhabitants.

Naturally, for the writer of *Hellenic Nomarchy*, these 'Hellenes' had to be attached to a homeland. On almost every page he writes of 'Hellas', in Greek, as Korais had written in French of *la Grèce*. Neither writer gives any precise sense of where the boundaries of this homeland might lie – and of course it existed on no political map at the time. By contrast, Rigas had been much more precise, in naming – and indeed mapping – the European and Anatolian provinces of the Ottoman Empire that were to comprise his 'Hellenic Republic'. Rigas had been prepared to work from the political reality that existed in his day. Korais and the author of *Hellenic Nomarchy*, both of them writing from beyond the empire's bounds, see no legitimacy in any of its institutions. Clearly echoing Korais's diagnosis of a national 'regeneration' already under way and crying out to be completed, the book ends with repeated calls for the 'restoration of the nation'.[23]

The anonymous author has more to say than either of his predecessors about ways and means, and about the practical resources available to the 'enslaved Hellenes' that might help them regain their liberty. Among these are the 'character' and 'morals' of the Greeks themselves.

Again echoing Korais, he insists that these have not been vitiated or diluted, despite the subjection of so many generations to the tyranny of foreign masters, going all the way back to the ancient Romans. In this he anticipates nineteenth-century ideas of 'national character'. Elsewhere, he draws on recent history to argue that some of his contemporaries still possess the fighting spirit of the ancient Spartans, who had defied the invading Persians to the last man at Thermopylae in 480 BCE. He cites episodes of heroic resistance by the mountain-dwelling Souliots against the campaigns of Ali Pasha over the past twenty years that were already becoming legendary. In the Souliots, he declares, may be seen the 'heroes and the honour of enslaved Greece, the starting point and facilitator of her coming liberation'. Then there are the mountain brigands, the klefts. The propensity of these men to wage guerrilla warfare had already attracted the admiration of Rigas. The author of *Hellenic Nomarchy* goes further, and is perhaps the first to extol the moral virtues he attributes to those outlaws, portraying them already as embryonic freedom fighters and the nucleus of a native fighting force that they would indeed become.[24]

Resources from abroad will be important too. But these are not the expected ones. We would be foolish to trust foreign governments to come to our aid, the author warns, because they are all of them run by 'tyrants', in their own self-interest. Why exchange one tyranny for another? This is a sideswipe at imperial Russia and the new French empire of Napoleon, although neither is named. The author places his hopes not in foreigners but in those Greeks, himself presumably included, who are studying or engaged in commerce in foreign countries – and to whom his book seems most of all to be addressed. He urges them at some length to go home and devote to the fatherland the skills they have acquired abroad. Another source of strength can be found in the very weakness of their enemies. The anonymous author of *Hellenic Nomarchy* is probably the first writing in Greek to draw attention to what would soon, in the west, become known as the 'Eastern Question'. The Ottoman Empire is so rotten within, it is ripe for the taking, he assures his readers. Earlier, he had produced statistics to show that, in many of its regions, the Orthodox Christian population amounted to some 80 per cent: the Greeks were not even outnumbered![25]

Something else that is new in this work, and a harbinger of divisions that would lie in the future, is its strong denunciation of internal enemies. The fellow merchant who had betrayed Rigas turns out to have been only the least of these. The anonymous author reserves some of his harshest words for the hierarchy of the Orthodox Church. *Hellenic Nomarchy* is one of the few Greek tracts of any period to echo the anti-clericalism of the revolutionaries in France. From the Ecumenical Patriarch (a 'ludicrous title'), through the corrupt workings of the Holy Synod, down to the ignorance and petty abuses of monks, the author has nothing but contempt for the clergy. Not only are they ignorant and self-seeking, but as part of the Ottoman system they are also traitors. The same goes for the Phanariot class and the primates. These are people who:

> for the greater unhappiness of our nation, an evil chance has made Hellenes, and have only been born upon Hellenic land, for no other purpose than to lengthen the time of our fatherland's slavery.

This, of course, was not how members of those elites were accustomed to think of themselves. The very concept of 'Hellenic land' would have seemed bizarre to most of them. People such as these, the author concludes grimly, 'will serve as examples of shame for those who come after'.[26]

We have been warned. The Greek revolutionary project, like all revolutionary projects, will be under threat from some of the most powerfully placed individuals and groups that it aspires to represent. The inclusive charter imagined by Rigas, the anonymous author's hero, has gone for good.

SOMETHING GROWING IN THE DARK

How much impact could these ideas have had on the ground? Of the disparate Greek-speaking populations of peasants, fishermen, farmers and monks, how many would have been engaged by any or all of these revolutionary programmes? In the case of Rigas, the real substance of what he had proposed would lie buried in the Austrian archives for almost a century. The original editions of the unsigned polemical pamphlets by Korais and of *Hellenic Nomarchy* survive today in very few copies. On the other hand, all of these were clandestine publications. To possess them was dangerous. Many must have been confiscated, hidden or destroyed. It is impossible to know how widely they were read, or how often their contents were passed on by word of mouth during the years leading up to the Revolution of 1821. The twenty-five volumes of the *Hellenic Library*, which included Korais's essays on education and language, were subsidized by a like-minded family of merchants and intended to circulate widely in the Ottoman Empire. These were not openly subversive and no attempt appears to have been made to suppress them. They were printed in runs of between a thousand and fifteen hundred, huge numbers for a Greek book at the time. Even if it is true that only half of those were actually distributed before the Revolution,[27] that still leaves a significant number in circulation. And they must have had some influence, because by the early 1820s the idea of a national revival had taken firm root, at least among educated supporters of the Revolution. But what of the population at large?

A valuable source of information is once again the foreign travellers who wrote up their experiences, sometimes in great detail. During the first two decades of the new century, thanks in part to the Napoleonic Wars blocking their access to other parts of Europe, more British travellers than ever before passed through the lands that they loosely referred to as 'Greece'. The twenty-one-year-old Lord Byron and his travelling companion John Cam Hobhouse first became aware of Korais, and the admiration in which he was held, while staying in the house of a local primate in the Peloponnese at the end of 1809. The very name of Rigas was sufficient to produce an 'ecstasy' in their host. From Hobhouse's diary we know that the lines later translated and made famous by Byron were already being sung, to the tune of the 'Marseillaise', in the Peloponnese, only eleven years after Rigas's execution:

> Sons of the Greeks, arise!
> The glorious hour's gone forth,
> And, worthy of such ties,
> Display who gave us birth.

Sons of Greeks! let us go
In arms against the foe,
Till their hated blood shall flow
In a river past our feet.[28]

The words are probably not, in fact, by Rigas. But the association with his name is just as important. Violence was in the air by that December of 1809. And we have the word of these and other travellers that the tune of the French Revolutionary anthem was on the lips of many patriotically minded Greeks.

Other foreign visitors, too, were hearing the same sort of talk at about this time. Henry Holland, whose book was published in 1815, thought it 'a matter of interesting speculation, whether a nation may not be created in this part of Europe, either through its own or foreign efforts, which may be capable of bearing a part in all the affairs and events of the civilized world'. On balance, and tentatively, based on the experience of several months travelling in the country in 1812, Holland concluded that it might.[29]

By the end of the first decade of the new century, it was evident that a seed of some kind had been fertilized and was growing. What it might lead to, and whether or not the new birth might be viable, or another stillbirth like the conspiracy of Rigas, nobody could tell. It was not just the Greeks who were being, in the expression of Korais, 'awakened'. The spate of travel books published, particularly in London, between 1800 and 1821 had the effect of raising consciousness there too. To a lesser extent the same was true in France and among the German states. Far more now than during the previous century, the writers of these books dwelt on the present state of the countries they passed through and the condition of their inhabitants. The result was that not only among Orthodox Greek speakers but far away in Europe, too, the sort of 'speculation' that had intrigued travellers such as Byron and Holland was beginning to grow.

In the west, Byron's poem *Childe Harold's Pilgrimage* would prove enormously influential when its first two cantos appeared in 1812. The book was an instant publishing sensation. Its appearance marked the beginning of its author's 'years of fame', as the first modern celebrity. But it was not just its author who 'awoke to find [him]self famous'.

Greece and the Greeks had overnight become famous too. The second canto of *Childe Harold* is the poetic travelogue of Byron's 'Grand Tour' in Greek lands. Included with the poem were the results of his investigations and speculations on the present and future state of Greece. *Childe Harold* would be followed, over the next few years, by a succession of swashbuckling best-sellers in verse. Known as Byron's 'oriental' or 'Turkish tales', all of them drew on his recent travels. These, as well as *Childe Harold*, would quickly be translated and admired all over Europe. Byron was not, at this time, a partisan for the Greeks (that would come later). Nothing that he wrote until after 1821 speaks out directly in favour of a Greek revolution. But in the minds of his readers, wherever they lived, the question had suddenly become topical. *Could* some kind of a Greek revival be possible, after all?

No such questions troubled the deliberations of the hard-headed politicians, monarchs, their advisers and diplomats who met, between November 1814 and June 1815, at the Congress of Vienna to determine the shape of Europe after the defeat of Napoleon. An essential article of the 'Concert of Europe' that would emerge from the Congress was the permanence of the frontiers that had been re-established at the end of the Napoleonic Wars. Indeed it was Klemens von Metternich, Chancellor of Austria and the chief architect of these arrangements, who a few years later would notoriously deny the existence of Italy as anything more than a 'geographical expression'. The Ottoman Empire was not represented at the Congress. The future of its European provinces seems not to have been on anyone's agenda there. But the principle that the boundaries of states throughout Europe could not be changed without the agreement of four (later five) Great Powers was implicitly extended to the Ottoman Empire too. By the time of Napoleon's final defeat at Waterloo in 1815, the future of the entire continent had been set in stone. Speculation was for poets and fantasists. This was the reality.

In the meantime, among Greek-educated elites the project for a Greek revival was quietly gathering momentum. Collaborative ventures, such as newspapers and learned societies, became more frequent. The first Greek newspaper had been established in Vienna as long ago as 1790. It had lasted for seven years, until the discovery of Rigas's conspiracy gave the authorities the excuse to close it down, although the newspaper itself had not been subversive. The year 1811 saw the establishment of its most authoritative and longest-lasting successor, the *Learned Mercury*. Appearing for the most part fortnightly over the next ten years, this attracted contributions from the leading figures in Greek education at the time. The subject matter of the newspaper was mainly 'philological', certainly not in any overt sense political. But many of those who contributed would later play their part among the intellectual leaders of the Revolution.

Among societies, the most prominent was the Philomuse Society, first established in Athens in 1813. One of its leading figures was Lord Byron's former tutor in modern Greek, Ioannis Marmarotouris. A parallel venture with the same name sprang up the following year in Vienna, and earned the patronage of Count Ioannis Kapodistrias, originally from Corfu but who at this time was attending the Congress of Vienna in the service of Tsar Alexander of Russia. All of these societies were at least overtly dedicated to the furtherance of education and the arts. To the extent that a Greek revival was also a political project, they had the potential to involve clandestine activity. But like the newspapers, they operated openly and their stated objectives were cultural rather than political.

Very different was the Society of Friends or Friendly Society, also known in English by its Greek name, *Philiki Etairia*. This was a secret society, dedicated to a war of liberation. A great deal has been written on the rituals, ranks and secret codes of the Society. Like other clandestine political groups elsewhere in Europe at the time, this one was based ultimately on Freemasonry. The place where it began is traditionally given as Odessa and the year as 1814. Odessa lay in the heart of the new 'borderland' that had opened up to the north of the Black Sea almost half a century before. Greek-speaking merchants had been encouraged to move there since the time of Catherine the Great, and now made up an influential community. In reality, the Society seems to have begun functioning as an organization only in 1817, and in Constantinople.[30] Part of the mystique that its founders cultivated lay in exaggerating the extent of its links to Russia. Supporters were encouraged to believe that the Society had the backing of the Tsar's government, which it did not. Liberation was the goal. But how was it to be achieved?

A series of rather wordy oaths sworn by initiates at different levels of the organization's hierarchy give the most reliable contemporary evidence. The most substantive passage is this:

> I swear that I will nurture in my heart unswerving hatred against the tyrants of my Fatherland, their supporters and those of like mind with them. I will act in every way towards their harm and towards their wholesale destruction, when the occasion should permit.

No room for compromise there. 'Nation' (*ethnos*), 'fatherland' and 'liberty' are frequently recurring terms. Members are described as 'Hellenes'. Foreigners may not be admitted. The purpose of the organization is 'the resurrection of our suffering Fatherland'. As once before in Rigas's constitution, there is much about procedure, protocol and the secrets of the society – which even during the years of its clandestine existence seem to have not been particularly well kept.[31]

The importance of the Friendly Society was out of all proportion to the number of its members. It has been estimated that, up to the middle of 1820, this stood at no more than seven hundred, rising to somewhere between two and three thousand in the final months before the Revolution began. Just over a thousand names have been preserved in an incomplete record. Of those, only a single individual is recorded as belonging to the rural peasantry. So it was nothing like a mass movement.[32] What is important about it, though, is the fact that it was an *organization*, and dedicated to revolution.

The nature of that organization was in some ways paradoxical. All the Society's elaborate *arcana* were designed to convince initiates that they were entering a hierarchical structure. The higher you ascended, the more mysterious it became. The greatest mystery of all, to which only the chosen few ever had access, was the identity of the *Archi* or supreme leadership. This was the real purpose of the whole machinery of secrecy: not so much to protect the identities of these unimaginably high-placed individuals, but rather to conceal from the membership how lowly they were in reality. The real structure was not top-down at all, but bottom-up. The instigators of the conspiracy were men of the emerging commercial middle class, and none occupied a distinguished position within it. They nonetheless succeeded in recruiting a membership just over half of whom were merchants, with significant numbers of doctors, teachers and, in the somewhat special case of the Peloponnese, landowners and members of the Church hierarchy.

This left a void at the very top. There was no plausible, highly placed leader, ready to take command when the moment for action came. None of the Society's inner circle was remotely in a position to take on this role. It was difficult enough for them even to gain access to the kind of person they needed. The most influential Greek anywhere in the world at this time was the Corfiot Count Ioannis Kapodistrias, who in 1816 had been promoted to serve as one of the Tsar's duo of foreign ministers. The initiated were encouraged to believe that he was indeed their hidden, unnameable leader. But despite repeated lobbying, Kapodistrias refused to have anything to do with the Society. Foreshadowing, in reverse, what would be said much later about the unification of Italy, Kapodistrias insisted, 'First we must make Hellenes, and then make Hellas.'[33]

In itself, the existence of the Friendly Society was more likely a symptom than a cause. Similar secret societies existed in other parts of Europe at the time. Underlying all of them was discontent with the settlement that had been reached at Vienna in 1815. Revolutions did break out – in Spain in January 1820, in the Kingdom of the Two Sicilies, with its capital in Naples, in June of the same year, in Sardinia and Piedmont in 1821. But these were peaceful putsches by 'constitutionalists' demanding political reform, not the kind of all-out war that the secret societies plotted. All would prove short-lived. Revolutionary change in most of Europe would have to wait until 1848.

So why was it different in the borderlands of the Ottoman Empire that would soon become Greece? There too, it might be supposed, the time of violent upheavals was over. Within the empire, centralized power was being steadily reimposed from the top – although this may not yet have been fully apparent to many people on the ground. The French Revolution had come and gone. So had Napoleon and his conquests. To many of the Orthodox population, the lure of liberty must have looked as illusory as the *Paternal Instruction* had warned, back in 1798. But some things *had* changed for good. For one thing, in this part of the world, there was no stable status quo to go back to. The past fifty years or more had seen a continuing process of change.

The uncertainties of the Napoleonic Wars had only increased the pace, and the level of uncertainty. The most fundamental change was in the way that people had begun to think about themselves. The fervour that had once been generated by *liberté, égalité, fraternité* may have died down, but far more people than ever before were coming to think of themselves as 'Hellenes'. Korais, in his 'Dissertation' in Paris in 1803, had testified to the new custom among shipowners and captains for naming their vessels after ancient heroes. The same thing was beginning to happen with personal names too. The adoption of ancient Greek names alongside traditional baptismal ones was a sign of the same process.

A huge shift in consciousness was occurring. It cannot have been uniform. Many parts of the population remained barely touched by it, if at all. Others rejected it. Of those who espoused it, the most vociferous were those living outside the Ottoman Empire, or who had business connections that enabled them to come and go. This new, inchoate, unevenly distributed consciousness of 'Hellenic' identity did not, in itself, make the disparate communities of the eighteenth century any more homogeneous in the first decades of the nineteenth. If anything, the new ways of thinking fragmented them still further. But, no matter how individuals or whole communities tried to accommodate themselves to it, change was in the air.

This is not to say that changing consciousness was sufficient to cause a revolution. The kind of violent upheaval that was to come can have been actively wished for by very few, surely. That was the lesson of gradualists such as Korais and Kapodistrias. Even after hostilities had begun, there were those who would argue that the Revolution had been unnecessary, that the goal of Greek self-government could have been achieved without it. Why, then, did the Revolution happen? And why did it break out when it did? Between 1815 and 1821 three things came together that need not have done. They were intrinsically unconnected. It was the combination that would prove combustible.

The first of these was long-term, and economic. Shipping and overland commerce that had been in the hands of Orthodox Christians in the European provinces of the Ottoman Empire had continued to do well during the Napoleonic Wars. With their end, commercial fleets belonging to western nations began to return to the eastern

Mediterranean. This was the time of increasing protectionism by national governments. Greek merchant houses both in the empire and abroad were badly hit by these developments. One historian even likens the situation to the economic crisis in Greece today.[34] Some of the foreign travellers noticed its effects too. Families and whole communities, which for two generations or more had been used to ever-increasing affluence, found their fortunes going into reverse. It was a failure of expectations. A generation was growing up in which it could no longer be taken for granted that the son would do better than his father, that the daughter would make a more advantageous marriage than her mother. In the worst case, destitution threatened. The best you could hope for was to hold your own. Half a century of upward mobility (for some) had come to an abrupt end. Individuals of means, determination and talent found themselves in a desperate situation.

That was not sudden. But it was insidious. Then, in the spring of 1820, two things happened that, between them, tilted the scales towards violence. Ali, the Albanian-speaking Muslim Pasha of Ioannina, came out in open revolt against the Ottoman Empire. And on 24 April the Friendly Society found the leader it had been looking for.

3

Born in Blood

1821–1833

It was, quite simply, a bloodbath.

To the extent that the Revolution had been planned, almost from the beginning events swung free of the planners' control. The plans had been hastily laid in any case. It was not a campaign fought by leaders with objectives. It was not a war between states or even between clearly recognized groups within one state. Historians outside Greece have usually called it a 'war of independence'. It was nothing so systematic. In Greek, traditionally, it is known as 'the Revolution', or more often just by the date, which resonates throughout all subsequent Greek history: '1821'.

Once the killing had started, it became a paroxysm, a manifestation of collective rage and fear that no power on earth could control. All sides (and there were many, in different places and at different times) resorted routinely to the most extreme violence imaginable. This was not war in its traditional sense of 'the continuation of diplomacy by other means'. It was a descent into savagery. The rational, liberal values championed by the Enlightenment were often invoked. But throughout the regions affected, there was all too little sign of these values in action. The story of the Greek Revolution is not one of rational actions and reactions. What happened was more like a real birth, or a cataclysm in nature.

Victims of this violence were more often than not civilians and those unable to defend themselves. Both sides routinely murdered prisoners and hostages, of all ages and both sexes. Undertakings of safe conduct were usually broken, unless foreigners were present to try to enforce them. After a skirmish both sides would collect the severed heads of their victims as trophies. All who dealt in death, from the Ottoman state executioners down to the Christian mobs that fell upon Muslim captives, suffered the same compulsion to compound the ultimate penalty with gratuitous forms of humiliation, sometimes too with hideous and prolonged suffering. It has been estimated that by 1828 the civilian population of the regions that would make up the Greek state had been reduced by 20 per cent since the outbreak of hostilities. Destruction of crops, flocks, mills and houses – the means of livelihood for an agricultural population – was on an even greater scale, up to 90 per cent in the case of livestock.[1] By the time it was over, no Muslims remained in most of those regions. Minarets were demolished, mosques turned into warehouses, town halls or (much later) cinemas. Often, today, only their orientation towards Mecca, at variance with the surrounding buildings, gives a clue to their original purpose. Monuments or inscriptions in the old Ottoman script, and gravestones or architecture from the Ottoman period, are hard to find throughout those parts of Greece that won their independence during the 1820s.

One of the first Greek historians of the conflict, writing a few decades afterwards, justified the behaviour of his compatriots on the grounds that 'The misdeeds of the Greeks are lessons of the Turkish school and begotten of slavery.'[2] Outside observers at the time were sceptical. Non-Greek accounts, more recently, have tended to show how symmetrical was the resort to extreme violence between the two sides. At the local level, this was undoubtedly true. But not all forms of violence were symmetrical. The Ottoman state established from the beginning a pattern of reprisals that probably exacerbated the threat it was attempting to control. Within a few weeks in April and May 1821 the work of more than a century was undone in the annihilation of the Phanariot class. Of all the executions carried out in Constantinople at that time, the most notorious was that of the aged Ecumenical Patriarch of the Orthodox Church, hanged from the gate of his own precinct on Easter Day, 22 April. More than a hundred prominent Phanariots were publicly beheaded in the city during those weeks.

It may have been a sign of panic on the part of the Ottoman government that these measures, disproportionate and indiscriminate as they were, were also damaging to the Ottomans' own interests. For several years afterwards it would prove impossible for the Ottoman state to fill some of its highest offices that traditionally had been held by Phanariots. The same kind of self-harming paroxysm would surface again a year later, when the mastic-growing villages of the island of Chios were razed, as punishment for an incursion by Greek insurgents from another island. The massacres on Chios between April and June 1822 were compounded by another institutional form of reprisal that was built into the Ottoman system: slavery. Tens of thousands of women and children from Chios glutted the slave-markets of the Levant during the summer and autumn of 1822. These events shocked the whole of Europe, to be immortalized in the famous canvas by Eugène Delacroix, *Scene of the Massacres of Scio*, completed two years afterwards. But closer to home, the ladies of high society in Constantinople had been accustomed to chew the mastic that is intensively cultivated only on Chios and which possesses medicinal properties. Now, thanks to Ottoman vengeance, they would have to do without.

By contrast, on the Greek side, there was no comparable state authority to carry out acts of punishment or reprisal on such a scale. Neither the Provisional Government nor the local leaders who exercised power in their regions would usually issue orders for atrocities to be carried out. Slavery, at least in theory, was outlawed by the Provisional Constitution of 1822. The fact that so many atrocities did take place has been attributed to a failure of leadership. George Finlay, normally the most judicious and still the most authoritative historian of the Revolution, is particularly scathing about the inability of even such powerful warlords as Theodoros Kolokotronis or Petrobey Mavromichalis to check them. But these leaders were anything but weak. They knew the men they commanded. As leaders, they understood the basis on which they enjoyed their men's trust and how fragile it was. Terms of surrender would be violated in Tripolitsa in October 1821 and in Athens in July 1822, on a scale that appalled Europe no less than did the Ottoman atrocities on Chios. But one must wonder whether *any* Greek leader, however talented and charismatic, could have restrained the mass bloodlust that broke out on those occasions, without immediately forfeiting all his authority.

Finlay believed that the 'true glory of the Greek Revolution lies in the indomitable energy and unwearied perseverance of the mass of the people'.[3] He had experienced the Revolution at first hand, and by the time he wrote his history had lived most of his life in independent Greece. His view has tended to prevail since. But even the canny Scot, whose personal motto was 'I'll be wary', romanticizes here. The grim truth must be that it was Finlay's hero, the 'mass of the people' themselves, driven no doubt by the most primitive human instincts under extreme conditions, who collectively fell victim to the pathology of violence – a pathology that infected Christian and Muslim populations alike. Out of this frenzy of terror, mutual hatred and bloodletting, the Greek nation state would in due course be born.

THE END OF THE FRIENDLY SOCIETY

Alexandros Ypsilantis (also spelt Hypsilantes) was the eldest son of a former prince of Wallachia who had fled to Russia at the start of the Russo-Turkish war in 1806. There Alexandros had received a military education and gone on to serve with distinction in the Russian campaigns against Napoleon. He had lost his right arm in a battle outside Dresden. Since then he had served as a member of the Russian delegation at the Congress of Vienna. By all accounts, Alexandros Ypsilantis enjoyed the confidence of Tsar Alexander. More recently, despite being no longer fit for active service, he had been promoted to major-general in the imperial army. He was now, conveniently for the emissaries of the Friendly Society, on leave. This was the man who in April 1820, aged twenty-seven, agreed to fill the vacuum at the top of the Society's ranks and become its long-sought leader. By the end of 1820, Ypsilantis had set up a secret headquarters at Kishinev (today's Chişinău, capital of Moldova), then just inside Russian territory and close to the border with Ottoman-controlled Moldavia.

Suddenly, to the minds of the Society's members, it seemed there was no time like the present. A leader was to hand. Ottoman forces were already on their way to lay siege to the rebel Ali Pasha in his capital at Ioannina. The whole of Roumeli (the mainland north of the Peloponnese) was becoming engulfed by a local war between competing Muslim powers: Ali versus the centralized authority of the Sultan. It seemed like the perfect moment to strike. But where, and how? At first the plan was to follow the example of Rigas. Ypsilantis was to go in disguise to Trieste and from there take ship for the Peloponnese. This was the one region where the Society's emissaries had been successful in recruiting most of the local Christian landowners, the 'primates', to the cause. Who knows how different the fortunes of Ypsilantis and the Friendly Society, or indeed the course of the Revolution, might have been if he had followed this advice? But at the last minute the plan changed. The Peloponnesians could make their own arrangements. The banner of revolt would be raised in the Danubian principalities instead.

Wearing Russian uniform and accompanied by only a handful of retainers, Alexandros Ypsilantis entered Ottoman territory by boat across the river Pruth on 6 March 1821. By evening of the same day he had reached Jassy, the capital of Moldavia. There he was made welcome by the Phanariot prince – who thereby reneged on his allegiance to his sovereign, the Sultan. Two days later a proclamation was printed, which in due course would be translated and published in the newspapers of Europe.

The Greek Revolution had begun.

By the end of his first day in Moldavia, Ypsilantis had already gathered a force of two hundred local supporters in arms. Within a week this number had quadrupled. By June, his army had swelled to something between five and eight thousand, including upwards of two thousand cavalry. This was a remarkable achievement in itself. Almost all of these had been locally recruited in the two principalities of Moldavia and Wallachia. Despite what the Ottoman authorities assumed, only a handful of Ypsilantis's officers, and no fighting troops, had accompanied him from Russia.

Even more remarkable was the composition of this army. At its heart lay a corps of five hundred educated Greeks from all parts of Europe – the very people who had once been addressed by the anonymous author of *Hellenic Nomarchy*. Known as the Sacred Battalion, they wore a black uniform and marched under a banner in Rigas's colours – red, white and black – but with a new symbol, the phoenix rising from the fire, and the slogan 'Out of my ashes I am reborn'. Far more numerous were willing recruits from all the language groups (or ethnicities) of the Balkans: Serbs and Bulgarians, Albanians and Vlachs (Romanians), Cossacks from the border regions with Russia. For the one and only time in history, this was the 'Orthodox commonwealth' in arms. Had it succeeded, Rigas's vision of a cosmopolitan 'Hellenic Republic' might have become a reality.

But Ypsilantis's enterprise was fatally flawed. The Friendly Society had been founded on the premise that its leadership enjoyed the support of Russia. But this had never been true. Ypsilantis may have believed that his own personal standing with the Tsar and his court would be enough to bring about a change. But with the worst possible timing, news of the revolt in Moldavia reached Tsar Alexander at Laibach (today's Ljubljana, capital of Slovenia), where he was attending one of the regular congresses of the 'Concert of Europe'. There, of all places, in the company of the representatives of the other Great Powers, it would have been unthinkable for the Russian autocrat to endorse a revolution in a neighbouring country. The purpose of these congresses was after all to reinforce the status quo that had been established in 1815. Tsar Alexander summarily dismissed Ypsilantis from the imperial service and stripped him of all his ranks and titles. He even went so far as to offer his support to the Ottoman government in putting down the rebellion.

Even then, Ypsilantis did all he could to keep up the pretence: the Tsar only said these things for show. Secretly, Ypsilantis claimed, his master had sent assurances that Russian aid would soon be on its way. But much of the momentum had been taken out of the campaign. The end came swiftly. On 19 June, at the battle of Dragashan, in Wallachia, the troops of the Friendly Society were routed by a much smaller Ottoman force. Ypsilantis slipped over the frontier to claim refuge in Austrian territory. The survivors of the army he had raised in the principalities were left to fend for themselves. Some fought on to the end, others were captured and executed. Ypsilantis himself was interned by the Austrians. A broken man, he would only just survive beyond the end of his incarceration, to die at the age of thirty-five.

The Greek Revolution in the Danubian principalities had been an ignominious failure.

*

In the meantime, at the southern end of the Balkan peninsula and in the Aegean, events had taken a very different turn. In the Peloponnese, and on the islands that were home to the biggest merchant fleets, local leaders had heeded the call of the Friendly Society in larger numbers than anywhere else. The reasons for this are not entirely clear. One may well have been the financial difficulties experienced by these groups at the time. For the islanders, trade had been bad since the end of the Napoleonic Wars. On the mainland, the wealthy landowners who depended on exports of products such as currants and silk were struggling too. Urged on by the representatives of the Society, some of these men were now prepared to tear up the decades-old agreements with the Ottoman authorities that had won them their privileges in the first place, and make common cause with former brigands such as Theodoros Kolokotronis, who now began to return from enforced exile in the Ionian islands.

As soon as news began to spread of Ypsilantis's revolt in Moldavia, uprisings in the Peloponnese broke out spontaneously in several places at once. The emissaries of the Friendly Society had originally set 25 March 1821 (6 April in the Western calendar) for the start of the Revolution. The date has symbolic resonance, as it coincides with the religious festival of the Annunciation. Ever since, 25 March has been commemorated as Greece's national day. But the oft-repeated legend that Bishop Germanos of Old Patras raised the standard of revolt on that day in the Monastery of Agia Lavra, high in the mountains above Kalavryta, is just that. The first towns in the Peloponnese to declare themselves free of Ottoman rule were Kalamata in the south and Patras in the north. Others soon followed. By the middle of April the whole region was in revolt.

This was not an organized military campaign, such as Ypsilantis had attempted in the principalities. It was guerrilla warfare, usually on a small scale. The leaders were local 'primates' and former brigands, aided after the first months by a steady trickle of idealistic volunteers from abroad, of whom more will be said later. With little coordination or agreement among guerrilla bands, in the mountainous terrain of the Peloponnese this kind of insurgency proved devastatingly effective.

Even now, not all the regional populations where Greek speakers predominated were ready to declare for the Revolution. In Roumeli, to the north, the situation was complicated by the Muslim-on-Muslim conflict between Ali Pasha and the Sultan's forces. In this part of the country, armed militias made up of Christians had for decades been recruited to keep banditry in check, largely from among the same brigands that they were meant to control. These militias had evolved a fluid system of switching allegiance among local centres of power. For as long as Ali held out in Ioannina, some of these bands could be bought over to his side, others by the Ottoman army. It was not until the summer that most of the local militias had come round to the new Greek cause. But as long as the Revolution lasted, many would never entirely give up their habit of making tactical alliances to secure their own local power bases.

Of key importance was the richest of the naval islands, Hydra, which joined the Revolution only after a coup d'état against the traditional oligarchy of shipowners. By the time the shipowners had regained control, there was no going back on the island's commitment to the Revolution. The fleets of armed merchantmen from Hydra, nearby Spetses and Psara on the other side of the Aegean, soon joined forces and proved more than a match for the Ottoman fleet. Particularly deadly, and particularly feared by the Ottoman sailors, were the Greek fireships – old hulks that would be coated in pitch, set alight and expertly set on course to collide with their targets, before the sailors abandoned them in small boats and escaped to safety. Within a few months these irregular fleets had all but gained control of the Aegean. Although they never quite managed to impose blockades sufficient to prevent enemy movements by sea, from the summer of 1821 onwards they were able to strike with impunity anywhere in the Aegean and even right round the coast, in the Ionian Sea to the west.

On many of the smaller Aegean islands, where Ottoman authority had always fallen more lightly than on the mainland, enthusiasm was more muted. The Roman Catholic communities established since the later Middle Ages on many of the Cyclades, including Syros, Tinos and Santorini, declined to risk their lives and livelihoods by supporting their Orthodox compatriots. Further north, on the mainland, on Mount Pelion, which for decades had been a centre of commerce and learning, an outbreak was quickly suppressed. The hinterland of

Salonica rebelled too. Here Ottoman reprisals were especially grim, but also effective. The same excessive measures that in the south served only to inflame revolutionary fervour, farther north had the opposite effect.

To the south and east, the Christians of Crete and of Samos enthusiastically joined the Revolution, though in the event neither island would become part of independent Greece until the twentieth century. In two other large islands in the Aegean, Lesbos and Chios, the Christian populations resolutely tried to avoid becoming embroiled – the former successfully, the latter not – with the catastrophic consequences already described. Revolts on the coast of Anatolia, at Ayvalık and Smyrna, were suppressed. Furthest away of all, on the island of Cyprus, where nobody rebelled, the leading churchmen were executed anyway, on the mere suspicion of having been in cahoots with the Friendly Society.

By the end of 1821, the countryside throughout the Peloponnese and the southern part of Roumeli had been subjected to what today would be termed 'ethnic cleansing'. Those Muslims who had not fled, been killed or, in a few high-ranking cases, ransomed, had taken refuge in a string of fortresses that went back to Crusader or Byzantine times. The decisive victory of the first year of the war was the submission of the fortified town of Tripolitsa, the capital of the Morea, in early October. After the town had capitulated, some eight thousand Muslim and Jewish inhabitants were slaughtered. In the language of the time, all Muslims were described as 'Turks', irrespective of what today would be called their ethnicity. Many of those killed, including probably all of the Jews, will have spoken Greek as their first language, most of the Muslims either Greek or Albanian. It was religion that determined who was to live and who to die. By the end of 1821 the nature of the conflict had been irreversibly defined. So, too, was the geographical heartland of the Revolution, which after many intervening changes of fortune would emerge more or less as the territory of the first independent Greek state at the start of the 1830s.

By this time its leadership had already passed into a new phase. Many, perhaps all, of those who had struck the first blows in March and April 1821 had been members of the Friendly Society. But the

Society as an organization had become bogged down with Ypsilantis in the campaign that would soon fail so disastrously in Wallachia in the north. In the Peloponnese, there was no direction from the top. No single authority was in charge. It was not until June that the Society's plenipotentiary arrived in liberated Greece, to claim control of events on its behalf. This was the younger brother of Alexandros Ypsilantis, Dimitrios. He too, like his brother, had a background in the Russian imperial army. Aged just twenty-five when he disembarked at Hydra, the younger Ypsilantis was received with rapturous enthusiasm – since it was believed that he brought with him the promise of Russian aid. Even the paramount warlords of the Morea, the warrior-chieftain of the Mani, Petrobey Mavromichalis, and the fifty-one-year-old former brigand Theodoros Kolokotronis, were prepared to place themselves under his command.

Sadly for Dimitrios Ypsilantis, the day of his arrival at Hydra was also the day of his brother's crushing defeat at Dragashan. It would not be long before the news had filtered through to the Peloponnese, where Dimitrios had in the meantime established his headquarters. Once it was known that the elder Ypsilantis had deserted the cause and sought refuge in Austria, and that the arrival of the younger did not signal a benign change in Russian policy, not only was it impossible for Dimitrios to assert the authority that he claimed on behalf of the Friendly Society, but the Society itself was beginning to seem like an irrelevance. Worse, it could even be seen as an embarrassment.

Enter the man who would do more than any other, in the early years at least, to shape the direction to be taken by the future Greek state. A descendant of the first and most distinguished of the Phanariot princes to rule in the Danubian principalities during the previous century, and still only in his late twenties, Alexandros Mavrokordatos had gained political experience in the service of his uncle, who had recently served the Sultan as prince of Wallachia. Mavrokordatos was one of a significant number among the leaders of the Revolution who had never previously visited the lands they were fighting for – a source of resentment for some among those that they led. Highly intelligent and a speaker of eight languages, Mavrokordatos immediately stood out as the only man of consequence in Greece who wore a European frock coat – while Dimitrios Ypsilantis, like his brother, sported imperial Russian uniform and almost everybody else (often including Western volunteers) dressed in the local Ottoman style. Mavrokordatos was a politician to his fingertips – and we will meet him again.

In the aftermath of the sack of Tripolitsa in October, while regional leaders jockeyed for power and influence, momentum was gathering for a general assembly of the whole liberated nation to take place. Dimitrios Ypsilantis encouraged this development, in the expectation that it would set the seal on his own supremacy. Mavrokordatos encouraged it too, but with a different goal in mind. While this assembly was in preparation, in early November, Mavrokordatos wrote at length and with remarkable candour to the chief representative of the Friendly Society. It was the mistakes made by the Society that had:

> aroused against us all the European Powers, which quite rightly thought we were the instruments of the Jacobins of Europe. These things alienated Russia, who in every other circumstance could willingly have aided us.

The answer, according to Mavrokordatos, was:

> to leave behind titles of 'leaders' and 'plenipotentiaries' and 'aides', to organize government by the local people themselves, under our guidance so far as possible ... to leave behind whatever makes the European Powers suspect us of Jacobin leanings ... to lay our just demands before Europe not with swollen words, but laconically as worthy of our ancestors and with moderation.

Above all, Mavrokordatos urged, it was imperative to 'do everything possible to bring people together in unity, so as to form the government'.[4]

The assembly duly took place. It ended with the proclamation of the first Provisional Constitution of independent Greece, near the site of the ancient sanctuary of Epidaurus, on 13 January 1822 (New Year's day according to the Orthodox calendar). This document drew heavily, just as Rigas's had done, on the French Revolutionary constitutions of 1793 and 1795. It established the name of the new country as Hellas and its citizens as Hellenes. Following the doctrine of the separation of powers that had first been implemented in the United States of America, it established an Executive and a Legislative Corps. Voted president of the first (on the American analogy, head of state) was Alexandros Mavrokordatos. President of the second (roughly equivalent to the US Speaker of the House of Representatives) was Dimitrios Ypsilantis. The Provisional Constitution makes no mention of the Friendly Society. At the same time, the red, white and black tricolour of Rigas was replaced by the blue and white colours, though not yet the design, of what would become the present-day Greek flag.

There was no mistaking who had come out on top.

From a practical point of view, this first Provisional Constitution would remain largely a dead letter. George Finlay, writing four decades later, would set the tone for historians who came after him: 'A good deal was done by the Greeks at Epidaurus to deceive Europe; very little to organise Greece.'[5] In many ways it *was* a deception. What the Provisional Constitution proclaimed was far more aspiration than practical policy, as all who set their names to it would have known very well. But from a political point of view, it was also a *necessary* deception, if a revolutionary movement was ever going to win acceptance in the climate of Europe in the first half of the nineteenth century. The Friendly Society had served its purpose. The Revolution was now on its way to becoming what one historian has more recently termed 'a European event'.[6]

WHAT KIND OF FREEDOM?

All this time, the Revolution in the south had benefited from the continuing campaign by the Ottoman army, further north, to subdue the rebellion of Ali Pasha. But in January 1822 the Sultan's troops entered Ioannina, Ali's capital. The veteran 'Muslim Bonaparte', as Lord Byron had styled him, was murdered by one of his captors on 5 February. The rebellion was over. The considerable military force that the Ottoman government had thrown into this conflict was now available to settle the affairs of the Greeks, and was already on their doorstep in strength. The first concerted counter-attack against the fledgling Greek state was launched with massive strength in July 1822.

One part of the Ottoman army marched south through eastern Roumeli and into the Peloponnese. Its aim was to relieve the besieged Ottoman garrisons of Corinth and Nafplio, join up with them and subdue the country in between. Another moved down the western side of the Pindos mountain range. Here the principal target was the trading port of Missolonghi, on which Mavrokordatos had concentrated his activities since his arrival the year before. Here too were besieged Ottoman outposts to be relieved, at Lepanto (today's Nafpaktos) and the Castle of Roumeli (today's Antirrio). In both campaigns the Greeks were heavily outnumbered.

In the west the Ottoman command had been assigned to Ali Pasha's replacement. Omer Vryonis, the new Pasha of Ioannina, had none of his predecessor's ambition, but would prove adept over the next few years at harrying the insurgent Greeks and exploiting the fluid loyalties of the local Greek- and Albanian-speaking militias. One of the few relatively conventional pitched battles of the war was fought on 16 July 1822. Vryonis's forces were met by a regular Greek force, made up of volunteers from western Europe and the Ionian islands, under the command of Mavrokordatos, outside the town and strategic river crossing of Arta at a place called Peta. The battle was a wipe-out. The foreign volunteers, sticking rigidly to their Western training, would not act without orders from their commander-in-chief, who was absent. The irregular militias, supposed to be providing cover in the hills, were impervious to orders from anyone and simply disappeared. The battle of Peta was a terrible blow to the Revolution, but even more so to the morale of those idealistic volunteers from abroad who had already begun arriving to join the cause. Most of all, it cast a blight on the whole concept of regular warfare and set back the creation of a national army, under a single command, for years.

On the other side of the country, the outcome was dramatically different. Mahmud Dramali, at the head of an Ottoman force some twenty thousand strong, including eight thousand cavalry, succeeded in penetrating into the Peloponnese. Here, resistance was in the hands of Kolokotronis and the local guerrilla 'captains'. Against all expectations, they prevented the attackers from entering Nafplio, and then decimated them in an ambush during their retreat north through the pass of Dervenakia. Coming just ten days after the defeat at Peta, this was a resounding vindication for the irregular tactics and ruthless methods of the guerrillas. Although many others played their part too, including the now eclipsed Dimitrios Ypsilantis, chief credit for the success at Dervenakia has generally gone to Kolokotronis. Justified or not (Finlay thought not), it certainly boosted that leader's political position among the other Greeks. By the late summer of 1822 no significant military threat to the Greeks existed down the entire eastern side of the country.

It took longer to secure the western flank. Mavrokordatos would redeem himself, in the months that followed the disaster at Peta, by his defence of the chief town of the region, Missolonghi. The surviving forces that remained loyal had regrouped there. Aided by torrential rain, by the arrival of ships from Hydra and by their own sheer determination, the defenders succeeded in breaking the Ottoman siege on 6 January 1823, which was Christmas Day according to the Orthodox calendar. This was the first of no fewer than three sieges that over the course of the war would make the name of Missolonghi famous throughout all of Europe. The end of this first siege meant that by the start of 1823 the precariously emerging Greek state had won itself a breathing space.

For reasons largely outside the insurgents' control, this breathing space would last a full two years. True, skirmishing on the borders continued throughout this period. Borders, except in the Peloponnese, were in any case porous and shifting. Outlying islands were especially vulnerable. Whole populations would be wiped out on Psara and Kasos in the summer of 1824. The same year would see the Ottomans regain control of Crete. But with these notable exceptions, from the beginning of 1823 until the spring of 1825, insurgent Greece enjoyed a period of relative security.

But not of peace. The stage was now set for an internal reckoning among the Greeks themselves. All could unite under the banner, 'Liberty or Death'. But now that it had been won, what *was* this 'liberty', exactly? What *kind* of freedom were they to enjoy in future?

One answer was based on the ideas of the Enlightenment. Mavrokordatos and those who thought like him were determined to promote a programme for centralized government, for modern, progressive institutions, the rule of law, democratic accountability – all of which had been enshrined in the Epidaurus Constitution (dismissed by Finlay and others as a 'deception'). For these men, the task was to turn that aspiration into reality. Historians today most often call this group 'modernizers'. Against them were ranged the traditional values and outlook of the local leaders collectively known as 'warlords'. For men such as Kolokotronis and Mavromichalis, freedom meant absolute self-sufficiency, the refusal to acknowledge any authority other than their own. Among their ranks, the leader was the strongest and the most charismatic, and the leader's word was law. Their power bases were local, or at the most regional. They had no great interest in widening the conflict, still less in encouraging foreign intervention – though they tended, not entirely consistently, to make an exception for Russia. Theirs was the concept of freedom captured in the oral tradition, in the songs of the klefts that first began to be collected, published and translated at just this time, and have been performed at national celebrations ever since.

These divisions came out into the open during April 1823. The occasion was a second National Assembly, held not far from Nafplio at a place known locally as 'St John's Huts' and for the occasion restored to its ancient name of Astros. New elections placed executive power in the hands of the most prominent warlords, Mavromichalis and Kolokotronis. Mavrokordatos was reduced to an ambiguous position. This reached the point of absurdity when Kolokotronis bullied him out of accepting the position of the President of the Legislative Corps, to which he had been elected. The separation of powers was not working well.

For several months, in late 1823 and early 1824, Greece had two governments, each attempting to face down the other from a different power base. Between March and June 1824 forces loyal to the rival governments took the field against one another. After an uneasy truce, and some opportunistic realignment of the contending parties, a second civil war broke out in the Peloponnese in November. One of the highest-profile casualties of these events was Kolokotronis's eldest son Panos, killed in battle by fellow Greeks outside Tripolitsa. Another, indirectly, was the most famous of all the foreign volunteers who came to Greece to aid the cause, Lord Byron.

Byron's death at Missolonghi on 19 April 1824 created a legend – but also served to obscure ever afterwards what had been his real contribution to the Greek struggle. Byron, too, arriving in Greece when he did, had to face the same dilemma as confronted the rival Greek leaders: what *kind* of freedom had he come to fight for? Having carefully weighed the alternatives, Byron opted to throw his celebrity reputation and his personal wealth behind Mavrokordatos and the modernizing shipowners of Hydra and Spetses. Byron lasted for only three months in independent Greece before succumbing to fever. But his strategic choice, and the flow of funds and the immense international publicity that came with it, had important consequences. One was that the second siege of Missolonghi was lifted at the end of 1823, without a shot being fired, on the mere report that the English lord had financed a squadron of Greek ships for the town's relief. Of even greater significance, in the long run, was Byron's decisive support for the modernizers against the warlords of the Peloponnese in the conflict that would drag on for the rest of the year.

By the start of 1825, the authority of a single, centralized government had been assured. In the process, the political leadership of the modernizers had passed from Mavrokordatos to a new figure. Ioannis Kolettis, now entering his fifties, had proved himself to be more ruthless and less squeamish during the civil wars than Mavrokordatos, when it came to directing the use of force against fellow Greeks. Kolettis had been born in Ali Pasha's fiefdom into a Vlach-speaking community. Taking advantage of the Greek education available through the Orthodox Church, he had gone on to study medicine in Italy and returned to serve as a court physician in Ioannina. There, Kolettis had learnt all about the intrigues necessary for survival in the court of Ali Pasha, and no doubt much also about his master's complex diplomacy with the rival powers of Britain and France during the Napoleonic Wars. In this way, Kolettis managed to combine a political legacy from Ali Pasha with a Western, modernizing outlook. From this time until his death in 1847, Kolettis and Mavrokordatos would remain bitter political rivals on the same, broadly modernizing side. More of a populist than the intellectually accomplished Mavrokordatos could ever be, it was more often than not Kolettis who would have the edge.

According to the bold reassessment of one Greek historian, writing in the twenty-first century, 'it was the outcome of the civil war that saved the Greek Revolution'.[7] In the sense that it determined the future shape and direction of the Greek nation state, this was true. But the price of that outcome was to open up a fault line in the fabric of Greek society that has never, since, gone away. On one side are the descendants of the 'modernizers' of the 1820s: political, statist, pragmatic and integrationist. Ranged on the other are traditionalists, nostalgic for the absolute freedom celebrated in the songs of the klefts and the brief moments of glorious self-sufficiency enjoyed by some of the warlords during the Revolution. Much that has happened in subsequent Greek history can only be explained or understood in terms of these dynamics, which first emerged during the struggle out of which the nation state was born.

But first, if the Revolution was to be saved, it had to survive.

ALL BUT EXTINGUISHED

No sooner had the modernizing central government gained the upper hand in the internal struggle with the warlords than the long-awaited Ottoman counter-attack began. Its effects would soon prove deadly. Back in 1822, the Sultan had relied on a two-pronged attack by land from the north. That strategy had failed. In 1825 the assault was renewed not only through the familiar land routes, but simultaneously from the south, by sea. Key players in this part of the story are Muhammad Ali, the Viceroy of Egypt, and his son Ibrahim. Muhammad Ali had begun life as Mehmet, an Albanian-speaking Muslim from Kavala, in the north of today's Greece. A decade earlier he had deposed and eliminated the Mameluke dynasty that for several centuries had ruled Egypt as a vassal state of the Ottoman Empire. During the intervening years, Muhammad Ali had thoroughly overhauled and modernized his armed forces along European lines, with some assistance from the West, particularly from France. Sultan and viceroy determined to work together to exterminate the threat from Greece. The Ottoman navy, based in Constantinople, was reinforced by a second fleet of transports and fighting ships from Alexandria, under the command of Muhammad Ali's son Ibrahim, who was appointed Pasha of the Morea.

Ibrahim began landing troops from Egypt at Modon (today's Methoni, in the southwest Peloponnese) on 23 February 1825. The twin fortresses in that area, Modon and Coron, had remained in Ottoman hands throughout the war. Relieving the garrisons, Ibrahim's fifty ships brought reinforcements on a scale not seen in this theatre of the war so far. A swift campaign drove the Greeks out of the neighbouring stronghold of Navarino, in an action that nearly cost Mavrokordatos his life. The anchorage of Navarino Bay, between the mainland and the island of Sphaktiria, for the next two years would provide a secure base for the combined fleets from Alexandria and Constantinople.

Meanwhile, to the north, a new commander-in-chief had replaced Omer Vryonis. Reshid Pasha, who had played a leading role in the battle of Peta, laid siege to Missolonghi at the end of April 1825. It was the beginning of the third, and final, siege that would last a whole year. Desultory fighting in the rest of southern Roumeli led to the collapse of the Greeks almost everywhere north of the Isthmus of Corinth. Only Missolonghi in the west and the Acropolis of Athens in the east still held out, and both were under close siege by the Ottomans. While Reshid and other local pashas ravaged Roumeli, Ibrahim embarked upon the systematic reconquest of the Peloponnese, burning and destroying crops and villages as he went. By the end of the summer of 1825 the Greeks had been forced to abandon Tripolitsa. At the height of Ibrahim's advance, Egyptian troops came within sight of the Greek stronghold and temporary capital of Nafplio. As George Finlay drily summed it up, 'The Egyptians carried on a war of extermination; the Greeks replied by a war of brigandage.' The result, he thought, must have seemed inevitable: 'Famine would soon consume those who escaped the sword.'[8]

Towards the end of 1825 all the efforts of both sides came to be concentrated on the besieged town of Missolonghi. On the Ottoman side, Ibrahim now joined forces with Reshid in Roumeli. The town was blockaded by both land and sea. For months Greek ships from Hydra and Spetses ran the blockade to keep the defenders supplied. Volunteers from Zante in the Ionian islands, officially proscribed from doing so by the British, who ruled the islands, contributed too. Hard pressed in its remaining stronghold of Nafplio, the Greek government was powerless to intervene, except by trying to raise money to keep the defenders supplied. But inexorably the noose tightened.

By mid-April 1826 the only choices facing those inside were to starve to death, to surrender or to try to break out. They chose the last. The attempt was made on the night of Palm Sunday, 22 April. It was an act of doomed heroism. Out of a population estimated at some nine thousand that had survived the siege so far, fewer than two thousand escaped with their lives. 'Ibrahim boasted of having taken 3000 heads, and from 3000 to 4000 women and children were made slaves.' Several hundred who were too weak to leave the town took a last refuge in the house of Christos Kapsalis, where Byron had lived and died two years earlier, and which in the meantime had been turned into a gunpowder store. There, the story goes, seemingly by common consent, and so as not to fall into the hands of the enemy, the elderly Kapsalis himself lit the match and plunged it into a barrel of gunpowder, killing everyone inside.

Even the normally reserved Thomas Gordon, who had himself served with distinction in Greece and became one of the Revolution's first historians, described the fall of Missolonghi as a 'glorious tragedy'. George Finlay, soured by thirty years of living in the country whose struggles he had witnessed in his youth, paid this tribute to the defenders: 'A spirit of Greek heroism, rare in the Greek Revolution – rare even in the history of mankind – pervaded every breast.'[9] In Greek, the 'Exodus of Missolonghi' would soon become the stuff of epic poetry and monumental painting. Ever since, the event has been commemorated in biblical terms. In 1937 the Greek government bestowed on the municipality the title 'Sacred City', by which name Missolonghi is still officially known today.

The months that followed were the darkest time for the Revolution. In Nafplio, Hydra and Spetses it seemed as though all was lost. Sooner or later, Ibrahim's forces were bound to return. Nafplio had much better defences than Missolonghi. But there could be no defence against starvation. Hydra and Spetses lived in daily expectation of a swoop by the Egyptian fleet, in a repetition of the wholesale destruction of their comrades-in-arms in Psara, where the entire community of the island had been wiped out in the summer of 1824. It is said that some of the leading citizens even contemplated flight to the British-ruled Ionian islands. For a few weeks, the whole population of Spetses, the smaller of the two communities, was evacuated to Hydra.

For more than a year after the loss of Missolonghi, things went from bad to worse. Repeated attempts to relieve the siege of Athens resulted in costly failures. Not even the arrival of high-profile foreign volunteers and an injection of money and ships from abroad could halt what seemed to be an inexorable slide in Greek military fortunes. Another outsider recruited in the desperation of the times was Count Ioannis Kapodistrias, the aristocrat from Corfu who for six years until his dismissal in 1822 had served as joint foreign minister of Russia. On 14 April 1827 a rancorous, third National Assembly, held at Damala (Troezen) in the northeastern Peloponnese, voted to offer the highest position of authority in the government to Kapodistrias. This was precisely the result that the Friendly Society had tried and failed to achieve almost a decade earlier. This time, perhaps surprisingly, in view of the situation in Greece, Kapodistrias accepted – though not immediately, and in the event he would not arrive for almost a year. The interim government, elected to serve in the meantime, had no grip on events. Lawlessness and starvation were everywhere; piracy flourished.

Two things combined to save the Revolution at this point. Neither could have been effective without the other. One was the dogged determination of a sufficient number of Greeks and their leaders to fight on. No doubt this resolution was fuelled by the refusal of the Ottomans to make concessions or grant terms to the insurgents – except in Roumeli where local arrangements applied and as a result the Revolution had already collapsed. The other was the success of Mavrokordatos, Kolettis, former Phanariots and men of education, merchants, shipowners and many others, in broadening the bounds of the conflict beyond their own shores. It was the international dimension that would make possible the decisive outcome of the Revolution – and also deepen the fault line that would be part of its legacy for the future.

THE INTERNATIONAL DIMENSION

From the very beginning, the Greek Revolution had never been a purely local affair, for Greeks alone. The Friendly Society had sought, and its leader had promised, military support from Russia. More unexpected, perhaps, was the 'Manifesto addressed to Europe by Petros Mavromikhalis' on 9 April 1821, just a week after his Maniat tribesmen had seized control of the town of Kalamata. Styling himself 'Commander-in-Chief of the Spartan Troops', Petrobey (as he is better known to history) called for 'the aid of all the civilized nations of Europe'. 'Greece, our mother,' he continued, 'was the lamp that illuminated you.' This is the language of indebtedness that goes back to the European travellers of the previous century. The time for repayment has come: 'Arms, money, and counsel, are what she expects from you.'[10] The language of the French Revolution had taken root in this remote outpost of Europe, six years after the final defeat of Napoleon.

Events were to prove that Petrobey was no great internationalist in practice. The manifesto was just as much of an imaginative creation as the Provisional Constitution of Epidaurus a few months later. But, remarkably, both were heeded. The Constitution would soon find its way to London and into the hands of the veteran political philosopher Jeremy Bentham, who returned it to the Greek government with a generous and thoughtful commentary. Bentham of course had no idea of the realities of the Revolution, or he might have saved himself the effort. But the point is that the great man even thought the document worthy of his attention. In the same way, and perhaps even more surprisingly, Petrobey's call for international aid also brought a response.

From all over Europe, and even as far as away as the United States of America, volunteers began arriving in Greece. Some of them we have met already. They included two of the earliest and best historians of the Revolution, Thomas Gordon and George Finlay, both of them Scots, as well as the more famous Byron ('half a Scot, by birth – and bred / A whole one').[11] The graves of many more are marked by a polyglot collection of memorials in the Garden of Heroes at

Missolonghi, still a beautiful and tranquil spot where the aura of history lies heavily. British adventurers Richard Church and Thomas Lord Cochrane were entrusted with high commands, the one on land, the other at sea. So was the French veteran of Napoleon's campaigns Charles Fabvier. Probably the most effective military contribution was made by Frank Abney Hastings. Dismissed from the Royal Navy for insubordination, Hastings would prove himself an ingenious naval strategist and went on to captain the world's first fighting steamship, the *Karteria*, until his death in 1828 in an attempt to recapture Missolonghi.

The philhellenes, as these volunteers have come to be known, were not mercenary fighters. Nor were they in Greece to serve their own countries. Indeed, particularly in the first years, they had often to evade the efforts of the security services at home, who did their best to prevent them from going. In most countries the authorities greatly feared the spread of the 'radicalization', as we would call it today, that they associated with any revolutionary movement. The philhellenes were never very numerous. The total number lies probably between one thousand and twelve hundred.

Some historians have suggested that modern 'humanitarian intervention' began with the philhellenes in Greece in the 1820s. But this is to misunderstand the motives of these volunteers. No less than those who a century later would volunteer to fight in Spain, the philhellenes were prepared to risk their lives in somebody else's war because they believed that they, too, had a stake in the conflict. In the language of the anonymous translator of Guys' travel book, of Petrobey Mavromichalis, and the poet Shelley, these philhellenes were moved to repay a debt that they felt they owed to the origin of their own civilization. This is what Shelley meant when he wrote, memorably, a few months after the outbreak of the Revolution in Greece, 'We are all Greeks.' The Ottomans stood in the way of an emerging new Europe, built on classical foundations, that the philhellenes saw as their own. This was the call to which the volunteers were responding.

This is not to suggest that the philhellenes were indifferent to the human suffering that some of them witnessed at first hand and many more read about in the safety of their own homes. The Swiss and the

Americans stand out in this respect. The Swiss banker Jean-Gabriel Eynard organized large-scale relief of famine in Greece during the winter after the fall of Missolonghi. Among the Americans, the energetic and humane Samuel Gridley Howe established a hospital on the island of Poros in 1827. Later, putting practical solutions ahead of veneration for the classical past, he would mastermind the demolition of the ruins of the ancient temple on the headland outside the port town on the island of Aegina, then the nation's capital, in order to provide a working harbour and employment for thousands of displaced workers who might otherwise have starved.

The direct effect of the philhellenes on the conflict was limited. They won no decisive battles. Almost a third of those who volunteered lost their lives, either in combat or from disease. But the very fact that they were there at all was the foot in the door that would lead to much wider and more effective international involvement.

It was not just boots on the ground that the philhellenes brought. Many more than volunteered in person fought a vigorous propaganda war in Europe and the United States, in those early days when the power of the press to influence public opinion was beginning to make itself felt. Philhellenic committees raised money to pay for three steamships, a huge frigate built in America and, for several months after the fall of Missolonghi, the first Greek regular army. Loans for the Provisional Government were raised from private speculators on the London stockmarket in 1824 and 1825. All of these initiatives were mired in scandal – in the countries where the funds were raised, not just in Greece – and the scale of waste was shocking. Even so, they undoubtedly helped keep the Revolution alive during its darkest years.

But there was a limit to what individuals and even the power of private capital could do. If the philhellenes were the foot in the door, the door had still to be prised fully open. It was Mavrokordatos, more than anyone, who saw what had to be done. And doggedly, peering through his thick-lensed spectacles and sporting his incongruous frock coat, Mavrokordatos worked to bring the European powers on board.

At first it seemed hopeless. When the 'Concert of Europe' held its fifth – and as it turned out final – congress, at Verona in the autumn of 1822, the Provisional Government of Greece tried to send a delegation.

But the Greeks were refused a hearing before they even arrived. Despite this, and unknown to the insurgents, a chink in the unity of the concerted powers was opening up at the Congress of Verona – which is why it would prove to be the last of its kind. The bone of contention was Spain, not Greece. But this was when Great Britain began to mark out a policy of non-intervention, and so to distance itself from the rest of the 'Concert'. One of the last acts of the ultra-conservative British Foreign Secretary, Lord Castlereagh, before he cut his throat in August 1822, had been to brief the Duke of Wellington, Britain's representative at Verona and no friend to the Greek cause either, that it might be necessary to recognize Greek ships on the high seas as belligerents. In March the next year this small step-change was announced by Castlereagh's successor as Foreign Secretary, George Canning. Although a Tory, Canning was of a very different stamp from his predecessor. A skilled orator, he commanded the respect of many in the opposition Whig party, not least among them Byron. Canning would go on to play a key role in the widening of the Greek conflict, during his tenure as Foreign Secretary, then briefly as prime minister until his death in August 1827, just two months short of the ultimate triumph for his Greek policy.

Recognizing the rights of belligerents on the high seas may not sound like much. It fell far short of formal recognition for Greece as an independent state. Great Britain was still neutral in the conflict. Nominally, at least, neutrality continued to be enforced in the British protectorate of the Ionian islands. But it meant that, legally, Greeks bearing arms were no longer to be regarded as pirates or criminals by the world's largest navy. This was recognition, of sorts. It conferred a degree of legitimacy on Greek actions.

Once the change in British policy was known, Mavrokordatos moved swiftly. In a series of letters written and despatched in June and July 1823, addressed to Canning and other highly placed British officials, he set out his vision for an alliance between a newly independent Greece and Great Britain. It was to be based on common maritime and trading interests. But Mavrokordatos went further. Like most Greeks up to this time, he had envisaged foreign support for the Revolution coming from Russia. Now Mavrokordatos realized that competition between that country and its European rivals would be the key. The Greeks held in their hands the solution to the notoriously insoluble 'Eastern Question'. A free and independent ally of Great Britain in the eastern Mediterranean would be the best guarantee of the balance of power in Europe, and put a limit to the expansion of Russia while the Ottoman Empire inevitably declined.

Mavrokordatos's first moves were made in secret. There were many in Greece at this time who would have been horrified by these proposals. Many others distrusted their author as an outsider, as a devious manipulator, and out for his own gain. (Only the last of these charges, the one that carried the most weight at the time, can safely be discounted from the perspective of history.) It was the rumour of these manoeuvres that provoked Kolokotronis to block Mavrokordatos's appointment as President of the Legislative Corps shortly afterwards, with the threat of violence. Canning, in any case, did not reply.

For the time being, Mavrokordatos had to be content with pushing forward the first application for a large foreign loan, not coincidentally to be raised in London. This move, unlike his previous one, had the full backing of the second National Assembly that had convened a few months before. Even Kolokotronis had voted for it at the time – although presciently the 'Old Man of the Morea' would confide his misgivings to Byron's emissaries who visited him not long afterwards, objecting that:

> Great Britain might thereby obtain an undue preponderance in Greece, which country he wished to be entirely unfettered, and that it might tend to aid the intrigues of Mavrocordato and the Phanariots, who . . . would contrive to appropriate to themselves the lion's share of it.[12]

Internationalization was always going to have its downside.

A year later, in August 1824, the first civil war had been won by the modernizers. The way was clear for a renewed approach to the British Foreign Secretary. This time it was done quite openly, in the name of the Greek government. By now the chink in the unity of the 'Concert of Europe' had widened still further. The contents of a secret Russian memorandum had just been leaked. The Russian initiative would have taken the steam out of the Revolution by dividing its gains into separate 'zones of influence' for the European powers, each zone to be still nominally subject to the Sultan. In this way the appearance of maintaining the status quo could just about be kept up. The newly empowered Greek government was quick to exploit the opportunity. Its letter to Canning took the form of a bitter denunciation of the Russian initiative and a request to the British for assistance. This time the Foreign Secretary did reply, although still without commitment. Mavrokordatos's policy of playing on the mutual mistrust between Russia and the Western powers was beginning to work.

By the time the arrival of Ibrahim and his Egyptian troops in the Peloponnese forced the issue, and with the ascendancy of the modernizers strengthened by their success in the second civil war, most of the Greek leaders had come round to the idea of trying to bring in one or more of the European powers. The question was, which one? So vital was this question that the very first signs of something like modern political parties beginning to emerge in independent Greece took the form of rival groups pushing for adherence to Great Britain (always, in Greek, called 'England'), France or Russia. Although they were never formally acknowledged under these names, for the next twenty years there would be an 'English' party led by Mavrokordatos, a 'French' led by Kolettis and a 'Russian' initiated by Kolokotronis. Few were as astute as Mavrokordatos, who saw that the answer lay not with any one of the three, but in playing off the interests of each against the others. This may explain why Mavrokordatos's strategy would soon be vindicated, even while his own political position within the government was eclipsed.

As the year 1825 progressed, with Ibrahim's troops closing in on Nafplio and Missolonghi, and with Athens under siege, competition among the rival parties reached fever pitch. One group was negotiating in secret with France to offer the throne of Greece to the French Duke of Nemours. Kolokotronis addressed a formal act of submission to Russia, which fell on deaf ears. A rare moment of agreement in July brought all the leaders together to sign a document that would shortly be carried to London. Dated 1 August 1825, this declared that 'the Greek nation places the sacred deposit of its liberty, independence, and political existence, under the absolute protection of Great Britain'.[13] Even though none of the three powers addressed in 1825 was yet ready to recognize any rights at all for the Greek insurgents, still less to intervene, the Revolution was entering upon an entirely new phase.

Instead of responding directly, the British Foreign Secretary despatched his cousin, Sir Stratford Canning, as ambassador to Constantinople. The ambassador was instructed to travel by way of the Ionian islands and Greece. While there, he was to confer with the Greek Provisional Government. On a deserted shore of the Peloponnese opposite Hydra, he met Mavrokordatos on 9 January 1826. Immediately afterwards the ships carrying both men were caught in a sudden storm. The ambassador's ship lost all its canvas and Mavrokordatos had to swim for his life when his foundered.[14] Still, a basis for international involvement had for the first time been set out. It involved a concession for which Mavrokordatos would not be easily forgiven once it became known at home. On the one hand 'Greece' (of unspecified extent) was to be emptied of 'Turks' (meaning Muslims). On the other, it must pay an annual tribute to the Sultan and remain part of the Ottoman Empire. This was not the complete independence that the Greeks had been fighting for. But for the next four years it would remain all that was on the diplomatic table. Mavrokordatos was diplomat enough to know how to be patient.

Back in London, the Foreign Secretary had waited until he heard the result of this meeting. Now, under the pretext of conveying congratulations to the new Tsar, Nicholas I, who had succeeded Alexander the previous December, Canning despatched the Duke of Wellington to Russia to agree a bilateral deal, based on these terms. On 4 April 1826, while the siege of Missolonghi was entering its final weeks, a protocol was signed in St Petersburg. The governments of both Russia and Great Britain undertook to mediate with the Sultan to achieve the settlement that Mavrokordatos had agreed to, on behalf of the Greek government.

In the meantime, the Ottoman position had hardened still further. Already, in 1824, the high-profile involvement of Byron and the raising of the first foreign loan for Greece in London had provoked strong protests from Constantinople. Top-down in its thinking as it was, the Ottoman government could recognize a reality that its European counterparts were at first reluctant to acknowledge. Even if these were the acts of individuals without official sanction, what kind of 'neutrality' was this? It was worse when the Russian proposals for partition became known in May that year. From this time on, even those voices within the Ottoman system that had advocated winning back the Greek insurgents by more lenient means were silenced.[15] It was the other side of the Greeks' own battle cry, 'Freedom or death'. Nothing less than total submission, annihilation if necessary, would do.

And even on the diplomatic front, for a time during the winter of 1826 and the first half of 1827 it looked as though it might have to be death. Indeed, its was the very starkness of this prospect, and the increasing likelihood of its happening, that gave a spur to the next round of diplomacy. Rumours were circulating in European capitals that Ibrahim intended to depopulate the whole of the Peloponnese and resettle it with Muslims from North Africa – in effect to reverse the 'ethnic cleansing' that the Greeks had begun in 1821. True or not, these rumours resonated powerfully. The fate of Missolonghi had left a deep mark throughout the continent. Byron's death there, two years before, had ensured 'recognition' for the name throughout the world. Athens, the very home of Western civilization, was under siege, and finally capitulated in May. Even hard-headed political leaders and their governments could no longer be indifferent to a vague sense that something of their own was being threatened – the more so in those countries where a pro-Greek press was free enough to express or mobilize public opinion.

This is not to say that there was anything like unanimity in favour of intervention. As early as January 1824, the US Congress had debated the issue, in response to strong public fervour for the Greek cause, and ruled out risking American lives by an early recognition of Greek independence. In France, where philhellenic sentiment reached a peak at this time, the government was secretly building warships for the Egyptian fleet and even sent French officers as advisers to accompany them when they went into service in 1827.[16] In Great Britain the ruling Tory party, with the exception of Canning, was in general hostile to anything that smacked of revolution. This was the instinctive response of the Duke of Wellington, whose role in the outcome would therefore become somewhat ironic.

Despite these conflicting currents, the mood among the Great

Powers was slowly shifting. The French government, too, had received appeals from Greece, and was piqued at being left out of the bilateral agreement drawn up in St Petersburg. Early in 1827 the French drew up their own draft of an international treaty. Finally, on 6 July, with Canning as prime minister, a tripartite treaty was signed in London by the representatives of Britain, France and Russia. The terms remained more or less as they had been before. There was some vagueness about how mediation was to be forced upon the warring parties, if the Sultan continued to rule out any foreign intervention in what the Ottomans considered to be their own internal affairs. Without too much attention being given to the precise wording of its mandate, the powers now dispatched a joint naval force to the Mediterranean to back up their words. It was a recipe for confrontation. And so it proved.

The battle that would decide the outcome of the Greek Revolution was fought in Navarino Bay on 20 October 1827. The British, French and Russian task force had only a third as many ships, but their fire-power was far superior. The combined Egyptian and Ottoman fleet was all but destroyed at its anchorage. At least one whole book has been written about the engagement. At the time and ever since, there has been intense controversy about who fired the first shot, and over the precise responsibility of the commander-in-chief, the Royal Navy's Admiral Edward Codrington. It was one of the very few set-piece battles in the whole of the Revolution. Navarino changed everything. And not a single Greek took part. That was the astonishing extent of the leverage that had been achieved by the determination of Mavrokordatos and others to internationalize their struggle.

From now on, the outcome of the Revolution would be indissolubly interwoven with the diplomacy and high politics of the European powers. But not of *any one* power. That, from the Greek point of view, was the beauty of it. Even while in Greece the rival parties came to blows over their preferred allegiances, the battle of Navarino had put in place a dynamic that could not be stopped, or resolved in favour of any one of the players. If the fate of the Revolution would now be decided far away from Greece, it would lie not in the hands of a single foreign country but in the interplay of each with its rivals. This was the true significance of the standing conference of the representatives of the three powers, known as the 'London Greek Conference', that first came together at the end of 1826 and would last right through to 1832. Between the summer of 1827 and the autumn of 1829 each of the three Great Powers in turn would take the lead in military operations to back up its diplomatic initiatives.

At Navarino, it was Great Britain that provided the largest squadron and the overall command. The consequence of that action was to remove all threat to Greece from the sea. A year later, in Britain, much of Canning's policy was reversed by the new prime minister, the Duke of Wellington. It was probably at Wellington's instigation that King George IV all but apologized to the Ottomans for the 'untoward event' at Navarino, in a speech to Parliament the following January. But the London conference was a kind of three-way seesaw. While British support for Greece flagged, that of France and Russia rose.

It was French troops, under General Nicolas Maison, who were entrusted with ejecting the last Ottoman forces from the Peloponnese in the summer of 1828. This was quite different from the intervention of the philhellenes, which still continued: General Maison was acting on direct orders from Paris. Then, from the spring of the same year until September 1829, Russia launched a new war against the Ottoman Empire. This was exactly what the Friendly Society had once conspired to bring about. But the circumstances were quite different now. It has been argued that Russia did more militarily than any other country to help the Greeks win their independence. And it is true that the Russian navy continued to be active in the Aegean, suppressing piracy.[17] But all the fighting in this new Russo-Ottoman war took place in the Balkans and the far shore of the Black Sea, in the Caucasus. The fate of Greece was only incidental to this latest bout in a series of wars that went back more than a century.

When Tsar Nicholas's forces reached Adrianople, today's Edirne, less than a hundred miles from the Ottoman capital, in August 1829, the effect was electrifying. For several weeks it looked as though the Russians would advance all the way to Constantinople. It was the turn of that arch-conservative, and no friend to Greece, the Duke of Wellington, to take a hand. 'We must reconstruct a Greek Empire,' wrote the prime minister to his Foreign Secretary, Lord Aberdeen, on

11 September; 'no Power of Europe ought to take anything for itself excepting the Emperor of Russia a sum for his expenses.'[18] In the event, it did not come to that. The Sultan sued for peace and accepted some fairly humiliating terms in the Treaty of Adrianople, signed three days after the Iron Duke's letter. They included accepting a deal for Greece along the lines that had been agreed between Sir Stratford Canning and Mavrokordatos at their meeting on that stormy day opposite Hydra, at the beginning of 1826. Greece would have self-government, but would remain a part of the Ottoman Empire, paying an annual tribute.

Even Wellington was now persuaded of the truth of what Mavrokordatos had first proposed to the British Foreign Secretary, back in 1823: the Ottoman Empire was on its last legs. Peace in Europe depended on finding a substitute to counterbalance the weight of Russia. Greece was the only option available. It was the British government, grudgingly, and motivated by distrust of its allies, that threw the final, unlooked-for ingredient into the mix. Why should not this new Greece be fully independent? That way, all three powers, as well as the Ottoman Empire, would be obliged to give up any pretension they may have had to rule Greece as their own dependency.

None dared object. The Sultan, for his part, was already bound by the terms of the Treaty of Adrianople, and so was obliged to accept whatever was determined. The Greeks were not asked either. The Protocol of London, signed on 3 February 1830, on behalf of the governments of Great Britain, France and Russia, declared for the first time, and under the guarantee of the three powers: 'Greece will form an independent State, and will enjoy all those rights – political, administrative, and commercial – attached to complete independence.'[19]

FINAL PUSH

Events in Greece by this time had come to revolve almost entirely around the personality and actions of one man. Kapodistrias had been elected to supreme authority at a moment of collective panic, when the life of Greece hung by a thread. The Third National Assembly, in 1827, had devised for him a title that had never been used in Greek before and never would be again. *Kyvernitis* in Greek is the exact equivalent of the Latin *gubernator*, from which the word 'governor' is derived. Originally meaning 'helmsman', *kyvernitis* today is used exclusively for the captain of a ship or an aircraft. Most accounts in English give Kapodistrias the title of 'President', but the Greek equivalent was already in use, under the provisional constitutions of the 1820s, for other roles at the top of government. The election of Kapodistrias was from the beginning an interim solution, an emergency measure that was not to last for more than a maximum of seven years. In Greek, Kapodistrias was never 'President' of Greece. He was its Governor, pending the final outcome of the Revolution.

It was never clear to whom Kapodistrias was answerable. Was it to the Great Powers that had acquiesced in his appointment? Or to the Greek people? Or to the Greek Provisional Constitution under which he had been elected, and which he then proceeded to abrogate? As a native of Corfu, born under Venetian rule, and an aristocrat, Kapodistrias was at once an insider and outsider. He was a product of the 'Orthodox commonwealth'. But he had spent most of his adult life and gained his political experience abroad, first in Russia and latterly in exile in Switzerland. It was this, above all, that gave him authority in the eyes of those who had elected him. Nothing in Kapodistrias's upbringing or his manners could have prepared him to fit into the world of the Peloponnese in the late 1820s. It was not his way, in any case, to fit in.

There is something enigmatic about Kapodistrias the man. The same can be said, even with the benefit of almost two centuries of hindsight, about the nature of his rule. An authoritarian, lonely, austere figure, he was seen by some (and is still) as the saviour of his country who brought order out of chaos. Support for this view can be found in the fact that his three and a half years in power were bookended by periods of violent anarchy. These had nothing of the character or excuse of the civil wars of 1824, in which real and inescapable tensions over the nature and purpose of the Revolution were being played out. The Peloponnese before Kapodistrias arrived in January 1828 had descended into armed chaos. When he sailed into Nafplio, escorted by warships belonging to each of the Great Powers, it was to find rival militias bombarding each other and the town from the two great fortresses that overlook it. This perhaps helps to explain why Kapodistrias never lost the devotion of a large section of the populace – and, in turn, he seems to have entertained a slightly romantic, certainly paternalistic affection for them. For most of the years that he ruled, the Governor was the nearest thing that existed to a guarantee of order. On the other hand, his distrust of the Greek leaders, even those who remained loyal to him, would be the cause of his downfall.

It was during Kapodistrias's rule that the last battles took place on the external front. These were an anticlimax. In the Peloponnese the business of mopping up the last Ottoman forces that had landed with Ibrahim in 1825 was in the capable hands of General Maison and his regular French force. In Roumeli, strenuous efforts were made during the first months of 1828 to regain a foothold, to retake Missolonghi and re-establish a Greek presence further north. The British phil-hellenes Frank Hastings and Richard Church played a large part in these operations, in one of which Hastings lost his life. But once Russia had declared war on the Ottoman Empire at the end of April, the formidable Reshid Pasha, who had subdued Missolonghi and Athens, was redeployed with all available troops to the Balkans. With the departure of Reshid, it was open season for the Greek- and Albanian-speaking militias, the latter part-Christian, part-Muslim, to fight it out or form new alliances as they saw fit.

The last battle of the war took place in September 1829 on the pass between Thebes and Livadia. It was not much more than a skirmish. Honours went to Dimitrios Ypsilantis, the brother of Alexandros who had begun the Revolution eight and a half years before. But now it made no difference. Thanks to the terms dictated by the Russians to the Ottomans at the Treaty of Adrianople that same month, the extent of territory that would become part of the Greek state north of the Isthmus would be determined not by military operations but by lines drawn on a map in a far-away part of Europe.

Kapodistrias's most important task was to carry forward the diplomatic campaign that Mavrokordatos had initiated in 1823. And even here, despite determination and persistence, his freedom for action would prove limited. The London conference had acquired the habit of reaching decisions without consulting the Greeks. Trained diplomat that he was, Kapodistrias should have been well placed to win maximum advantage for his country. But his very advantage turned out to be a handicap. The Governor had acquired his diplomatic skills in the Russian service. The British and the French could never be persuaded that he was negotiating sincerely on behalf of Greece, rather than as a secret arm of the Russian interest. Sadly, Tsar Nicholas seems not to have trusted him either, although he had granted him an honourable discharge from his service in order to take up his position in Greece. For all his efforts on the diplomatic front, it is hard to point to any element of the final settlement that was due to the initiative of Kapodistrias himself.

It was his actions at home that made the most impact. Critics, such as George Finlay, accused Kapodistrias of being a tyrant and motivated by selfish ambition.[20] On the positive side, he promoted education and encouraged the founding of new schools using the latest experimental methods from Britain and continental Europe. He introduced Greece's first modern currency, based on a coin called the phoenix, and an embryonic national bank. He organized the judiciary. He began work on a much-needed land registry – which remains much-needed and incomplete at the time of writing, almost two centuries later. He also introduced that staple of every Greek *taverna* and restaurant in later times, the potato.

All accounts agree that Kapodistrias tended politically towards the sort of autocracy that he had been used to in Russia. To that extent, his whole Governorship ran counter to the democratic and pluralist tenor that had been emerging throughout the Revolution. His politics could not have been more different from those of the Friendly Society, which had once tried to recruit him as its leader. Under Kapodistrias, Greece moved backwards politically. He has been called an 'enlightened despot', and this seems not far from the mark.[21] Although only in his early fifties, Kapodistrias was already an anachronism in independent Greece. Perhaps the most lasting legacy of his rule has been as a role model for authoritarianism that could be emulated by would-be 'saviours' of their country in the future.

By the start of 1831, Kapodistrias was attempting to face down two separate rebellions from opposite sides. On one side were the shipowners and merchants of Hydra, on the other the proud warriors of Mani, led by the Mavromichalis family. The nub for both groups was taxation. The central government looked to the wealthiest of its subjects to provide essential funds for its own operations. The Maniats, in particular, had never paid any taxes to the Ottomans, and refused to do so now to the agents of Kapodistrias. The shipowners of the islands had had arrangements of their own, before the Revolution, that had worked well for them. Now they too were threatened with impositions that they had never had to pay before. Far from subsidizing a common treasury, these and just about every other interest group in the land looked to the government as a source of further wealth to be milked. They had a case, too – since these were the people whose livelihoods had borne the brunt of a decade of war. The devastation of ten years had impoverished everyone, the central treasury included. The rebellions against Kapodistrias were in essence tax revolts.

But they were not only about money. Mavrokordatos, who had always been close to the entrepreneurial middle class of the islands, by this time had emerged as the leader of political opposition to the Governor. Kapodistrias's refusal to reinstate the Provisional Constitution under which he had been elected was a step too far for Mavrokordatos. Suspicion that the Governor was prepared to allow a free hand to Russia contributed as well. Matters came to a head when the Hydriot Admiral Miaoulis defied the government. His ships were cornered in the harbour of Poros by a Russian squadron. Rather than submit, Miaoulis blew up the flagship of the Greek fleet, the *Hellas*, which had been built at great cost with money raised by American philhellenes. It was an absurd waste.

By the end of the summer, both rebellions had been quashed. But Kapodistrias's victory was not to last. Petrobey Mavromichalis and two of his relatives were still being held by the government in Nafplio, effectively as hostages, in October. Petrobey was the head of his clan and the undisputed leader of the Maniats. It seems that he had not been directly involved in the tax revolt. It is not clear whether his brother Konstantinos and his son Georgios had been either. But Petrobey was in prison, with the other two under a loose form of arrest, being allowed to move freely only within the walls of the town, and each of them always accompanied by an armed guard.

Early on the morning of Sunday 9 October 1831, as Kapodistrias was about to enter the church of St Spyridon in a backstreet of Nafplio, Konstantinos and Georgios were waiting for him on either side of the door, armed. Both were under guard, but evidently not restrained. There was something almost stage-managed about what happened next. The Governor saw them, hesitated, then went forward, almost as though willingly, to his death. He fell on the spot. The hole allegedly gouged by one of the bullets fired at him is today pointed out to tourists in the doorway of the church. One of the assassins was lynched on the spot – further proof that although he had alienated the leaders, Kapodistrias still commanded the loyalty of many people on the street. The other assassin was caught and after due process executed.

More than a century later, writing at another turning point in Greek history, in 1944, the poet and novelist Nikos Kazantzakis would recreate these events for the stage and represent Kapodistrias's death as a Christ-like act of sacrifice for the sake of his divided nation. At the time, reactions by those whose politics could loosely be termed liberal and progressive were intemperate. The assassins were hailed in some quarters as the heirs of Harmodios and Aristogeiton, the tyrant-slayers of classical Athens. The octogenarian Korais, he who had been the first to articulate the idea of Greece as a modern nation, unforgivingly complained in print that the murderers had saved 'the transgressor against Hellenic laws from a punishment more just than death: expulsion in disgrace from Hellas'.[22]

Once it was known that the Governor had been assassinated, anarchy returned to the Peloponnese with a vengeance.

For more than a year after that, the political life of independent Greece fragmented. No group or leader could afford to recognize or allow any other to become dominant. It was like a violent caricature of the rivalry among the Great Powers, which the most far-sighted of the revolutionaries had been so successful in exploiting. The last of a series of National Assemblies ended in ignominy in August 1832, when armed soldiers 'burst into the hall of the assembly . . . and carried off the president and several deputies, as hostages for the payment of their arrears'.[23] The ill-fated gathering took place in a shanty-town on the fringe of Nafplio, which had been founded by Kapodistrias to house refugees from the fighting elsewhere in Greece. Its name, Pronoia, means 'Providence'. Kapodistrias had been a great believer in Divine Providence. Whether any of those present on that August day was alert to the irony is not recorded.

The Revolution ended as it had begun, with the near-total collapse of civil order. This time the violence was not between Christian Greeks and Muslim Turks, but among fellow Greeks and fellow Christians. True, it was on nothing like so horrific a scale. But lives were still being lost, and many more livelihoods went with them. The very last hostilities took place in the town of Argos, not far from the capital, Nafplio, on 16 January 1833, only days before the arrival of the country's new king, with an army of Germans to restore order.

It had taken some time for the three Great Powers to follow through after the London Protocol of 1830. Upheavals in France, Belgium and Poland, and a change of government in Great Britain, had already drawn attention away from Greece, before the assassination of Kapodistrias. But it was once again in Europe's northern capitals that the fate of the new nation would be decided. And it is at least possible that recognition of this fact was one of the causes for the mayhem on the ground.

It was not until early in 1832 that the reconvened London conference agreed to offer the throne of Greece to Otto, the underage second son of King Ludwig of Bavaria. The previous favourite for the role, Prince Leopold of Saxe-Coburg, had turned it down after prolonged deliberation. Leopold would earn his place in history as the first King of the Belgians instead. All parties professed themselves satisfied with Otto's appointment. The Greeks, once again, had not been consulted – but by this time no individual or group within Greece had the authority to represent the country anyway. Otto, like the barbarians of Cavafy's famous poem of the next century, could be seen as 'some sort of a solution'.

A new protocol, signed by the Great Powers in London in May 1832, updated the terms of the settlement that had first been set out in 1830. Otto would become king when he reached the age of majority in 1835. A Bavarian regency would hold power until then. This time the frontiers of the new state were more generously drawn than they had been at first, though they would still leave three times as many Orthodox Greek speakers outside it as lived within it. The northern frontier was to run from just south of Volos in the east to just south of Arta in the west. It was also finally determined which islands were to be incorporated into the new state. Those nearest to the mainland on the Aegean side, as far north as the Sporades, were in; Crete, Samos and Chios, larger islands that had all played a part in the Revolution, were excluded. For the first time in the 3,500-year recorded history of the Greek language, Greece existed as a political entity on the map of Europe.

With the arrival of Otto, aboard a British warship, at Nafplio on 6 February 1833, the new birth had been delivered. Nobody's brain-child, an unplanned offspring, it was unavoidably the child of its two parents, Europe and the Ottoman Empire. But like any human child, it was also a new entity, which was bound to grow up to define its own unique, unforeseeable personality.

4

First Steps

1833–1862

It was one of those winter days that in Greek are called 'halcyon'. The sun was warm, the sea calm and intensely blue. Three thousand troops, mercenaries recruited from the German states, had already landed. More than seventy ships, of several nations, rode at anchor off Nafplio, their rigging decked out with flags. Cannonade after cannonade saluted the arrival of the young king-to-be. White smoke drifting from the guns obscured the distant view. The entire populace had come out to greet the new arrivals where they came ashore, near the prehistoric walls of Tiryns, and escort them into town. It was a scene of brilliant colour and noisy rejoicing, a triumphant end to twelve years of war. Tall and slim in his sky-blue uniform, escorted by mounted hussars, and followed by the three Bavarian regents who would hold power until he came of age, the seventeen-year-old Otto rode at the head of the procession.

All the political and military leaders of the Revolution were there to honour the occasion. Kolokotronis, in his flamboyant helmet, seemed to be looking away. Mavrokordatos, in top hat and thick spectacles, and Kolettis, in his red fez, had both half-turned to cast a look of quizzical awe upon the sovereign they would from now on be required to serve. These men, who had so recently shaped the future in this part of the world, had already begun to move on, yielding their places to the new men of destiny, while on the edge of the scene camels waited patiently to be loaded with their burdens. So, at any rate, the moment came to be depicted, very shortly afterwards, on a canvas more than four metres long and two high that hangs today in the Neue Pinakothek in Munich. The artist, Peter von Hess, had been one of the arriving party.

George Finlay, another eyewitness, devotes to the scene a rare lyrical passage in his *History of the Greek Revolution*. 'The uniforms of many armies and navies, and the sounds of many languages, testified that most civilised nations had sent deputies to inaugurate the festival of the regeneration of Greece,' he wrote almost thirty years afterwards. Finlay went on to recall, from that time, the 'hope that a third Greece was emerging into life, which would again occupy a brilliant position in the world's annals'. Writing in Greek, only a year after the event, and so without the benefit of hindsight, the young, European-educated Panagiotis Soutsos included his own evocation of the scene in the first novel to be published in the independent kingdom. His fictional hero then goes on to this passionate avowal:

O King of Greece! old Greece bequeathed the lights of learning to Germany; through you Germany has undertaken to repay the gift with interest, and will be grateful to you, seeing in you the one to resurrect the firstborn people of the earth. [1]

The language of Europe's indebtedness to Greece, which had begun with the European travellers of the previous century, had well and truly entered the modern Greek consciousness. It was there to stay. So was the idea that the future of Europe and the future of Greece were already intertwined. It was no more than a logical consequence of the way in which independence had been won. So too was the theme of 'regeneration' or 'resurrection' that dominates both these accounts.

Those Greek leaders who had ridden the tiger of revolution and survived had pulled off an extraordinary coup: to persuade three of the most conservative regimes in modern times that theirs was not a liberal, national revolution at all (which of course it was), but rather the restoration of an ancient status quo. It had worked. In the climate of 'Restoration' throughout Europe, the birth of an all-new Greek state could be made to look like the ultimate restoration – of something even older than any state that existed.

It was no such thing. With recognition of Greek independence in 1830, a new dynamic entered European geopolitics: that of the nation state. A year later would come recognition of the continent's second, Belgium under King Leopold. The far-reaching effects of this change would not begin to become apparent until 1848, the year of revolutions across the continent. Only with the successful 'unifications' of Italy and Germany, during the 1860s, would the nation state begin to emerge as the new model, which would go on to sweep away the multi-national empires of the nineteenth and early twentieth centuries – and would still be proving its tenacity during the first decades of the twenty-first century.

Greece was the pioneer.

At the time, though, in the political climate of the early 1830s, the success of the entire project depended on playing this down. Indeed, so effective and so pervasive has been the official narrative that took root at this time, that historians of nation-building in Europe have yet to give the achievement of Greek independence in 1830 its proper due. They have not been helped by Greek historians, who until the late twentieth century would almost always prefer to present their country as a special case, uniquely ancient and therefore like no other. It was during the first twenty years of the life of the new kingdom that enduring concepts of the Greek state, and of the wider, harder-to-define Greek *nation*, would be hammered out. And they are still with us today.

UNDER WESTERN EYES

The choice of Otto of Bavaria to be the first king of Greece had been dictated largely, if not entirely, by considerations of *Realpolitik*. Chance played a part, too. The second son of Ludwig I happened to be available. The Bavarian royal house of Wittelsbach was free of close ties to any of the three rival powers that had undertaken to act as guarantors for the new kingdom. The choice could therefore be acceptable to all. No one seems to have given much thought to the personal qualities of the individual chosen. Otto has been described as 'vainglorious, stubborn and frivolous' in his youth, latterly as suffering from 'incurable irresoluteness'.[2] Any other monarch appointed in these circumstances would have had no choice but to learn on the job, just as Otto would have to do. It remains an open question how far the political direction of the country he ruled for nearly thirty years was shaped by the character of its king. For all his faults, Otto fared a great deal better than Kapodistrias had done before him. There is no doubting the deep affection that he developed for his adopted country, whose national costume he would continue to wear, even in exile back in his native Bavaria, to the end of his life.

When the offer came, in 1832, there was one particularly compelling reason for the young prince to accept it – or, rather, for his father to accept on his behalf. Bavaria had been the only state in the world during the previous decade where philhellenism went right to the top of government and informed many aspects of state policy. The word itself meant originally 'a love of anything Hellenic'. Before the Revolution it had been applied to those inspired by the ideas of Winckelmann. Philhellenism in Germany meant most of all an admiration for the achievements of *classical* Greece. And nowhere were those achievements more conspicuously admired than in the Bavarian capital, Munich – as is still apparent today, in many of the city's monuments that date from the first half of the nineteenth century.

Ludwig took a personal interest in Otto's kingdom. He it was who appointed the three regents (all Bavarians, naturally). Ludwig even intervened in practical decisions, such as the site for the royal palace in Athens. It was his decision that his son would rule without the benefit of a parliament or constitution. The terms of the 1832 treaty did not specify any limits to the monarch's powers. Given the state of lawlessness and the impasse into which the political process had degenerated, Ludwig ensured that Otto would be adequately supported. Hence the three thousand German troops who paved the way for his arrival and would remain for several years afterwards. Hence a smaller army, too, of qualified advisers brought in to help set the country on its feet.

For most of its first decade the Greek kingdom would be governed more like a colony than the sovereign independent state described in the treaties. This aspect has been much discussed by historians, and indeed has left its mark in popular memory, which labels the period, more ruefully than affectionately, as the 'Bavarocracy'. But the significance of these arrangements is more than just political. If it is in the nature of colonial rulers to impose something of their own upon the ruled, in this case that something was the German philhellenism that prevailed at Ludwig's court in Munich. The first steps of the infant Greek nation state were taken under the care of a highly protective nanny, one who had modelled her own life on an idea of what her young charge ought to grow up to become. And of course, as the saying goes, 'nanny knows best'.

Greece was to become Western, European, modern. But paradoxically, the way to achieve this was by turning backwards, to the remote past: 'It was the ancients leading the moderns towards modernization.'[3] Part of the price of becoming modern was that Greece and Greeks were now expected to live up to the narrative that had served them so well during the Revolution. The rulers and most of the elite among the ruled agreed on this. The new state must be in every possible way 'Hellenic'. And we must remember that the adoption of this ancient name was itself a very *new* development, codified for the first time in the Provisional Constitution of 1822. Not only that, the new state must be in every way also 'national'.

Nationalism as an ideology had become most fully developed and articulated in the German states during the Napoleonic Wars, when German speakers had been living under French rule. Most of the Bavarians who came to Greece in 1833 would have been brought up in this climate, whether or not they shared the aspiration for a united Germany. Here, in Greece, was the perfect opportunity to try out ideas that would have no place at home until three decades later. Once again, the infant Greek state was a pioneer – though the less happy metaphor of a 'guinea pig', frequently heard in the wake of the 2010 financial crisis, may also come to mind. If so, it has a long pedigree.

Even before Otto came of age, the Regency had laid the foundations for a national army, and for national administrative, judicial and education systems that reached, at least in theory, into every corner of the kingdom. There was to be a National Bank. A policy was developed for how to deal with the 'national' lands, which had formerly belonged to the Ottoman state or Muslim landowners. The national currency, the phoenix, which had been established by Kapodistrias, was renamed after an ancient Greek coin, the drachma.

Many of these initiatives, begun in the early years, would take decades to bring to fruition. Land distribution would not be completed until the early 1870s. It would take as long before the drachma would replace the traditional Ottoman coinage in daily use throughout the kingdom – another reminder that intentions are not the same as results. But the determination was there at the very beginning. And all of these nationalizing programmes would eventually be realized.

Highest priority of all was given to the national army. The purpose of investing so heavily in the military was not to protect the country's external borders, since these were internationally guaranteed. The enemy was within. Like Kapodistrias before them, the Bavarians were determined to put an end to the local power bases of the war-lords and irregular militias loyal only to their own leaders. In creating a national army they set about ensuring a monopoly on the use of force within the kingdom, perhaps the most essential of all the pre-requisites for a modern, functioning state. This, too, would take many decades to bring to fruition. But it would not be long before the new national institution grew more powerful even than the Bavarian dynasty itself, and would eventually prove its undoing. Between 1843 and 1974 the army would repeatedly intervene in the political life of Greece. That is another legacy of the Bavarian decade.

Even the Orthodox Church was nationalized. The overwhelming majority of Greek citizens suddenly found themselves cut off from the rest of the 'Orthodox commonwealth'. But in the eyes of the Bavarians – and of many Greek patriots too, such as Korais in Paris – the leadership of that commonwealth, and especially the Ecumenical Patriarchate with its seat in Constantinople, had become tainted by the loyalty it was obliged to maintain towards the hated Ottoman Empire. The measure would prove controversial. After all, it had been in the name of their religion that most of the fighters in the Revolution had risked their lives and taken part in the massacre and expulsion of Muslims. The formal rift between the 'Autocephalous Church of Greece', based in Athens, and the Patriarchate in Constantinople would last only until 1850. But even today the Archbishop of Athens and All Greece holds ecclesiastical authority over those parts of the country that comprised the kingdom in the nineteenth century, while the Patriarch retains jurisdiction over the rest. Church and state have never been fully separated in Greece. The identification between the two goes back to the Revolution. But it became institutionalized under the Bavarian Regency, with the creation of the 'autocephalous', national Church in 1833.

In no other sphere was the identity of the new kingdom given such visible and durable form as in the plans to develop Athens as its capital city. The decision to move the capital from Nafplio was taken in 1833. The last Ottoman troops in Athens had held on long enough in the fortified citadel of the Acropolis to surrender to the Bavarians rather than the Greeks, and had just been escorted over the frontier. The inauguration of the new capital took place in December the following year. The main part of the town was even more of a ruin than the ancient temples above it. Athens had been besieged and ransacked twice by Greek forces and once by the Ottomans in the course of the Revolution. To build a modern capital city here would be an extraordinary act of faith.

The new layout of the town plan and the scale of its public buildings were out of all proportion to the size or the resources of the little kingdom. Even though much would be watered down in the process of implementation, it is still impressive how much of that original ambition came through. The cityscape of the new capital would not be fully realized until the turn of the next century. But once again, and often literally, the foundations were laid during the first decade of Otto's reign. It was not just a question of building. It was also about preservation. The whole rationale behind the choice of Athens as the capital lay in the pre-eminence of its monuments and the city's role in the history of ancient Greek (and therefore also of all European) civilization. These ruins must become the focal point. Paradoxically, and exactly like the nation itself, Athens was to be at once a perfectly modern city and the reincarnation of its long-lost ancient glory. The preservation and the fullest possible display of everything that remained of that glory were therefore central to the new government's plans.

To this end, new institutions implanted a newly coined word into the Greek language, and a new concept into the hearts and minds of citizens. The word was 'archaeology'. Coined from Greek roots, meaning 'the study of antiquity', this term had only very recently entered the vocabulary of Western languages. Used in this sense, it was every bit as much a neologism in Greek. An 'Archaeological Service' was founded right at the beginning, in 1833. The next year saw the first of a series of 'archaeological laws' passed. The Athens

Archaeological Society and the *Archaeological Journal* appeared on the scene in 1837. Archaeology was the new science that would provide the link between planning for the future and uncovering and exhibiting the ancient past. So far so good. But there was a casualty. The logic of a national revival, and of the seamless juxtaposition of the new and the ancient, was that all trace of human activity in the city over the intervening two thousand years must be expunged. Almost more breathtaking even than the programmes for preservation and for new building was the extent of the destruction that followed as a consequence.

It is often said that dozens of beautiful and historic Byzantine churches were levelled in the first years of the Greek state to make way for the new Athens city plan. The extent of the damage has been exaggerated: many 'gems', such as the Kapnikarea church in Ermou Street, would be reprieved. It was on the Acropolis itself that the most radical obliteration of 'all the remnants of barbarism' took place.[4] Work began almost immediately after the transfer of the capital. What had been a crowded citadel, with streets, houses and gardens huddled against the ancient buildings, was cleared of everything that dated from later than Roman times. The ground was literally cleared down to the bedrock, on which visitors walk today, and which had probably never been fully exposed at any previous time in more than three millennia of human occupation. In 1843 the small mosque that been built inside the shell of the Parthenon disappeared. The most conspicuous landmark in Athens, the 'Frankish' tower built by Florentine dukes in the fourteenth century, lasted until 1874. The programme set in motion by the Bavarian architect Leo von Klenze, and enthusiastically endorsed by the leading Greek intellectuals of the day, had developed a momentum of its own. Photographs dating from the second half of the century show huge heaps of spoil banked against the southern walls of the Acropolis, where it had been cleared from the top and tipped over, to be carted away. Archaeologists today spend much of their lives sifting such evidence. But the legacy of the 1830s was to rid the city of everything that threatened the seamless juxtaposition of the very old with the very new.

Wide, straight boulevards were laid out. New buildings began to rise. First and largest was the royal palace. The foundation stone was laid in 1836. Massive, and compared by some to a barracks, Otto's palace was completed in 1842. (Today the building houses the Greek Parliament.) It was followed in short order by Greece's first and, for almost a century, only university – and an observatory. The priorities of the new state could not have been more eloquently set out. With the exception of the neo-Byzantine Orthodox cathedral, completed in 1862, all these public buildings would be designed in the classical style – and all, not excluding even the cathedral, by German-trained architects, most of them either German or Danish. Private dwellings followed this principle too, starting with the grandest of them all, built in 1842 across the square from the royal palace, which in due course would become the Grande Bretagne Hotel. On a more modest scale, 'neoclassical' dwellings would spring up in the centre of Athens and most provincial towns, to dominate the Greek urban landscape until the zealous march of concrete obliterated most of them between the 1950s and the 1970s.

Whether public or private, the design of these buildings revived the *form* of classical architecture. But they did so in the *spirit* of the Romantic-inspired Gothic Revival in other countries at the same time. This was a homage to the past that only superficially looked like the neoclassicism of the previous century in Europe. It was not that Greece lagged behind. The architects were perfectly well aware of the Romantic movement and its appeal to indigenous traditions. But in Greece the indigenous tradition was identified directly with the ancients – again, with nothing intervening allowed to obtrude. So it followed that the palace, the observatory, the Academy, the National Library, the national Parliament (in due course), the Archaeological Museum, the Polytechnic, the Athens Municipal Theatre, the Zappeion Exhibition Hall must all of them look like the temples that had once graced the landscape of ancient Greece.

Even the language of the new state underwent the same treatment. Here the obstacles were more formidable. Languages have a life of their own, in a way that buildings do not. The backlash would come later in the century. But during the first decades of the kingdom, no effort was spared to make the national language, in its written form, *look* as much as possible like its ancient predecessor, despite the many differences of vocabulary, grammar and syntax. There are also important differences in pronunciation, but these were never considered, because only the *written* form of the language was affected. There was no suggestion of reforming the writing system, which remained (and still remains largely today) the same as for ancient Greek. Just as in the buildings, it was the visual that counted. In this case, except at the very beginning, the architects were not Germans but European-educated Greeks.

The same law that in 1834 established seven years of compulsory schooling also stipulated that children must learn to read and write according to the rules of ancient, not modern, Greek. It quickly became fashionable in all walks of life, not just among the educated, to replace common words for everyday things, and everyday elements of grammar and syntax, with their ancient equivalents. Although it never became official policy in the nineteenth century, this was essentially the programme that had been advocated by Korais from Paris in the first years of the century, to 'correct' and 'powder the face of' a modern language that over the centuries had lost most of its ancient graces. Both in Korais's theory and in daily usage, this was as cosmetic a procedure as it sounds – very much the equivalent of the practice of sticking ancient pediments on modern buildings, as the poet George Seferis was caustically to observe a century later.

By the 1850s, Panagiotis Soutsos, the novelist and poet who had extolled the arrival of Otto and the Bavarians, would go farther and announce the literal 'resurrection of the ancient Greek language'. 'The language of the ancient Greeks and ourselves will be one and the same,' Soutsos proclaimed in a pamphlet of 1853; 'their Grammar and ours will be one and the same.'[5] That future tense perfectly captures the spirit of the times: tacitly conceding the opposite of what it seems to promise. Once again, the way to the future is by *appearing* to resuscitate a vanished past.

But this was to prove a revival too far. Korais himself had accepted that the resurrection of a dead language would be impossible. It was Korais's piecemeal, cosmetic approach that would carry the day for most of the nineteenth century. Before long this hybrid written form (compared by Seferis to the 'buildings of the Athens Academy') would come to be known by the name *katharevousa*, which means literally a language 'in the process of being cleaned up'.

All of these radical innovations were top-down. Most of them were started by the Bavarians, who had set out with the preconceptions of European philhellenes about ancient Greece and used them to lay the foundations of a functioning modern state. Those Greeks who supported them and carried them out had been educated in Europe. For them, no less than for the Bavarians, it was natural to see the new Greece as a *Western* country and to do everything in their power to make it at least *look* like one. Nation-building was essentially therefore state-building. The Greek nation would be defined by the Greek state.

But not everyone thought this way – or if they did, not all of the time.

EASTERN HORIZONS

The process of state-building initiated by the Bavarians was only ever one side of the coin. The state's new institutions might be defined as 'national', but the nation itself was much harder to pin down. The borders of the state had been fixed, but they were also arbitrary. Until the last minute, before the 1832 settlement, it had been uncertain which Greek populations were to be included within them. Approximately three times as many people who could qualify to be called 'Hellenes', in terms of their language, religion, or both, lived outside those borders: in the Ionian islands to the west (still ruled as a protectorate by Great Britain), and in the Ottoman Empire to the north, south and especially to the east. It was inevitable that the establishment of the kingdom would be seen in many quarters as unfinished business. And indeed this view has prevailed in Greece ever since. A popular history of the Revolution written for children and published in 2013 has the subtitle: *The Beginning that was Never Completed.* [6]

During the Revolution there had been many who thought that the struggle must go on until the whole of the Greek-speaking, Orthodox world had been liberated. The historic capital of that world had for centuries been Constantinople. The name means 'City of Constantine', and has traditionally been abbreviated in Greek to 'City'. Constantinople was (and remains) the seat of the Ecumenical Patriarchate of the Orthodox Church. In the 'Orthodox commonwealth' of the eighteenth and early nineteenth centuries there had only ever been the one 'City'. Athens, with a pre-Revolution population of around twelve thousand, had never counted as one of its centres. No wonder that when the move of the national capital from Nafplio to Athens was first mooted in 1833, the veteran revolutionary leader Ioannis Kolettis objected on the grounds that the only possible capital for Greece would be Constantinople. For as long as that was not available, Kolettis protested, the state should have no capital at all. On the first occasion that the anniversary of the outbreak of the Revolution was celebrated in Athens, five years later, there were spontaneous cries from the crowd: 'To the City!'

The long-term aspiration to win Constantinople goes back before the start of the Revolution in 1821. From as early as 1824 the rapidly expanding press in Greece would take up the cause.[7] After 1833, those who were most discontented with the Westernizing rule of the Bavarians were the leaders of the so-called 'Russian' party, also known as 'Napists'. Grouped around the veteran warlord Theodoros Kolokotronis and his son Gennaios, these were the inheritors of the ideal of self-sufficiency extolled in the songs of those mountain brigands and later guerrilla fighters, the klefts. This was the faction that most consistently looked to the east, both for protection by Russia and to expand the gains of the kingdom at the expense of the Ottoman Empire.

Right at the beginning, the new government determined to make an example of these dissidents. Kolokotronis and some of his associates were arrested just seven months after the arrival of the Bavarians. In 1834 they were subjected to a show trial and condemned to death. This was a risky procedure, as the condemned men were among the most widely revered heroes of the Revolution. Probably it had always been part of the plan that Otto would show clemency, as indeed he did after they had served a year in prison. At the same time, severe curbs were placed on what had initially been a free press. But beneath the show trial and the magnanimity of the pardon, which was in reality a show of strength, lay the fault line that had first opened up during the civil wars of ten years earlier. Kolokotronis and his associates had plotted treason against the *dynasty*. They had sought to mobilize a popular appeal to Russia to have Otto and the regents removed. They had stirred up brigandage in the countryside. This was a threat that the Bavarians had to face down, if they were to survive. But Kolokotronis had remained loyal to an idea of the *nation* that was defined primarily by the Orthodox religion and far transcended the bounds of the Greek state.

The arrest, trial and imprisonment of Kolokotronis showed up the fault line in its starkest form. But by no means all who shared these wider aspirations were opposed to the Bavarians or their state-building enterprise. In the same novel by Panagiotis Soutsos that includes the enthusiastic description of Otto's arrival, a peasant states his simple faith in the powers of the new king: 'the reach of his hand can stir into action the entire Hellenic race, from the Bosphorus to Crete, the nod of his head a signal for general revolution'. It was in this spirit, rather than one of antagonism, that the crowd celebrating the anniversary of the 1821 Revolution chanted the slogan, 'To the City'. The next year, when Sultan Mahmud died, even Otto himself entertained a notion of taking ship for Constantinople to claim the throne as his successor – or so one account by a contemporary would have us believe.[8]

It was not long before an opportunity arose to test the possibilities for this way of thinking in the world of international politics. In 1839, Mahmud's successor, Sultan Abdulmejid, faced a challenge from the Viceroy of Egypt, the same Ibrahim who had ravaged the Peloponnese and helped to subdue Missolonghi. For a time, Great Power diplomacy was in disarray. In Athens, secret societies sprang up, modelled on the Friendly Society that had helped trigger the Revolution. One of these was the work of 'Napists', who believed in closer ties to Russia and a more belligerent attitude towards the Ottoman Empire. Kolokotronis's son Gennaios was among its leaders. The Philorthodox Society would quickly be discredited as being no more than another conspiracy to oust King Otto. Much about it remains mired in accusation and counter-accusation to this day. But there seems little doubt that the main purpose of the Philorthodox Society was to organize clandestine warfare in neighbouring Ottoman provinces, with a view to annexing them to Greece.

Soon afterwards, revolts broke out in Thessaly and in Crete. The

Athens press showed a rare unity and despite severe curbs on its freedom agitated for war. For a short time in 1840 and 1841 it looked as if conditions might be right for Crete, at least, to be united with Greece. While the Great Powers disagreed among themselves, and the future of the Ottoman Empire remained in doubt, there might be room for even larger gains for Greece. Otto himself, caught wrong-footed at first, became an enthusiastic convert to the cause. Indeed this was one of the few occasions in his reign when the Bavarian monarch made himself genuinely popular among his subjects – at least if we may trust the evidence of a press whose circulation was tiny outside elite circles in the capital.

What happened next should have been a warning to Otto and his advisers. The crisis would be resolved, once again, far away in the capitals of Europe. By 1841 the Great Powers had lined up once more behind their old policy of maintaining the integrity of the Ottoman Empire. Otto was caught between two fires. The powers felt he had let them down by putting his own country's interests ahead of the 'Concert of Europe'. But at home, this was exactly what public opinion expected of him, and he had failed to deliver. It was time for a reckoning. Otto's days as an absolute ruler, unfettered by a constitution or parliament, were numbered. The semi-colonial 'Bavarocracy' was about to give way to something more like home rule. And it was the instinctive pull of the young kingdom towards the east – towards the mother, if one may risk stretching the biographical parallel so far – that provoked the change.

It began as a financial crisis. With the settlement of 1832 had come a dowry, in the form of a new loan of sixty thousand francs, underwritten by the Great Powers. Service payments on the debt had been one of the largest items in the state budget ever since. Every year the state had been obliged to ask for an additional loan to meet them. In 1843, in the wake of the recent international crisis, the powers turned tough. Instead of agreeing a further loan to meet the shortfall, as they had done before, they reconvened the London conference that had guaranteed Greek independence in the first place. In desperation, Otto imposed austerity measures that were instantly and deeply resented. But the measures were still nowhere near enough. In the summer of 1843 the king was forced to agree to humiliating terms.

Part of the country's future tax revenue was to be appropriated by the creditors, to be paid directly to their agents in Athens. Further austerity to the tune of 3.5 million francs was to be imposed as well. Both the circumstances and the conditions are uncannily similar to those of the so-called 'third bailout' in July 2015 – when once again a Greek government would be obliged to surrender its fiscal autonomy to its European creditors.

In 1843 it was a way of showing that the Great Powers' guarantee was for the kingdom, not for any particular king, if he failed to toe the line. It was now the turn of Otto's internal enemies to strike. On the evening of 14 September, Dimitrios Kallergis, captain of the cavalry unit stationed in Athens, attended a performance of the recently premiered opera by Gaetano Donizetti, *Lucrezia Borgia*. (That was how 'civilized' Athens had become in the ten years since the arrival of the Bavarians.) Afterwards, the captain went to his barracks. 'After a few moments of uncertainty, he stammered a few incoherent words, raised his sword, then shouted, "Long live the constitution."'[9] Cavalry and infantry marched together on the palace. Through a window they handed a set of demands to the king. It was a bloodless revolution. The demands had come from the politicians, who had been sidelined by Otto's autocratic rule. But it was the military, the very force that the Bavarians had created as the instrument of their new order, that carried it out and ensured its success. Otto would keep his throne, for now. But it was the army and the politicians who dictated the terms. The decade of autocracy was at an end. Greece would have its first constitution since winning independence. According to some, the day after the coup (3 September in the calendar of the time) marked the true end of the Revolution. One of the main streets in central Athens still bears this date as its name. The open space in front of the palace, which until then had been known, rather charmingly, as the 'Garden of the Muses', would be renamed Syntagma, or Constitution, Square.

Elected representatives from all over the kingdom began arriving in Athens in November 1843. The work of drafting the constitution was completed by the end of March 1844. Of more lasting influence even than the changes to the way the country was governed was a single phrase, which came to be uttered during the course of these deliberations, and from then on would come to enshrine all the inchoate hopes, longings and aspirations that had been the flipside of state-building from the beginning: the 'Grand Idea'.

The immediate context was a proposal to restrict full political rights to those who had been born within the kingdom. This would have been a further nationalization, along the lines of what had already happened to the Orthodox Church. Its effect would have been to narrow the definition of the nation even further within the limits of the state. Presiding over the Assembly was the now seventy-year-old Kolettis, who still wore the kilt of his native Epirot mountains, a region that remained under Ottoman rule. Along with his rival Mavrokordatos, who had been born in Constantinople, and many other prominent members, the Assembly's president risked being excluded under this proposal. Kolettis was credited by contemporaries with an unerring instinct for the popular mood, and the skill to turn it to political advantage. During the Revolution he had been the principal architect of victory for the modernizers in the civil wars of 1824. He was still a formidable force, twenty years on.

In a speech delivered to the Assembly in January 1844, Kolettis began by invoking the oath that he and many others, no longer living, had sworn in the early days of the Revolution, 'the oath in support of liberty for the fatherland, by which we swore to make every sacrifice, even of our very lives, for the liberty of Hellas'. He went on to define the place of the fatherland in the world of his day:

> Through her geographical position Greece [Hellas] is the centre of Europe; standing with the East to her right, and to her left the West, she is destined to enlighten, through her decline and fall, the West, but through her regeneration the East. The first of these missions was accomplished by our forefathers, the second is now assigned to us.

This was a reassertion of the international dimension of the Greek struggle. Far from being alone in the world, Greece was its very centre. Kolettis continued:

> . . . in the spirit of this oath and of this grand idea, I have been observing the plenipotentiaries of the nation come together to decide no longer just the fate of Hellas but of the Hellenic race.[10]

Far from defining the nation by the borders of the state, Kolettis was drawing upon the nationalist language of the day, to lay claim to an ethnic, race-based identity. That much is clear. What is less clear is how, exactly, this identity connects with the phrase, left oddly hanging in the air, 'this grand idea'.

The same words occur again a few lines later, this time to deplore 'how far we have diverged from that grand idea of the fatherland, which we saw first expressed in the song of Rigas'. This was a reference to the 'Battle Hymn', the only part of Rigas's doomed political programme that had been widely disseminated. Today we know a good deal more about the content of that programme than Kolettis or his contemporaries could have done. The 'Hymn' does not in fact set out any clear 'idea of the fatherland' at all. But it *is* addressed to all the diverse populations of the Ottoman Empire. The geographical reach of Rigas's 'Hymn' goes all the way from Belgrade to Egypt. Rigas had of course *not* been promoting the cause of any one ethnic or racial group, quite the reverse. But in the new world of the 1840s this could easily be ignored. After all, Rigas had apparently been calling for the liberation of the entire empire ruled from Constantinople. This, too, would become attached to the meaning of the 'grand idea'.

Within a very short time the 'Grand Idea', now usually embellished with capital letters, would come to stand for a whole new mission: not merely to 'civilize' the East but to extend the borders of the state to encompass all the members of the nation, wherever they might be found. By the end of the 1840s so powerful had this sense of mission become that a new political line-up began to emerge. The declining and never institutionalized 'English', 'French' and 'Russian' parties were being subsumed into a new binary opposition: not between those for and against the Grand Idea itself, but rather between competing policies for achieving it. Mavrokordatos would become the first of a series of leaders over the next eight decades to advocate a 'softly-softly' approach, consolidating gains already made and working through diplomatic means to expand the kingdom in the long term. Kolettis, who served as the first prime minister to be elected under the Constitution of 1844, would come to be identified with a more gung-ho attitude, though his speech to the Assembly had been carefully couched.

From the death of Kolettis in 1847 until the early 1920s the 'Grand Idea' would be shorthand for a programme of national expansion. Horizons were opening up towards the East. Why should not the young Greek kingdom grow up to become an empire like its ancestor the Byzantine, an *eastern* Christian power with its capital at Constantinople?

A NEW NARRATIVE FOR THE NATION

By the early 1850s, the Western-oriented Greek state was becoming harder than ever to reconcile with a more widely diffused Greek nation, most of it still subject to the Ottomans, and whose heartland belonged to the East. The state had been built on a narrative of revival that brushed aside more than two thousand years of intervening history. The nation had not yet established a clear narrative or a political programme at all.

The project started by the Bavarians had already come under attack – ironically enough, from within Bavaria itself. In 1830, the year when Greek independence was first guaranteed by the powers, and well before a Bavarian had been named as the country's first king, a young Austrian schoolteacher named Jakob Philipp Fallmerayer published in Munich the first volume of a study entitled *History of the Morea Peninsula during the Middle Ages*. Volume 2 would complete the story six years later. This was forensic history, written with a political agenda. Fallmerayer's target was not directly Greece itself, which barely existed in the 1820s when he had embarked on his work. What had aroused his ire was the climate of philhellenism that prevailed everywhere in his adopted country of Bavaria. Philhellenism, Fallmerayer set out to prove, was based on a false premise. Every trace of the spirit of ancient Greece, every drop of blood of the ancient Greeks, had been wiped out by successive conquerors of the Peloponnese over the centuries: Romans, Goths, Slavs, Albanians. A revival or resurrection was therefore a logical impossibility, because there was nothing left to revive.

Fallmerayer's thesis is unprovable and in any case irrelevant, since nobody nowadays thinks that culture is determined by race. But his broadside did highlight a vulnerable spot in the national narrative. It was all very well to celebrate the 'revival', 'regeneration' or 'resurrection' of the long-lost civilization of the ancients, even to design a capital city as its visual representation. But sooner or later those with a historical cast of mind were bound to ask: yes, but what happened in between? After all, according to most histories published during the first half of the nineteenth century, including Greek ones, the glorious era of classical civilization had ended when Philip II of Macedon, the father of Alexander the Great, defeated an alliance of the Greek city states at the battle of Chaeronea in Boeotia. This had been back in 338 BCE. The gap from there to the outbreak of the Greek Revolution in 1821 was a long one. It would need some explaining.

Other historians found less contentious ways to tell the story.[11] But the gap once opened up could not be closed again – even if the building and landscaping programme for Athens, or plans for language reform, carried on blithely oblivious. By the start of the 1850s, the new nation and the new state were in need of a *national* history of their own. It was not just the 'missing' centuries that had to be bridged, but the ever more apparent lack of fit between the two components of national identity: nation and state. The gap was not just historical, it was geographical and conceptual: between 338 BCE and 1821 CE, between Athens and Constantinople, between two different ways of thinking about what it meant to be Greek.

The challenge was taken up by two men of intellect who came from opposite ends of the old 'Orthodox commonwealth'. Spyridon Zambelios was an aristocrat from Lefkada in the Ionian islands. Konstantinos Paparrigopoulos had been born in Constantinople. Those of his family who had survived the Ottoman reprisals of 1821 had found refuge in Russia and wound up in Athens after independence. Born in the same year, 1815, both men had studied and travelled in western Europe in their youth. Zambelios, with the advantages of his class, would establish himself in the mid-1840s as amateur philosopher, historian, folklorist and novelist in Corfu, still the capital of the British protectorate of the Ionian islands. Paparrigopoulos had to earn his living, first as a schoolteacher and then, from 1851 until his death forty years later, as Professor of History at the University of Athens.

The new history emerged, without warning, almost fully formed. It was Zambelios who took the decisive step. His purpose, he declared in a book of over seven hundred pages published in Corfu in 1852, was 'to touch upon that obscure and unexplored period, during which civilization's most chosen race mysteriously passes from its ancient to its modern stage of liberty'. This was, for the first time, to tackle the 'missing' centuries head on. There were two ways to do it. Zambelios's book has as its main title *Folk Songs of Greece*. The oral traditions of the common people, largely overlooked by Greeks until now but already the subject of much scholarly activity elsewhere in Europe, would provide one avenue. A collection of songs transcribed from the oral tradition makes up the book's final part. The other avenue, which takes up proportionately far more space, announces itself as a 'Historical Study concerning Medieval Hellenism'. Together, the unofficial, popular record preserved in the oral tradition of the songs and the recorded history of the Byzantine centuries would fill the gap.[12]

Greek historical thinking had all of a sudden moved on. The established narrative of the sudden rebirth of 'Hellas' was beginning to be overlaid by the *longue durée* of what Zambelios termed 'Hellenism'. This is another of those words, like 'archaeology', that *look* ancient but were actually new at this time, at least with the meanings they have since acquired. *Hellenismus* had recently begun to appear in German history-writing. Zambelios was the first to apply the term systematically to an overarching concept of identity based on the continuity of the Greek language. Today, in Greek, 'Hellenism' is defined as 'the totality of Greeks living throughout the world, the Greek nation' or 'Greek civilization and the totality of Greeks as bearers of that civilization'.[13] Zambelios was the first to divide the history of newly named Hellenism into three periods: ancient, medieval and modern. Christianity, he declared, had 'become a component of Hellenism'. The 'medieval Hellenism' that had resulted was as much a constituent part of the identity of the modern Greek as his ancient birthright: 'We, like it or not, are children of the Middle Ages ... [W]e cannot lay down that eastern character that links us with the Byzantine Middle Ages'.[14] It was the beginning of a far-reaching synthesis.

Paparrigopoulos, the professional historian, had published history books already – the first of them, indeed, a response to Fallmerayer.

But it was only after reading Zambelios's book that his own ideas changed radically. The very next year Paparrigopoulos brought out a much slimmer volume, disarmingly entitled *History of the Greek Nation, from the Most Ancient Times until Today, for the Instruction of Children*. Essentially, the story that Paparrigopoulos now told for the first time, and in only two hundred and thirty pages of large type, followed the lines that Zambelios had set out more elaborately the year before. The difference was that Paparrigopoulos took the proposition to its logical conclusion: he told the story from beginning to end (and left out the folklore – he was a professional, after all). Avoiding, for the time being, the more abstract-sounding 'Hellenism', Paparrigopoulos told the story of the Greek *nation*. And he defined his subject too, succinctly, on the very first page: 'The *Greek nation* is the name for all those people who speak the Greek language as their own tongue.'[15]

This was the narrative that would later be elaborated into a five-volume work with the same title, which would appear between 1860 and 1874. No longer a children's book, this was still accessible, narrative history addressed to the widest possible readership, uncluttered by information on sources or abstruse points of academic debate. The five volumes consolidate and carry forward the new thinking that had emerged in the early 1850s. Paparrigopoulos was the first Greek historian to mobilize another new concept that had developed in German history-writing in recent decades. 'Historicism' defines history as process. The theory of evolution had not yet been born, but German historicism intellectually belongs to the same stable: everything that happens in history is part of a continuously evolving pattern of change. It was Paparrigopoulos's unique achievement to tell the story of the Greek 'nation' as the continuous narrative of a continuous process of historical development. His *History* is a systematic application of the new horizons of historicism to the historical record preserved in the Greek language over three millennia. Deservedly, it has been hailed by one modern historian of ideas as 'the most important intellectual achievement of nineteenth-century Greece'.[16]

In the new scheme of things, 'revival' was replaced by 'continuity'. The newly reclaimed centuries, and particularly the millennium that had been dominated by the Greek-speaking emperors of Byzantium, far from an embarrassing lacuna to be glossed over, now became the formative stages of a centuries-long process that had finally been vindicated by the Revolution of 1821 and the establishment of the new kingdom.

Everything else followed from that simple definition on the first page of Paparrigopoulos's book for children in 1853. If language is indeed the sole defining condition for the nation, then it must follow that the Greek nation is as old as the language. And so was born the compelling and durable narrative of a long-lived nation struggling to achieve its ordained purpose through the flux of historical change, sometimes triumphant as in the classical period and the Revolution of the 1820s, more often a victim of others' triumphs, but always holding on to a fundamental 'national character' that would be progressively refined in the crucible of history. It was a bold and moving concept. It chimed with the way in which national histories were being written in other parts of Europe. And by the time the main part of the work was finished in 1874, it would have turned into the necessary intellectual underpinning for the Grand Idea. The state was no longer at odds with the claims of the nation: it existed to serve them. The Greek state was finding its place in a historical scheme of things that was infinitely older, and had a far wider geographical reach. It was acquiring a destiny beyond its current borders, which would encompass all the Greek-speaking populations of the Ottoman Empire.

By that time, there would be a new dynasty on the throne and the history of the young kingdom would have embarked on its next phase. But first we must return to the 1850s, to see how that story ended.

REALITY CHECK

The Protocol of London, back in 1830, had promised the Greek state nothing less than 'complete independence'. Its first decade, under the tutelage of the Bavarians, had not felt much like that. Bavarian influence had ended with the putsch of 1843. With the exception of the king himself, his immediate family and a few close associates, the remaining Bavarians had been sent home. But if nanny had been sacked, the parents – that is to say, the Great Powers – became more watchful than ever. Events of the early 1840s should have been a warning to Otto and his ministers. Worse lay in store for them.

Before another opportunity could arise to test the limits of the Grand Idea in practice, Otto's nationalism collided with that of another famous and much more powerful advocate of the doctrine, the British Foreign Secretary, Viscount Palmerston. The inventor of 'gunboat diplomacy', and the determined enforcer of the rights and freedoms of British subjects around the world, Palmerston was more than a match for the little kingdom. Otto and the British Minister in Athens cordially loathed one another. Individual Britons, including the Minister himself, had been cavalierly treated. By 1850 several complainants had gained the attention of the Foreign Office in London. One of those was George Finlay, the historian, part of whose land had been expropriated without compensation to make way for the new Royal Garden (now the National Garden), next to the palace.

The issue that finally provoked the British government to action was the attack on the house of a Jewish merchant during the Easter celebrations in 1847. Don Pacifico had been born in Gibraltar and so was entitled to the protection of the British Crown. After claims for compensation had been ignored for more than two years, Palmerston ordered the Royal Navy into action. In January 1850 the port of Piraeus was blockaded. When Greek captains refused to abide by the blockade, several ships were seized by force. The standoff lasted for four months, until French mediation brought about a settlement.

The 'Don Pacifico affair', as it has been known ever since, was the sharpest humiliation yet for the Greek kingdom. Otto and his ministers had relied once again on the competing interests of the Great Powers to work to their country's advantage. But this was a new situation, when one of the powers was prepared to act unilaterally to defend what it saw as its own interests. The affair set an ugly precedent. No less ugly was the element of latent anti-semitism that the attack on Pacifico's house had brought to the surface, giving the lie to the generalization sometimes heard that there is no anti-semitic tradition in Greece. There would be repercussions in Britain, too. Called to account by Parliament, Palmerston would give his most eloquent and fullest defence of the principles that had informed his action. Not everyone at home was impressed. The British satirical magazine *Punch* carried cartoons showing Greece as the underdog, one of them with the caption, 'Why don't you hit one of your size?'[17] The Don Pacifico affair took place midway between the two 'opium wars' against China in the 1830s and the 1850s. It could be that Greece got off relatively lightly – saved by its small size from a fate even worse.

Memories of this episode were still fresh three years later when a new international crisis erupted in the Levant. This one began as a dispute between Russia and France over the guardianship of the holy places in Jerusalem. Since Jerusalem was part of the Ottoman Empire, it was the Ottoman government that had to adjudicate. When the Sultan came down on the side of France, the signal was given for yet another in the long-running series of wars between the two empires, the Russian and the Ottoman. War was declared in October 1853. For Otto, and for many in the Greek government and the press, this was the ideal opportunity. The last time these rivals had gone to war, Greece had benefited greatly from the terms of peace. That had been in 1829. Now independent, what could be more natural than for Greece to pledge its support for Russia against their common enemy? Once again, there ought to be rewards if the right side won.

By the end of 1853, Greek irregular bands had crossed into Ottoman-controlled territory north of the frontier. In a re-run of what had happened during the crisis of the early 1840s, revolts broke out in Epiros to the north and Crete to the south, in both cases backed by Athens. But this was to reckon without the other two guarantor powers. France was by this time well launched into its 'Second Empire', under Napoleon III. In Great Britain, Palmerston's party, the Whigs, were still in power. Britain and France together determined that Russia must not be allowed to dismember the Ottoman Empire – now for the first time dubbed 'the sick man of Europe'. Back in the 1820s, Mavrokordatos had tried to persuade a British Foreign Secretary that a strong and independent Greece would be the best solution to the 'Eastern Question', standing between a crumbling Ottoman Empire and Russian expansionist ambitions. In 1829 the Duke of Wellington had come close to wishing that solution into being. But times had changed. The preferred solution to the 'Eastern Question' was once again what it had been all along: to keep the 'sick man' alive. It was the only way to preserve peace in Europe – even when, in this case, it meant going to war with another European power to preserve it.

Britain and France joined the war on the Ottoman side in the spring of 1854, and shortly afterwards sent troops to land in the Crimea. This was where most of the fighting would take place. In Greece, the diplomatic representatives of the two powers had already demanded that Otto declare neutrality and withdraw all Greek irregulars from Ottoman territory. When Otto refused, a joint British and French naval squadron was despatched to Piraeus, to protect the Ottomans' flank. Once again the chief port of Greece was blockaded. This time the port itself was occupied too. Otto was left with no choice but to back down. In the aftermath, it fell to the hapless Mavrokordatos, the most moderate and diplomatically able of the political leaders available, to form a government and enforce a deeply resented neutrality.

This time the humiliation was complete. There were no saving graces. To compound matters, the occupiers justified their actions under the terms of the 1832 treaty of guarantee. This authorized the guarantor powers to intervene to ensure the annual service payments and secure the capital of the loan of sixty thousand francs that had come with the guarantee. The threat to sequester part of the revenues of the Greek state in 1843 had never been implemented. Now it was – to justify what would otherwise have been, in legal terms, an act of aggression. The financial state of the kingdom had not improved in the meantime. The measures had the effect of rubbing the offending youngster's nose in the consequences of its own precocity: how could a state that had never yet balanced its books possibly be allowed to raise an army or fight to extend its borders?

The Crimean War ended in exhaustion in March 1856. Russia was marginally the loser. The Treaty of Paris affirmed the territorial integrity of the Ottoman Empire. For Greeks, it looked as though the Grand Idea was off the agenda for the foreseeable future. Britain and France kept up their blockade and occupation of Piraeus for a full further year, until a Control Commission had been put in place to oversee the latest rescheduling of Greece's debt. By the time the blockade was lifted, Otto's reputation in the eyes of his subjects was in tatters.

*

It was not Otto's fault. It is difficult to see what any Greek government could have done, caught between a groundswell of public opinion at home and the exercise of *force majeure* by two of the guarantor powers – whose own policies in the Crimean War have not stood up well to the judgement of history either. There were many reasons for what happened next. This was only one of them.

Otto had married Amalia of Oldenburg on a trip back to Germany in 1836. Twenty years later it was evident that the couple would have no children. There would be no successors to 'Otto I' in a direct line. Then there was religion. Otto was Catholic, his queen Lutheran. Both had willingly embraced many of the habits of their adopted country, including its language and style of dress. But neither of them was prepared to convert to Orthodoxy. The fact that the titular head of the Orthodox Church in Greece belonged to the rival and traditionally distrusted branch of Christianity was a constant source of dissatisfaction in many quarters. It was a particular provocation to the pro-Russian 'Napists', the very group that had most to smart about, during the Crimean War and after.

Then, in 1859, came a new threat to the 'Concert of Europe', one that would soon prove fatal. It was the turn of another small kingdom in southern Europe to take on the mighty – and this time to prevail. The Kingdom of Sardinia and Piedmont became the spearhead of the long-simmering movement for the unification of Italy into a new nation state. The name for this movement, 'Risorgimento', means 'revival'. This time, it was a different ancient civilization that was to be revived – the empire of Rome. One of the movement's ideological leaders, Giuseppe Mazzini, had studied and admired the 'revival' of Greece in his youth. The Italians were rewarded with French support at a crucial early stage of their struggle, earned through the canny alignment of the Sardinian kingdom during the Crimean War. The Kingdom of Italy was proclaimed in Turin, the capital of Piedmont, in 1861. But this was explicitly a provisional solution. The nation's true capital was declared to be Rome. It would take another ten years before that declaration could become a reality, and Italian unification complete. But already the parallel with the Greek case was glaring for any Greek who had sufficient education to read a newspaper. The Italians, by 1861, had reached much the same point as the Greeks had done back in 1833. The new Kingdom of Italy, just like theirs, had set its sights on an ancient imperial city for its future capital – after all, for a thousand years, had not Constantinople been known as the 'New Rome'? And no one seemed to be preventing them. Why could not Greece do the same?

This was the opportunity that might just have saved Otto his throne. There was little enough that impoverished Greece could have done to help the Italians – though individual volunteers did take part, just as Italians had done in Greece in the 1820s. But Otto's family, the Wittelsbachs, had close ties to Austria. And it was against the rule of Austria, imposed over much of northern Italy since 1815, that the battles of the Risorgimento were being won. When the crucial test came, the Greek royal government threw its support behind Austria, when it could once and for all have proclaimed its own revolutionary credentials and a common purpose shared with the architects of a united Italy. The 1860s were to become the decade of the two great 'unification' movements that together would mark the turning point between the old Europe of multi-ethnic empires and the post-1918 continent of nation states that we know today. Otto *could* have led the Greeks to claim their share of ownership in this project, whose day was about to dawn. They had been the pioneers, after all. Of all the mistakes of a troubled reign, this was perhaps the greatest.

As always, there were more immediate flashpoints, too. Even after the constitution had come into force in 1844, Otto had never lost his taste for absolutist government. There was widespread interference and intimidation in the parliamentary elections of 1859. Unrest among students at the University of Athens, that summer, marked the entry into politics of a force that every succeeding generation of Greek politicians would have to reckon with. By the first months of 1861, Otto's refusal to accept even modest reforms had the effect of bringing together almost the entire governing class against him. In February, a disaffected university student, a fervent supporter of the Grand Idea, narrowly failed to assassinate Queen Amalia.

Early in 1862 rioting broke out in a barracks in Nafplio. The political climate was deteriorating. In the autumn the king and queen set out in their yacht for a tour of the Peloponnese. The aim was to show themselves to their people and take the temperature of public opinion.

While they were gone, several provincial garrisons revolted. The *coup de grâce* came on 22 October. Just as had happened back in 1843, it was the national army, recruited and drilled in discipline by the Bavarians, that rebelled against the Bavarian sovereign. This time, it was not the generals but middle-ranking officers who took the lead. That, too, was to set a precedent for the future. The next day a new 'revolutionary government' was proclaimed in Athens. When the king and queen sailed back into Piraeus, they were tactfully intercepted by a British warship. None of the three guarantor powers would support the king's right to his throne any longer. Otto left Greece as he had arrived, as the guest of the British Royal Navy.

Greece, according to Otto's British nemesis, Lord Palmerston, had 'come of age'.[18]

Palmerston's verdict may have been premature. But what had been achieved in almost exactly thirty years? Evidence for attitudes at the time is oddly mixed. Many of the initiatives of the 1830s were still forging ahead at the time of Otto's expulsion. Centralized political and administrative institutions, many of them still incomplete, would continue to be consolidated over the following decades. But politically, Otto had been an anachronism, just as Kapodistrias had been before him. The role of enlightened despot ruling over a small and not fully independent state, to which German princes had become accustomed during the preceding centuries, had been coming under pressure in the German states, even in 1833. Thirty years later, the descendants of those princes were being rolled up into the new *Reich*, another nation state in all but name. In Greece, the progressive politics that had been marked out by the first Provisional Constitution of 1822 had effectively been put on hold from the arrival of Kapodistrias in 1828 until now. That would be an important task for the next dynasty to make good.

Change in Greece had been fundamental and irreversible – at least in Athens and the larger towns. But for the great majority, in villages scattered over mountain valleys and islands, life had still probably changed very little. It was, inevitably, the elites that were driving the forces of change, and themselves changing with them.

Among those elites, by the early 1860s, dogged optimism went hand in hand with an almost mystical hope for a better future. The Grand Idea provided a focus for those hopes. But alongside them went an undercurrent of public disillusion, sarcasm and on occasion even self-disgust. Newspaper editorials from the last months of Otto's reign catch this new mood:

> Greece herself, of which the European world had dreamed as the unifying centre between the East and the civilization of the West, has today become so degraded as to be considered a burden by the European world, as an obstacle to the future of the East.

The same newspaper even considered that the nation, in its 'progress towards civilization' since the Revolution, had managed to lose 'a large part of the advantages it had possessed before'. This sort of self-lacerating gloom was not just a passing phenomenon. A full decade later an assessment of yet another 'crisis' would starkly sum up the mood, which had still not lifted: 'Greece since her liberation has achieved nothing worthy of note.'[19]

One of the underlying causes of this soul-searching, though it does not emerge explicitly from these diatribes, was that all this time, while the young Greek kingdom had been taking its first steps, its old rival the Ottoman Empire had not stood still. Beginning in 1839, and followed up in 1856, the reforms known collectively as *Tanzimat* ('reorganization') had guaranteed new political and legal rights to non-Muslim subjects of the empire. In its own way the 'sick man of Europe' was modernizing too. These reforms had a far more immediate impact on the lives of the three-to-one majority of Orthodox Greek speakers who were still subject to the Ottomans than anything said or done in the kingdom, or in the name of the Grand Idea. By the 1850s the Phanariot class, which had been all but extinguished in the paroxysm of reprisals that took place in 1821, had found its way back to something like its former favour. Orthodox Christians could once again occupy high positions in the reformist Turkey of Sultan Abdulmejid.

The greatest failure of Otto's Greece, wrote George Finlay shortly before the king's expulsion, was that the aftermath of the Revolution had 'not created a growing population and an expanding nation . . . [N]o stream of Greek emigrants flows from the millions who live enslaved in Turkey, to enjoy liberty by settling in liberated Greece.'[20] Instead, citizens of the kingdom would still often leave to seek their fortunes in the modernizing and growing cities of the Ottoman Empire: Constantinople, Smyrna, Salonica. It would not be until the 1870s that the conurbation consisting of Athens and the port city of Piraeus would begin to experience comparable growth.

In October 1862, Greece was once again leaderless. Another breakdown of civil order, like the one that had followed the assassination of Kapodistrias, seemed all too likely. Thanks to a new historical narrative, and the popular appeal of the Grand Idea, the nation was rapidly acquiring a new past. But what about its future? In the race to 'modernize' (that is, to become more like western Europe), there was no telling which would get there first: the ageing 'sick man of Europe' or the new 'model kingdom in the East', as Greece was about to be dubbed by its next king-to-be.[21]

5

Ideals and Sorrows of Youth

1862–1897

At the end of 1862 no one could have told who would next sit upon the vacant throne of Greece. Greek public opinion had fixed upon the person of Prince Alfred, the second son of Queen Victoria of Great Britain. An election to choose a new sovereign was called by the Provisional Government that had ousted Otto, and carried out during December. From almost a quarter of a million votes cast, 95 per cent were for Alfred. It was a choice that at the time took observers by surprise. The reasons for this sudden enthusiasm are still not entirely clear. A British-born monarch might perhaps have been expected to rule with more respect for parliament and the constitution than Otto had done. There was also the question of the Ionian islands. Agitation had been gathering pace, during the previous decade, for an end to the British protectorate and for union of the islands with Greece. It was beginning to be rumoured that after almost fifty years the British were ready to give them up. Perhaps the election of a monarch from the British royal family would encourage the government led by Lord Palmerston to cede the islands to Greece? If this was the thinking, it worked – though not in a way that anyone could quite have foreseen.

In hindsight, the most remarkable aspect of this election is that only ninety-three individuals, a negligible percentage, wanted to see the monarchy replaced by a republic. However low Otto's stock had fallen latterly, and despite the unhappy precedent set by his reign, two principles had become deeply embedded in an electorate that had been enfranchised only twenty years before. One was the monarchy as an institution. The other, that the head of state should be an outsider, above and beyond the intense rivalries of Greek political life.

The time would come when both principles would be fiercely contested, but not until the next century.

The polls had not yet closed when news reached Greece that the three guarantor powers had 'signed an engagement, declaring that no member of the imperial and royal families reigning in France, Great Britain, and Russia could accept the crown of Greece'.[1] Queen Victoria in any case let it be known that no son of hers was going to risk sharing the fate of the luckless Otto. By the time the election result was announced in February 1863, it was already a dead letter. The Greeks were not to be allowed to have the candidate they had voted for. But the vote for Prince Alfred gave the British government the leverage it needed, in effect to choose the next sovereign for Greece. The choice would then have to be ratified by the Greek National Assembly. This had been a mere formality in 1832, but no longer. The sweetener that would persuade the Assembly to accept Great Britain's choice would be the Ionian islands.

That left only one problem: to find a suitable candidate. Christian William Ferdinand Adolphus George Glücksburg was (like Hamlet) prince of Denmark, and probably even younger, at seventeen. His sister, Alexandra, was about to marry Edward, Prince of Wales, and would become a future Queen of the United Kingdom. William (as he was generally known) was the same age as Otto had been when he had been nominated for the Greek throne. His name had been on the list of candidates for election back in December, and had garnered precisely six votes. The offer to the Danish royal family came not from Greece, but from the British government. In Athens it was evident to the members of the National Assembly which way the wind was blowing. Less than two months after the announcement of the result of the election, and even before Prince William had formally accepted the offer of the throne, the Assembly elected him unanimously as king. Of the prince's five given names only the last could be readily assimilated into Greek, being also the name of a much venerated saint in the Orthodox calendar. Probably for this reason, when the Danish prince duly entered into his kingdom on 30 October 1863, it was under the royal name of George I.

With the arrival of King George, Greek governments at once achieved a degree of self-determination that had been denied them ever since the later stages of the Revolution. The constitution ratified in 1864 was the work of a *Greek* assembly. Twenty years before, Otto had dictated changes to its predecessor. Subsequently he had found ways of manipulating it to his advantage. This time the National Assembly determined that the monarch would have no rights over the constitution itself. King George bound himself to accept the new state of affairs in a public speech delivered on his very first day in office. Sovereignty, this time, rested ultimately with the people. The Constitution of 1864 went further than its predecessor to give the vote to almost all adult males (women would have to wait until 1952). At the time, it established one of the most democratic political systems in the world. Once again, Greece was a pioneer.

Another innovation was the royal title. This, too, was the work of the National Assembly. Otto had been crowned 'King of Greece' (Hellas). His successor, even before his identity had become known, was to be 'King of the Hellenes'. Just so far had the Grand Idea advanced in little short of twenty years. In French, the international language of the time, the true significance of this change was easily missed. It related not to the status of the monarch, as the equivalent change had done in France some years before, but to that of his subjects. Only the Ottoman ambassador to London, ironically enough himself a Greek-speaking Orthodox Christian, realized the implications and saw fit to challenge it. But the new title was nodded through with a minor tweak that affected only the official translation.[2] Unwittingly, the Great Powers had invested the new king with a title to rule over the entire Greek nation.

And indeed, during the reign of King George, the kingdom would expand. In its first year, the British made good on their promise and the Ionian islands became part of Greece, in June 1864. For Great Britain, having ruled what was nominally a 'protectorate' for half a century through the Colonial Office, this act marked a first rehearsal for the era of decolonization that would come a century later. For Greece, a half-century of expanding the frontiers of the state had begun.

That half-century coincides almost exactly with the reign of the new king.

THE POLITICS OF EXPANSION

For someone who presided for so long over the fortunes of his country, and did so without any of the ruptures that would mark the reign of every other Greek monarch, before or after him, George I has attracted remarkably little attention from historians. Only one biography of him exists, and it is more than a hundred years old. His personality is hard to gauge, perhaps a little colourless, if one may judge by the few private letters that have found their way into print.[3] But King George was neither an empty figurehead nor an autocrat. From the beginning he accepted constitutional limits to his power that Otto would never have countenanced. But he retained the right to appoint governments and prime ministers. Not always obviously or directly, King George seems to have kept a hand on the helm of the ship of state throughout his reign. His marriage in 1867 to Grand Duchess Olga, the niece of the Tsar, ensured that the queen and their future heirs would share the same Orthodox religion as their subjects. This removed at a stroke a grievance that had dogged the reign of his predecessor. From then on, the King of the Hellenes would be linked dynastically to the ruling families of two of his kingdom's three guarantor powers – an enviable prospect for stability compared to Otto's always tetchy relations with those same powers. If Greece's second monarch never attained the popularity of the leading politicians who brought their decrees to him to sign, he was never as divisive either, or as his own royal successors would prove to be. So it is hard to tell to what extent the successes and failures of half a century may have been due to the only public figure who oversaw all of them.

Between 1864 and 1882 Greece had no fewer than thirty-three different administrations, several of them 'unity' governments that were effectively leaderless. It was not until 1875 that the principle became accepted that the task of forming a government must be given to the leader who enjoyed the 'declared confidence' of the Chamber, that is to say, a parliamentary majority. And even after that, it was not always applied in practice. Parties were loose groupings of patronage networks dominated by charismatic individuals – no great change there, from the time of the Revolution. In the 1870s there were four of these, then five. Something for the first time resembling a two-party system would emerge only after 1880. But that had less to do with party organization than with the personal qualities of the two arch-rivals who between them would dominate and divide the political landscape of Greece throughout the last two decades of the century, very much as Gladstone and Disraeli had done in Britain before them.

In many ways, these two men were the inheritors and perpetuators of the old fault line that had opened up within the leadership of the Revolution in the 1820s. On one side of this fault line lay outward-looking engagement with the West, on the other the traditional ideal of defiant self-sufficiency, coupled with yearning for expansion towards the East. In their case, it was not only a matter of political choice, it was also dynastic.

Charilaos Trikoupis was the nephew by marriage of Alexandros Mavrokordatos, the modernizing leader who had done more than anyone to engage the European powers in the Greek struggle during the 1820s. His father, Spyridon, had been a loyal supporter of Mavrokordatos during the Revolution and afterwards throughout a long career in public service that included more than a decade as his country's ambassador in London. The elder Trikoupis is still remembered as the author of the most authoritative history of the Revolution in Greek, written and published in London at the time of the Crimean War. Charilaos, much like his uncle Mavrokordatos before him, gained political and diplomatic experience while employed as the secretary of his father's embassy. Nepotism was nothing unusual at this time. Nor were those who benefited always undeserving.

Theodoros Diligiannis also had a famous and influential uncle. Kanellos Deligiannis had been a wealthy landowner in the Peloponnese. He, too, had distinguished himself during the Revolution – as one of the chief supporters of Kolokotronis, against Mavrokordatos and the modernizers during the civil wars of the 1820s. The slight change of surname between generations is revealing: 'Dili-' is meant to sound more like ancient Greek than 'Deli-', a frequent prefix in Greek surnames, which comes from Turkish. Historians in recent years have devoted far greater attention to the career and ideas of Trikoupis than of his rival. Diligiannis had a gift for the popular touch, as Kolettis had once done. He could easily rouse the enthusiasm of audiences, in a way that did not come naturally to the more intellectual Trikoupis, any more than to Mavrokordatos before him.

In the rhetoric and the political careers of these two men the shadow of the old fault line can be traced through the latter years of the nineteenth century. But this time the tremors would be contained within the parliamentary system. There was no fracture of the wider community, as there had been before and would be again. The parties led by the parliamentary rivals were not consistently aligned with ideological positions, or deeply rooted in opposing popular attitudes. Trikoupis is often described as 'progressive' and Diligiannis as 'conservative'. But neither man was above changing his policies according to circumstances, nor were their followers any less averse to switching their allegiance. Diligiannis's often-quoted remark that he was against everything that his rival was *for* reveals the limits of the party system in Greece at this time.

And so for the time being the fault line remained active only on the surface. One reason for this may have been to do with the personality of the king and the way he exercised his constitutional role. But whatever the causes, this was a time of rare unanimity about the nature and purposes of the Greek nation state. The combined edifice of the Grand Idea and the new historical narrative, which had been rounded off with the publication of the fifth volume of Paparrigopoulos's *History* in 1874, had made sure of that. Throughout the reign of King George there was only ever the one policy on offer: to expand the state and bring as much as possible of the Greek nation within its borders. This goal shines through the policy statements of Trikoupis, often represented as the champion of moderation and restraint, just as it does through the more belligerent tones of Diligiannis. At an early stage of his career, during the 'Eastern Crisis' of 1876, Trikoupis is on record as saying, 'The national idea of Hellenism is the liberation of Greek land and the establishment of a unitary Greek state that includes the entire Greek nation.'[4]

Today, Trikoupis is chiefly remembered for his far-sighted investments in infrastructure – roads, railways, harbours, the Corinth Canal – and for introducing a measure of industrialization into an economy that had always been primarily agricultural. The most visible present-day homage to this legacy is the three-kilometre-long Charilaos Trikoupis Suspension Bridge that elegantly spans the entrance to the Gulf of Corinth and links the Peloponnese with the road networks of northwest Greece, opened in 2004. But what is easily forgotten in the twenty-first century is that, at the time, the purpose of all this expansion at home was to create the springboard for expansion abroad. This was the driving force behind almost all Greek policy decisions during this period.

After the peaceful absorption of the Ionian islands in 1864, opportunities to make further territorial gains would arise on no fewer than four occasions before the end of the century. Historians tend to play up the *failures* of Greek politicians at these testing times. But the difficulties they faced were formidable, and also more interesting, in the insights they can offer into the changing dynamics of the international stage at the time, and the ways in which successive Greek administrations learned (or failed) to adapt.

Some of these difficulties were already familiar. The guarantee by the Great Powers, which protected the state's integrity, at the same time prevented it from encroaching on that of any other. A national army that had been created for the purpose of restoring *internal* order, and had now deposed a sovereign, had never been designed to wage an aggressive war. The state was poor in resources. Even after the enforced restructuring of the late 1850s it was still heavily in debt. The 'sick man of Europe', the Ottoman Empire, was perhaps not so sick after all, and very much larger and more powerful, hemming in the little kingdom on three sides.

But perhaps the greatest difficulty of all was new. It came from an entirely unexpected quarter. What had been achieved in Greece since 1830 was now being emulated all over the continent. Nationalism along ethnic lines was now sweeping the board. Although politicians still paid lip service to the 'Concert of Europe' that had been established at the end of the Napoleonic Wars, the new and shifting reality was better represented by the phrase that came to be heard more often in the second half of the century: the 'balance of power'. The 'unifications' of Italy and Germany during the 1860s had changed the map of Europe for good. The new German Reich, built out of Prussian military defeats inflicted on Austria and France, came into existence in 1871 as already another Great Power. Anything was possible. And the claims of ambitious new nation states could no longer be denied or ignored, after the Prussians had entered Paris, in January of that year.

It was not just in the West that this was happening. In the European provinces of the Ottoman Empire, populations that had won a degree of autonomy, short of independent statehood, were more and more coming to resemble nation states in the way they defined and governed themselves. This had been the case with Serbia since 1829. Then in 1859, in the wake of the Crimean War, the Danubian principalities also became autonomous, and adopted the name 'Romania'. The largest group of all were the Slavic speakers of the Balkan mountain range and the hinterland of the Black Sea, who now began to press for recognition and self-government as Bulgarians.

In the 1860s, Greece was still the only fully independent state in southeast Europe. But others were looking to copy its example. The national rivalries that today are almost synonymous with the name that the region would acquire in the twentieth century were just beginning. The 'balkanization' of the Balkans goes back no further than the middle of the nineteenth century.[5]

The first victim of this development was the 'Orthodox commonwealth'. The spiritual and cultural unity of the Orthodox Christian world had been severely shaken by the Revolution of 1821 and the Ottoman reprisals of the same year. Since 1833 it had been divided by the unilateral action of the Greek state in establishing a national Church. Now came demands, first heard in 1860, for the Bulgarian-speaking community in Constantinople to have a Church of its own, too. This might have seemed a minor matter of ecclesiastical jurisdiction. Its magnitude became apparent a decade later, when in March 1870 the Ottoman government formally recognized a separate communion to be known as the 'Bulgarian Exarchate'. In retaliation, two years later, the Ecumenical Patriarchate excommunicated the followers of the rival Church. A new and bitter antagonism had come into play.

The Bulgarians were not the only ones. At the same time, the newly established principality of Romania was building its identity on the

Wallachian language, from this time onwards known as Romanian. What remained of the eighteenth-century Greek-educated elite that had ruled over Wallachia and Moldavia for a century was now cast as the oppressor, resented even more than the Ottomans, because closer to home. If there had ever been a possibility of the 'Orthodox commonwealth' coming together into a political force that might have played its part in determining the future of the whole region, as Rigas Velestinlis and others had once envisaged, it was during the 1860s that it vanished for good.

The other issue that was changing was the attitude of Russia. Defeat in the Crimean War had given a new *ethnic* edge to the way in which Russian elites saw themselves and their place in the world. Leo Tolstoy's great epic of the Napoleonic Wars, *War and Peace*, was written and published in serial form during the 1860s, and anachronistically projects the changing attitudes of his own day onto the earlier period. Russian state policy, and so far as one can tell public sympathies too, were moving away from supporting the *Orthodox* populations of eastern Europe in favour of those that shared a Slavic *language*. In this way 'pan-Slavism' was born. At the same time and for much the same reason, the influential strand in Greek public opinion and political life that had maintained a 'Russian' party in existence for more than thirty years quickly tailed off. Russia was now supporting Greece's rivals. And the fact of these new rivalries had yet to be faced. The Ottoman Empire was no longer the only enemy. From the 1860s onwards, just when the citizens and the political leadership of the Greek state had come together in the determination to realize their Grand Idea, the rules of the game had morphed into something more like three-dimensional chess.

The first opportunity came in 1866. In September of that year a 'General Assembly of Cretans' unilaterally declared the union of Crete with Greece. Of all the Ottoman provinces in Europe throughout the nineteenth century, Crete was always the most unstable. The island's Orthodox majority had all but succeeded in bringing about union in the first years of the 1821 Revolution. They had rebelled again in 1841 and most recently in 1858. Unlike almost every other revolutionary movement in modern times, what the Cretan revolutionaries fought for, no fewer than seven times during the nineteenth century, was not autonomy, or self-determination, but *Enosis* – union – with Greece. The repeated demands coming from Crete would have placed any Greek government in a difficult position. This one, remembering what had happened during the Crimean War, maintained a fig leaf of official neutrality. At the same time, for the next three years Greek ships ran the Ottoman blockade to transport volunteers and arms into Crete and refugees, made homeless by the fighting, out.

This was one of many occasions in the century when Greek irregulars went into action beyond the frontiers. Some of these men were subjects of the kingdom, others of the Ottoman state. It was clandestine, it was against the 'rules' of warfare. It was controversial within Greece too. More often than not it would lead to an upsurge of brigandage at home, demonstrating the uncomfortable truth that Greek governments still did not have a monopoly on the use of force within their own territory. This lesson was hideously brought home when a group of aristocratic British travellers was captured and several of its members murdered by brigands only a few miles from Athens, a year after the end of the revolt in Crete, in 1870. On the other hand, it had been irregular guerrilla warfare that had won the initial battles of the Revolution. Greek governments and public attitudes would remain ambivalent about irregular warfare until beyond the end of the century.

During the Cretan revolt, the Great Powers became involved, as they always did. Russia was still on the cusp of its shift towards the later policy of pan-Slavism and so, for a time, encouraged the insurgents and appeared to back the hopes of the Greek kingdom. For the first and only time during the nineteenth century a Greek government made serious attempts to build alliances with its not yet fully independent Balkan neighbours. The only concrete result was a secret treaty with Serbia whereby each country would support the regional claims of the other against the Ottoman Empire. The treaty would prove short-lived and of no help in solving what was now becoming known as the 'Cretan Question'. But the very possibility that such alliances could be contemplated shows awareness of how the political world of southeast Europe was changing. For the first time the Greek state was obliged to recognize the existence of others in its own likeness. International relations were no longer only a matter of treating with the Great Powers. Mutual self-interest and mutual help could be negotiated among emerging states in their own backyard. It was a possibility that would not be fully exploited until almost half a century later, and even then, not for long.

The longest and bloodiest of all the Cretan revolts would drag on until the beginning of 1869. By that time, the Ottomans had regained the upper hand. Once again a conference of the Great Powers brought a resolution – just in time to prevent open war between Greece and the Ottoman Empire. Humiliatingly, the Greek government was excluded from the conference, and had no choice but to accept the terms handed down from Paris. It was scarcely a better outcome than in 1841 or 1854.

When the second opportunity arose, almost a decade later, the political complexities were even more challenging. The first signs of a new 'Eastern Crisis' came in 1875. That summer, local rebellions broke out at the opposite end of the Balkans from Greece, in Herzegovina and Bosnia. In May the following year, Serbia and Montenegro declared war on the Ottoman Empire. At the same time, the Bulgarian provinces rose in revolt. The first round of hostilities was won by the Ottomans. Reprisals against their Bulgarian subjects provoked the high-profile campaign by the British Leader of the Opposition, William Gladstone, against 'Bulgarian atrocities' – meaning violence against Christians. In Greece, opinion was deeply divided. Were these Bulgarians, who had dared to create their own Church in defiance of the Ecumenical Patriarchate, fellow Christians to be supported in their bid for freedom from the traditional enemy? Or were they in their own way as great a threat to Greece and Greek interests as the Turks?

In April 1877, Russia went to war with the Ottoman Empire, championing the rights of a Slavic population as it had never quite done for the Greeks. Once again secret societies and open committees sprang up in Athens. Greek consuls in many Ottoman provinces began stockpiling arms and supplying them to local Christian armed bands. Once again volunteers and brigands (the distinction between them often unclear) crossed over Greece's northern frontier to strike at the Ottomans' rear while they engaged the Russians. By the beginning of 1878 even the normally cautious King George had taken personal charge of preparations for war, and was supported by cheering crowds in Athens. For the first time in Greece, conscription was introduced. The purpose of all this activity was not to aid fellow Christians, whether the Russians or the Bulgarians. It was to stake a claim to as much Ottoman territory as possible, before the fighting stopped and the inevitable peace conference apportioned the spoils.

At the beginning of February 1878, a Greek army more than twenty-five thousand strong crossed the frontier into Thessaly – only to discover that the war was already over. The Russians had once again come close to Constantinople, and the Ottomans sued for peace. The Greek army had hastily to be recalled, without firing a shot. Elsewhere – in Thessaly, Macedonia, and once again in Crete – fighting by Greek volunteers and irregulars continued for several months, aided and abetted by unofficial committees in Athens.

The peace that followed was almost as messy as the war. The Treaty of San Stefano (the name given by Europeans to a suburb of Constantinople) created a large new principality of Bulgaria, but gave nothing to either Greece or Serbia. It was time for the new Great Power of the decade, Germany, to take a hand. The Kaiser's foreign minister, Otto von Bismarck, convened a conference in the German capital. The treaty that emerged from the Congress of Berlin, in July 1878, would determine the political contours of southeast Europe for a generation. Bulgaria was reduced in size and split into the separate principalities of Bulgaria and Eastern Rumelia, neither of them fully independent. In recognition of what had by this time become a reality in all but name, Serbia, Montenegro and Romania were all granted independent statehood. Greece was promised territory to the north of its original frontier. Two by-products of the negotiations, which would have repercussions later, were the right given by the treaty to Austria to occupy and administer the Ottoman provinces of Bosnia and Herzegovina, and a separate bilateral agreement with the Ottoman Empire that gave Great Britain similar rights in the island of Cyprus.

The territorial gains promised to Greece would not materialize for another three years. When they did, they would prove less than had been promised. It would take a further round of negotiations in Berlin, and a second general mobilization of troops in Greece – ordered by King George with the backing of his prime minister, the supposedly anti-war Trikoupis – before the Ottomans would agree terms. By a settlement of 2 July 1881, Greece gained some 213,000 square kilometres in Thessaly and the southern part of Epiros. For the first time, the Greek state took on responsibility for a sizeable Muslim population, a first foretaste of things to come. The acquisition of Thessaly was the second and last territorial gain for the Greek kingdom in the nineteenth century. First the Ionian islands and now this new northern province had been secured by diplomatic means, not war. This time, though, it had been a close-run thing.

The young kingdom was learning, as well as growing. By the early 1880s it had acquired new territory – but also new enemies. Chief among them were the recently created Bulgarian principalities. And behind Bulgaria stood the might of Russia. All at once the policy of the Great Powers, of keeping the 'sick man of Europe' on his feet, began to seem not so perverse after all. What would become of the Orthodox Greek speakers of the Ottoman Empire, if the empire were to collapse and a rival Orthodox nation was in a stronger position to take over? The question would have been incomprehensible before 1860. Now, two decades later, it was urgent.

It was the Bulgarians who opened the way for Greece's third opportunity. A revolution in Plovdiv in September 1885 unilaterally brought the separate principalities of Bulgaria and Eastern Rumelia together under the control of the government in Sofia. Both Serbia and Greece saw this as a threat. But Greece at this time had no common frontier with Bulgaria – Ottoman Macedonia lay in between. It was the Serbs, a fellow Slav nation, that went into action, only to be roundly defeated by the Bulgarians. In Greece, as it happened, Diligiannis had recently come to power and now found himself trapped by his own warmongering rhetoric. As hostilities wound down, and the principalities of Bulgaria and Eastern Rumelia became a unified nation state in all but name, Diligiannis tried to wrest territorial gains from the Ottomans in compensation. Unable to back down, and with an army mobilized on the frontier, the Diligiannis government found itself forced into the same position as King Otto's during the Crimean War. The navies of two old Great Powers, Britain and Austria, and two new ones, Germany and Italy, blockaded Greece for thirty days in May and

June 1886. There were to be no gains this time. Diligiannis was obliged to hand over the reins to his arch-rival Trikoupis.

By the time the final opportunity of the century presented itself, in 1897, Trikoupis's ambitious programme of expanding both infrastructure and the armed forces would have led the country into bankruptcy. Before we come to the rollercoaster of triumph and disaster that would be Greece's *fin de siècle*, we need to look beyond the boundaries of the state and explore the wider horizons of the nation – as so many in Greece itself were beginning to do at this time.

THE NATION AND ITS LIMITS

Nowhere else was local agitation for union with Greece so strong as it was in Crete. 'Union or death' had been inscribed on the revolutionary banners of 1866, a variation on the war cry of 1821, 'Liberty or death'. 'Union', or *Enosis*, had already proved a potent recruiting agent in the Ionian islands. At the time and ever since, the Cretan struggle has been presented as a two-way fight between a patriotic people and its foreign oppressor. In reality, somewhere between 25 and 40 per cent of the Cretan population were Muslims. These people had their own patriotism. Descended from native Cretans who had converted to Islam since the seventeenth century, they were proud of their local, *Cretan* traditions. Most spoke the Cretan dialect of Greek as their first language, and seem to have had little knowledge of Turkish.

According to Paparrigopoulos's definition, the Turcocretans, as they were known, ought to have been part of the 'Hellenic nation'. But in Crete throughout the nineteenth century the cleavage ran between religious communities, not language groups. The Turcocretans, as Muslims, looked to the Ottoman Empire for protection and were loyal to its institutions. Union with a state that had killed or expelled all its Muslim population was hardly an option for them. So the Turcocretans, despite their Greek speech, were as much the enemies of the insurgent Cretans as the officials and the military sent from Constantinople. The Cretan revolutions of the nineteenth century were in reality a prolonged intercommunal struggle.

Moving eastwards from Crete, distant Cyprus presented something of a special case. Here the Greek-speaking Orthodox population made up a larger proportion of the total than in Crete, around 80 per cent. The minority Muslims spoke Turkish among themselves, though Greek was used throughout the island. The advent of British rule in 1878 was generally welcomed at first. But here, too, the first calls for *Enosis* would be heard before the end of the century, although the movement would not gain momentum until well into the next.

In the Greek-speaking enclaves of Anatolia – Pontos and Cappadocia – there could never have been much prospect of union with Greece. Greek schools were founded for the better-off, who in this way learned to think of themselves as Hellenes. For the rest, 'Greek and Turkish peasants alike were socialized through their respective faith and measured their status against a dominant local Muslim governing hierarchy.'[6] Not much room for change there. In Cappadocia, and also in Constantinople, there were sizeable communities of Orthodox Christians who used the Greek alphabet – but the language they spoke and wrote was Turkish. Attempts during the second half of the century to persuade the Karamanlides, as these people were known, that they were 'really' Greek seem to have made little headway. It is still unclear exactly how members of these communities thought of themselves in the nineteenth century.

Moving to the western seaboard of Anatolia, another kind of evidence comes from population growth and settlement patterns. In the *vilayet* (administrative division) of Aydin, the region that includes the city of Smyrna, the Greek Orthodox population was growing exponentially. This affected not just the city, where the Greeks had become the largest group by the turn of the century, but the rural areas too – particularly along the expanding network of railways. Most of these settlers came from the Greek kingdom, particularly from the Aegean islands. Other emigrants were setting out at the same time from Greece for America. For many of the poorest in Greece, as the state's population grew, the national economy could not offer the opportunities, or sometimes even the means of subsistence, that were to be found beyond its borders. It seems that the 'land of opportunity' for Greeks of the kingdom, in the late nineteenth century, was as likely to be found in the Ottoman East as westward across the Atlantic.

This particularly applied to the wealthy business community of Alexandria and a smaller one in the Egyptian capital, Cairo. Greeks had begun moving there in significant numbers early in the century. The American Civil War of the 1860s led to a boom in the international market for cotton grown in Egypt. Many Greek fortunes were made in those years, including that of the Benakis family, who would later provide a prominent mayor of Athens and whose private art collection would become the origin of the Benaki Museum. After the bombardment of Alexandria in 1882 by the British Mediterranean Fleet, Egypt passed under direct British control. The Greek community continued to thrive, often strengthening its ties with expatriate Greeks in London, Liverpool and Manchester, until new political conditions in the late 1950s and early 1960s caused most of their descendants to leave for Greece.

Another magnet that drew incomers was the 'city of the world's desire' – Constantinople, the Ottoman capital. Here, many Greek families claimed ancestry going back to Byzantine times. After the Ottoman conquest of 1453 the city had been deliberately repopulated with Orthodox Christians. In the second half of the nineteenth century, out of a total of just over one million, approximately a quarter of its inhabitants were Greeks.[7] These were the people most immediately affected by the series of reforms to the Ottoman system, known as *Tanzimat*, that had begun in 1839 and had been given a new impetus, partly in response to pressure from the empire's European allies, in the wake of the Crimean War in 1856.

In April 1861 a group of prominent citizens met in a fashionable house in Pera (today's Beyoğlu, then the 'European' quarter of the city) to create a literary society. The Greek word for 'society' (*etairia*) was still capable of causing jitters, forty years after the Friendly Society (*Philiki Etairia*) had lit the fuse for the Greek Revolution. So a different, less subversive-sounding, Greek word had to be found instead: *syllogos*, or 'association'. In this way the Hellenic Educational Association of Constantinople was born.[8] It would prove to be the longest-lasting and the most influential of dozens of such ventures in the Ottoman Empire over the next half-century. By establishing, funding and organizing schools, the *syllogos* movement would become one of the most influential channels for disseminating secular and progressive ideas among the Greek-speaking communities of the empire. It was in large part thanks to the Educational Association that ideas of 'national regeneration' and 'national duty' came to be disseminated wherever educated Greeks were to be found within the empire.

These *syllogoi* usually had close and friendly links with like-minded individuals in the Greek state. But they did not function as the state's agents. It would have been impossible for them to do so openly in any case. Occasionally they did arouse the suspicion or hostility of the Ottoman authorities. But these suspicions seem to have been largely unfounded. Children whose parents had been brought up to think of themselves as *Romioi* in Greek, and in official Ottoman terminology as *Rum*, went to schools where they learnt that they were Hellenes and heirs of two great past civilizations. But in all civic respects they remained *Rum* (meaning Christian Orthodox subjects of the Ottoman state). Leading members of the *syllogoi* were often themselves highly placed stakeholders in the Ottoman system and in Ottoman society. And they were not the only ones.

The roll call of senior Ottoman officials in the second half of the nineteenth century who were Orthodox Greeks is a long and distinguished one. These were men of talent and distinction, no less than the Phanariots of the previous century had been. For obvious reasons they have been largely elbowed out of later national histories, both in Greece and in Turkey. Politically, they had no heirs beyond the early 1920s. If any of them committed their intimate thoughts to paper, these have yet to come to light. They include Alexandros Karatheodoris (or Karateodori Pasha), whose father had been personal physician to the Sultan and first president of the Educational Association. His mother was a distant relative of Alexandros Mavrokordatos. Karatheodoris served on two occasions as the empire's foreign minister, and established himself throughout a long career as one of its most trusted and successful ambassadors. As chief Ottoman representative at the Congress of Berlin in 1878, he is credited with the revisions of the Treaty of San Stefano that were most favourable to the empire.

Surprising though it might seem, a succession of Ottoman ambassadors to Athens were themselves Greek-speaking Orthodox Christians.

The careers of these men show no sign of divided loyalties. It had been Konstantinos Mousouros (or Musurus Pasha), the long-serving Ottoman ambassador to London, who had taken exception to the new royal title that was proposed for King George, before his accession, and succeeded in having its official translation into French altered. His translations of Dante's *Divine Comedy* into Byzantine Greek verse were published in London in the 1880s. No friend to the Greek kingdom, Musurus Pasha must have been nonetheless one of the most able and learned Greeks of his day.

Other spheres in which Greeks came to occupy positions of power and influence in the empire were the traditional one of commerce and the new one of banking. The chief banking institutions in Constantinople had been founded, and were largely run, by Greeks. Even the Sultan's court banked with Greek firms. This was the cutting edge of modernization. The activities of these individuals and institutions financed the industrialization of the Ottoman Empire. They also aided projects nearer home, such as the *syllogoi* and the schools that they founded. Some of them invested in the Greek kingdom, too. Much of the 'foreign' investment that made possible Trikoupis's infrastructure projects actually came from wealthy Greeks of the Ottoman Empire. It is hard to tell how far these actions may have been motivated by national solidarity and how much by hard-headed speculation.

Best known among the bankers was Andreas Syngros, who married into the Mavrokordatos family, making him a distant relative by marriage of Karateodori Pasha. After making his fortune as one of the leading financiers in Constantinople, Syngros moved to Athens in the 1870s. There he would become a prolific benefactor and philanthropist, remembered not least in the wide avenue named after him that leads from the centre of Athens to the sea at Phaliro. But Syngros was the exception. Most of these men retained their Ottoman citizenship. They might travel the world or settle in places such as London or Alexandria. But they saw no reason to become subjects of the King of the Hellenes.

Certainly, no one in the Ottoman capital was talking of *Enosis*, meaning union with Greece. This was the view of one Greek banker in Constantinople, vouchsafed in French to a visiting archaeologist in 1861:

The Hellenes (as the inhabitants of the independent kingdom are known throughout the east) are like great children. Just because they put something in their mouth, they're persuaded it's easy, then that it's already come to pass . . . Let them say what they like, we wouldn't for anything want them here in Constantinople. At least the Turks don't get in the way.[9]

Such offhand candour is rare. But it does seem that most educated Constantinopolitan Greeks tacitly distanced themselves from the Grand Idea emanating from the Greek state. For them the future lay not with the dismemberment of the Ottoman Empire, but rather with the continuation and deepening of the reform process that had begun in 1839. In this way, given time, the empire would be reconstituted as a modern European state. As that happened, progressively, Greek talent and Greek wealth would have ever more to give and also to gain.

When Sultan Abdul Hamid unveiled a new constitution in 1876, nineteen Greek deputies (among a total of 130) attended the first session of a short-lived Ottoman parliament. In a document addressed to the British Foreign Secretary some of these new parliamentarians expressed themselves in favour of a 'unitary Helleno-Ottoman nation', a strong and united eastern state including Christians and Muslims, which would be sufficient to counterbalance the power of the West and especially the expansion of the Slavs.[10] It had never before seemed more possible to be those seemingly contradictory things, Hellenic and Ottoman, at once. Hellenism (as defined by Zambelios and Paparrigopoulos) and Ottomanism (as defined by the *Tanzimat* reform programme) could yet learn to co-exist.

These ideas survived even the dissolution of parliament and suspension of the constitution in the face of the empire's defeat by Russia in 1878. For the next thirty years the Ottoman state would return to its old autocratic ways. Even so, at least until 1912, many Greek individuals and institutions would keep faith with their Ottoman identity – *Rum* in the official terminology of the state, but Hellenes at home and among themselves.

That left one area of the Ottoman Empire where no room for compromise existed. All that remained of 'Turkey in Europe' after the

Treaty of Berlin of 1878 was the swathe of territory that stretches westwards from Constantinople along the northern shore of the Aegean and across the southern Balkan peninsula to the Adriatic. In Greek, as in European languages, these regions were known by their ancient names: Thrace, Macedonia, Epiros, Albania.

It is hard to find evidence from these regions for the kind of passionate devotion to the idea of *Enosis*, among local Greek speakers, that undoubtedly existed at different times in the islands. And if Greek was widely spoken, and probably even more widely written, in all these areas, it was as one of a number of languages that had co-existed for hundreds of years. For a great many people living in these regions, it was enough that they were Orthodox Christians. Pressure to declare themselves as Greeks, or Serbs, or Bulgarians, Romanians or Albanians, almost invariably came from outside, and during the late nineteenth century was on the increase.

For this reason, evidence collected and published at the time by national governments and pressure groups has to be taken with a pinch of salt. Particularly in Macedonia, widely differing statistics were circulated by all the interested parties.[11] From the 1870s onwards, Greek and Bulgarian organizations mobilized local armed gangs to intimidate villagers in favour of one side or the other. Churches that celebrated the liturgy in Old Church Slavonic and whose priests were appointed by the Bulgarian Exarchate were targeted by Greeks. Those that kept the Greek liturgy and remained loyal to the Patriarch were attacked by supporters of the Exarchate. In communities where most people were bilingual, these tactics were often effective. Whole villages would change allegiance for the sake of peace – and then change back again, when a different group of armed men rode in. This became a territory riven by terrible choices for individuals, families and communities – choices over which, more often than not, they themselves had little control.

For all the claims and counter-claims, the contest for Macedonia that was about to begin would be not so much about hearts and minds as about language and education. If people could be persuaded, or if necessary induced by threats, to worship in Greek and to learn to read and write in that language, then they could be brought within the fold of the Greek nation. 'National expansion' began to acquire a whole new dimension. What individuals caught up in this process thought about the matter at the time hardly ever made it onto the record. Those in a position to write down their thoughts for posterity had already taken sides – the moment you put pen to paper you were identified as either 'Greek' or 'Bulgarian' by your choice of language.

In the towns and in Salonica, the largest city of the region, educated Greeks did express their opinions. Educational and cultural associations sprang up here too. Like their counterparts in Constantinople, these had to be politically neutral as far as the Ottoman state was concerned. But they could be as vicious as they liked about rival Orthodox ethnic groups. *Syllogoi* in these regions were much more politically active than in the Ottoman capital. For example, at Raidestos (today's Tekirdağ) on the Sea of Marmara, a newly formed Educational Association set out its programme in 1871: 'The Greek muses would within a short time transform the numerous Slavs, who live here, from enemies to genuine children of the Church and of Hellenism, if we act expeditiously within the short time we have at our disposal.' The aim was to 'hellenise' wherever possible, as quickly as possible, in the face of a Slavic threat that had 'become all the more aggressive because of the lethargic intellectual state of the people'[12] – a telling admission that the patriotic enthusiasm of the Association's founders had shallower roots in the community than they might have wished.

This was a local initiative. But in all these regions the activities of local groups tended to be eclipsed, if they were not actually directed, by pressure groups based in Athens. By far the most influential was the Athens-based Society for the Dissemination of Hellenic Learning, established in 1869. Athenian newspapers throughout the 1880s published regular reports and comment under the heading 'From Macedonia'. In one of these, the writer even proposed that in the worst case this 'utterly Hellenic' region would be better served by becoming independent, rather than be swallowed up by Slavs or Austrians. It was from Athens, not from the region, that the most strident calls for union with the Greek kingdom came.[13]

In Salonica itself, now at its heyday as one of the great cities of the Ottoman Empire, Greeks were outnumbered by both Muslims and Sephardic Jews, the latter group being the largest. The Jews still spoke a dialect of Spanish that their ancestors had brought with them from Spain at the end of the fifteenth century. Others had arrived as fugitives from more recent persecutions in Christian states. They can have had little desire to be absorbed into another one, especially if they recalled how the Jews of Tripolitsa had been massacred along with the Muslims in 1821. The first Greek newspaper in Salonica appeared in 1875. Subject, of course, to Ottoman censorship, its editorials promoted good relations with the city's other communities and favoured the 'Hellenic Ottomanism' that was emerging in Constantinople, rather than the expansionist or anti-Bulgarian policies of Athens.[14]

No wonder, then, that when the revolution of the Young Turks came to be proclaimed in Salonica on 23 July 1908, and constitutional rights promised to all the subjects of the empire, the city's Greeks would be as jubilant as everyone else. No wonder, either, that both before and after that event, Macedonia would become the crucible in which the future of the Greek state and the Greek nation would be forged for the twentieth century and beyond.

TRIUMPH AND DISASTER

On 25 July 1893 the Corinth Canal was formally opened. King George was present. So was Andreas Syngros, who had stepped in to rescue the project when the French company in charge of construction had gone bust. Steamships of the Royal Hellenic Navy fired salutes. It was a paler echo of the day in 1833 when Greece's first king, Otto, had stepped ashore. Or so it appears in the oil painting by Munich-trained Konstantinos Volanakis shortly afterwards. For the first time it was possible to sail from the Aegean to the Ionian sea, from Piraeus to Patras, less than a hundred miles away, without having to go the long way round by Cape Matapan and the notoriously stormy waters off the southern tip of the Peloponnese. Almost ten years in the making, the Corinth Canal was the most spectacular of the many infrastructure projects initiated by Charilaos Trikoupis.

On that July day the prime minister who had dominated Greek public life for over a decade was out of office. The king had dismissed

Trikoupis two months before, along with the government that he led, essentially for trying to borrow the country's way out of debt. The 1880s had been a decade of frenetic borrowing and spending. A final restructuring of the debts that had been inherited from the time of the Revolution, in 1878, had given Greece access for the first time to international capital markets. Faced with the choice, early in his premiership, of investing in infrastructure or in the armed forces, Trikoupis had elected to do both. It was borrowed capital that made it possible. According to one contemporary commentator, the country had been effectively insolvent throughout this boom decade.[15]

Dismissing the architect of boom and bust had been a mistake, as the king soon found out. Foreign investors had even less confidence in the short-lived administration that took over. The crunch came that summer. The smoke of cannons had scarcely cleared from the mouth of the Corinth Canal when the price of Greece's staple export, currants, plummeted. In November, Trikoupis was back as prime minister, to face the music. The words he is supposed to have spoken in parliament on 22 December 1893 may be apocryphal: 'Unfortunately, we are bankrupt.' But there was no denying their truth. Once again, Greece was an international pariah. Once again, control of the country's finances was about to pass into the hands of foreign creditors.

Greece was down, but not out. At the same time that French and British bankers were squeezing what returns they could from a crippled national economy, another Frenchman was putting the finishing touches to a visionary idea. Baron Pierre de Coubertin was an educational reformer who held a passionate belief in the moral and physical benefits of sport. His idea, first put forward a year before Greece declared bankruptcy, was to recreate the ancient Olympic Games as a modern international athletic competition. In the summer of 1894 the first International Olympic Committee was formed. Thanks in large part to the energetic representations of Dimitrios Vikelas, a Greek businessman and writer who had lived for most of his adult life in London and Paris, Athens was chosen as the first venue for the Games.

Trikoupis, now in failing health and soon to depart office for good, tried to object. At the very least, he insisted, the Greek state would put no money into it. But Coubertin had good connections with the royal family and other prominent Greeks. The first modern Olympics went ahead. They began on the official anniversary of the start of the Revolution, 25 March 1896, which was 6 April in the Western calendar. It was Easter Monday. The symbolism was perfect.

The Games proved a resounding success. The climax, four days later, was the twenty-five-mile race from the Bay of Marathon to the newly rebuilt Panathenaic Stadium near the centre of Athens. Devised to recapture a glorious moment from the ancient wars between the Greeks and the Persians, this was the first ever 'Marathon'. (No such race had existed in antiquity.) More than eighty thousand people crowded into the stadium to watch Spyridon Louis, a Greek former soldier, cross the finishing line as the world's first Marathon winner. The two royal princes, Constantine and George, leapt from their father's side to join Louis as he completed the final stretch. It was a moment of triumph for a kingdom that was not much older than its king. The following day, far away in the French Mediterranean resort of Cannes, Charilaos Trikoupis died.

In some ways, the triumph of the Athens Olympics was a throwback to the early years of the kingdom. The new-old cityscape of Athens, to which the rebuilt stadium itself was but the latest addition, was still being shaped according to plans that had been drawn up by German architects back in the 1830s. Foreign visitors could not fail to be impressed by the seamless superimposition of the very new upon the foundations of the very old. The revival of the Games and the revival of Hellas could be seen as all of a piece. It was the culmination of a process that had begun with the Revolution and the philhellenic blueprint for the kingdom that had come with the Bavarians.

But this late in the century, the reality had moved on. Greeks had lost nothing of their fierce pride in their ancient Hellenic heritage. But they no longer saw their country as its literal revival – any more than Coubertin and the first International Olympic Committee really believed that the modern festival they had devised was going to recreate the athletic contests of antiquity. Zambelios and Paparrigopoulos had filled in the missing centuries that separated the classical period from the modern. Byzantium had been rediscovered. There was more to the Greek nation, nowadays, than a willed act of revival – be that never so well intentioned or triumphantly carried through. Whatever the revival of the Olympics meant for the world of sport, for Greece it was the revival of a revival, the embodiment of a mindset whose heyday had been sixty years earlier.

Even while the Olympics were going on, beyond the kingdom's borders, to north and south, intercommunal violence was getting out of hand. In Macedonia, armed bands of Greek- and Bulgarian-speaking Christians clashed with one another and terrorized the populace into taking sides between them. In Crete, Greek-speaking Christians clashed with Greek-speaking Muslims. In both regions, intercommunal murders were becoming a daily occurrence. The country districts were becoming ungovernable. In Greece it was not humanitarian concern for the victims that drove the public mood, but fear that the nation's long-term goals were being usurped by rivals. With every new settlement imposed on Crete by the Great Powers in concert with the Ottoman government, the more likely it seemed that the 'Great Island', which had so nearly become part of Greece in the 1820s, would slip finally from the country's grasp. If the Bulgarians were to gain the upper hand in Macedonia, both the land and its people might be lost to the Greek nation for ever.

It was to forestall these perceived dangers that a group of young army officers, at the end of 1894, had set up yet another secret society, distantly modelled on the Friendly Society. It would not be long before the National Society, as this one was called, emerged from the barracks and from the shadows to become a highly vocal pressure group. Its leader was the far-from-military figure of Spyridon Lambros, Rector of the University of Athens, a prolific academic historian of Byzantium, tutor to the heir apparent and (briefly) a future prime minister. By October 1896, the National Society had come out into the open, fund-raising through the press to pay for irregular military operations, and even addressing a set of demands to the king. Other groups, more shadowy, were more extreme still. Within months of the ending of the Olympic Games, it really did begin to look as though the Grand Idea was about to be realized. The fourth and last opportunity of the century had well and truly arrived.

As it happened, Diligiannis was once again in power. But the popular mood that was gathering by the first months of 1897 was more than even this seasoned populist could control. With the sporting

1. Ali Tepedelenli, Pasha of Yanya [Ioannina], known as Ali Pasha (c. 1740–1822)

2. Rigas Velestinlis, also called Pheraios (1757?–98), was the first to devise a constitution for a future Hellenic Republic in 1797.

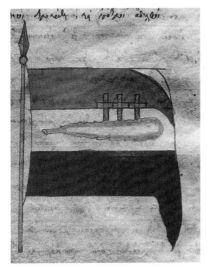

3. The tricolour banner of Rigas's Hellenic Republic, showing the club of Hercules and three crosses.

4. Adamantios Korais (Coray) (1748–1833), the ideological 'father of the Greek nation'.

5. *Karaiskakis' trophy from Arachova*. Watercolour of 1827. The text reads 'Trophy of the Hellenes against the Barbarians. Commander in Chief [Georgios] Karaïskakis, erected in the place [called] Plovarma'.

6. Theodoros Kolokotronis, drawn from life (pencil sketch by Karl Krazeisen, 14 May 1827).

7. Count Ioannis Kapodistrias, former foreign minister of Russia, Governor of Greece 1827–31, painted by Sir Thomas Lawrence, 1818–19.

8. Peter von Hess, *Entry of King Otto of Greece into Nauplia on 6 February 1833* (1835), detail.

9. King Otto of Greece as a young man (*left*) and as king, wearing national costume, (*right*) in a rare early photograph (daguerrotype) of about 1848.

10. Alexandros Mavrokordatos (1791–1865), prime minister of Greece 1833–4, 1841, 1844, 1854–5.

11. Ioannis Kolettis (1773–1847), prime minister of Greece 1834–5, 1844–7.

12. Leo von Klenze, *Ideal View of Athens with the Acropolis and the Areios Pagos* (1846).

13. The same view as it actually was at about the same time. F. Stademann, *Panorama von Athen* (Munich, 1841).

14. (*left*) King George I of the Hellenes (reigned 1863–1913).

15. (*below*) Konstantinos Volanakis, *The Opening of the Corinth Canal* (1893). The most ambitious of the infrastrucure projects initiated by Charilaos Trikoupis (*below, right*), it also contributed to Greece's bankruptcy later the same year.

16. Prime ministers and rivals: (*left*) Theodoros Diligiannis (1824–1905); (*right*) Charilaos Trikoupis (1832–96)

17. Paul Mathiopoulos, *Panepistimiou street* (1900–1910). 'Gentlemen and ladies wearing the latest fashions from the west could stroll or sit outside in cafés described by an American visitor as "like those in Paris", while horse-drawn omnibuses rumbled slowly past' (p. 171).

18. Georgios Jakobides (Iakovidis), *Pavlos Melas* (1904), based on a photograph taken shortly before Melas was killed in an ambush while fighting in Macedonia.

19. Pericles Giannopoulos, who committed suicide in a bizarre manner in 1910. Charcoal drawing by Sophia Laskaridou, 1897.

20. The future rivals: (*right*) Eleftherios Venizelos (1864–1936) and (*left*) King Constantine I of the Hellenes (reigned 1913–17, 1920–22), pictured at the time of the Balkan Wars.

21. Previously unpublished images of the Balkan Wars (1912–13). Serres (*left*) had been captured by Bulgarian forces in 1912 and then by the Greek army in 1913. The village of Doxato (*right*), near Drama, was destroyed in fighting between Greece and Bulgaria in June 1913.

victory in the Marathon fresh in people's memories, an appetite for winning carried all before it. Crete was relatively quiet, after the latest outburst of violence that had swept the island the previous spring and summer. Once again the Great Powers had intervened with the Ottoman government to cobble together a settlement. It was not working particularly well, but not necessarily worse than its predecessors. Then in February 1897, Greece took a step that no Greek government had openly authorized since the Revolution.

An armed flotilla under the command of Prince George, the king's second son, sailed from Piraeus to Chania, at that time Crete's capital. The prince spent less than twenty-four hours ashore. Three days later, a Greek expeditionary force landed troops. A proclamation by Colonel Timoleon Vassos, aide-de-camp to King George, announced the military occupation of Crete in the name of his sovereign. This was too much for the Great Powers. With the consent of the Sultan, control of Crete was parcelled out to the navies and marines of Great Britain, France, Russia and Italy. Crete was on the path, not to *Enosis*, but to autonomy.

Not even this modest setback was enough to dampen the enthusiasm of the National Society, an enthusiasm that now had the royal family, the press, the armed forces and an initially more cautious government firmly in its grip. Athens was convulsed by jubilant mass demonstrations. People of all classes came out on the streets to demand war. The scenes would be a foretaste of what would happen in many western European cities in 1914. During March 1897 forty-five thousand infantrymen and five hundred cavalry mustered in Thessaly and Epiros, along the Greek – Ottoman frontier. In overall command was the heir to the throne, Prince Constantine – he who less than a year before had sprinted alongside the Marathon victor towards the finishing line. Raids by Greek irregulars into Ottoman territory during April provoked the Sultan to declare war on 17 April.

The war of 1897 lasted barely over a month. The Greek army was outnumbered and outclassed by Ottoman forces that had recently benefited from German training and equipment. The leadership shown by the future Greek king and his staff officers came in for particularly harsh criticism. It was a rout. The victorious Ottoman armies pursued their attackers far inside Greek territory. The towns of Larisa and Tyrnavos, and the Greeks' forward base at the port of Volos, were all taken. The whole of Thessaly was overrun. More than a hundred thousand refugees were displaced. Even Lamia, the first town inside the pre-1881 border, was abandoned by the Greek army, as it fled southwards to prepare for a last stand near the site of the ancient battle of Thermopylae.

It was once again intervention by the Great Powers that saved Prince Constantine and his troops from this ultimate test. In the course of negotiations that would last for the rest of the year, the Sultan was induced to relinquish almost all the gains his army had made at the expense of Greece, in return for payment of a huge indemnity and some minor adjustments to the frontier. A seventeen-year-old cadet at the Ottoman military high school in Monastir (today's Bitola in North Macedonia), thwarted from volunteering by the brevity of the campaign, is said to have learnt the bitter 'lesson that the European great powers intervened when the Ottomans won, but failed to intervene when they were defeated'. The cadet's name was Mustafa Kemal, later known as Atatürk, the father of the modern Turkish nation.[16] It was not only the fortunes of Greece that would be determined by the outcome of that short-lived campaign.

But there was another lesson to be learned from the debacle of 1897. Almost seventy years after the treaty guaranteeing Greek independence had been signed, it was still proving its worth. The existence of the Greek state had never been a matter for Greeks alone, to defend by themselves. Now, as the century neared its end, all the world could see that Greece's place was assured, on the map of Europe and among the nations that would forge the continent's future. Whatever exactly 'Europe' might come to mean during the century ahead, Greece must be an integral part of it. However galling it might seem to a patriotic new generation of Ottoman officers, the achievement of the Greek Revolution and the decades that had followed it could not be reversed by force of arms.

Even so, the cost to Greece was high – as it had been before and would be again. Since the exchequer was bankrupt, it was the Great Powers themselves that had to pay the indemnity to the Sultan. To cover this, and other outstanding debts, the powers the next year established an International Financial Commission – a step that effectively took the national economy out of the control of the Greek government. It was the third time this had happened since independence. It would not be the last.

For Greece, the defeat of 1897, following hard on the heels of bankruptcy in 1893, was the greatest of the national humiliations of the nineteenth century. Of all the lessons learnt by the young kingdom the bitterest was the obvious one: that on its own it possessed neither the military nor the economic strength to take on a much larger enemy.

The disaster of 1897 has been called a posthumous vindication of Trikoupis's policies.[17] In itself, a disaster on this scale is a strange sort of vindication. The only advance for the Greek nation was that Crete the next year would be declared an autonomous principality, under Great Power protection and with Prince George of Greece as head of state. It is true that during the years that followed, many of the initiatives set in motion by Trikoupis would be given new impetus. The rewards to come, in 1912 and 1913, would be spectacular. But through the greater triumphs and the worse disasters of the next quarter-century, the bitter truth that had been learned in 1897 would remain as immutable as the laws of physics.

6

Military Service

1897–1913

In Athens and throughout the Greek kingdom the shock of defeat ran deep, and would last for years. Compared to later defeats to be suffered in the 1920s and the 1940s, the actual damage done in 1897 was very limited. But a whole set of assumptions, built up over half a century at least, had been suddenly called into question. Everybody was looking for scapegoats. Even the king and the royal family came in for the kind of vilification that had last been heard during the final years of King Otto's reign. Might King George and his sons go the same way? Every aspect of the Greek state and all of its institutions were on the rack. Communal soul-searching and self-loathing reached depths they never had before. Only one actor in the drama was exempt from blame. It 'was the *state*', as one apologist for the war put it shortly afterwards, 'that had been defeated and not the *nation*.'[1]

The nation floated free. The more threatened, or unreachable, this extra-territorial entity came to seem, the more exalted it became in the imagination of those still smarting from defeat. This new attitude found a passionate and articulate spokesman in a young diplomat, activist, writer, diarist, society figure and future victim of political assassination, whose career had been just beginning in 1897. Ion Dragoumis likened the relationship between state and nation to that between a garment and its wearer. The Greek nation had clothed itself in the garb of many different political systems in its three-thousand-year history. The present kingdom was just the latest of these. All were transitory and ultimately expendable. What mattered was the nation.[2]

State and nation had never been so far apart, or seemed so hard to reconcile, as they did at the turn of the twentieth century: the state too weak to expand, the nation too physically dispersed and politically inchoate ever to coalesce into the unitary state that for more than half a century had been the goal of the Grand Idea. What nobody could have predicted was the deadly tussle between these two concepts of what it meant to be Greek, or the series of conflicts that would eventually bring very nearly the entire Greek nation within the borders of a Greek state that had greatly expanded in the meantime.

DOLDRUMS AT HOME

Athens in 1900 was a place of extreme contrasts. The city's population had increased tenfold since it first became the capital in 1834, from about twelve thousand to a little over a hundred and twenty thousand inhabitants. It had not yet joined up with the port of Piraeus, which had grown in the same period from almost nothing to some fifty thousand. Even so, the combined population of Athens and Piraeus stood at less than one-fifth of that of Constantinople, and a quarter of that of Smyrna. In the city centre the wide boulevard that runs past the grand neoclassical-style buildings of the Academy, the University and the National Library, and today carries six lanes of congested traffic, was an elegant open space. Gentlemen and ladies wearing the latest fashions from the West could stroll along the boulevard or sit outside in cafés described by an American visitor as 'like those in Paris', while horse-drawn omnibuses rumbled slowly past. Photographs of the time, and paintings in the impressionist style by the Paris-trained painter Paul Mathiopoulos, convey a sense of 'grace, gentility, and contentment'.[3]

But only a few hundred metres away, on the west side of the city, were suburbs where hundreds of mostly single young men had migrated from the country in search of work. Since the 1880s, violent crime in Athens had far outstripped that of other European capitals. It has been estimated that the murder rate was more than fifty times greater in the last two decades of the nineteenth century in Athens and Piraeus than it was in London, Paris, Berlin or Amsterdam.[4] Violence even reached to the very top. In 1898 the king himself narrowly survived an assassination attempt. Diligiannis was not to be so lucky.

Forced to resign after the debacle of 1897, Diligiannis was once again serving as prime minister in 1905 when he was fatally stabbed on the steps of parliament. His assassin was a professional gambler, aggrieved by measures that had been announced against gambling houses. The fact that such measures had had to be taken was another symptom of the corrosive malaise of the time.

In districts such as Psyrri, in the shadow of the ancient temple known as the Theseion, and in the port of Piraeus, there flourished a whole underworld of hashish dens, brothels and petty criminality. Traditional codes of social behaviour, which had developed over centuries in small communities in the mountains and islands, became adapted to the deprived environment of a new urban underclass. Male heroism was still a matter of display and based on shared ideas of honour. But the 'hero' was now the *mangas*, the spiv or 'wide boy', who lived by his wits and had nothing but contempt for the better-off or the obedient wage slave. The *mangas* was expected to cock a snook at authority, to be quick with a knife and ruthless in avenging insult. He had to be capable of consuming prodigious quantities of hashish and alcohol, while all the time exercising the rigorous self-control prized by his rural forebears. His dealings with women would be casual, often violent, exploitative, and designed to show off his callousness and sexual prowess. This underworld generated its own special language, partly as a code to escape detection but also as a form of group solidarity.

In makeshift hashish dens, drinking houses and oriental-style cafés, known as *café-aman*, the men of this underworld would give expression to their own distinctive version of pride and melancholy in songs accompanied by a local variant of the Turkish long-necked lute, or *saz*, known in Greek as a *bouzouki*. This was the beginning of a culture of music and song that would later come to be known by the enigmatic term *rebetika*. Admired both in Greece and abroad, from the 1970s onwards, as the Greek equivalent of American Blues, this tradition and the urban underworld that gave it birth would come to be equally detested by nationalists and by the left for its alleged introversion and defeatism. At the time, these earliest known songs of the *rebetika* tradition were a symptom and a particular manifestation of a wider climate of violence, criminality and despair, whether real or imagined, that permeated the Greek capital around the turn of the century.

In these conditions an alternative for many was to leave the country altogether. Since the 1890s a new destination had opened up for young Greek men in search of work. Many had already sought better chances than could be offered by the subsistence economy of their home villages or the elusive promises held out by Athens and Piraeus or even, latterly, the great Ottoman cities of Constantinople, Smyrna and Salonica. Now, they began to establish Greek-speaking communities all over the world. The greatest number went to the United States – where among other things they brought with them the songs of the Greek underworld. It was in New York and Chicago that the foundations would be laid for the commercial success of *rebetika* through the fast-developing industry of sound recording. Emigration peaked in 1907, when thirty-six thousand individuals left – almost all of them single men in their twenties and thirties.[5]

At the opposite end of the social spectrum the climate of those years found more intellectual and aesthetic outlets. At a time when old certainties were so widely felt to have failed, young people, in particular, were casting around for something to replace them. This was the background to the first appearance of a women's movement, in a society that had always rigidly separated the male sphere, outside the home, from the female one, within it. *The Ladies' Magazine* had been founded in Athens as far back as 1887 and would run for twenty years. Its editors, its contributors and its intended readers were all women. The magazine's founding editor, Callirhoe Parren, is recognized as Greece's first feminist, and the country's first woman writer to be published in her lifetime. Many of the magazine's editorials called for political change to give rights, such as the vote, to women – something that would not happen for another half-century. The war of 1897 and its aftermath gave a new impetus to the movement, with so many women mobilized as nurses or in charitable organizations.[6]

After 1900, other, newer ideas arrived from France. Among them were French translations of German philosophy, particularly extracts from the works of Karl Marx and Friedrich Nietzsche. Socialism made its first appearance in print in Greek. There was not yet a political party, but a Socialist Movement was founded in 1902 and an extended manifesto published in 1907.[7] In France itself the period known as the '*fin de siècle*' had given rise to the movements known as '*décadence*' and 'aestheticism'. Their adherents placed the highest value on art and personal pleasure, while affecting boredom or disgust with the everyday world. These attitudes chimed readily with the mood of some among the educated young of Athens in the years after the defeat of 1897. In 1906 a twenty-two-year-old student at Athens University seemed to glorify them in a novel, published under the pseudonym of Karma Nirvami. *Serpent and Lily* tells the story of a young couple who prefer to commit suicide rather than consummate their love, and suffocate in the voluptuous aroma of exotic flowers. Hard on the heels of the novel came a polemical essay by the same hand. Here the cause of the fictional hero's trouble was diagnosed in a phrase translated from the French of an earlier era, 'The sickness of the century'. Much later, after the Second World War, the author of this work would achieve international fame under his own name, as the creator of *Zorba the Greek* and *The Last Temptation of Christ*. Such was the precocious literary debut of Nikos Kazantzakis.

Life seemed to imitate art. The 'sickness' took hold. The very public suicide of two young lovers in the Athens First Cemetery, a few years later, seized the newspaper headlines and has been credited with 'heralding the beginning of an epidemic of suicides in Greece'.[8] Superficially, this might be compared to the soaring suicide rates reported in the country since the financial crisis that broke out in 2010. But those who took their own lives over a hundred years ago seem to have been driven by an urge to assert their individuality – in some ways not unlike the antisocial behaviour of the *mangas* in his own sphere. Whether in fiction or in reality, self-destruction needed to be staged, as an aesthetic act.

In another high-profile incident, art and life came together in a manner at once bizarre and tragic. Pericles Giannopoulos was a newspaper columnist and essayist, forty years old in April 1910. Dressed in a white flannel suit with matching gloves, Giannopoulos commandeered a horse and rode it into the sea at a gallop. Far out from the shore, he raised a pistol, held it to his temple and pulled the trigger. His body was recovered two weeks later. Not long before his suicide, Giannopoulos had published a manifesto, full of heavy bold type and block capitals, in which he celebrated the 'Hellenic Spirit' or 'GREEK-NESS'. To be Greek, according to Giannopoulos, was to be human. But only the Greek, it seems, possesses this quality fully, because:

the DESTINY of the Greek in this World, was and is in every age, TODAY and TOMORROW:

THE HUMANIZATION OF THE UNIVERSE[.][9]

Giannopoulos differed from his contemporary Dragoumis in many things. But both men were reacting to the extreme contrasts of Athenian life as they experienced them in the first years of the century. In particular, they were infected by the climate of defeatism that had begun in 1897, which seemed to blight their whole generation. Desperate for solutions, however extreme, they were drawn, like moths to a flame, towards new ideas about nationalism, art and aesthetics. Giannopoulos revered the spirit of ancient Greece, Dragoumis a more elusive 'national soul'. But the ideas themselves, and in the case of Giannopoulos the actions too, came from a western Europe that both men distrusted profoundly. Their understanding of the Greek nation derives not from Greek antiquity but from the contemporary mystical nationalism of Charles Maurras and Maurice Barrès in France. This is the origin of Dragoumis's assertion, in 1913, that 'the Nation is the new religion'.[10] The style of Giannopoulos's death comes straight from the heart of literary and intellectual Paris. The ideas and the actions are of a piece with the cafés, boulevards and omnibuses of Athens, and their misty evocation in the impressionist oil paintings of 'Paul' (not Pavlos) Mathiopoulos.

Public life during the first years of the century was marked by more conventional signs of disaffection. Until 1906, short-lived governments came and went, much as they had done in the early years of King George's reign, before the rise of Trikoupis and Diligiannis. Opposition deputies filibustered. Newspaper editorials thundered that the plight of the nation was going unaddressed.

Organized political protests in 1901 and 1903 turned violent and left several people dead on the streets of Athens. It was, of all things, the question of the Greek language that brought demonstrators out onto the streets. The linguist Giannis Psycharis, back in 1888, had come out stridently as the champion of the spoken, or 'demotic', variety of Greek as the proper written language for the nation. Psycharis had also been the first to claim that the language question was a political one. Now, it was. Supporters of his radical ideas had begun to serialize a translation of the Christian Gospels into a form of everyday colloquial Greek, offending both traditional religious and traditional nationalist sensibilities. Other factors were involved too. But the publication of the translation in the newspaper *Acropolis* was provocation enough for a mob of university students to ransack the paper's offices and wreck the printing presses. Two years later, a translation of an ancient Greek tragedy set off more violence, though on a smaller scale. On both occasions, it was conservative-minded students who took to the streets, aided and abetted by some of their professors. In the new, febrile atmosphere, anything that threatened the idealized integrity of the nation was enough to provoke a frenzy. Now, more than ever, the choice of which variety of Greek to use in public was a profession of faith in the nation. If you were a demoticist, as proponents of the spoken language were called, you revered the everyday spoken form of Greek as the living repository of the nation's very 'soul'. If you belonged to the opposite camp, you saw any slackening of the hold of ancient Greek over the modern language as a betrayal of your birthright as a Hellene.

It was not all bad news during those first years of the century. The economy recovered strongly during most of the fifteen years after 1897. Fiscal discipline had been imposed by the International Financial Commission. Its early forecasts even had to be revised upwards – in marked contrast to what has happened since 2010. It has been suggested that, by 1912, Greeks were in general better off than their parents' generation had been. In education, the expansion sponsored by Trikoupis during the previous two decades was beginning to pay off. By 1907 just over 40 per cent of the population over the age of eight could read and write – double the percentage of thirty years before. Allowing for the very limited opportunities available for girls, this probably means that more than half of adult males in the Greek kingdom were literate by the first decade of the twentieth century.[11]

But it was not in Greece, it was beyond its borders, that forces were at work whose effects would soon change the face of the entire region for ever.

ACTION ABROAD

To the south, in Crete, the Christian majority was as determined as ever to pursue union with Greece. Never mind how much the self-confidence of the Greek state had been dented at home, no such misgivings seem to have reached across the Cretan Sea. The island's Christians were just about the only people anywhere to have gained by the war of 1897. Nominally the 'Cretan State' was still part of the Ottoman Empire. But the last Ottoman troops had been withdrawn in 1898 on the insistence of the guarantor powers. A multinational force, gathered from Great Britain, France, Russia and Italy, had been keeping the peace between the Christian and Muslim communities in the meantime. In these circumstances, no government in Athens, with memories of defeat still fresh, could risk accepting Cretan demands for *Enosis*, however much it might wish to.

So it was left to the Christians of Crete themselves to make the running. By 1905, Prince George, the island's governor, had alienated their political leadership to such an extent that a number of them blockaded themselves and their armed supporters in the village of Therisos in the foothills of the White Mountains and threatened all comers. The revolt of Therisos ended without bloodshed, but it cost the prince his job. Its leader was a forty-year-old lawyer from Chania who had first come to prominence during the revolt of 1897. This drastic act marked the first step along a path that would lead to the eventual union of Crete with Greece. It would also launch the political career of the most famous, as well as the most controversial, Greek statesman of the twentieth century: Eleftherios Venizelos.

Macedonia, in the opposite direction, was a slowly erupting volcano. Here, the Ottomans were still in charge – though not always in full control. Intercommunal violence between Greek speakers and Slavic speakers had only worsened since the 1880s. By now, Greece was in competition with both Serbia and Bulgaria to claim the 'national consciousness' of local communities throughout the region. A movement had even emerged among some Slavic speakers for an independent Macedonia. The Internal Macedonian Revolutionary Organization (IMRO) had been founded in Sofia, the Bulgarian capital. Its programme was more Bulgarian than its name suggests, but its methods were revolutionary enough. In April 1903 a splinter group of the organization set off a series of massive bombs in Salonica. Despite several days of panic, and a heavy-handed crackdown by the police, the bombers failed to spark the more widespread reprisals that might have fuelled a more general revolt.

Then on the night of 2 August, after concerted preparations, the main body of the organization orchestrated an uprising in villages across the region of Monastir. The movement was ruthlessly put down and its leaders were executed by the Ottoman authorities – aided by Greek irregulars and the Greek Orthodox bishop of Kastoria. The event has been known ever since as the Ilinden Uprising, from the Bulgarian for St Elijah's Day, when it happened. It is today commemorated as the national day of North Macedonia, whose claim to the name of 'Macedonia' was contested by Greece from 1992 to 2018.

As these details suggest, it was not the fate of fellow Orthodox Christians that aroused the indignation of Greeks in the region and in Athens. Ilinden was read as a warning signal: without equally determined action on their own part, the whole region might soon come to be dominated by the Bulgarian Church (the Exarchate), by the Bulgarian language, and ultimately by the principality – not yet an independent state – of Bulgaria itself. The Athens government no more had the resources or the diplomatic leverage abroad to risk open intervention in Macedonia than it did in Crete. It had little stomach for a fight anyway. But under pressure from the press and prominent individuals, a Macedonian Committee was formed in Athens, early in 1904.

Under cover of the consulate in Salonica, serving Greek army officers were sent into the country as agents. Bands of irregulars, led by these officers, confronted the *komitadjis*, as their rivals, recruited and controlled by IMRO, were known. The commanders were answerable to the Macedonian Committee in Athens. Successive governments were always able to deny any control over them, when challenged by the Ottomans and the Great Powers: all this armed activity by Greeks in Macedonia was merely self-defence by the local population. And such was the extent of violence in the countryside that the claim, even though manifestly far from being the whole truth, proved durable over several years.

Today the building near the seafront in Salonica that used to house the Greek consulate is home to the Museum of the Macedonian Struggle. This is the name by which the conflict has ever since been known in Greek. It was an unofficial, undeclared, clandestine war. It had no defined beginning or end. Conventionally it is dated by the acute phase that began with the establishment of the Macedonian Committee in Athens in 1904 and ended in 1908. But smaller-scale hostilities had been going on for a decade before that, and would continue until the map of the entire region was changed irrevocably in 1912. The campaign was fought against adversaries who used exactly the same methods of intimidation, extortion, torture, assassination of rivals and tactical denunciations to the Ottoman authorities. Its objectives were limited. There could be no question, as there was in Crete, of *Enosis*, or annexing territory to Greece. Rather the aim of the insurgents was 'to conquer the territory of the souls' – meaning to instil so far as possible Greek 'national consciousness' among the local peasants, who persisted in identifying themselves by their religion, not language or nationality.[12]

Since no other methods were feasible, the Macedonian Struggle was also a vindication of the old guerrilla tactics that had been used to such devastating effect during the Revolution of the 1820s, and sporadically in conflicts beyond the borders ever since. In a deliberate evocation of that resonant past, many of the volunteers dressed in the kilts, zouave jackets and crossed bandoliers, shepherd's cloaks and heavy shoes, called *tsarouchia*, favoured by the mountaineers on the other side of the Pindos range – the 'national' costume that had become synonymous with the heroic deeds of the klefts and armed militias of old. This time the distinction was clearer, if never openly acknowledged, between the volunteer bandsman and the professional brigand. The first would still be drawing his Greek army pay. The second would be every bit as voracious for booty and cash retainers as his predecessors had been in the 1820s. Ever-present danger forced the two types of combatant to work closely together. The volunteers had grudgingly to learn from the local brigands the basics of survival in conditions that were often extreme. And the brigands resented having to take orders, especially when these involved being exposed to enemy fire – a hazard traditionally shunned in this type of warfare.[13]

The most famous of all the volunteers was also one of the shortest-lived in the field. Pavlos Melas was the son of a politician and was married to the sister of Ion Dragoumis, who was himself engaged in the 'Struggle' as a senior consular official in Macedonia. A dashing figure, and like his brother-in-law feted in Athenian society, Melas was placed in command of the first Greek band to enter western Macedonia, in February 1904. Eight months later, he was dead, ambushed by an Ottoman patrol that had mistaken his men for a group of Bulgarians they were hunting down. A photograph of the handsome captain in his guerrilla outfit, taken shortly before his death, became the subject of a much-reproduced oil painting. Orally composed, anonymous folk songs lamented his death in the style traditional for a hero. Ever since, in Greece, the name of Pavlos Melas has served as an emblem for the Macedonian Struggle. At the time both name and image helped draw new recruits to the cause. Today, his memory is perpetuated in the name of the municipality of present-day Salonica that for many decades housed an army camp named after him, and of the village where he died – Statista, near Kastoria, now called Melas.

Over the next few years, in Athens, hatred of Bulgarians and all things Bulgarian reached fever pitch. 'Monsters spewed up by the Volga and out of hell' is just one description preserved by the parliamentary record, from 1904. Newspapers had a field day: Bulgarians were 'deceitful, savage, uncivilized, immoral, untamed by religion, like wild animals, ravening for blood'. Setting a tone that would soon become respectable in high literature too, one editorial in 1903 held that 'The nation once described by Byzantine historians as polluted and hateful to God has remained just the same, down to our own times.'[14] The best-known, and enduring, example of the trend in literature is the novel for children *In the Time of the Bulgar-Slayer*, by Penelope Delta. Published in 1911, this story takes its readers back almost a thousand years, to the victorious campaigns of the Byzantine emperor Basil II, who died in 1025 after having subdued much of the Balkans, earning in the process the sobriquet that gives the book its title. The 'Bulgar-Slayer' had already been recreated as an epic hero in verse by the great poet of the age, Kostis Palamas, in a poem written while the Macedonian Struggle was at its height.

By the time these literary works had brought the thousand-year-old

'Bulgar-Slayer' back to public consciousness in Athens, the most important event of the decade had already begun to transform the geopolitics of the entire region. This, too, took place in Macedonia. But it had nothing to do with the ethnic struggle going on there. It was in Monastir and Salonica that the revolution of the 'Young Turks' was first publicly proclaimed on 23 July 1908. Disaffected elements within the Ottoman army demanded the restoration of the abortive Constitution of 1876. Sultan Abdul Hamid quickly made the necessary tactical concession and by the next day the rejoicing had spread from Macedonia to the capital and throughout the empire.

In Salonica, Olympos Square on the waterfront by the harbour, with its open views across the Thermaic Gulf towards the home of the ancient gods, after which it had been named, overnight became *Plateia Eleftherias*, or Liberty Square. Although much changed in appearance, the square still bears this name today, even if few among the crowds that daily pass through it probably make the association with the liberty promised by the Young Turks in 1908. It was there, a few days after the revolution, that Enver Pasha, one of the leaders, addressed a delirious crowd with these astonishing words, if a contemporary French eyewitness is to be believed:

> Citizens! Today the arbitrary ruler is gone, bad government no longer exists. We are all brothers. There are no longer Bulgarians, Greeks, Serbs, Romanians, Jews, Muslims – under the same blue sky we are all equal, we are all proud to be Ottomans![15]

Elections were announced throughout the empire, and duly took place a few months later. Once again Ottoman Greeks took their places in an elected parliament in Constantinople. Even in strife-torn Macedonia the rival Bulgarian and Greek committees suspended hostilities. In Salonica, representatives of the two communities were seen side by side. No longer the 'sick man of Europe', the Ottoman Empire from now on was going to be different. The leaders of the 'Young Turks', men such as Enver Pasha, were indeed young – but the name of the movement in Turkish means actually not 'young' but '*new*'. The official name for the movement was 'Committee for Union and Progress'. It was all about modernization.

It is worth pausing at this point to look at some of the ways that

Greeks reacted at the time, both Ottoman and Greek subjects. Because of what happened later, most of these reactions have been relegated to footnotes in history, if not forgotten altogether. But for at least a few months in late 1908 and 1909, it really must have looked as though the entire political dynamics of the region had been reset.

Writing only three weeks after the Young Turk revolution, the Greek ambassador to Constantinople gave a cautious welcome to what he called 'the cooperation of the two nations [i.e. Greeks and Turks], in freedom – that is to say, true equality of citizenship and respect for acquired rights and privileges'. But he also warned that the new spirit of 'blood brotherhood' might be a pretence, or only skin-deep. Real change – meaning presumably real benefit to the Greek community – would prove impossible if it turned out that the Young Turks were aiming to assimilate the Christian nationalities, 'and especially Hellenism', into a dominant 'Turkism'.[16]

Not everyone was so guarded. From the most unlikely quarter came this, from Venizelos, writing in a Cretan newspaper in January 1909:

> All of Hellenism . . . felt very deeply . . . that the success of the Young Turk movement has saved not only the Turkish State, but also Hellenism, from dismemberment and catastrophe . . . [T]he establishment of a constitutional regime in Turkey was, under a different form, the realization of the Great Idea.

No less passionate a nationalist than Venizelos, Dragoumis confided to his diary, at about the same time, 'The Grand Idea is at an end.' Dragoumis now saw the political future of Hellenism 'in a state more restricted than Byzantium'. He went on:

> The Turkish [Ottoman] state has the same capital city as Byzantium used to, and for as long as that state exists, the City [Constantinople] will be a Greek capital city also, especially now that Turkey has (or claims to have) a constitution.[17]

Dragoumis had served for two years in the embassy in Constantinople, from 1907 to 1909, and so had been there at the time of the revolution. Together with another veteran from the consular service in Macedonia, Athanasios Souliotis-Nikolaïdis, during the next few years Dragoumis would support semi-official Greek efforts to find common ground with the Young Turk movement in a partnership against Bulgarian nationalism. The Constantinople Organization lasted from 1908 until 1912. During the same years, Greek deputies continued to participate actively in the newly reconstituted Ottoman parliament. Their aim, they said in a statement, was 'to establish, along with other nationalities of our common fatherland [i.e. the Ottoman Empire], the Constitutional Ottoman State, participating in the same duties and rights and genuinely contributing to the strength and well-being of the State'.[18] This new form of Ottomanism was particularly strong in Constantinople itself and in some nearby regions with large Greek Orthodox populations, such as the island of Lesbos, also known by the name of its capital, Mytilini. The lack of any apparent communal desire there for *Enosis* with Greece at this time is in marked contrast to other large islands farther south, such as Samos and Crete.[19]

As the century's first decade moved towards its close, many Greeks must have been wondering whether the Grand Idea might not turn out to mean something quite different from what everyone had been supposing for more than half a century. It might not be necessary to fight at all. It was not just Greeks who thought this way. Foreign observers of Ottoman society in the early 1900s thought that, given 'progress' and the rule of law, the Christians of the empire already had the upper hand.[20] For the Greeks of the wider nation, beyond the Greek state, 'Hellenic Ottomanism' might yet turn out to be the answer. The state and the nation need not, after all, be collapsed into a single political entity. A Greek kingdom growing towards maturity, and a modernized, rejuvenated Ottoman Empire could live side by side. Was not this, in practice, what had mostly been going on ever since the start of the *Tanzimat* reforms in 1839?

From the perspective of today, it requires an effort of imagination to set aside all that we know of twentieth-century history and see those possible vistas as they must have appeared at the time. By the same token, it would have been hard for a contemporary observer to predict what the next few years would hold in store – for the Greek kingdom, for the Greeks of the Ottoman Empire, or indeed for the empire itself.

CALLED TO ARMS

The first ominous signs appeared less than three months after the Young Turk revolution. On the empire's fringes there were those ready to take advantage of the new regime. On 5 October 1908, Bulgaria declared full independence. Prince Ferdinand, from being nominally a vassal of the Sultan, became overnight 'Tsar of all the Bulgarians', a title clearly echoing that of George I of the Hellenes, and with much the same implications. Then the next day Austria announced the unilateral annexation of Bosnia and Herzegovina. The two provinces had been under Austrian administration since the Treaty of Berlin in 1878, while remaining formally part of the Ottoman Empire. These moves together provoked the first of a series of new 'eastern crises' that over the next few years would tear up that thirty-year-old treaty and pave the way for the First World War.

In Crete, the moment suddenly looked too good to miss. For Venizelos and the local Christian leadership, the Young Turks might be good for Greek interests in theory and somewhere else, but not on their own turf. The future of Crete lay with the Kingdom of Greece, they had never harboured any doubts about that. Within days of the Bulgarian declaration, the local administration in Crete once again declared *Enosis* with Greece. The capital, Chania, broke out in celebration. Modern assessments, and some made at the time, suggest that if the government in Athens had pressed the case it might have been able to annex Crete in 1908. But it was a hard calculation to make. The prime minister, Georgios Theotokis, of an old aristocratic family from Corfu, was cautious, and referred the matter to the guarantor powers. The status quo in Crete would last a few years longer.

All of these developments were damaging to Ottoman prestige, at a time when the grip on power of the new rulers within the empire was still fragile. Just how fragile was demonstrated a few months later. In April 1909 a counter-coup in Constantinople not only briefly overturned the Young Turk regime, it restored the full powers of the Sultan and announced a return to pre-1839 Sharia law. This would have been a reversal of the entire programme of modernization that had been going on for more than half a century. Ten days of violent confrontations in the capital ended with the Committee of Union and Progress back in control. This time the Sultan was deposed and replaced by a puppet figure. The leaders of the Young Turk revolution had consolidated their hold over the empire. But the events of April 1909 in Constantinople had shown for the first time the depth and breadth of opinion among the empire's majority Muslim subjects, especially Turkish speakers. These were the people 'left behind' (in today's parlance), and largely left out, by a process of reform that had always been driven by a desire to placate and 'catch up' with European ideas and European powers.

Over the weeks and months that followed, the Young Turk movement adapted its outlook to become more and more the champion of this dominant group. In less than two years the regime would become almost as authoritarian as its predecessors had been. At the same time it developed a new hard line in its dealings with the large Christian populations living both within and beyond its borders. 'Ottomanism' had not yet given way to the Turkish nationalism that would emerge a decade later. But, whether or not this had been the intention from the beginning, the misgivings of the Greek ambassador at the time of the 1908 revolution would soon prove justified. The 'Ottomanism' of the Young Turks was becoming increasingly identified with Islam and the Turkish language. It was a vicious circle: the more the Christian populations, inside and outside the empire, insisted on their own *national* rights and claims, the more the leaders of the Turkish-speaking Muslim majority reacted by pushing their own. And the more Turcophone and Islamist the governing party became, the more it was bound to alienate those of other languages and faiths, entrenching their nationalist, separatist identities still further.

In the meantime, voices in Greece were calling for their own version of renewal. In a series of editorials from October 1908 onwards, the outspoken editor of the Athens daily *Acropolis*, Vlasis Gavriilidis, called for what he called a 'peaceful revolution'. It may have been as early as that same month that a group of junior army officers began meeting in secret in Athens, to hatch a conspiracy of their own, on the example of the Young Turks.[21] Dissatisfaction with the failure to secure Crete gave impetus to these plans during the months that followed. Economic woes would turn out to be short-term, but were strongly felt at the time. Protesters were taking to the streets.

Responses at the highest level of government were curiously demoralized. Prime Minister Theotokis did his best to evade his responsibilities by offering to resign at the end of March 1909, and finally succeeded in doing so in July. By this time a new Cretan crisis was brewing. The last detachments of the international peacekeeping force were due to leave the island at the end of the month – with no real plan in place for how peace was to be maintained thereafter. A new attempt to declare *Enosis* was on the cards. And this time the recently restored government of the Young Turks would be unlikely to take it lying down. The leader of the opposition, Dimitrios Rallis, took several days to accept the king's mandate to form a minority government, and then did so only on conditions. Even King George himself, quite uncharacteristically, seemed ready to give up. His popularity had not recovered after the defeat of 1897. His sons, who held prominent positions in the army, were being openly criticized. Feeling himself poorly served by his ministers, and despairing of support from the powers over Crete, the king confided to the British Minister in Athens his thoughts of abdicating – that he might take all his family and 'just go and never come back'.[22] In August, rumours of similar conversations within the palace were leaked to the press. By now the conspiracy in the army was an open secret. Not coincidentally, British warships once again appeared off the port of Piraeus. It was beginning to look like a re-run of the last days of King Otto. Nobody in Athens, it seemed, wanted to take responsibility. All that anyone could agree on was that things were in a mess.

Into this vacuum, in August 1909, stepped the junior officers of the Athens garrison. Their conspiracy had only really got going in July. Known as the Military League, it quickly emerged from the shadows, thanks to smart liaison work with the like-minded editor of a daily newspaper. The League's demands for reform within the armed forces and the civil service were widely publicized, although its membership remained secret. It is doubtful whether the government, without a majority in parliament, could have carried through these reforms even if it had been willing to bow to pressure – which it was not.

The conspirators took advantage of a public holiday, the Feast of the Dormition of the Virgin, to act. In the early hours of 28 August (or 15 August according to the calendar in use in Greece at the time), the greater part of the garrisons stationed in Athens marched out of the city and took up a position on a low hilltop among the foothills of Mount Hymettos, called Goudi. Today the area is home to several military hospitals and the Medical Faculty of the University of Athens. Then, it was a strategic spot, overlooking one of the main routes out of Athens towards the north and east. At Goudi the League set up an armed camp, in a show of strength some three thousand strong, including officers and men. Soon they were joined by a cavalry detachment from Kiphisia to the north. Before dawn, the League had delivered its ultimatum to the government.

Within hours, the Rallis government resigned and a new administration was sworn in, promising to address the demands of the military. It was not the first time in Greece that the army had forced a change of government, and it would not be the last. But Goudi was the first occasion when the military acted alone. It was a bloodless coup, and in its execution entirely successful. In these respects, it was similar to the Young Turk revolution. Its supporters would invariably dignify this one, too, with the name of a 'revolution'. But the Military League had much shallower roots than the Committee for Union and Progress. Its demands were parochial by comparison. Most were about procedural matters within the armed forces. Those that touched on wider issues were so bland as to mean little.[23] By itself, the League achieved nothing more than the overthrow of a government whose democratic legitimacy was questionable and its replacement by another whose legitimacy was even less. It established a precedent that would be followed all too often throughout the decades that followed. Within a few months the movement had run out of steam. But not before it had engineered the one event that would prove to be its lasting legacy. It was at the invitation of the Military League that a new figure, and a whole new style of government, came to dominate the political life of the Greek kingdom.

Even today, the name and legacy of Eleftherios Venizelos are capable of arousing deep divisions in Greece. No Greek politician ever gained so much respect among the leaders of the Great Powers of his day. None, with the possible exception of Kapodistrias, ever divided opinions and loyalties so much among his own people. Love him or loathe him, Venizelos did more than anyone else to change the physical map of Greece for ever. But it was not just the map that was changed: minds and whole ways of thinking would never be the same again either. The consequences of those changes have still not fully bedded down, a century later. As a person, Venizelos remains inscrutable. He left hardly any diaries or private papers to give a clue to his thoughts and motivation as they developed. As a politician, he combined the diplomatic skills and patience of a Mavrokordatos with the popular appeal of a Kolettis or a Diligiannis. What his opponents have condemned as reckless, unprincipled opportunism, to others appears as the pragmatism of the consummate tactician. Then there is the hagiography: with almost religious devotion, Venizelos has been hailed as the messianic visionary, the redeemer of the nation whose deep-laid plans would have triumphed on every side, but for the envy of smaller-minded spirits. However one evaluates his contribution today, it is a fact that, for at least a generation, Greek society would become polarized between 'Venizelists' and 'anti-Venizelists'.

One reason for this may be that, like Mavrokordatos and Kapodistrias before him, Venizelos was at once a Greek and an outsider. With the arrival of Venizelos from Crete, the wider, distant *nation* had taken over the running of the *state*. And not everyone liked it.

Even with the backing of the Military League and the reluctant acquiescence of King George, there was something crablike about Venizelos's rise to power. A first visit to Athens to confer with officers of the League and politicians was supposed to be a private one, out of the public eye. In an interview published in *The Times* of London, Venizelos flatly denied what was in fact the truth: that he had been invited to Athens by the Military League to be canvassed as a future prime minister.[24] On that occasion, he stayed in Athens for only three weeks. But while he was there the next steps were all mapped out – and seemingly on *his* initiative. The only way to resolve the impasse that had led to the coup was by a thorough revision of the constitution. Until a new Constituent Assembly could be elected, a caretaker government would be formed. The Military League would disband in the meantime.

All this duly happened, but in slow motion. The elections to the Constituent Assembly, which would replace parliament for the duration, were delayed until August 1910. Venizelos stayed away – first in

Crete, then on holiday in Switzerland. But his name had been included in the ballot for the district that included the capital, and in the event he topped the poll. The new assembly met for the first time on 14 September. Four days later, Venizelos disembarked from a specially chartered steamer at Piraeus. From there, he went straight to the centre of Athens to address a throng of some ten thousand people in Syntagma Square. The subject of this first public speech in Greece was the rather abstruse one of the precise terms of reference for the new assembly. Such was the power of his oratory and his personality that Venizelos easily carried the day. A month later, the new arrival from Crete was sworn in as prime minister of Greece.

It was a moot point whether the new premier could command a majority in an assembly that was divided fairly evenly between those who supported him and those who did not. A week after his appointment, Venizelos persuaded the king to grant him a dissolution. A new election was called, for what was now to be a 'Revisionist National Assembly', on 11 December. During the weeks before the election, two remarkable things happened: Venizelos established his own political party, and the three existing parties that among them had returned more than 50 per cent of the previous assembly decided to boycott the contest.

The result was a foregone conclusion. It has been termed a 'constitutional coup' and a 'parliamentary dictatorship'.[25] Venizelos's new Liberal Party was based closely on the model of the party of the same name that he had already led in Crete. In no time the rudiments of a party organization were set up all over the country. The Liberals brought to Greek politics for the first time the elements of a disciplined, organized party structure. Control was firmly exercised from the top. Venizelos was consolidating his power base in the country. On the opposite side, the electoral boycott by the existing parties was the first of several such fateful actions in Greek parliamentary politics – a tactic that has invariably proved self-defeating. Quite what the three party leaders hoped to achieve by their action is unclear. Technically, Venizelos had violated the Constitution of 1864 by asking for a dissolution, and the king by granting it. This was because a Constituent Assembly, unlike a normal parliament, could not be dissolved except by itself. But boycotting an election was never going to undo what had been done.

The election of 11 December 1910 swept Venizelos to power with an overwhelming majority. This gave him a mandate to oversee revision of the constitution and reform of anything else that the 'Revisionist National Assembly' took within its sights. Change was on the way. But it had not been done, quite, within the letter of the law.

The months that followed saw an unprecedented bustle of legislative activity. The revisions to the constitution were completed quickly. Mostly they were designed to streamline the business of government. Individual and civic rights were strengthened – but new provisions allowed for exceptional circumstances when these could be suspended. An innovation was that for the first time the notorious 'language question' became a matter for formal legislation. Venizelos himself was sympathetic to the reformers who were pushing for demotic, the spoken language, to be enshrined as the official language of the state. But, ever the pragmatist, in the face of entrenched opposition he allowed this article to go onto the statute book instead: 'The official language of the state is that in which the constitution and the texts of Greek legislation are drawn up; all intervention leading to its corruption is prohibited.'[26] The formal split between demotic and *katharevousa* (the officialese of the constitution itself and the legal profession) would last until 1976 – a harbinger and perhaps a symptom of the much deeper split in Greek society that would be opened up by Venizelos's initiatives a few years later, and would take as long to heal.

The revised constitution came into effect in June 1911. For the next nine months, the Revisionist Assembly continued to govern, now formally reconstituted as a regular parliament. During that time an astonishing 337 new laws were passed. Many of these, too, were about streamlining government. There were also social reforms. These included breaking up the huge landed estates in Thessaly, where the peasants who worked the land were still little more than serfs. Astonishingly, the country's most agriculturally productive province, acquired in 1881, was still bringing no gain to the national economy thirty years later. Conditions in prisons and access to justice were improved. Trade unions were recognized and restrictions placed on the exploitation of women and children in the workplace.

Much of what was achieved during the first eighteen months after Venizelos came to power can be put down to his own huge investment of personal energy, charisma and sheer political competence. By the time a new parliamentary election was held in March 1912, the economy was in surplus – a minor miracle that remains to be fully explained. Money was at last available for military and civilian projects that went back to the time of Trikoupis in the 1880s. Military missions from Great Britain and France had arrived to overhaul the organization and equipment of the navy and the army respectively.

It is easy with the benefit of hindsight to put all this activity down to a long-term strategic vision, as though Venizelos could have foreseen the opportunities and the challenges that would emerge later in that same year, 1912. But nothing that Venizelos either did or proposed was as radical as the changes that Enver Pasha and the Young Turks were bringing about in the Ottoman Empire, to say nothing of the seismic shift that Mustafa Kemal (later known as Atatürk) would set in motion after the First World War. All Venizelos's constitutional and legislative initiatives were carried out in the spirit of *revision*, as he himself had insisted in his first public speech in Athens in 1910. In modernizing the country's infrastructure, economy and armed forces, so as to be ready to fight for the Grand Idea, he was doing neither more nor less than fulfilling the programme that had been laid down by Trikoupis more than three decades before. The achievement of Venizelos's early years in power lay in streamlining the mechanisms for getting things done and then doing them. If Venizelos had a 'vision', it was the old one of the Grand Idea, which had been tarnished but not discarded after the defeat of 1897. And that vision, even if it had lost some of its appeal, was still not controversial, let alone divisive, in 1912, any more than it had been fifteen years earlier.

At the time of the parliamentary election in March that year, Greece was better equipped than ever, whether for peace or war. The 'old' parties, realizing their mistake in boycotting the last election, returned to the fold for this one. But they now stood no chance. Venizelos and the Liberals swept all before them. The new mandate was as great as before. And this time, no one could cast aspersions on its legitimacy.

By the summer of 1912, Greece was ready, even if no one yet knew exactly for what.

INTO BATTLE

On the external front, events had been moving rapidly since the last months of 1911. European colonial expansion into the continent of Africa had all but ended before the end of the previous century – there were few lands left to conquer. The Mediterranean coast of Africa and its hinterland had once upon a time all been part of the Ottoman Empire. The French had taken control of Algeria after 1830, the British of Egypt in 1882. The first decade of the new century saw Morocco divided between France and Spain. That left just one stretch of African coastline still in Ottoman hands – the provinces then known as Tripolitania and Cyrenaica, today as Libya. And there was one European power that had come late to the game. Outliers of the Ottoman Empire had been picked off with impunity in 1908. Now it was the turn of Italy to stake a claim, to that part of North Africa that conveniently was also the closest to its own shores.

War between Italy and the Ottoman Empire in North Africa began on 29 September 1911. The campaign in the African provinces did not go well for the Italians. So, early the next year they extended the sphere of their operations into the Aegean. The Dodecanese, the twelve islands closest to the southwestern tip of Anatolia, including Rhodes, with their overwhelmingly Greek Orthodox population, were unilaterally annexed. Italian occupation of these islands would last until the Second World War. Italian warships appeared off the Dardanelles. The 'Ottoman endgame', or 'War of the Ottoman Succession', had begun.[27]

This was the background to a series of bilateral talks, many of them secret, among the rival Christian states of the Balkans. A formal pact was signed between Bulgaria and Serbia in March 1912. Using the correspondent of *The Times* as a backchannel, Venizelos began his own cautious overtures to the government in Sofia. With public opinion in Greece still gripped by the heroic figure of the Byzantine emperor Basil the 'Bulgar-Slayer', and with low-level guerrilla actions continuing against the Bulgarian *komitadjis* in Macedonia, it was a high-risk strategy. But the war with Italy was showing up, by the day, just how weak the Ottoman Empire might now be. The original inclusive spirit of the Young Turk movement had largely evaporated by this time. Greece signed a treaty of mutual support with Bulgaria on 30 May. Venizelos now turned his attention to reaching a similar understanding with Serbia.

On their own, these diplomatic moves were not enough to make war in the Balkans inevitable. But the Ottomans were under pressure on another front. In the empire's provinces that bordered the Adriatic, it was the turn of Albanian speakers to demand independence and a nation state of their own. A sustained uprising against Ottoman rule had begun in January. The Christian states of the region had no reason to be sympathetic towards the Albanians. The territory claimed for a new Albania would be at the expense of Greece, Serbia and Montenegro. And the Albanian national movement was not based on a shared religion, as all of theirs had been, since Albanian speakers were fairly evenly divided among Orthodox, Catholics and Muslims. But just as had happened in 1821, when the revolt of Ali Pasha had given cover for the Greek insurgents of the Peloponnese, the action of the Albanians tied down numbers of Ottoman troops during 1912.

And then in Constantinople yet another coup d'état temporarily ousted the Young Turks from power. For several months, from July to October, the Ottoman capital was reduced to a state of 'virtual civil war'.[28] Hostilities with Italy and with the Albanian insurgents ended in concessions by the Ottoman government in September. The empire's weakness was evident for all to see. Even so, most of Europe seemed to be taken by surprise when the First Balkan War broke out. When it did, the immediate expectation was that the Ottomans would see off this threat, as they had so many others.

Montenegro declared war on the empire on 8 October 1912. Greece, Bulgaria and Serbia followed ten days later. Much as they had attempted to do fifteen years before, two Greek armies struck northwards across the mountain passes, one into Macedonia from Thessaly, the other, in the west, into Epiros. The larger of the two forces, in Macedonia, was again commanded by Crown Prince Constantine. At the same time, the Greek fleet quickly gained control throughout the northern and eastern Aegean. Between October and December, one by one the islands of Samos, Lemnos, Thasos, Samothrace, Mytilini (Lesbos), Chios, Tenedos and Imbros raised the

Greek flag. All but the last two of these would remain in Greek hands from that time on. At the battle of the Dardanelles, fought near the entrance to the straits on 16 December 1912, Admiral Pavlos Koundouriotis, aboard the 'dreadnought' *Averof*, led the small Greek fleet to victory and imposed a blockade on the approach to Constantinople from the Mediterranean.

A simultaneous thrust by Bulgarian land forces was directed southeastwards towards Adrianople (Edirne) and Constantinople. As there was little, if any, coordination among the high commands, this undoubtedly helped the Greeks win their greatest prize in Macedonia. On 8 November the army led by Prince Constantine entered Salonica, beating a Bulgarian division by only a matter of hours. Four days later, on a bitterly cold day of rain, the Crown Prince was joined by his father, King George, and Venizelos. The three rode in triumph through streets decked out with blue and white Greek flags, to the cheers of the city's Greek inhabitants. True, they made up only about a third of the population, and the rest probably stayed indoors out of the rain. But for Greece and for most Greeks it was their greatest victory since the glory days of the Revolution. The Greek state had acquired its second great city, later to be dubbed its 'co-capital'. This was what the Grand Idea had always been about – and until now had so often failed to deliver.

By the end of November the Balkan allies were winning on almost all fronts. Only the Greeks, bogged down for the time being outside Ioannina, the chief town of Epiros, refused to join a general armistice that was agreed at the beginning of December. Representatives of the belligerents and of the Great Powers were called to London for a peace conference. Not to be left out, even though his country had not laid down its arms, Venizelos took the train from Salonica to Paris and arrived in London on 12 December. It was to be expected that once again the future of Greece would be determined in one or more of the capitals of the Great Powers. This was what had always happened until now. This time, Venizelos was determined to be there in person. He was a natural negotiator. He would be in his element.

In the event, things turned out rather differently. The first round of talks, in December 1912 and January 1913, was fractious from the beginning. Negotiations were fatally derailed on 23 January when in

Constantinople the ousted Young Turks took back control in a bloody counter-coup and immediately repudiated the peace terms that had just been handed down from London. Venizelos took this as his cue to head for home. What he took back with him were not terms for peace, but something potentially even more enticing and more far-reaching. Within days of his arrival in London, Venizelos had been introduced to David Lloyd George, then Chancellor of the Exchequer, later to become prime minister, and to the First Lord of the Admiralty, Winston Churchill. A series of private meetings had mapped out the possibility of a future 'entente' with Britain, and perhaps also with France. It was the fullest version yet of the kind of alliance that Mavrokordatos had first proposed to Foreign Secretary Canning almost a hundred years before. And this time, here was the democratically elected prime minister of Greece himself to put the case in person. Lloyd George was impressed. 'He is a big man, a very big man,' he is reported to have said, the day after Venizelos left London. Much of Venizelos's foreign policy over the next ten years would be grounded in the prospects held out in these formative discussions in London, in the shadow of the abortive Balkan peace conference.[29]

In the meantime, all this was to be kept top secret. It was only with difficulty that Venizelos extracted permission to share what had been discussed in London with his king. On his way back to Athens he stopped off in Salonica just long enough to do so. It would prove to be his last opportunity. Less than two months afterwards, on 18 March, King George set out for his usual afternoon walk to the city's most famous landmark, the White Tower on the seafront. He was accompanied by a single aide. At a discreet distance followed two Cretan gendarmes. He was returning when a young man got up from the bench where he had been sitting, just after the king had passed, and shot him at close range in the back. The king died instantly, six months short of the jubilee that would have celebrated fifty years of his reign. No political motive for the assassination has ever been proved, though plenty were suspected. The assassin, Alexandros Schinas, was officially described as a 'dipsomaniac' and a vagrant, and died shortly afterwards in police custody.

King George had lived to see the country that he ruled more than double its size and population. The Ionian islands had been added to

Greece in the first year of his reign. Less than a fortnight before his death, Greek troops had finally entered Ioannina, on 6 March 1913, bringing to an end the triumphant successes of the First Balkan War. Peace had not yet brought stable frontiers. But by far the greatest expansion of the Greek state that ever took place, bringing it very nearly to its present extent, had been achieved during the reign of the former Danish prince who had reinvented himself as King George I of the Hellenes.

How much of his briefing from London Venizelos ever felt himself empowered to share with King George's successor, who now came to the throne, we may never know for sure.[30]

The war in the Balkans had been won decisively by the Christian states. But for the first time in the history of the region there was to be no lasting peace settlement imposed from above by the European powers. They did try nevertheless. In parallel with the conference that Venizelos had attended in London, in December 1912 and January 1913, the 'London Ambassadors' Conference' brought together the representatives of Britain, France, Russia, Germany, Austria and Italy. Their remit was to revise the terms of the previous settlement, which had been worked out at the Congress of Berlin in 1878, so as to fit the new realities of the Balkans. The best they could do was to lay down terms for the exhausted belligerents, more or less in line with the military situation on the ground. The Treaty of London, signed on 30 May 1913, was one of the very last acts of what remained of the 'Concert of Europe'.

It was also one of the least effective. Even before the treaty was signed, the victorious Balkan states were already at loggerheads. Bulgaria had gained an Aegean coastline in Thrace and territory that brought its frontier to just west of Constantinople, but lost out in Macedonia, which was mostly partitioned between Serbia and Greece. On the same day that the treaty was signed, a new government took power in Sofia. Venizelos in the meantime had signed a bilateral treaty with Serbia. The stage was set for the Second Balkan War to begin.

Bulgaria went into action first, at the end of June 1913, with simultaneous attacks on Greek and Serbian forces in Macedonia. This

Second Balkan War was shorter, and even messier, than the first. Greece and Serbia were fighting to keep the Bulgarians out of Macedonia. Bulgaria was the enemy, and anyone could join in. The Young Turks, once again led by Enver Pasha, seized their opportunity and clawed back Eastern Thrace, including Edirne, from the Bulgarians. Romania, having taken no part in the First Balkan War, now grabbed a share of Bulgarian territory along the river Danube.[31]

It was all over quickly. Hostilities ended on 30 July, just over a month after they had begun. The Romanian capital was chosen as the place to settle the terms of peace. The Treaty of Bucharest was signed by the delegates of Greece, Bulgaria, Serbia, Montenegro and Romania on 10 August. Some of them seem to have hoped that the Great Powers would intervene to revise the treaty in their favour. But the divisions among the powers were almost as great as among the regional rivals. And so, for one of the few occasions in the history of the region, the map of southeastern Europe was redrawn by the Balkan states themselves. A separate Treaty of Athens, signed between Greece and the Ottoman Empire in November, brought Crete at last within the kingdom. Greece had now increased its land area by 68 per cent. In less than a year the country's population had increased from 2.7 to 4.8 million.

By the time these treaties were signed, Greece had a new monarch. Fair-skinned and fair-haired, standing a head taller than most of his troops, Constantine had acquitted himself well as commander-in-chief. His failures of 1897 could at last be forgotten and forgiven. Forty-four years old when he came to the throne, Constantine was more than twice the age that either of his predecessors had been on their accession. He had political and military experience behind him. Already related, through his parents, to the royal families of Great Britain and Russia, he was married to the sister of Kaiser Wilhelm of Germany. If dynastic relations still meant anything in the unpredictable world of European politics, King Constantine brought to his role the widest and deepest connections with the royal houses of the Great Powers of any Greek monarch so far.

Greece had triumphed in war. The king was secure upon his throne. In Venizelos he had a prime minister with a rock-solid parliamentary majority, ruling under a newly revamped, modernized constitution.

The king had proved his worth in the field, Venizelos in diplomacy and statesmanship. Together they had steered the Greek state to victory. What had seemed scarcely conceivable only a few years before was now entering into the history books. The Ottoman presence had been rolled back out of Europe. The Greek state had reached out to embrace the far-flung nation. How much more would it take to turn the Grand Idea into political reality at last?

7

The Self Divided

1913–1923

The human cost of the two Balkan wars of 1912 and 1913, on all sides, has ever since been overshadowed by the far greater destruction of life caused by the global conflict that was soon to follow. But these wars had an even more devastating, and longer-lasting, impact on the *civilian* populations of the regions where they were fought, and sometimes far beyond. Hundreds of thousands of Muslims were permanently displaced from Europe. Christians, too, in huge numbers were forced from their homes because they spoke the wrong language and used the wrong form of the liturgy in church. Many thousands of those were never able to return either.

Muslim refugees began to crowd into the Ottoman capital, Constantinople. For a time they seemed to threaten public order. Encouraged to move on, many of them ended up in the countryside of western Anatolia, which happened to be the area with the greatest concentration of Greek-speaking Orthodox communities. Within a year, in a domino effect, all along the Aegean seaboard of Anatolia, Muslims who had fled from the Balkans as refugees were turning on the Greek inhabitants, in revenge for the losses they had suffered themselves, and often with the connivance of the local Ottoman authorities. A new wave of emigration began, as whole Greek towns and villages were razed. During the first half of 1914 thousands of Anatolian Greeks abandoned their homes to seek refuge in Greece.

Of course, not all the Muslims of southeast Europe were able to flee, or perhaps wanted to. By the time the Treaty of Bucharest was signed, Greece had acquired a Muslim population of some 350,000. Before 1912 the only significant Muslim minority in the Greek state had been concentrated in Thessaly, incorporated in 1881. Now Muslims made up not far short of 10 per cent of the state's newly increased population. And it was not only Muslims who suddenly found themselves nationals of a country they had not chosen, and to which they had no natural allegiance. Many Christian families who spoke a Slavic language, if they did not migrate to Serbia or Bulgaria, found themselves in a different kind of minority status – one that would store up problems for later. Others spoke Albanian or Wallachian, rather than Greek. Then there was the sixty-thousand-strong Jewish community of Salonica, most of whom spoke the Spanish dialect known as Ladino or Judaeo-Spanish. How were all these new citizens to be assimilated?

Almost at once, people began to speak of 'Old Greece', meaning the state within its pre-1912 frontiers, and the 'New Lands' that had been added since. To some extent, and in certain contexts, these terms can still be heard today. Once the euphoria of victory had begun to wear off, officials and soldiers sent to serve in the New Lands sometimes displayed a shockingly colonialist mentality towards their newly acquired fellow citizens. A senior army officer with an upper-class Athenian background wrote home from Salonica in May 1913: 'How can one like a city with this cosmopolitan society, nine-tenths of it Jews. It has nothing Greek about it, nor European. It has nothing at all.'[1]

At the same time, more than two million Greek-speaking Orthodox Christians remained outside the borders of the state. There were communities in Romania, Bulgaria and newly emerging Albania that now found themselves in the position of endangered minorities. But by far the greatest number were to be found in the Ottoman Empire. There, the attitude of the Young Turk government had hardened still further. The Young Turks had already established the principle of an exchange of minority populations in their separate treaty with Bulgaria at the end of 1913. Venizelos was obliged to consider similar proposals for the Greeks the following year.

It was a highly volatile situation. If a third Balkan war were to break out, anything could happen. And then, on 28 June 1914, in Sarajevo, a Serbian nationalist called Gavrilo Princip fired the fatal shot that killed the heir to the Austrian throne, the Archduke Franz Ferdinand. Time and again in recent years a crisis in the Balkans had threatened to upset the ever more fragile balance of power in the whole of Europe. This time it did. A month after the assassination, on 28 July, the empire of Austria-Hungary declared war against Serbia. Within days, this third Balkan war had escalated to become the 'Great War', the 'war to end all wars'.

TAKING SIDES

The outbreak of war pitted the Great Powers of the European continent against one another. It was the outcome that almost exactly a century of concerted diplomacy had been designed to prevent. During the first days of August 1914, Europe split into two great alliances, each determined on the annihilation of the other. On one side was the Triple Entente, consisting of the empires of Great Britain, France and Russia; on the other the Central Powers, namely, the German Reich and the empire of Austria-Hungary.

Like it or not, there was little chance that Greece would be untouched. For the Greek government the choice lay between seizing an opportunity and minimizing a threat. Both were huge, and existential, choices. In a clash of giant empires, a small state such as Greece, even doubled in size as it was, could easily be snuffed out.

It came down to three choices. Few in Greece favoured an alignment with the Central Powers. Even if there had been strong ideological reasons or compelling grounds of self-interest for wishing to, the simple realities of geopolitics ruled out that course. As King Constantine explained candidly to his brother-in-law, the German Kaiser, just after the outbreak of war, 'the Mediterranean is at the mercy of the united fleets of England and France'; Greek shipping, Greek islands and Greek ports would face annihilation.[2] That reduced the options to two: either to enter the war on the side of the Entente or to remain neutral. There were perfectly good, rational grounds for either course. The trouble was, how to choose between them?

In favour of the Entente were both geography and historical ties. Russia had not been much of a friend to Greece of late, but all three members of the alliance just happened to be the same powers that had signed the Greek state into existence almost a century before.

Once the Ottoman Empire came in on the side of the Central Powers in November 1914, suddenly the biggest geopolitical forces on the continent were lined up in a way that Greeks had been dreaming of ever since the days of the Friendly Society, in the run-up to the 1821 Revolution. It was exactly this that had failed to happen in the 1850s, when two of the country's 'protecting powers' had ganged up on the third, and imposed neutrality on Greece by force. Now that all three were aligned, and the traditional enemy in the opposite camp, why would a Greek government hold back from joining them? It was the very thing that Otto and the political leaders of his day had most longed to do.

Victory by the Entente would surely bring about the long-anticipated dissolution of the Ottoman Empire. The 'Eastern Question' would be solved at a stroke – and in just the way that Mavrokordatos had first boldly proposed to the British Foreign Secretary of his day, George Canning, as long ago as 1823. The Russians could be expected to help themselves to Constantinople, so the most cherished prize of all would probably still be out of reach. But David Lloyd George and Winston Churchill, in their meetings with Venizelos in London at the end of 1912, had held out the prospect of other gains in Anatolia, not least an enclave that would include the city of Smyrna. Smyrna at the time had the largest concentration of Greeks of any city in the world. The Balkan wars had gifted Greece with control of almost the entire Aegean, including the largest of the islands close to the Anatolian coast: Lesbos, Chios and Samos. To gain a foothold on the mainland was not necessarily an unrealistic ambition. Building on the successes of the two Balkan wars, to fight alongside the Entente would bring a triumphant conclusion to the work of the Revolution that had begun in 1821.

There would be defensive advantages too. Of the other Balkan states, only Serbia was so far involved in the war – and under attack by Austria. Bulgaria, Romania and Montenegro were neutral, Albania not yet fully recognized as a state. Whatever Bulgaria did would be crucial. The sea-based power of the Entente would probably be a better protection against Bulgarian designs on Salonica than any pressure the Central Powers could bring to bear. And there was another aspect to the role of the Entente as 'protecting powers'. These potential allies had a proven track record of violating Greek sovereignty in the name of the original treaty of guarantee. Greek ports had been blockaded no fewer than three times in the previous century: in 1850, from 1854 to 1857, and again in 1886. This consideration seems not to have figured in initial Greek discussions about policy, but perhaps it should have. It would not have been for the most high-minded of motives, but there would have been a certain political logic in siding voluntarily with the Entente rather than risk the country being hijacked by those powers and forced into hostilities against its will.

The case for neutrality was equally rational, and a good deal simpler. A country the size of Greece, with its limited military strength, could hardly hope to influence the outcome of a European war. To commit to one side would make the Greek people hostage to forces and events they would never be in a position to control. Why risk everything that had been achieved in almost a century for future promises that depended on the outcome of an uncertain conflict, were vague and in any case might never be delivered? In the best case, full, legal neutrality ought to guarantee the integrity of the state's newly established borders, whatever the fallout might be beyond them, once the war was over. In the worst case (although this scenario would only begin to emerge later), some of the recent gains might have to be traded – but there could surely be no risk to the kingdom within its pre-1912 borders? And then there were the Greeks of the Ottoman Empire. Greek neutrality would save them from becoming hostages in their own homes. Greek lives, Greek property, Greek well-being, at home and abroad, would all be preserved. The terrible human cost of war would be avoided. After all, unlike Serbia or Belgium, Greece was not directly threatened by any of the Central Powers.

It was an impossible choice. The story of Greece during the First World War, and what has been euphemistically known ever since as the 'National Schism' (with capital letters) is too often reduced to the personal rivalry between two men: Venizelos, the elected head of government, and King Constantine, the crowned head of state. Personal chemistry and the obstinacy of charismatic individuals certainly played their part, just as they had done in the civil conflicts of 1823 and 1824, during the Revolution. Then, too, there had been a wider war going on, and then, too, the country had split apart. But just as in those internal conflicts of the 1820s, the 'Schism' was not only about individuals and those who followed them. It was not just a tussle over sovereignty or the right to rule. It was not, fundamentally, even about rational decision-making – because both decisions were based on perfectly rational foundations, even if the means used to try to impose them were anything but. It was the very nature of the choice that was bound to split Greece apart – because the war itself had split apart the European continent, and with it European civiliza-tion. Greece, created in the particular circumstances of the 1820s and nurtured as it had been ever since, could not help but be a microcosm of that riven continent and that civilization divided against itself.

It was no accident that among those who had the highest responsi-bility for making the decision, some had close personal and professional links to one side or the other of the European divide. Venizelos had cut his diplomatic teeth in Crete dealing with the guarantor powers during the island's fifteen-year period of autonomy. Those powers were Brit-ain, France, Russia and Italy. Venizelos's first foreign language was French. His first visit to London had brought him close to Lloyd George and Churchill. Venizelos was an islander through and through. His geopolitics were based on the sea. He thought as they did.

On the other side, King Constantine was married to the sister of Kaiser Wilhelm of Germany. He had been trained at the German Military Academy, and had a profound respect for German military methods. Chief of his General Staff, and therefore one of his leading advisers, was General Ioannis Metaxas, a capable officer who had undergone the same training and come out of it with similar views. Venizelos's foreign minister at the start of the war, Georgios Streit, was himself descended from a German family that had come to Greece with King Otto, and he had studied law in Germany. All of these men were fluent in German. They felt at home in a German environment. They sincerely believed that the war would be won by the German military machine.

This did not make these men any the less 'patriotic', as would be claimed. They were all of them part of a Greek elite that had grown up in a kingdom shaped by the Revolution, by Great Power involve-ment in it *and* by the formative role of German nineteenth-century philhellenism. It was in the nature of the modern Greek kingdom for its elites to be plugged into *all* the major languages and cultures of

Europe – which were now fatally at war with one another. It was as much a symptom as a cause of the divisions that followed, that each side conversed more easily and more frankly with the diplomatic representatives of one or other of the warring powers than they did with each other.

But there was a deeper cause of division. All along, hidden beneath the surface of the remarkable unanimity of the previous half-century, the old fault line from the 1820s had not gone away. Then, it had been between rival concepts of what it meant to be free. Now, after almost a hundred years of a free Greek state, it was about what it meant to be *Greek*. For the one side, what mattered above all else was to liberate the nation. For the other, it was to preserve the state. And from 1915 until 1922, Greece's own microcosm of the First World War would be fought between those who viscerally identified with each of these two incompatible choices.

THE FAULT LINE REOPENS

In August 1914 the agreed policy of the Greek government was for neutrality. It was Venizelos who broke ranks first. On 18 August, less than three weeks into the war, he made an offer to each of the Entente ministers in Athens: Greece would join with them if invited. At the time, while the Ottoman Empire and most of the Balkan countries remained neutral, none of the Allies was enthusiastic about opening a new front in southeast Europe. The overture was politely rebuffed. But once the Ottoman Empire had come into the war on the side of the Central Powers in November, military planners in the Entente capitals began to think again. Would Greece, after all, be willing to come to the aid of Serbia, the British Minister asked Venizelos? If it was solely to fight against the Austrians, then no, replied Venizelos. But the Greek minority in the Ottoman Empire was coming under ever greater pressure. If the empire were to be attacked, and dismembered after the war, the future liberation of this population might be worth some sacrifices in the Balkans. On this basis, the Entente then put a formal offer to Greece on 24 January 1915.

This offer brought Venizelos into direct conflict with the king and the General Staff. At the time they were horrified at the idea of giving up any territory to Bulgaria (still neutral) in return for much bigger but possibly indefensible gains in Anatolia in future. This scepticism seems justifiable – though it is one of the ironies of the 'Schism' that the time would come when King Constantine and the same advisers would be content to surrender even more of Macedonia, once Bulgaria had joined the Central Powers, in their determination to frustrate Venizelos's plans.

Then in February came the start of the Dardanelles campaign. Would Greece send divisions to Gallipoli, to support the Allied landings? Venizelos was all for it. For a time, even the king and his advisers were tempted. Although he had been crowned 'Constantine I of the Hellenes', the king enjoyed the mystique that associated his name with that of the last emperor of Byzantium. Particularly in the army, where his popularity was greatest, it was common to refer to him reverently as 'King Constantine XII' – that is, of the Byzantine Empire. The objective of the Dardanelles campaign was to seize the Ottoman capital. Surely the emperor-in-waiting should be there, at the head of his troops, as *stratilatis*, or 'victorious commander', an old Byzantine title that his supporters had already begun adopting for Constantine?

In the event, it would prove to be a non-issue. The Gallipoli landings, as we know from hindsight, would end in ignominy, one of the most disastrous campaigns, for the Allies, of the entire war. And in any case Russia would soon veto any participation by Greece. 'Tsargrad' had already been promised to Tsar Nicholas II. But before any of these things could happen, on 6 March 1915 the king took the advice of his Chiefs of Staff and overruled his prime minister. Thwarted and furious, Venizelos submitted his resignation. At a press conference the next day, he declared, 'with tears in his eyes', 'Tomorrow the Allies will be masters of the Dardanelles, and the day after of Constantinople; our flag will not participate in the liberation of the city of our dreams . . . [T]he harm is irreparable.'[3]

From this time onward, a proxy war began to be waged in the Athenian press. Numerically, newspapers were about equally divided between support for Venizelos and support for the king. The Venizelist press ramped up its rhetoric about liberating Constantinople, fulfilling the Grand Idea and abolishing tyranny in 'lands utterly Hellenic' in the Ottoman Empire. The other side adopted a more soothing tone, dampening expectations about the Grand Idea and reassuring its readers that the country had been saved from certain disaster thanks to the wise intervention of the monarch.[4] The battle lines that from now on would define the 'Schism' were being drawn. At the same time King Constantine, ruling through a rapid succession of prime ministers, became in effect the leader of a political party. Around the banner of 'anti-Venizelism', the political survivors of the 'old' parties that had been sidelined after the coup of 1909 regrouped to form a new 'Party of Nationalists', under the leadership of a talented parliamentary orator, the ill-fated Dimitrios Gounaris.

Venizelos was soon back. On 13 June 1915 his Liberal Party won the first election that had been held for three years – with a reduced majority, to be sure, but still with a convincing mandate to govern. The king's illness during that summer was perhaps more serious than was given out at the time. It appears that his health never really recovered. Even once he was well enough to swear in the new government, an event that had to be delayed until the end of August, Constantine's reluctance to work once more with Venizelos was palpable. Within days he was confiding to the German Minister in Athens his frustration with a man 'who as late as yesterday declared that he was . . . convinced as firmly as a rock of the final victory of the Entente'.[5] The king was just as convinced of the opposite. He had no intention of bringing his country into the war. But he did believe sincerely in the superiority of German arms. Cooperation with Venizelos would surely be impossible. And so it proved.

When Bulgaria mobilized its forces a few weeks later, on 21 September, it was immediately apparent that Greece's old Balkan adversary was preparing to enter the war and join with the Central Powers. Greece responded with mobilization of its own. This was an uncontroversial precaution. The Bulgarians were known still to have designs on regaining the Aegean coastline that they had won in the First Balkan War and lost in the Second, as well as on Salonica, which had so nearly become theirs in 1912. The priority of the Entente powers was quite different. For them, the entry of Bulgaria into the war presented a new threat to Serbia, which had so far managed to withstand repeated onslaughts by the much more powerful Austro-Hungarian Empire.

At once, and once again without consultation, Venizelos made an offer to the British and French: Greek troops would be available to help defend Serbia if the Bulgarians were to attack. But the king, not the prime minister, was commander-in-chief. Within twenty-fours Venizelos had been forced to rescind his offer. He took his case to parliament. On 4 October 1915, the day that Bulgaria formally declared war against the Entente (though not against Greece), Venizelos won a vote of confidence in the chamber. But the king would not be overruled by parliament either. Ignoring the principle of the 'declared majority', he now dismissed his prime minister.

For the Entente, the overriding concern was the defence of Serbia, which during the next few weeks came under simultaneous attack by Austria from the north and by Bulgaria from the east. King Constantine may have thought himself well rid of Venizelos, as he boasted in a private telegram to Berlin. But he could do nothing to prevent the landing of thousands of British, French and colonial troops at Salonica, beginning in October 1915, under the overall command of the French general Maurice-Paul Sarrail. Meanwhile, in a last-ditch attempt to match coercion with inducement, in October Great Britain made a formal offer to the Greek government of sovereignty over Cyprus if Greece would join the Entente. Not even this was enough to win over either Constantine or the minority government that had been sworn in after the forced resignation of Venizelos. So the British and French settled for coercion pure and simple. They proceeded to occupy islands and strategic positions all over Greece. These included Souda Bay in Crete, the fortress of Karabournou that guards the entrance by sea to Salonica, and the whole of Corfu, in due course to house the army and exiled government of the defeated Serbs. Lemnos, in the northern Aegean, became the home to a new British naval base established at Moudros. All of these actions took place in defiance of the will of the Greek government, and in flagrant violation of the country's declared neutrality.

By this time, King Constantine had been obliged to call a new parliamentary election, since his government had lost a vote of confidence. The election took place on 19 December 1915. According to Venizelos and his supporters, this was unconstitutional because his party still enjoyed a majority and his policy had been upheld by the chamber as recently as October. Also, an election carried out under conditions of general mobilization could not be a fair one. It was an unfortunate irony that Venizelos had himself come to power through a similar tactic on the part of Constantine's predecessor, King George, in 1910. Even more unfortunate was Venizelos's decision to repeat the response of the offended parties then: to boycott the election. It is true that participation in the election of 19 December was much lower than it had been six months previously. But it is impossible to know whether this was because voters (who had to be male) were absent serving with their army units, or actively heeded the Liberal call for a boycott. In any case, the result was the immolation of Venizelos's party as a parliamentary force. Whether this was the intention or not, it was inevitable that the action from now on would have to be conducted outside parliament.

During the first six months of 1916, tensions continued to rise. The flashpoint came at the end of May. By this time, the Serbs had been defeated by Austria and Bulgaria and their country overrun. The remnants of the Serbian army had been first evacuated to the safety of Corfu, then brought by sea to Salonica to regroup alongside the French and British forces already there. The 'Macedonian Front', as it was becoming known, had become even broader, with the arrival of reinforcements from Italy (now a belligerent on the side of the Entente) and from Russia. A new corps made up of Greek volunteers, mostly recruited from the 'New Lands', brought the number of Allied forces on the front to six. Officially, Greece was still neutral, but still also fully mobilized for war. From the point of view of the Entente, the armed forces of the Greek state represented a potential threat to their rear. On the other hand, as seen by the Central Powers (particularly Germany, Austria-Hungary and Bulgaria), the neutrality that the Greek government continued ever more desperately to protest was fast becoming a bad joke, since in their eyes that government had lost control of strategic parts of its territory to the enemy.

At the end of May 1916, it was the turn of the Germans to make demands. The Greek frontier fortress of Rupel must be surrendered to Germany's ally, Bulgaria. When the king's government complied – to the consternation of the Venizelists, who could do nothing to stop it – the Entente powers stepped in with a show of British and French naval force close to Athens. A diplomatic 'Note' delivered by the representatives of Great Britain and France on 21 June demanded that the Greek army be disbanded at once, and the government itself resign, in favour of a 'non-political' one that would give the Allies a free hand. This was a blatant intervention in the internal affairs of the country. To justify it, the text of the 'Note' invoked the rights of the 'protecting powers' that went back to the treaty of guarantee for Greece in 1832, and were supposedly enshrined in the Constitution of 1864. King Constantine had no choice but to comply.

This intervention by the Entente powers did more than anything else that had happened so far to swing Greek public opinion against them. That meant also against Venizelos, and behind the king and his government. It only made matters worse when Venizelos expressed in a telegram to the prime minister of France his gratitude that 'the Protecting Powers have acted like parents in the fullness of their rights'.[6] King Constantine's boast to the Kaiser at being rid of his prime minister had at least been expressed in private. But Venizelos's telegram was leaked to the press.

The 'Note' had been meant to remove the threat to the Entente forces from their rear, by demobilizing the Greek army. But an unintended consequence for Greece was to turn loose upon the country thousands of armed men fiercely loyal to their commander-in-chief, the king, and now subject to no official control or discipline. For almost a year the 'Reservists', as they were called, became a byword for violence and terror. The establishment of a rival 'National Reservists League', loyal to Venizelos, was the clearest sign yet that what was beginning was nothing less than a civil war.

In August the imminent entry of Romania into the war on the side of the Entente changed the balance of forces on the Macedonian Front. Fighting began in earnest between General Sarrail's forces and those of Bulgaria, Austria and Germany. Over the next few months the French, the British and the regrouped remnants of the Serbian army, with their other allies, made modest gains in western Macedonia. At the same time Bulgaria proceeded to annex the eastern part of the region unopposed, its forces uprooting the Greek-speaking population as they went. In early September the strategic town of Kavala surrendered, along with an entire Greek division that was supposed to be defending it. 'Neutral' Greece was being carved up between the two sides in the European war, while its own army had just been stood down and the country's leaders were at each other's throats.

On 27 August 1916, Venizelos addressed a mass demonstration in the centre of Athens. He still offered cooperation with the king, who he claimed had been led astray by his General Staff. But he also hinted plainly at other measures. Two days later it became apparent what this might mean. In Salonica, officers of the Greek divisions stationed there, members of a recently formed 'Committee for National Defence', staged a show of strength and repudiated their allegiance to the king and the government in Athens. This action is often described as a coup d'état, though the officers were in no position to set up their own 'state'. They carried the day only thanks to active support from General Sarrail. It was far from being a popular uprising, and of course it was condemned as the highest form of treason in Athens.

This was Venizelos's moment. But even now he hesitated to act. Finally, on 25 September, he took ship for Crete, from where he had started out. There, outside the capital, Chania, in the tradition of that island's century of revolutions, Venizelos staged a demonstration in arms, and announced a new 'Provisional Government of the Kingdom of Greece'. A proclamation addressed 'the Nation, which is called, in the absence of the State, to answer a national emergency', and explained: 'Whereas the State has betrayed its obligations, it remains to the Nation to act in order to achieve the task assigned to the State.'[7] From now on, and to some extent for decades afterwards, the 'Schism' would lie between 'Old Greece' – the kingdom as it had been before 1912 – and the 'New Lands' acquired during the Balkan wars.

NATION VERSUS STATE

From Crete, Venizelos made his way through the islands to Salonica. Greece's second, newly acquired city was to become the seat of the Provisional Government. For the next eight months Greece would have two governments, one in Athens, the other in Salonica. It was a re-run of what had happened in 1823 and 1824. And just as had happened then, each government denounced the other as illegitimate. The Provisional Government of Salonica declared war against the Central Powers in November, whereas the 'official' government in Athens remained neutral. In December 1916, from Salonica the king was declared to be deposed, while in Athens he reigned and the Archbishop of Athens and All Greece carried out the *anathema* of Venizelos, excommunicating him from the Church and burying his effigy under thousands of stones ritually thrown by loyal citizens.

Again, just as had happened in the 1820s, the forces of one government took the field against those of the other. At the beginning of November the town of Katerini in Macedonia, near the former border with Old Greece, was captured by National Defence forces after an armed skirmish. Only French intervention to establish a demilitarized zone along the old frontier prevented many more such actions. Then at the beginning of December, civil war came to the streets of Athens. Because the calendar in use in Greece at the time was thirteen days behind the Western one, the episode has ever since been known in Greek as the 'November events'. King Constantine's government was effectively under siege from British, French and Italian ships anchored off Phaliro and Piraeus. Demobilization was not enough to satisfy the Entente powers. That part of Greece which had not joined with Venizelos and the Provisional Government in Salonica was not merely to be neutral, as it had always asserted its right to be, it must be neutralized.

On 1 December the commanders of the fleets gave an ultimatum for the government to hand over its arsenals and heavy munitions. What happened that day bears striking parallels with another confrontation in the centre of Athens, on almost the same date twenty-eight years later, that would mark the start of a new phase in the last and most violent of all Greece's civil wars. Now, on Friday, 1 December 1916, a force of three thousand Allied troops, most of them French, landed to seize the contested depots and supplies. They found the disbanded Greek army waiting for them. The first shots were fired at around eleven in the morning. Fighting between Allied and Greek troops broke out at several places in the city. The foreigners were driven back. Shells fired from the Allied ships began to burst in the city centre.

King Constantine had won at best a pyrrhic victory. A compromise saw the Allied troops withdraw to their ships and only a part of the contested armaments surrendered, for the time being. But the events of that Friday became the signal for a rampage throughout the city against anyone and everyone suspected of Venizelist sympathies. Venizelos's own house was attacked and looted. The Grande Bretagne Hotel was raked with gunfire. The mayor of Athens, the widely respected Greek-Egyptian cotton millionaire and benefactor Emmanuel Benakis, was dragged from his home by the enraged mob. His daughter, the novelist Penelope Delta (author of *In the Time of the Bulgar-Slayer*), was convinced they were taking him to the Ilissos river to lynch him, as had apparently already happened to others. Next day she went to the city's prison, 'not knowing whether we would find him alive' – though in due course he would be released unharmed.[8] The arrested Venizelists were accused of high treason. Others were murdered or beaten up, their property ransacked. An official report published in Paris two years later put the number of dead during two days of violence at thirty-five, with almost a thousand imprisoned. The printing presses of Venizelist newspapers were destroyed, their editors were among those jailed. Unable to hit back at the 'protecting powers' that had invaded their capital, the mob and the Reservists took their revenge on their own people. Although no evidence was ever found to corroborate this, it was claimed that the Venizelists had been planning an uprising to coincide with the landing by the hated foreigners.

The actions of the Reservists during those two days, and continuing at a lower level for months afterwards, have been described by a respected academic historian writing a century later as 'proto-fascist' and a 'pogrom'.[9] A favourite target for the Reservists were refugees, often destitute, who had fled persecution in Anatolia for the safety of free Greece, and were now lumped together with the Venizelists. This was because support for Venizelos's policies was highest in the newly acquired territories and among those groups who looked to him for the future liberation of their homelands. Many in the anti-Venizelist camp already despised these incomers from beyond the frontiers as 'unknown faces, outsiders, refugees, Cretans', 'a rabble for hire', 'scoundrels'.[10] So much for the Grand Idea and the unity of the nation.

The violence was not all on one side. Venizelos's Provisional Government imposed martial law upon the areas it controlled. Pockets of resistance were ruthlessly crushed. Notorious cases were in the Chalkidiki peninsula near Salonica, and at the village of Apeiranthos on the island of Naxos, where women and children were among the victims. There were even disturbances in Venizelos's native Crete and in Samos.

The 'November events' and their aftermath had the effect of polarizing Greece irreparably. Up to this point, the Allied powers had held back from formally recognizing the Provisional Government in Salonica. They did so now. At the same time they began to impose a tight blockade on Old Greece. To humiliation was added widespread starvation. There were reports of military supplies being looted by desperate citizens. The king's government had almost no freedom for action left. Instead, all but abandoning the fig leaf of neutrality that was its only remaining rationale for existing, the king and his ministers seem to have placed their hopes on an offensive by the Germans and Bulgarians to dislodge the Provisional Government from Salonica – and presumably to hand most of Macedonia to Bulgaria if they had won. An old tactic was revived. Irregular volunteer fighters were sent over the border to destabilize the enemy, without the government being accountable. Only, this time, the 'border' was the demilitarized zone between Old Greece and the New Lands. The methods that had once been directed towards expanding the kingdom were now turned against the rival Greek government in the north.

In May 1917, Greek troops raised by the Provisional Government saw action for the first time on the Macedonian Front. By the following month their strength had risen to sixty thousand. As far as the internal affairs of Greece were concerned, the Entente powers now felt confident enough to impose their will upon the whole of the divided country. Once again the key decision was taken in London. A conference held there at the end of May determined that King Constantine must be deposed, by force if necessary. The demand was made, once again, in the name of the 'protecting powers'. The king left Greece, with his immediate family, on 15 June. He had not formally abdicated. With the approval of the Allies, his place on the throne was taken by his second-born son, Alexander.

The way was now open for Venizelos to return to Athens as leader of a reunited Greece. After almost three years of bitter division over the issue, Greece had made its peace with the Triple Entente – and become for the first time formally a belligerent in the world war. The 'National Schism' was, supposedly, over.

It was nothing of the sort. The crowd that Venizelos addressed in Syntagma Square, in the centre of Athens, at the end of June 1917, was much smaller and more subdued than the one that had cheered him there when he first took office in 1910. Even while he was speaking, armed French troops occupied every rooftop and every strategic point in the city. Local sensibilities (no less racist, in the language of today, than anywhere else in Europe at the time) were particularly offended by the fact that many of those troops came from France's African colonies. Venizelos had acted in the name of the 'Nation'. But who were the masters now? Not even *his* rhetoric could disguise the fact that it was the 'protecting powers' that had brought him there. It had been ever thus for Greece, of course, since the 1820s. But this was all the more reason for resentment by those who resented it.

In his speech, Venizelos looked forward to the 'unity of spirit' of the Greek people. Apart from those with the highest share of responsibility, he declared, there would be no reprisals. But the circumstances were far from normal. Well-meaning words went nowhere. Parliament was dissolved – but with a renewed mobilization of the whole country, there could be no question, now, of a general election. Instead, the last but one parliament, which had been elected two years earlier, *before* the election of December 1915 that the Liberals had boycotted, was brought back to life – earning it the nickname of the 'Lazarus parliament'. In this artificially resuscitated chamber Venizelos won a vote of confidence at the end of August 1917.

Leading members and supporters of the previous government were rounded up and exiled to Corsica – an act that showed the hand of France at the highest level. Lower down the scale, and despite Venizelos's earlier promises, wholesale purges were carried out of the armed forces, the civil service, the judiciary and even the Church. The Archbishop who had pronounced the *anathema* was dethroned and replaced by a Cretan who was a friend and supporter of Venizelos.

Through the last months of 1917 and the first of 1918, while the Allies prepared for their next offensive on the Macedonian Front, Greece was more divided than ever. In May 1918 three Greek divisions took part in the Allied victory over Bulgarian forces at Skra di Legen, just inside the present-day boundary between Greece and North Macedonia. All three divisions had been raised in the New Lands. Earlier in the year, in Old Greece, whole units had mutinied and been subjected to exemplary punishment. In these and other punitive measures, the role of Cretan gendarmes was prominent: these tough mountaineers were greatly feared by other Greeks, and ferociously loyal to their compatriot Venizelos. Even as a superficially united Greece contributed significantly to the Allied war effort, to the rear a savage and undeclared civil war was still going on.

It was against this background that the decisive breakthrough on the Macedonian Front was made in September 1918. Greek troops made up one-third of the forces engaged on the Allied side. On the same day that the Bulgarians sued for a separate peace, in Berlin the German High Command came to the conclusion that the war was lost. It ended first in the East: in the armistice signed with the Ottoman Empire at the British naval base at Moudros on the island of Lemnos on 30 October. The final armistice, on the Western Front, followed on 11 November. The next day, the first of the victorious Allies marched into Constantinople. Since Russia had abandoned the war after the Bolshevik Revolution in 1917, no one was talking, now, of 'Tsargrad'. Instead, a combined British, French and Italian military administration was put in place, which would last for almost five years. Greek troops, too, were allowed to play a small part, and received a rapturous welcome from the city's Greek population. With them went the 'dreadnought' *Averof*, which had won battle honours in the First Balkan War.

By this time Venizelos was already in London. Even before the armistice, he had presented to the British prime minister, Lloyd George, his detailed proposals for the dismemberment of the Ottoman Empire. Based on the meetings he had had with Lloyd George, then Chancellor of the Exchequer, back in 1912, these envisaged the Ottoman heartland of Anatolia being divided three ways, with the whole western section, bordering the Aegean, going to Greece. His country had made its contribution to the Allied victory, even if only by the skin of its teeth. Venizelos was in early with his claim for a share of the spoils.

The peace conference began in Paris in January 1919 and lasted for a whole year. Its effects would transform the map of Europe and the Middle East, replacing age-old empires with the still-evolving patchwork of nation states that we know today. The best-known product of the conference was the Treaty of Versailles. This was completed relatively quickly, in June. Negotiations for peace with the Ottoman Empire would drag on for more than a year after that.

Most of this time Venizelos spent away from Greece, at the negotiating table, where he excelled. The young British diplomat Harold Nicolson was sufficiently overawed to declare, 'He and Lenin are the only two really great men in Europe.' Hearing Venizelos speak, Nicolson had been struck by 'a strange medley of charm, brigandage, welt-politik, patriotism, courage, literature – and above all this large muscular smiling man, with his eyes glinting through spectacles and on his head a square skull-cap of black silk'. The British Foreign Secretary, Lord Curzon, too, was impressed by Venizelos's 'inexhaustible eloquence'.[11]

Through diplomacy, persistence and adroit footwork Venizelos secured two huge gains for Greece, both in land and in prestige. The first was a mandate to occupy Smyrna and the *vilayet* of Aydin in western Anatolia, in May 1919. The second was the award of an even larger slice of Ottoman territory in Anatolia, together with most of Thrace, excluding Constantinople, by the terms of the Treaty of Sèvres, a little over a year later. Both of these apparent gains, as events turned out, would prove disastrous for Greece – for reasons that were not really foreseeable at the time. Both gains came about, not as a result of feats of arms, but of an assiduous policy of pursuing tactical alliances and exploiting the divisions among rival, greater powers. It was in essence the same tactic that had worked with such brilliant effect in the 1820s.

On 12 August 1920, two days after signing the Treaty of Sèvres, Venizelos was ready to leave Paris. His work there was done. The Greek administration of Smyrna was now a little over a year old. One hundred thousand copies of a coloured map of 'Great Greece' were being printed in England, and would soon be reproduced on post-cards too. Coloured orange were Greek territories that almost completely encircled the Aegean Sea, with a gap for an international zone around Constantinople and another in the southwest corner of Anatolia and the islands of the Dodecanese, which the treaty had assigned to Italy. The map also featured a personification of Greece as a long-haired maiden carrying aloft a huge Greek flag in one hand, while in the other she held a placard that read, 'Greece is destined to live and will live'. In the top left corner appeared the bearded, mus-tachioed head of Venizelos with his signature flat-lensed spectacles. This was a new Greece 'of two continents and five seas', a favourite expression used by Venizelos and his supporters. All of this new 'Great Greece' defined by the Treaty of Sèvres was already occupied by Greek troops, with the exception of parts of Thrace, which very soon would be.

The state had achieved the greater part of what it had been trying to achieve ever since it had first come into existence – to expand so as to embrace the entire nation. And Venizelos was confident that where Greeks still lived outside its borders, either those borders would be extended eventually by the same diplomatic means, or people would be induced to move home: Turkish-speaking Muslims into the rump Ottoman state in central Anatolia, Greek-speaking Christians into the Greek-controlled areas.

On that August evening in 1920, as Venizelos prepared to board his train at the Gare de Lyon in Paris, the Grand Idea had been realized. Then two gunmen ran up and opened fire. The attackers turned out to be former Greek army officers who had been cashiered in the recent purge. The smouldering Greek civil war had reached as far as Paris, the capital of the civilized world. With terrible inevitability from that moment on, the whole mirage began to fold up and dissolve.

THE END OF THE GRAND IDEA

Venizelos escaped with light injuries, and spent only a few days in a Paris clinic. The day after the attack, when the news reached Athens, the city was convulsed by a wave of violence against known anti-Venizelists. It has been described as a repeat of the 'November events' of 1916, although on a smaller scale. At its height, Ion Dragoumis, by this time one of the most eloquent of Venizelos's critics, was dragged from his car and shot dead by agents of the security forces. It happened in broad daylight on a busy street, close to the site of today's Athens Hilton. The city's mayor, Emmanuel Benakis, was accused of complicity. Dragoumis had been apparently unmoved when Benakis had been threatened by the lynch mob in 1916. Now, the fortunes of civil war were reversed.

This was the climate in Athens when Venizelos returned from his triumph at Sèvres. The first thing he had to do was face a parliamentary election. The life of the 'Lazarus' parliament had been artificially prolonged twice already, because of the continuing state of martial law and mobilization to keep the army in Anatolia. There had not been a fully contested election since June 1915. So martial law was lifted, and an election called for November. The opposition politicians had finally been allowed to return from their exile in Corsica. The 'Party of Nationalists', which had been founded by Dimitrios Gounaris in 1915, was now renamed the 'People's Party'. In his first campaign speech, in October 1920, Gounaris spoke of 'obliterating the tyranny' of the present government. In future the country would be 'decontaminated to remove the pestilence of tyranny'.[12] It was not an auspicious start.

Matters were complicated further by the sudden and unexpected death of King Alexander from sepsis, after being bitten by a pet monkey in the grounds of the royal estate at Tatoï, outside Athens. The young successor to Constantine had acted, for the most part obligingly, as a figurehead during his three-year reign. The election had to be postponed for another week, to allow for the obsequies, and for a regent to be sworn in. By the time it took place, on 14 November, the contest was no longer merely a referendum on the performance of Venizelos's government. Out of the blue, and beyond the wildest hopes of his opponents, there was now a real alternative. The election became a two-way race between the charismatic opponents who had faced one another down over the last decade: Venizelos and the exiled King Constantine.

Neither of the two could be described at this time as close to the people. Constantine had been languishing in Switzerland since 1917. Venizelos had spent most of his last three years in power abroad and had only just returned. Distance from the flesh-and-blood protagonists only helped to foster the climate of almost religious fanaticism that had built up around each of them since the 'November events'. A pro-Venizelos newspaper compared its hero to Christ and Mohammed, a prophet sent by God at a new critical moment in human history to enlighten mankind. For his supporters Venizelos was a Messiah, the representative of Divine Providence on earth. Predictably, for his enemies, he was a 'false prophet' and 'fake Messiah', a deranged mental cripple driven by 'Satanic inspiration'.[13]

The Liberals lost. Constantine returned to Greece and his throne, after a hastily arranged referendum that produced an implausible 99 per cent of votes cast in his favour. Even before the ballot had opened, a diplomatic 'Note' on behalf of the governments of Great Britain, France and Italy informed the new Greek administration that 'the restoration to the throne of Greece of a King, whose disloyal attitude and conduct towards the Allies during the war caused them great embarrassment and loss, could only be regarded by them as a ratification by Greece of his hostile acts'.[14] Unfair – possibly. Interference in the country's politics – certainly, but this was nothing new. A separate communiqué made it clear that if Constantine were to return as king, there would be no financial assistance from the Great Powers either. The warning could not have been clearer.

Astonishingly, and despite its own manifesto commitment to end the occupation of Ottoman territory in Anatolia and bring the troops home, the new government decided to continue the campaign, even though it now meant going it alone.

Shortly before his fall, Venizelos had pleaded with Lloyd George to authorize a new advance eastwards by the Greek army, to enforce the terms of the Treaty of Sèvres. Since the Greek landings in Smyrna in May 1919 – and indeed, to a significant extent, because of them, as can be seen in hindsight – a new force had entered the politics of the defeated Ottoman Empire. Mustafa Kemal we have already met as the seventeen-year-old military cadet from Salonica, too late to enlist in the war of 1897 and bitter about the intervention of the Great

Powers to bail out Greece in its defeat. Kemal had served with distinction during the world war, in the successful Ottoman resistance to the Gallipoli landings and on the Russian and Mesopotamian fronts. His future title of Atatürk (father of the Turks) had yet to be earned.

In May 1919, just four days after Greek troops disembarked in Smyrna, Kemal had taken advantage of a posting to the interior of Anatolia to put himself at the head of a new movement that was preparing to fight back against the dismemberment of the Ottoman Empire. In September 1919 a first congress of Turkish Nationalists had drawn up and proclaimed a 'national pact'. This was to become the blueprint for the Republic of Turkey as it still exists today.

Defying the authority of the puppet Sultan in Constantinople, whose government was controlled by the occupying powers, Kemal and the Nationalists soon set up a rival Provisional Government in Ankara. Once the terms of the Treaty of Sèvres became known, the Nationalists determined to repudiate it. Belatedly, the time had come for the Turkish-speaking Muslims of Anatolia to do what the Greeks had done a century before them. The Ottoman Empire was a thing of the past. The modern Republic of Turkey would become a secular nation state, on the European model and based upon the Turkish-speaking heartland of Anatolia, together with a tiny corner of Europe surrounding Istanbul, which would no longer be a capital city. And, as with so many nation states before it, the supporters of this one were ready to kill and if necessary to die, to liberate their land from foreign occupiers: in reality, this meant the victors in the world war. But the mandate that Venizelos had accepted, to occupy Smyrna and the *vilayet* of Aydin, meant that Greece had become their proxy. The war between Greece and the Turkish Nationalists that lasted from 1919 to 1922 has ever since been known in Turkey as the country's 'war of independence'. Greece and Turkey, as modern nation states, have each fought a 'war of independence' against the other.

Such hindsight was not available in the first months of 1921. A new government was in power in Athens, united by nothing so much as resentment against the Venizelists who had victimized its members and their supporters over the last three years. Venizelos himself had prudently left the country, but continued to watch affairs closely.

Kemal's new power centre in Ankara looked to most observers like just another insurgency. It had no international recognition. The entire logic of the Paris Peace Conference – a flawed logic, as we now know – had been predicated on the victors dictating terms to the vanquished. Germany had seen the Rhineland occupied and was crippled by hyperinflation, partly as a result of having to pay swingeing 'reparations'. The empire of Austria-Hungary had been carved up. Whatever the peace conference decided about the remnants of the Ottoman Empire, this was the new international order, and must be obeyed. It was in this spirit that Venizelos wrote to Lloyd George in October 1920. Kemal's threatened defiance was simply a matter of enforcement. Provided that at least one of the leading signatories to the Treaty of Sèvres was prepared to give him the necessary authority, Venizelos had been prepared once more to send in Greek troops as enforcers.

This was the strategy that the new royalist government in Athens also determined to pursue, early in 1921. It remains something of a puzzle why they did it. The strategy was a legacy of the hated Venizelos. It also depended completely on British support. That support had now been withdrawn, after the return of King Constantine. It has been suggested that it was fear of their internal enemies, the Venizelists, as much as antipathy to Kemal's Turkish Nationalists, that drove them. The new regime in Greece had to show the world, and especially Great Britain, that it could do just as well without Venizelos. If it failed to act against Kemal, it might itself be toppled. If that were to happen, the 'Venizelist terror' would be back. Even a military defeat in Anatolia might be the lesser evil, compared to that.[15]

So it was once again a deeply fissured body politic that went to war against Kemal in the spring of 1921. It was also an army that within the last few months had been thoroughly purged of officers who had been promoted by the previous regime – many of them on the strength of battle honours they had won on the Macedonian Front in 1917 and 1918. A first Greek offensive in March was driven back. It was an inauspicious way to celebrate the centenary of the outbreak of the Greek Revolution. A reshuffle brought Gounaris, the leader of the rebaptized People's Party, back to head the government. Undeterred by this first failure, it seems to have been Gounaris's idea to send

King Constantine himself to Smyrna, to take up what this time would be no more than a symbolic high command. The day chosen for him to sail was another anniversary. It had been on 29 May 1453 that Constantinople fell to the Ottomans, and the last Constantine to occupy the Byzantine throne had died in battle. On this day in 1921 his spiritual heir, still known to some fancifully as 'Constantine XII', set out to fulfil the old prophecies about the return of 'the City' to Orthodoxy. Never mind that Constantine, although only in his early fifties, was 'a tired and sick man, without his old stubbornness and will'.[16] On 10 July two Greek armoured columns struck eastwards towards Kemal's provisional capital, Ankara.

The battle of the Sakarya river has been described as the 'last real battle of the First World War'.[17] It was fought in the intense heat of the central Anatolian plateau in late August and early September 1921. The Greeks had stretched their supply lines to their limit. The Turks had the advantage of being able to draw on ever more recruits from farther east. But they, too, were short of food, weapons and ammunition. The Provisional Government in Ankara did not yet have anything like the resources of an organized state. The Greeks had better organization and stronger forces. The outcome remained in doubt until the very end. Kemal even made contingency plans to abandon Ankara. But it was the Greeks who broke first. After almost three weeks of fighting, the order was given to retreat. The Greek army had come within fifty miles of Kemal's provisional capital. Now, there was nothing for it but to retrace its steps.

The endgame dragged on for a whole year. The Greek army remained dug in along the same defensive line that it had held before the campaign began, some two hundred miles east of the Aegean coast. In Athens, the Gounaris government won a vote of confidence in November and made desperate overtures to the British Foreign Secretary, Lord Curzon, for mediation with the Turkish Nationalists and a loan to cover the soaring costs of keeping an army in the field. Some half-hearted efforts were made on the British side, but nothing came of them. Among increasingly desperate measures to raise revenue, in spring 1922 all banknotes in circulation were called in, to be cut in half. The Greek government eventually fell in May 1922, and a new coalition came to power – united, to the extent that it was, by its opposition to 'Venizelism'.

With the war on the battlefield stalled, and no honourable end to Greece's Anatolian campaign in sight, the fault line between state and nation began to widen still further. All the viciousness that been stirred up by the simmering civil war of the past six years and more began to rise to the surface. In August a notorious editorial in the pro-government newspaper *Kathimerini* carried the headline, 'Homeward . . .'. There must be 'no more blood wasted in continuing the adventure imposed upon the people by the man who, unhappily for Greece, still lives' – meaning, of course, Venizelos. It was time for 'Asia Minor' (as Anatolia has historically been known in Greek since Roman times) 'to be given up to its noble inhabitants', an expression that seems to annul the very distinction between Greek Christian and Turkish Muslim upon which Greek national identity had been founded from the beginning. For Georgios Vlachos, the editor of the newspaper, who later claimed to have been writing at the behest of Gounaris, what was at stake was no longer the future of the 'liberated' nation but the honour and prestige of the Greek *state* and its institutions, the army especially.

Perhaps most chilling of all, though also prophetic, were the words of the High Commissioner of Smyrna, Aristeidis Stergiadis, the most senior Greek civilian official in Anatolia. Asked, when it was already too late to avert a humanitarian disaster, why he did nothing to help the Greek population to flee the city, Stergiadis is said to have replied, 'Better they stay here and be massacred by Kemal, because if they go to Athens they'll turn everything upside down.'[18] It was a fear that would linger, long after the bitter outcome of the 1922 campaign.

The end came suddenly, during the same hot weeks of late summer that, a year before, had seen the battle of the Sakarya river. The Turkish assault began at dawn on 26 August 1922, along a broad front. Two days later the Greek army was in full retreat. By 8 September the remnants of the defeated army had fallen back to the immediate hinterland of Smyrna. The order was given to bypass the city to the south and embark from the port of Çeşme, separated by only a narrow channel from the Greek island of Chios. It was an inglorious end to almost a century of expansionist dreams. The Grand Idea was dead.

The next day, 9 September, the vanguard of Kemal's army entered Smyrna. The date is still celebrated in the city, where Dokuz Eylül (9 September) University was founded as recently as 1982. The agony of the Greek and Armenian populations of Turkey was about to begin. Armenians, having nowhere else to go, were systematically murdered in their homes. For more than a week, Greek women and children from the interior had been streaming into the city. The famous 'Quay' of Smyrna, more than a mile of waterfront lined on the landward side with grand buildings in the neoclassical style, was jammed throughout its length by a desperate crowd of refugees. Allied warships stood off in the bay. Their crews were under strict orders to pick up only their own nationals. By night Turkish searchlights swept the crowds. Machine-gunners and snipers randomly opened fire into this mass of humanity, and picked off those who tried to swim towards the safety of the ironclads. Only the timely intervention of an American philanthropist, who chartered a fleet of merchant ships, enabled many thousands to escape before Kemal's deadline passed for all Greek subjects of the former Ottoman Empire to leave the city. Most of those were women, children and the elderly. Men of military age had already been rounded up, to be conscripted into labour gangs and put to work in the interior.

The city itself would soon be engulfed in flames. The fire that destroyed the greater part of 'infidel Smyrna' during three days, beginning on 13 September, has been variously blamed on arson by Armenians, Greeks, the victorious Turkish army or the irregulars that followed in its wake. Whether intended or not (and there are indications that it may have been), the effect of the fire was to cleanse the city of almost all visible signs of a Greek, Christian and European presence that went back centuries and had made Smyrna one of the greatest cultural meeting places and commercial centres of the Levant.

It is not known how many Christians – Greeks and Armenians – lost their lives in and around Smyrna and in other parts of Anatolia between 1921 and 1923. The number is generally reckoned to run into hundreds of thousands. Even this huge toll reflects only one part of the total losses, on all sides, during the twelve-year 'War of the Ottoman Succession' that was only now coming to an end. It has been estimated that by 1923 the total population that had been living within the borders of the empire in 1911, Muslim and Christian combined, had fallen by some 20 per cent – a casualty rate, including flows of refugees both into and out of the empire, of one in five.[19]

In the annals of the modern Republic of Turkey, which would be formally inaugurated just over a year later, the taking of İzmir (Smyrna) marks the crowning victory of the nation's 'war of independence'. For Greeks, the destruction of the city and the mass killings and deportations that followed are remembered as the horrific climax to the 'Asia Minor Catastrophe', often shortened to just 'the Catastrophe'.

RETRIBUTION

In Greece, at the time, the response was swift and deadly. The ashes of Smyrna had barely had time to cool before army officers among the troops evacuated to the nearby islands of Chios and Lesbos formed a Revolutionary Committee on 26 September. The Committee demanded the resignation of the entire government and the immediate abdication of King Constantine, as collectively responsible for the disaster. Before the ships carrying the revolutionaries had even reached Piraeus, a panic-stricken government had conceded all their demands. King Constantine left the country on the last day of the month, this time for good. His eldest son inherited the throne as George II. Some twelve thousand of the troops that had been so recently defeated outside Smyrna now marched into Athens. The Revolutionary Committee took over the government. The opportunity for a catharsis that might have swept away the vicious divisions of the last few years seemed quickly to fade. Within weeks the dominant forces behind the new military government emerged as loyal to Venizelos. The former prime minister himself kept his distance from Greece, but agreed to represent the regime abroad.

In the meantime, and in the face of horrified pleas from foreign governments and their representatives in Athens, a show trial was set up to convict the five politicians and one military commander deemed the most to blame for the disaster. The 'Six', as they have been remembered ever since, were shot by firing squad on the hilltop of Goudi, where the whole cycle of triumph and disaster had begun with the putsch back in 1909 that had first brought Venizelos to power. So ended the careers of former prime minister Dimitrios Gounaris; Foreign Minister Georgios Baltatzis; Minister for War Georgios Theotokis; Petros Protopapadakis, who had had the misfortune to be prime minister at the time; Nikolaos Stratos, a bitter personal enemy of Venizelos who had just had the portfolio for foreign affairs thrust upon him; and the army Chief of Staff, Georgios Chatzianestis.

The charge of high treason on which the 'Six' were convicted by a court martial was of course absurd. Nobody, the condemned men included, had ever had the slightest desire or intention to damage, let alone destroy, their country and its interests. But both the charge and the savagery of the sentence reflected exactly the language of accusations and counter-accusations that had been flying between Venizelists and their opponents since the early years of the First World War. 'Treason' had come to stand for the wrong interpretation of where the country's interests truly lay. The 'Six' were obvious scapegoats, judicially murdered in a paroxysm of collective humiliation and revenge for failure. And, as has been observed, this bloodletting would only serve to leave the question of real blame for the catastrophe festering below the surface – for generations afterwards.[20]

This opens up the question of Venizelos's own share of responsibility. For those who had feared and loathed his policies and his influence from the beginning, or been victimized during the years of the 'Venizelist terror', it was axiomatic that the arch-culprit had to be Venizelos himself. Since at least 1915 he had been routinely branded a 'traitor' by his opponents. For the rest of his life, and long after it ended, this substantial section of Greek society could not forgive Venizelos and his supporters, either for the national humiliation in Anatolia or for the execution of the 'Six'. More sober historians, not otherwise hostile to Venizelos or his legacy, at the time and since, have also been reluctant to absolve him.

Something like a consensus has emerged that the root cause of the disaster lay in Venizelos's decision to accept the mandate of the Allies and land troops in Smyrna in 1919. By the time of his electoral defeat a year and a half later, he had compounded the error by failing to recognize the true nature of the Turkish nationalism that he was up against. His plan for a new military campaign against Kemal in the interior of Anatolia was therefore doomed from the beginning. Its eventual failure was the fault of Venizelos, who had started it, not of his successors, who had merely pursued it to the bitter end. And anyway, a Greek enclave in western Anatolia would never have been viable (as General Metaxas had warned back in 1915). No frontier in that region would have been defensible against attack from the east by the Turks. To have cut off Smyrna from its Muslim Turkish hinterland would have made no economic sense either. Within a few years, if Greek rule had continued, Smyrna would have lost all reason to exist.[21] So it has been persuasively argued.

There is inevitably something speculative about all such questions. But, to take the second point first, compare the fortunes of Salonica. The physical setting and economic history of both cities are very similar. So, even, was their traditional urban layout, before each was destroyed by fire, the one in 1917, the other in 1922. The Greek population of Smyrna was larger both as an absolute number and as a proportion of the total than was the Greek population of Salonica. Salonica, too, has been to various degrees cut off from its hinterland since it became part of Greece in 1912. This includes the half-century when the 'Iron Curtain' that divided Europe during the Cold War ran just fifty kilometres to its north. Greece's frontiers in Macedonia and Thrace, established between 1913 and 1923, would prove impossible to defend on the one occasion when they were attacked, in 1941. Imagine that a Greek frontier in western Anatolia had been negotiated between Venizelos and Kemal, and consolidated by a much less drastic movement of populations than in fact took place. After all, Venizelos's diplomacy with Kemal's representative İsmet Pasha at Lausanne in 1923, and with Kemal himself in 1930, would prove his pragmatic skill in negotiating a settlement in circumstances much less favourable to Greece than existed in 1920 and 1921. Ironically enough, had that happened, Greece's Anatolian province, adjacent to neutral Turkey, might have been the only part of the country to escape occupation by Axis forces twenty years later.

And then there is the fateful decision to go into Anatolia at all, in 1919. The key lies in the fact that Venizelos only, and always, went into action when he was assured of Great Power backing.[22] He had that backing in 1919. He had it also in 1920 when he ordered his troops to extend their zone of occupation, both in Anatolia and in Thrace. He was *seeking* it again at the time when he fell from office. Without far more robust guarantees than were available to his successors, Venizelos would never have pressed ahead with the offensives of 1921. But even without those guarantees, it is remarkable how close that campaign came to success. The battle of the Sakarya river was very nearly won by the Greeks. The Turks had made preparations to abandon Ankara. Even Kemal himself seems to have experienced moments of despair, and might have given up the struggle.[23] Allied forces, even though they no longer actively supported the Greeks, remained in control of Constantinople and the straits between the Aegean and the Black Sea. Their resolution to retain that foothold in former Ottoman territory had not yet been tested. (When it was, in the Chanak crisis of September and October 1922, the climb-down that followed would cost the British prime minister, Lloyd George, his job.) From a purely military point of view, the balance of advantage was still with the Greeks, even at the time of the Turkish counter-offensive in August of that year. If the morale of the Greek troops had been better, it has been suggested, that battle could well have gone the other way.[24]

So defeat in Anatolia was still not inevitable, three years after Venizelos had first committed Greek troops, and almost two years after his own fall from power. Even without the logistical and diplomatic advantages that would have been available to Greece in the meantime if Venizelos had retained the premiership, the supposedly 'doomed' tactic of defeating Kemal by military force still came closer than is often realized to success.

Venizelos's fundamental mistake, if there was one, goes much farther back. His brilliance at negotiating with foreign statesmen had not been matched by his political skills at home. It was Venizelos who forced the 'National Schism' upon the country by his early insistence that Greece should join the Triple Entente. Even the Entente powers themselves thought this premature. He could have bided his time. He could have worked with King Constantine and the General Staff. He could have directed his genius for persuasion where it was most needed, which was also the place closest to home. The loss of trust between these two camps seems to have come about very early on, and the consequences of that loss would prove irreparable. The whole logic of Venizelos's expansionist plan for the state was based on his Cretan, outsider's perception of the *nation*. If he was to prevail, he would have had to sell that perception to the leaders and the populace of an Old Greece who had become used to the comfortable certainties that had grown on them since the arrival of the Bavarians in the 1830s.

Entirely indicative is the perception of General Metaxas, King Constantine's former Chief of Staff and the future dictator who would lead Greece into the Second World War. Writing in a private letter, at the moment in July 1914 when war seemed finally inevitable, Metaxas had confided, 'In the midst of this great disaster, I hope for our dear *little* Greece to be spared.'[25] Much the same view, shorn of its evident personal sincerity, could be read daily in the royalist press throughout the height of the 'Schism'. Venizelos and his supporters would rant against what they saw as small-minded parochialism, while they championed, instead, the boundless horizons of the 'Nation'. Where Venizelos failed was in not recognizing, and giving them their due, the passion and sincerity of those who wished to preserve intact a 'small honourable Greece'. Seemingly unable to understand the perspective of his opponents, Venizelos resorted to means that were the very opposite of diplomatic. Once he had concluded, probably around the summer of 1915, that the only way to gain his objectives was by overthrowing the constitutional basis for the government that he led – by repudiating the authority of the king – every step that Venizelos took would strengthen his hand abroad, but weaken it fatally at home.

It was there, back in 1914, if not even earlier, that the seeds of the disaster lay. But on one thing Venizelos cannot be faulted: he had fully absorbed the lesson of 1897. Every one of Greece's military advances and diplomatic gains between 1912 and 1920 was made in alliance with foreign partners. Military and diplomatic campaigns were run in tandem, each feeding into the other, and each responsive to opportunities and constraints experienced by the other. In 1921 and 1922, even if it was a close-run thing, it was the unwillingness or inability of the royalist Greek government to restore that partnership that made the difference – and must indeed have made itself felt, down to the morale of the humblest conscript facing the Turkish barrage in August 1922. Greece had been created in the first place, and had expanded its borders since, through diplomacy as much as on the battlefield. The immediate cause of the 'Catastrophe' was the failure of diplomacy. And that was a mistake that Venizelos himself would never have made.

It was Venizelos who represented Greece at the peace talks, arranged under the auspices of the recently formed League of Nations in the Swiss lakeside town of Lausanne. His negotiating hand was weak. Mustafa Kemal's representative, İsmet Pasha, later known as İnönü, was intransigent, and in a position to push through his side's demands. A full peace treaty would take until the following July to hammer out. Its terms would include international recognition for Kemal's Turkey as the newest among several new nation states created after the First World War – a process of nation-building throughout the continent that had begun with recognition of Greece almost a century before.

But the most pressing question weighing upon the negotiators at Lausanne, when they met in November 1922, was how to deal with an immediate humanitarian crisis. Some eight hundred thousand Greeks had already fled from Anatolia. A quarter of a million more were streaming out of Eastern Thrace, evacuated by the Greek army in October. İsmet made it plain that the new Turkish government was not prepared to have them back. The upshot was a bold plan. At the time, it was unprecedented on such a scale. The Convention of Lausanne, signed on 30 January 1923, would set a baleful legacy for the resolution of future conflicts throughout the remainder of the twentieth century and beyond.

The opening article of the Convention set out starkly what had been agreed by the Greek and Turkish plenipotentiaries:

As from 1st May, 1923, there shall take place a compulsory exchange of Turkish nationals of the Greek Orthodox religion established in Turkish territory, and of Greek nationals of the Moslem religion established in Greek territory.

These persons shall not return to live in Turkey or Greece respectively without the authorization of the Turkish Government or of the Greek Government respectively.

The only exceptions allowed were for Greeks living in Constantinople, the islands of Imbros and Tenedos, which were awarded to Turkey, and the Muslim community of western Thrace, which remained part of Greece.[26]

At a stroke, almost the entire Greek nation had now to be crammed within the existing borders of the Greek state. In a way that had never been intended, the Grand Idea, which had been left for dead on the battlefields outside Smyrna, would be fulfilled after all. But the rupture that had opened up during the First World War would not be healed for another half-century.

8

Starting Over

1923–1940

For the first time in Greek history the overwhelming majority of Greek speakers were now citizens of the political state that had been created out of the Revolution of a hundred years before. As a result, the two decades after 1922 present many parallels with the earliest years of independence, back in the 1830s and 1840s. Once again, everything had to be built almost from scratch. Once again, just as during the time of the Bavarians, the quest was on: how to be at once *Greek* and *modern*, which really meant western European. New ideas, new openings towards Europe, and particularly the West, were everywhere. Just as had happened then, the eastern heritage of Byzantium and Orthodox Christianity was once again eclipsed in favour of a redefined direct line leading from the high points of classical Hellenic civilization to the present day. It made sense: the geographical heartland of that ancient civilization, with its rival centres of Athens and Sparta, coincided as neatly as it ever had with the now more or less fixed frontiers of the Greek state. Historical memories of the Byzantine millennium were too painfully linked to those eastern horizons that had been lost for ever when the Greek army scuttled out of Anatolia.

The two decades that followed the 'Catastrophe' of 1922 were a time of remarkable renewal. They had to be. The political foundations of the state had been all but broken. The economy was in ruins. Economically and socially, Greece was a poorer, more backward country during the interwar period than it had been before the decade of upheavals.[1] The same had been true a century earlier, when it emerged from the devastation caused by the Revolution. In both periods, authoritarian government was either a reality or an ever-present threat, more than at most other times in Greece's modern history. Once again, just as in the 1830s, when people spoke of the 'nation' what they meant was the state. Renewal during the 1920s and 1930s would be concentrated, to an unprecedented and eventually extreme degree, on the Greek state and state institutions.

RECOVERY AND RENEWAL

The resettlement of the refugees from Turkey after 1922 has rightly been called the 'Greek state's greatest peacetime achievement'.[2] But, like other achievements of the Greek state in its nearly two-hundred-year history, this one was built upon international cooperation. An international relief effort was coordinated by the recently established League of Nations. Headed by the American diplomat Henry Morgenthau, it would last for seven years. A mediating role at the Lausanne conference had been played by the Norwegian former polar explorer Fridtjof Nansen, in his capacity as the League's first High Commissioner for Refugees. Foreign loans, brokered by the League, would be necessary too. Once again, the way forward for Greece would not be a matter for Greeks alone.

Exactly how many people came to Greece as refugees between 1922 and 1925 will never be known. The most reliable estimates put the number at between 1.3 and 1.4 million. That is equivalent to just over a quarter of the total population of the country before they arrived. The same proportion of new arrivals in the United Kingdom in 2019 would give a total of sixteen million migrants to be absorbed over a three-year period. For the United States the figure would be a staggering eighty million. The Lausanne Convention had stipulated that they were to be 'exchanged' for approximately one-third as many Muslims living in Greece, making a net influx into Greece of around one million. According to the census of 1928, the first to be undertaken after the exchange, one in five of the population of the Greek state was by that time a refugee.[3]

The country was transformed – not just demographically, but socially, politically, economically, even in its physical appearance. Shanty-towns sprang up all round the cities of Athens, Piraeus and

Salonica. Throughout the New Lands of Macedonia, Epiros and Thrace, the islands of the northern and eastern Aegean and Crete, as well as in Thessaly, which had been acquired by Greece as far back as 1881, Muslim families and communities that had been settled for generations were forced to leave, to make way for whole new settlements of incomers. Most of the minarets, which dotted the rural landscape and in older drawings and photographs dominate the skyline of Salonica, were torn down; mosques were converted into warehouses or cinemas. As for the displaced Muslims, few Greeks, either at the time or, it has to be said, since, were sorry to see them go. In Crete, the enforced departure of the 'Turcocretans', whose language was the island's dialect of Greek, was recorded by the art historian and novelist Pantelis Prevelakis, who had been an eyewitness:

> The army threw a cordon round the Turkish quarter, secured the entry to the harbour, and then called the Turks to pass in single file into the tenders . . . Fainting from grief . . . they came out of their houses with torn clothes, their hands bloodied; the women had thrown off their headscarves. They filed between a double line of soldiers, like thieves who had been caught red-handed, glancing sideways with reddened eyes, their mouths tight with the passion of their feelings.

Almost a century later, descendants of these people have retained their Cretan language and some Cretan customs, in the homeland to which they were displaced in western Anatolia.[4]

In Greece all eyes were on the plight of those arriving. Ambassador Morgenthau described what had already become a familiar sight, in the harbour of Salonica, in November 1923:

> I saw seven thousand people crowded in a ship that would have been taxed to normal capacity with two thousand. They were packed like sardines upon the deck, a squirming, writhing mass of human misery. They had been at sea for four days. There had not been space to permit them to lie down to sleep; there had been no food to eat; there was not access to any toilet facilities. For those four days and nights many had stood upon the open deck, drenched by an autumn rain, pierced by the cold night wind, and blistered by the

noonday sun. They came ashore in rags, hungry, sick, covered with vermin, hollow-eyed, exhaling the horrible odor of human filth – bowed with despair . . .[5]

This was more than a year after the rout of the Greek army in Anatolia and the burning of Smyrna. Conditions must have been unimaginably worse for all those who had fled from Smyrna, western Anatolia and eastern Thrace in the immediate aftermath of these events. What Morgenthau was witnessing was the Lausanne Convention in action: the consequence of the relatively orderly evacuation of Greek populations from further east, who had not been directly caught up in the fighting. Also on these ships would have been some of the men of military age taken as prisoners of war. Those who had survived notorious conditions in labour gangs in the interior of Turkey had finally been released after the Treaty of Lausanne brought an end to hostilities in July 1923.

It is often said that the refugees brought with them new skills, extra manpower, a broader outlook on the world, and even (this last is certainly true) spicier and more exotic tastes in food – all to the long-term benefit of Greece. It cannot have felt like that during the 1920s. Like most migrants in many different historical crises, these ones did not easily adjust to their new homes. Their arrival was greeted with a corresponding amount of fear and mistrust. The kind of abuse that had first been heard in Athens during the civil war of 1916, directed against those who had already fled from Ottoman persecution, became intensified in the 1920s. The incomers were not 'real' Greeks at all, but 'Turk-spawn', not real Christians but 'baptised in yoghurt'.[6]

They came from all social classes. Some had left behind towns and cities, others were farmers or pastoralists. Many found themselves resettled in environments to which they were unsuited: former city-dwellers in agricultural communities or vice versa, or farmers faced with types of soil, terrain and climate of which they had no experience. Some Orthodox Christians expelled from the interior of Anatolia spoke not Greek but Turkish. Others, such as the Pontians from the region around Trebizond on the Black Sea coast, brought with them a dialect that enthusiasts like to claim is closer than any other to ancient Greek, but was (and is) hard for Greeks from any-where else to understand. For the next twenty years, 'refugees' as a category would stand out as an unassimilated (and huge) factor in Greek social and political life. One of the most notorious of the refugee settlements, on the outskirts of Piraeus, would later enter the mythology of the Greek left under the nickname of Kokkinia (Red-Town), a name that even today has all but eclipsed the official Nikaia (after Nicaea, home of the Nicene Creed, today's Turkish city of İsnik). True assimilation can probably be dated from as late as the 1980s.

Other groups that remained in place, though they were much smaller, would prove even harder to assimilate. If the exchange of populations had relieved the Greek state of the need to find an accom-modation with most of its Muslim subjects, there remained (and remains today) a Muslim minority in western Thrace, protected, and to some extent isolated from the rest of the country, by the terms of the Lausanne Convention. The Muslims of western Thrace are the only officially recognized ethnic minority in Greece. Other Muslims exempted from the exchange were the Albanian-speaking Tsamides, or Chams, of Epiros. In other parts of the same region were (and still are) communities of Vlachs, Christians who speak a language close to Romanian. Jewish communities had existed for centuries in several parts of Greece and were Greek-speaking (these were the Romaniot Jews). But the community in Salonica, still more than fifty thousand strong in the 1920s, maintained a distinct identity linked to its Spanish-derived language as well as the Jewish religion. Macedo-nia, in the 1920s and 1930s, would continue to be home to many who had previously adhered to the Bulgarian Church, and who still spoke their own Slavic dialect. No Greek government has ever recognized this group, known colloquially as 'Slavo-Macedonians', as an official minority, although between the wars they may have numbered as many as a quarter of a million.[7]

The state was now home to far fewer unwilling subjects than it had been between 1913 and 1923. But all of these groups that remained, no less than the incoming refugees who were regarded as ethnically Greek but often despised for being 'other', would come under intense pressure to assimilate during the next two decades.[8] Even after the distinction between the state and the wider nation had been all but erased, the centralized state would struggle to impose homogeneity upon its diverse subjects. When something approaching homogeneity did come, it would be due not to the Greek state but to its total collapse during the 1940s, to the horrors of a world war and a brutal occupation. Most of those divergent groups, for different reasons, would pay dearly for their difference when that time came.

Despite these formidable challenges, the rest of the 1920s saw some remarkable successes. The refugees were housed, and the worst of the damage to the economy was repaired. Young intellectuals and artists of the upcoming generation were being formed in a crucible of competing ideas and impulses. Writing during the next decade, one of their number, Giorgos Theotokas, in his panoramic novel *Argo*, depicted the young university students of that time as 'Argonauts', who argued passionately over every new philosophical, political or artistic idea or movement, but were united by a melancholy determination to live up to the 'great name' they had inherited. For these young men, and a smaller number of women, now was the time:

> . . . to free themselves from a sterile past, to gaze out to sea, to live once more the life of the spirit, no longer as humble imitators of their great ancestors and belated disciples of foreigners, but as explorers, as conquerors, as true Hellenes.[9]

Theotokas was looking back at the formative years of what would prove to be an extraordinarily creative generation, not just in literature but in all the arts. In literature they have come to be known as the 'Generation of the Thirties'. But they had been formed during the previous decade, in the immediate aftermath of the Asia Minor Catastrophe. Theotokas's own debut came in 1929, in the form of a polemical manifesto for a new era of the arts in Greece. Entitled *Free Spirit*, the book begins with the author imagining himself looking down at the European continent from an aircraft far above. From such a height, the distinctions between one country and another begin to fade. *Free Spirit* argues that Europe, for all its tribal differences, is a single entity, and that Greeks ought to go out and embrace their destiny within it. The Catastrophe had blown away an entire world. Just as the rest of Europe was reinventing itself after the trauma of the Great War, the creative energy of the young in Greece was ready to seize the moment: 'The time is ripe for bold pioneers,' Theotokas concluded.[10]

An early poem by Theotokas's friend, the poet George Seferis, kicks over the traces of traditional verse-making to celebrate a symbol of these modern horizons in their city. The poem is entitled 'Syngrou Avenue, 1930', and it evokes the wide, straight boulevard that had recently been completed to link the centre of Athens with the sea at Phaliro, named after the banker and benefactor from Constantinople, Andreas Syngros.[11] Both writers had been born and had spent their earliest years as citizens of the Ottoman Empire – Seferis in Smyrna, Theotokas in Constantinople. Both had recently settled in Athens after studying in Paris. Odysseus Alepoudelis was still there at the end of the 1920s, imbibing the spirit of newly minted Surrealism and translating the poetry of one of the movement's champions, Paul Éluard. When he returned to Greece and began publishing his own exuberantly surrealist poetry in the 1930s, Alepoudelis would adopt the pseudonym of Elytis, partly in homage to Éluard. Later in the century, Seferis and Elytis would each be awarded the Nobel Prize for Literature, in 1963 and 1979, respectively.

These are some of the best-known names. But there were many others. The turn of the decade saw an unprecedented spate of published poetry and fiction that experimented with new ideas and new techniques that were causing excitement (and often outrage) in Paris, London or New York. The same thing was happening in the other arts. In 1925, Dimitris Pikionis returned to Greece after studying in Paris and Munich to become one of the leading influences on Greek architecture for many decades. Pikionis is best known for his landscaping of the lower slopes surrounding the Acropolis of Athens in the 1950s. In painting, Nikos Hadjikyriakos-Ghikas, the surrealist Nikos Engonopoulos, Giannis Tsarouchis and Giannis Moralis were all undergoing their formative experiences at this time. The composer Nikos Skalkottas was scraping a living in Berlin, determined to follow in the footsteps of the musical avant-garde led by Arnold Schoenberg, before returning to Greece in 1933. Dimitri Mitropoulos, best known as the conductor of the New York Philharmonic in the 1950s, was also an avant-garde composer and followed a similar path until his departure for the United States. All of these innovators in the creative arts, some sooner, some much later, would achieve international recognition on a scale never achieved by any other Greek generation before or since.

And it was not only the young. Nikos Kazantzakis, now in his forties, had turned to Communism, and in 1928 published an account of his travels in Soviet Russia. At the same time he was starting to work on what may well be the longest poem ever published, his sequel to Homer's *Odyssey*. Another larger-than-life figure from the same generation, Angelos Sikelianos, with his American wife Eva Palmer, instituted festivals of ancient Greek drama at Delphi in 1927 and 1930. The performances were intended to recreate the total experience that ancient drama must once have been, matching the words of the text to music and dance as well as the visual elements of staging. Ancient theatre in this way became an ultra-modern art form. For the first time the new medium of cinematography was used to capture a performance of an ancient Greek play performed in its original setting. Although they had no immediate sequels, these Delphic festivals were the distant precursors of the international arts festivals that since the 1950s have flourished all over the world, not least in Greece itself, at the theatres of Herodes Atticus in Athens and at Epidaurus.

During the later 1920s and 1930s, Greek cultural and intellectual life was infused with an abundance of youthful energy. The same could not be said for the political class or political institutions. It was an ageing generation that was in control. And even proper control proved hard to establish during the first years after the Catastrophe, as the divisions of the previous decade continued to play out.

POLITICIANS AND GENERALS

The military that had been so roundly defeated abroad had returned in 1922 to take charge at home. It was a 'revolutionary' government that had executed the Six in November of that year. Then in October 1923 came an attempt at a counter-revolutionary coup by officers loyal to King George II. The attempt failed. But it was to prove the first of many such interventions during the interwar period. It was the army, not the politicians, still less the public at large, that first made an issue out of the monarchy in Greece.

Traditionally the armed forces had been fiercely loyal to the throne – and during the Balkan wars to their commander-in-chief, Crown Prince Constantine. But going all the way back to the discontents that had led to the first coup of 1909, there had been a small coterie who had wanted to do away with the monarchy altogether. The division between these two groups had been magnified out of all proportion by the series of purges and counter-purges of the officer corps that had begun in 1916. For every senior officer on active service there was at least one more who had been removed from the same post, waiting in the wings. Throughout the interwar period Greece had in effect two corps of senior officers, while there were only enough jobs for one. The rivalry between them was no longer in any meaningful sense between political allegiances: it was simply a matter of keeping your job (if you had one) or getting it back (if you didn't). Over the next twenty years it was support for the monarch or support for a republic that would prove to be the way to do this. Political leaders almost invariably, throughout those years, would find themselves in hock to the bitterly opposed factions of the military.

Return to nominally civilian rule at the end of 1923 did nothing to change this. In a typically self-defeating gesture the first parliamentary election held since the Catastrophe, in December, was boycotted by all the parties of the royalist, anti-Venizelist opposition. For a few brief weeks at the start of 1924, Venizelos was back as elected prime minister. But not even he had the authority to put the army back in its box. The monarchy was abolished by a vote of yet another Constituent Assembly in March. After a referendum to confirm the vote, Greece became officially a republic in April. For the next half-century the monarchy would become one of the most fiercely contested issues in Greek political life.

Nobody seems to have been very surprised, let alone roused to protest, when in the summer of 1925 General Theodoros Pangalos abolished the Constituent Assembly and soon afterwards set himself up as President. As a young officer, Pangalos had been one of the architects of the 1909 'revolution' at Goudi that had brought Venizelos to power. Pangalos lasted only a little over a year, before being ousted by a rival general. Georgios Kondylis would soon bow to pressure and reinstate parliamentary rule. For a few months in 1927 the main parties tried setting their differences aside and ruling in coalition. But by early the next year that was not working well either. The stage was set for the elderly Venizelos to present himself as the only leader who could reunite the fractured nation.

Venizelos had declared repeatedly that he had retired from politics. But then, in April 1927, he returned from self-imposed exile to his old home in Crete. A year later, he placed himself at the head of a newly invigorated Liberal Party. On 19 August 1928, a few days short of his sixty-fourth birthday, his party was elected to power with the biggest landslide in Greek electoral history. Together with smaller splinter groups, the Venizelists had captured 223 seats out of 250. Writing when it was all over, Theotokas chose to place the scene of Venizelos's return to parliament close to the climax of his novel:

> [He was] tall, straight, robust and slim, his cheeks glowing, in the pink of health, smiling in all directions an enigmatic smile that combined fatherly tenderness, womanly vanity and superior irony; autocratic and affable, easy-going, open-hearted, intimate and fearsomely strong-willed, effortlessly master of himself and all around him, a hard man but one of uncommon grace, exquisite cunning and flexibility: this was Prime Minister Eleftherios Venizelos, son of Odysseus, full of sinew, passion, strength, spirit and above all artistry.[12]

It was a moment of delirious triumph for supporters such as Theotokas and most of those who, like him, had been displaced from the new Turkey. It marked the start of the only stable, democratically elected government to hold power in Greece between the two world wars. Here, finally, was the opportunity for reconciliation that had eluded all parties for so long. Statesman of world stature that he undoubtedly was (never mind the hyperbole), Venizelos now held in his hands the mandate to heal the split that he himself had played such a large part in creating. His programme, he declared, would change the face of Greece and make the country 'unrecognizable'. It was the beginning of what has been called a 'second Golden Age of

Venizelism'.[13] The hopes and aspirations of Theotokas and his generation seemed about to be fulfilled.

It began well enough. An ambitious programme of economic and social reforms revived and carried forward initiatives that went back almost twenty years, to Venizelos's first period in office, and had since stalled. Brigandage, that scourge of rural life in Greece that the Bavarians had first tried to kill off a century before, was finally eradicated. A social security system that still exists today was inaugurated. A new Agricultural Bank, reforms to land tenure, reclamation of marshes, all boosted the prosperity and life chances of a population that still primarily lived off the land.

Still bolder initiatives came in foreign policy. Security had yet to be fully guaranteed within the new frontiers of the state – as had been shown by incidents involving Italy in 1923 and Bulgaria in 1925. From the moment of the Greek defeat in Anatolia, Venizelos had accepted the geopolitical realities of the new Greece. Systematically he set about creating regional alliances with former rivals and enemies. One by one, he mended fences with Italy, Albania and newly christened Yugoslavia. Romania had already been brought on side by the previous government. Venizelos did his best to reach an understanding with Bulgaria, too. The most dramatic of all these diplomatic achievements was a far-reaching 'Pact of Friendship, Neutrality, Conciliation and Judicial Statement', signed at the end of October 1930 between the two modern republics, Greece and Turkey. This was the policy that would lead to the establishment of a 'Balkan Entente' in 1934, consisting of Greece, Romania, Turkey and Yugoslavia. Only Bulgaria, of the regional powers, remained unreconciled, though relations were at least better than they had been.

On the wider stage, Venizelos's visits to Paris and London, early in his premiership, were designed to rebuild good relations with the remaining 'protecting powers' from the previous century, without being as dependent as in the past. Russia, now the Union of Soviet Socialist Republics, had by this time long renounced all obligations inherited from the former tsarist regime. With Britain and France what mattered to Venizelos was not so much hundred-year-old guarantees as capital investment and (as ever) the availability of loans. On these fronts he was successful, too – although his determination to follow Great Britain in adhering to the gold standard would soon prove the undoing of his country, and his government.

Part of that undoing, too, lay in another of those foreign-policy achievements. To reach a diplomatic understanding with Mustafa Kemal's Turkey, only eight years after their respective citizens had been murdering one another in their homes as well as on the battlefield, was a remarkable feat. Venizelos had to use all his oratorical skills to persuade parliament and public opinion that the traditional enemy must now become a friend. It was necessary to protect the integrity of the state. The price was the outstanding claims of the refugees. Effectively, those who had lost everything in their flight to Greece had to renounce any possibility of future compensation. But there was more to it than money. Although the wording of the settlement actually made it possible for individuals once again to move between and buy property in the two countries, its political impact was the exact opposite: one in five of the Greek electorate had now to come to terms with the reality that the homes they had lost were lost for ever. Up to now, the refugee population had voted, almost to a man, for the Liberals or other pro-Venizelist parties. No longer. The electoral cost of this would not be counted for another two years, by which time further disasters had beset the Liberal government.

Venizelos's government had been only a little over a year old, in October 1929, when the Wall Street Crash brought the international banking and financial systems tumbling down. While the world's most advanced economies were gripped by the Great Depression, Greece had at first been let off relatively lightly. Then in September 1931 Britain abruptly left the gold standard. The value of the pound plummeted. At once the drachma and the Greek economy came under intolerable pressure. For the second time in its history the country was obliged to default on its external debts, in effect to declare bankruptcy. This happened on 25 April 1932. The government, despite its huge majority in parliament, was already tottering. A series of bad harvests had worsened the economic crisis. Scandals and splits within the Liberal Party had weakened Venizelos's authority. He himself was not implicated in any wrongdoing. But Venizelos had never been one to consult or confide in his ministers. Lack of trust and a degree of personal arrogance had left him increasingly isolated as he approached his seventieth year.

Nothing damaged Venizelos's electoral chances more than the failure of his economic policy of pegging the drachma to sterling and the gold standard, and the fallout from his rapprochement with Ankara. The collapse of the international tobacco trade, heavily concentrated in the New Lands where Liberal support had always been strongest, added to the turmoil. Recognizing that the tide was turning away from him, Venizelos fought the election campaign of September 1932 on a ticket that explicitly reopened old wounds: what he called the 'civil war continuing since 1915' must now be won, either by conciliation or by the victory of one side.[14] Politically, after Greece's second bankruptcy in 1932, the chance to heal the rift that went back to the First World War had all but vanished. Far from dampening down the old divisions, or trying to bridge them, politicians and their supporters in the military, on both sides, now began to vie with one another to rekindle the hatreds of almost twenty years before. It made matters worse that all the political leaders of any consequence were of an age to have been shaped by the polarization of that time. While the young people of the generation of Theotokas and Seferis were transforming the arts in Greece, the political class seems to have been starved of new blood or new ideas.

The election resulted in a close tie between the Liberals and the People's Party, now led by Panagis Tsaldaris, 'an essentially well-meaning, provincial lawyer with none of Venizelos's charisma, energy, or vision'.[15] All the advantages that had been gained by the spectacular victory of the Liberals four years before had been dissipated. First Tsaldaris and then Venizelos formed a precarious government that fell at the first vote of confidence. A new election in March 1933 again brought equal numbers of votes to both sides, but this time the electoral system gave a majority to the People's Party. Enter, once again, the generals.

The military had been sidelined as a political force during Venizelos's four-year term of office. Now, they were back. On the day after the election, one of the Liberals' most vigorous supporters in the armed forces staged a military coup to try to overturn the result.

Nikolaos Plastiras had form: he had been one of the two officers who seized power and created the 'revolutionary' government after the defeat of 1922. Like most such attempts between the wars, this one petered out after a few days from sheer lack of support. Venizelos was still politician enough to distance himself from the officers who had acted in his name.

But the political world was slipping inexorably beyond the control of parliament and towards violence. In June the same year, Venizelos and his wife narrowly escaped assassination when the car carrying them was chased by gunmen and shot through with bullets on the road between Athens and Kiphisia. The government was accused of dragging its feet, when little seemed to be done to bring perpetrators to justice. During the next two years, while the People's Party was in power, fist fights broke out in parliament. Venizelos did nothing to calm matters by thundering from the wings about an impending 'explosion, which could take the form of a most savage civil war'.[16]

On 1 March 1935 the explosion came. Plastiras tried again. And this time his attempt had the full support of his political master, Venizelos. In conception and execution, it was a textbook case of a general (and a politician) fighting the last campaign instead of the next one. Exactly as had happened in 1916, the coup attempted to set the New Lands against Old Greece, with simultaneous uprisings in Crete, the islands and Macedonia. Rather than challenge the government directly, the conspirators seem to have aimed once again to divide the country and set up their own administration in the 'co-capital' of Salonica. Fighting broke out in the north. For a few days, the Tsaldaris government was paralysed. This has led some to suggest that 'with better planning and leadership' the coup 'might have succeeded'.[17]

But Plastiras failed. Both he and Venizelos fled the country. They were tried and condemned to death in their absence. Venizelos would never return, and would die in Paris a year later. But Plastiras still had a future in Greek politics. Three lower-ranking conspirators, less fortunate, were subjected to show trials and executed. Others were publicly humiliated. All senior ranks of the military were purged, along with the civil service and the judiciary. If Venizelos had set out to take the country back to 1916 by endorsing Plastiras's action, their enemies in revenge had taken it, instead, back to 1922 and the execution of the Six.

The dust had barely settled from those events when a half-hearted election campaign took place under martial law. This was lifted only just in time for the election itself, on 9 June. Venizelists, subjected to intimidation just as they had been in 1916, repeated the classic, self-defeating mistake of boycotting the contest. This time it hardly mattered. The anti-Venizelists in the military were in no mood to rely on any political party, not even the one that had brought them back from the wilderness. These were men who had been marginalized for a dozen years and had only recently been swept back into positions of power by the tide of reprisals against the perpetrators of the failed coup. The only way to put an end to Venizelism for good would be to abolish the republic and bring back King George II from his exile in England. Nobody necessarily thought that restoration of the monarchy would heal the divisions, or bring any more stable government. On the contrary, it was to be the proof of who was in charge now, one in the eye for the hated Venizelists. The old 'Schism' was back in strength.

Its first casualty was the prime minister, Tsaldaris. The leader of the People's Party had been elected as the undisputed master of the chamber. But this did not prevent the chiefs of the armed forces from intercepting him in his car on his way into Athens, on 10 October 1935, and politely demanding his resignation. Later, it would be the parliamentary system itself that would fall victim to the same inveterate rivalries within the officer corps that had been simmering for twenty years.

The arrest of the elected prime minister by the military was in effect another coup d'état. This one brought to power General Georgios Kondylis – the same man who had toppled the unloved General Pangalos and had since changed sides and become a royalist. Kondylis's personal ambitions would fare no better on this second attempt. With the backing of the royalist faction in the military, his first act was to reimpose martial law. Under these conditions a rushed referendum on restoring the monarchy was held on 3 November. The result was an implausible 97.87 per cent of votes cast in favour of the king's return.

King George II of the Hellenes landed at Phaliro on 25 November 1935. Greece's first republic since independence had lasted for eleven and a half years. It has been dubbed, in a classic modern study, 'stillborn'. It had been founded on political expediency and jockeying for position within an officer corps whose ranks and whose political heft had been unnaturally swollen by the civil strife of the 1910s. Its roots were shallow and it failed to create long-lasting institutions. Neither the role of President nor the elected second chamber, which would be abolished along with it, ever attracted individuals of stature or achieved much influence. Had Venizelos chosen to run for President himself, as had briefly been a possibility at one time, things might have turned out differently. As it was, the demise of the republic was part and parcel of a wider political failure. The drift towards authoritarianism had been encouraged at different times and in different ways by both political factions. By 1935, there was a real fear of renewed civil war between them.[18]

The second King George was a very different man from the first, and still more different from his father. He had first come to the throne in 1922, when King Constantine had been bundled out of the country in the wake of the defeat in Anatolia. He had reigned for only eighteen months before sharing the same fate, though in his case without ever abdicating his throne. The experience had left him understandably embittered. Returning to the country that had already rejected him once, he was distrustful of the Greeks in general and Greek politicians in particular. Greece, he was once reported as saying, 'could not be regarded as a Western country. Greeks were Orientals and looked upon soft treatment as weakness.'[19] His parents and grandparents had been Danish, Russian and German. The first King George had set himself assiduously to become a leader of his people. After him, King Constantine had made himself more Greek than the Greeks, winning the hearts and minds of the soldiers he led into battle. The second King George was the first monarch since Otto who in his own eyes and those of his subjects seemed an outsider.

During his exile in England, he had made many friendships there, including with the British royal family, to whom he was also related. It was inevitable that he would find it easier to confide in the British Minister, Sir Sydney Waterlow, than in his own compatriots – just as both his father and Venizelos had done with rival foreign diplomats during the First World War. The return of King George ensured that Greece would enjoy good relations with Great Britain for as long as he remained on the throne. The mutual trust and reliance between the restored king and the British Foreign Office might have seemed to bring benefit in the short term to both countries. But, however well intentioned it may have been on both sides, this closeness would exert an extraordinary and distorting effect on Greek political life through-out the next decade.

To his credit, the king started well. He dismissed Kondylis and insisted on a free and fair parliamentary election. This was held in January 1936. For once, nobody boycotted it. The result was yet again an even draw between the Venizelists and the anti-Venizelists, led by the People's Party. Parliamentary government had been restored, but the impasse had not been resolved. There was a difference, though. This time, the balance of power was held by a party that until now had played only a marginal role in Greek politics. This is where the Communist Party of Greece (or KKE, to give it its Greek initials) enters the story.

THE FAULT LINE SHIFTS

The Socialist Labour Party of Greece had been launched in 1918. The initiative had been encouraged by Venizelos, who was seeking at the time to boost working-class support for his side of the 'National Schism'. Then in 1924 the party changed its name to the Communist Party of Greece, or KKE. At the same time it became an affiliate of the Comintern, the international body founded in 1919 by the Russian leader Vladimir Lenin. The ideology of the KKE would be rigidly aligned to the Soviet model – as indeed it remains to this day, long after the demise of the Soviet Union.

Over the next decade, a handful of communist deputies some-times won seats in parliament, but made little impact. Greece had almost no 'proletariat' to speak of, in the sense of an urban, indus-trial working class. But Communism found adherents in the tobacco industry, where large numbers were employed on low wages, and trade unionism was just beginning. It also began to have an appeal among a small number of intellectuals. Until 1935 the Comintern, perhaps influenced by lingering echoes of Russian pan-Slavism from the previous century, supported a separate state for the 'Slavo-Macedonians' of Greece's northern provinces. That, taken together with its renunciation of nations and nationalism in principle, was enough to alienate most shades of opinion among Greeks.

As an international movement that was putting down roots in Greece, however shallow, Communism had begun to alarm the Greek political establishment before the end of the 1920s. A knee-jerk reaction to a phenomenon that was feared but not well understood was a new law against the 'special offence' of subverting the 'established social order', brought in by Venizelos in July 1929. Known ever since as the 'Idionym' law (from the word for 'special' in Greek legalese), this measure was mainly directed against communists and trade unionists. It has often been held up, particularly by the Greek left, as proof of Venizelos's tendency towards authoritarianism. For the first time, it criminalized political opinions. During the remaining three years of Venizelos's term of office, some fifteen hundred people fell foul of this law. In 1931 the penalty of internal exile – usually to a remote island in the Aegean – was re-introduced specifically for this type of offence. Both the penalty and the 'Idionym' law itself would remain in force until 1974, by which time the number of actual or supposed communists had multiplied exponentially, and the number of internees in proportion.

In 1935 the Comintern changed its stance. Two years earlier, Hitler had come to power in Germany. Now, communists were encouraged to participate in a broad 'anti-fascist' front. Calls for Slavic speakers in Macedonia and Thrace to have their own state were dropped. The way was open for the KKE to win its fifteen seats in the Greek parliament. The risk that the communists might seize power in Greece and overturn the 'established social order' – something that so far had happened only in Russia, and under the very particular pressures of a world war – could easily be exaggerated. But during the first months of 1936 that order was indeed under very grave threat. To understand why, we have to look at what was happening in the Greek economy during those years.

Beginning with the Wall Street Crash in October 1929, Greece's agricultural exports had taken a severe hit. By 1932 production in tobacco, wine and currants had halved. Thousands of workers had been laid off. The total volume of foreign trade in 1932 had dropped by just over 60 per cent from the level of three years before. Gross National Product fell by a third, while unemployment grew by the same factor.[20] As international markets collapsed or were drastically reshaped, Greece, like other countries, was forced back on its own resources. 'Autarky' – self-sufficiency – became the watchword. In its last months Venizelos's Liberal government took a set of measures that were the polar opposite of economic liberalism. Tariffs were imposed on imports; domestic production was deliberately increased by government action. The state had never before intervened so drastically in managing the economy. And it really was the *state* that was intervening, not the government, once the measures had been set in place. Throughout the years of increasing political chaos between 1933 and 1936, the management of the economy was in the hands of those who would now be called 'technocrats' – officials of the Bank of Greece and the Agricultural Bank, and senior civil servants. Short-lived governments did little more than look on.

And the remarkable thing is that it worked. By 1935 observers both at home and abroad were astonished by the 'remarkable recovery from the crisis' and the 'perceptible atmosphere of prosperity [that] prevails compared to two or three years ago'. Intervention by the Agricultural Bank to promote new, more productive strains of wheat greatly reduced Greece's endemic reliance on imported cereals. But the very success of the economic upturn brought with it new instability and would play its part in realigning the fault line running through Greek social and political life during those years. In the new conditions, under protectionism and state intervention, the rich got richer and the poor poorer. As one historian puts it, 'It was economic *growth* which taxed the capacities of the existing system and pointed the way to an eventual realignment of political forces.'[21]

As inequalities grew, the state apparatus was less and less able to cope with the fallout. In 1935 and during the first months of 1936, strikes and demonstrations became frequent. In May 1936 a strike by tobacco workers in Salonica brought the city to a standstill. After more than a week of escalation, a mass demonstration on 9 May was confronted by the armed gendarmerie. Thirty-two people were killed, and more than three hundred injured. The British Minister, Sir Sydney Waterlow, had written to the Foreign Office just one month before these events:

> As new issues take shape, new lines of cleavage may be expected gradually to cut across the old, turning old hatreds into new channels . . . Perhaps the problem is insoluble: it may well be that parliamentary government will break down altogether.[22]

He was right. Four months later, it did. The blow, when it came, would come not from below, from the communists or the working class, but from above.

The name of Ioannis Metaxas has been a recurring, but mostly low-key, presence in these pages so far, going back all the way to his formative experience as a young army officer in the disastrous war of 1897. To most Greeks who followed public events during those years, he would have appeared in much the same light. Metaxas in the early months of 1936 was a man whose day was about to dawn. It happened that several of the elderly figures who had dominated Greek politics for two decades or more died during those months: the exiled Venizelos in March, then Tsaldaris, the leader of the People's Party, in May. General Kondylis (who had toppled two governments, once acting as a Venizelist and the second time as a royalist) had preceded them at the end of January. As luck would have it, in April the same fate befell the caretaker prime minister appointed by the king to oversee the stalemate in parliament until a proper government could be formed. Metaxas, aged sixty-five that month, was not the youngest among these men, but would prove still to have five years of life left in him. How Metaxas would use those years probably not even he could have foreseen.

For one thing, he hardly looked the part that he was about to play. 'General Metaxas is far from being endowed with the physical qualities necessary for success as a dictator,' wrote Waterlow's successor as British Minister in 1939. 'His short, corpulent, ill-dressed figure could never evoke popular enthusiasm.'[23] 'General' Metaxas had not worn a uniform since he had briefly served as Chief of Staff to King Constantine at the beginning of the First World War, and never would again. Propaganda photographs seem to glorify rather than to hide the paunch, the receding hair, and especially the rounded, chubby cheeks. His propagandists would promote Metaxas as a genial, paternal figure – the very antithesis of the fire and steel associated with Hitler, Mussolini or Stalin.

But Metaxas possessed steel of a different sort. Born into an aristocratic family from the Ionian islands, but in a country that from the beginning had never recognized aristocratic titles, Metaxas nurtured a lifelong veneration for Greece's only official hereditary institution, the royal family. He was no less devoted to the military discipline in which he had been trained as a young staff officer in Germany. Politically, his overriding concern had always been for the integrity of the Greek state. During the First World War, Metaxas had been the most articulate advocate for neutrality. Later, almost alone on the royalist side after Venizelos's electoral defeat in 1920, he had stood out against continuing the war in Anatolia. With a mixture of tenacity and shrewdness, Metaxas had established his own political party and stubbornly kept it going ever since. As capable of pragmatism as Venizelos, he had been the first political figure on the anti-Venizelist side to recognize the republic – a position that he had also been the first to repudiate, when the tide swung back after the failed Venizelist coup in 1935.

But, unlike Venizelos, Metaxas had never had much luck with the voters. His 'Party of the Liberal-Minded' (often misleadingly translated as 'Freethinkers') was neither named nor presented in a way that would easily appeal to those implacably opposed to Venizelos's 'Party of the Liberals'. In 1936, Metaxas's party won fewer seats than the communists. If the electorate had never warmed to Metaxas, neither had he to them. By this time he had come to despise the entire parliamentary system, as it had evolved in Greece over the last two decades. In this he was by no means alone. Venizelos had effectively reached the same conclusion when he gave his blessing to Plastiras's attempt to seize power by force.

So how it did happen? How did this unlikeliest of characters become, in effect, dictator for life on 4 August 1936?

The parliamentary arithmetic at the end of January allowed for only three possibilities. Either the Liberals or the anti-Venizelist bloc led by the People's Party could form an alliance with the communists to form a majority. Or the two great blocs, which between them held most of the seats, could settle their differences and work together to keep the communists out. An understanding between the anti-Venizelists and the communists was out of the question – their ideological differences were just too great. That left a Liberal–communist alignment, or one between the Liberals and the anti-Venizelists. Both were tried. And both fell at the same hurdle.

It took less than a month after the election for the Liberals and the communists to come up with a set of compromises that would allow them to form a government. But the military chiefs of staff would have none of it. The minister for military affairs in the caretaker administration visited King George to break the news. The king summoned Metaxas and placed him in charge of the ministry instead. Within days Metaxas had also been appointed deputy prime minister. The character of the caretaker government had changed. And it was the veto by the generals that had changed it.

Then on 13 April 1936 the interim prime minister, Konstantinos Demertzis, died. King George now exercised a prerogative that still existed, under the Constitution of 1864. He appointed as prime minister a man whose party held only seven out of three hundred seats in the chamber: Ioannis Metaxas. In hindsight it seems extraordinary that two weeks later Metaxas went on to win a vote of confidence with an overwhelming majority. In this way the deputies of the established political parties willingly sleepwalked towards the abolition of the democratic institution that they had been elected to serve.

Five days after winning the vote, Metaxas declared a parliamentary recess, to last until September. Events now moved rapidly. A wave of strikes, culminating in the violence in Salonica in May, gave credence to fears that a general uprising organized by the Communists was imminent. Metaxas did everything he could to ramp up those fears. They may have been genuinely shared by King George. Diplomatic observers at the time thought the risks were being much exaggerated, a view shared by historians since. Then in July came the second serious attempt by the political parties to form a government.

But this one, too, it soon turned out was no more acceptable to the armed forces than the previous deal with the communists had been. The price exacted by the Liberals for shoring up the anti-Venizelist bloc was to be the reinstatement of all those purged from the armed services in reprisal for the Venizelist coup attempt the previous year. This put the jobs of many serving officers on the line – the ones who had been drafted in to replace them and in many cases had themselves been the victims of previous purges.

The king appeared to accept the proposals of the party leaders to form a coalition. But it seems that this was the moment when he and Metaxas decided to act. The occasion and the pretext were provided when the General Confederation of Greek Workers called a twenty-four-hour general strike for Wednesday 5 August. The day before the strike was due to begin, martial law was declared, articles of the constitution were suspended, and parliament was dissolved. Soon afterwards, all political parties were disbanded, including Metaxas's own. The 'Regime of the Fourth of August' had begun.

Such was the climate of the time that no show of strength was even necessary. The day passed peacefully. There was no resistance. By the time anyone was minded to protest, it was too late. The reason that Metaxas and his spokesmen would give for their intervention, tirelessly and repetitively over the next days, months and years, was that it had been necessary to forestall a violent takeover by the communists.

The reality was different. What seems fundamentally to have motivated Metaxas, and enabled him to persuade the king to back him, was the fear that the old civil war of 1916 would be revived within the army. If the grand coalition of Venizelist and anti-Venizelist parties had been allowed to go ahead, there was a real prospect that the two rival corps of officers would have ended up fighting it out between them. Added impetus to these fears came from what had just happened in Spain.

Only two weeks before Metaxas's seizure of power, Spanish military units based in Morocco and in the Canary Islands had declared war on the Popular Front government that had recently been elected to power in the Spanish Republic. The Spanish Civil War that began in July 1936 would soon play out as a proxy war between Communism and Fascism. But that would not have been immediately obvious during its first weeks. What thoughtful Greek observers would have seen happening in Spain was a war waged by one half of the country's armed forces against the other. Perhaps the same thing really could have happened in Greece? We will never know. But we can at least judge by results. The intervention of General Franco in Spain in July 1936 started a civil war. That of General Metaxas in Greece, three weeks later, did not. On the other hand, whatever may have been the motivation of Metaxas and King George II, the consequence of their action in the long run would be not to prevent civil conflict, but only to postpone it.

The effect of the Metaxas regime would be the equivalent of pouring a deep layer of concrete over the shifting fault line that divided Greek society. When the plates began to move again, the nature of the forces driving them would have changed. The concrete did not suppress or diffuse the pressures that were building up. But it did make them split along a different axis. The KKE, a largely imaginary threat invented to excuse the seizure of power in 1936, would in the short term be almost destroyed by the Metaxas regime. But the rhetoric of that threat would go on to nourish the creature it was meant to destroy. Communism was not a significant force in Greece in 1936. Ten years later, it would have become one.

The Greek left, which despite official persecution would go on to dominate the country's intellectual life from the 1940s onwards, would paradoxically emerge as an unintended beneficiary of the Metaxas regime. Modern notions of left and right entered Greek politics with the imposition of a manifestly and extreme right-wing dictatorship in 1936. When the fault line once again broke through the concrete, in the next decade, it would be along the right–left axis that Greece would split apart, in the country's second civil war of the twentieth century.

THE 'NEW STATE' AND THE 'THIRD GREEK CIVILIZATION'

The regime began by establishing complete control over the press and communications. By the evening of the first day, the police had visited the offices of all the country's newspapers and delivered instructions on what they would and would not in future be allowed to publish. The latter included the instructions themselves. The public was not even supposed to know that the newspapers they read had become mere instruments of the regime – although this was a secret that could hardly be kept for long. Later in the month, a new 'Undersecretariat of Press and Tourism' was formed. Its remit was defined as:

> Instruction of public opinion, i.e. matters pertaining to the Greek and foreign daily and periodical press, Congresses and Exhibitions of all kinds, the Theatre, cinema, gramophone records, every form of advertisement, lectures, publications and in general printed matter of every kind, performances whether live or reproduced by mechanical means, so as to comply with the framework of national traditions and aspirations, including control of radio broadcasts.[24]

Beneath its innocuous-sounding name, the 'Undersecretariat' was modelled along the lines of the notorious Propaganda Ministry of Joseph Goebbels in Berlin. Indeed, most of the rhetoric and many of the methods adopted by the Metaxas regime are immediately recognizable as ready-made borrowings from Nazi Germany and Fascist Italy. New media were to be exploited to the full for the purposes of control and to promote the regime's message throughout the population. Before long, slogans would appear everywhere – even stamped on lightbulbs, postmarks on letters, and all over the countryside. Other echoes of the Nazis were the short-lived Labour Battalions and Metaxas's most cherished creation, the National Youth Organization (known by its Greek initials EON). Young people were encouraged, and after 1938 effectively forced, to join EON. Summer camps became compulsory and included political indoctrination. The young members of EON (numbering one million by 1939), and workers conscripted into the Labour Battalions, learned to give a variation of the Nazi salute – though it is said that the 'Leader' himself never returned it.

Metaxas and the elderly appointees who made up his government (hardly any ministers had a background in politics) made no distinction between the nation and the state. For them, the supreme value was the corporate state. Metaxas's belief in the 'State' was obsessive.

It was a fixation. The state was 'a living organism', it had an existence of its own, interests of its own. It was founded upon 'an organized national mass'. In the early months of the dictatorship the regime began to promote what it called the 'New State'. The language used by Metaxas in his first address to the students of Greece's second university, in Salonica, is chilling:

> I forbid any of you, male or female, to have any ideas other than those of the State. I require you not only to have the same ideas as the State, but to believe in them and to work accordingly with enthusiasm. If any of you have different ideas he or she had better not be educated.[25]

Just as Hitler had proclaimed the Third German Reich and Mussolini the Third Rome, Metaxas in a speech in June 1937 came up with the 'Third Greek Civilization'. This was not so much intended to describe present conditions as to represent a goal for the future. It was to be 'a civilization superior to those of the past and capable of keeping our nation among those who wish, are able, and are worthy to live'.[26] The model from the past chosen by the regime and its ideologues was not democratic Athens, but militarist, corporate, disciplined Sparta – which in turn had been the inspiration for militarist traditions in Germany that went back well before the Nazis.

But there was more to the Regime of the Fourth of August than ideology and slogans. Its domestic policies (including repressive measures taken against communists) were mostly not new, but built on and intensified efforts that had begun under Venizelos. Indeed, there was more continuity between the four-year period of stable parliamentary rule under Venizelos and the authoritarian regime of Metaxas than is often realized.

First of all, state institutions were further strengthened. The civil service was increased. So was the police. The regime embarked on an ambitious series of public works. A series of laws did much to resolve the crisis in labour relations that had resulted from the economic recovery since 1932, and that none of the previous elected governments had proved capable of handling. Strikes were declared illegal, but so were lock-outs by employers. Both sides in industrial disputes were forced to accept compulsory arbitration. An eight-hour working day was introduced. The social security system, another embryonic legacy of the Venizelos years, was considerably extended. These and other measures were intended to bring about 'social reform' and 'a just distribution of wealth', in this way addressing the most glaring of the grievances of workers and the unemployed who had suffered disproportionately during the years of recovery.[27] State-driven measures to increase employment seem not to have been very successful, and tax rates rose. But the drive to increase wheat production, initiated in Venizelos's final year in office, continued to such an extent that output doubled between 1936 and 1938 under Metaxas, with a corresponding further reduction in reliance on imports.

Much of the new legislation was aimed directly at the disaffected peasantry and agricultural workers. In subjecting all social classes to the *diktat* of the corporate state, Metaxas was trying to neutralize the perceived threat from below by presenting himself as the 'Leader' of the oppressed. Elaborate public occasions, speeches and radio broadcasts promoted the dictator as the 'First Peasant' and 'First Worker'. However quaint or even absurd these period postures seem today, they are of a piece with Metaxas's championship of the spoken language, or demotic Greek. Metaxas was the first to commission an official grammar of spoken Greek, bucking a trend that for much of the twentieth century linked demotic with the political left and the official form of the language, known as *katharevousa*, with the right.

The most effective internal measures taken by the Metaxas regime were those directed against the communists or, increasingly, against dissenters of any kind. Metaxas's favoured instrument of oppression was not the army but the police. His Minister of Public Security, Konstantinos Maniadakis, was the most feared man in Greece. As well as being head of the rural gendarmerie and the city police force, Maniadakis also ran an efficient service of underground surveillance. Thousands of communists were rounded up, interrogated, dosed with castor oil, and in many cases sent to detention camps on remote islands. The price for release was to sign a 'Declaration of Repentance'. In 1940 the regime boasted that forty-seven thousand individuals had signed these declarations – a figure more than three times the recorded membership of the KKE in 1936.[28] As for the party itself, by that time it had been driven underground. Its leader, Nikos Zachariadis, and the members of its Central Committee were in prison. The threat that had provided the pretext for the regime to seize power had been extinguished, if it had ever existed. On the other hand, thousands who had been victimized by the regime had been given an outlet for their new sense of grievance in future, one that might never otherwise have occurred to them.

In hindsight, it is hard not to see the imposition of dictatorship in Greece in 1936 as part of the slide towards totalitarianism that was happening all over Europe at the time, and would culminate in the Second World War. It was not only in Greece that parliamentary democracy had first come under threat and then, increasingly, become discredited. Mussolini had held sole power in Italy since 1922, Stalin in Russia since the mid-1920s, Hitler in Germany since 1933. Other countries were jumping on the bandwagon. To many in Greece during the second half of the 1930s, it must have looked as though the political chaos of the last few years, and the impasse of the hung parliament of 1936, had shown up the limits of a system that was crumbling not just at home, but all over the continent. When everything else had been tried and failed, perhaps their portly, self-proclaimed 'Leader' and the authoritarian methods of these seemingly unstoppable rising powers really did represent the way of the future?

Certainly, there was little overt resistance. A widespread view seems to have been that while it left much to be desired, the 'New State' was still to be preferred to the chaos that had preceded it. At least no one was talking, now, of the risk of civil war. Organized attempts to overthrow the regime and restore parliamentary government were made on only two occasions. Both came in 1938. Both were brief, half-hearted and decisively put down. By the autumn of that year it was obvious to all that Metaxas was there to stay.

Resistance was not conspicuous in the world of the arts and intellectuals either. This was in marked contrast to what would happen later, under the dictatorship of the 'Colonels' in the late 1960s and early 1970s. Few prominent figures in the arts at this time identified with Communism. Exceptions were the poets Kostas Varnalis and the young Giannis Ritsos, and the historian Giannis Kordatos, who in the 1920s had written the first Marxist history of the Greek Revolution. Ritsos circulated some of his poems in underground publications, such as the communist newspaper *Rizospastis* (*The Radical*). But much of his work had no overt political content and appeared in mainstream periodicals that were subject to censorship. For the most part, writers and intellectuals kept their distance from the regime. The spectacle of public burnings of books, and the banning of some of their own previously published work, was hardly likely to endear them. And the sentiment seems to have been mutual: 'Though I honour and respect pure intellect,' Metaxas once said in a speech, 'I have to admit that I communicate better with people of practical professions.'[29]

This is not to say that artists and intellectuals were either won over or submitted to coercion, as happened in the Soviet Union and Nazi Germany at this time. There was no mass exodus, either, as there was from Germany. Poetry, fiction, visual arts, theatre and cinema (the last two tightly controlled by the regime) had already embarked on their own, subtler, quest for autarky – seeking the indigenous roots of a uniquely Greek character, history and culture – and carried on in the same direction. The avant-garde, experimental techniques, whether in writing, painting or music, that had burst upon the Greek scene at the end of the 1920s, became fused during the last years of the decade with an agenda of national self-discovery. The novel known in English as *Zorba the Greek*, written by Nikos Kazantzakis in the early 1940s, provides as good an example of this trend as any. The regime itself is best understood as an expression (crude and plodding by comparison) of this same quest.

There was one section of Greek society that would not be reconciled to the regime – nor the regime to it. This was the urban underclass, whose distinctive voice had first begun to be heard in the first decade of the century. Its numbers had been hugely swelled, and its repertory of self-expression greatly extended, by the arrival of the refugees in the 1920s. Many of those who were destitute drifted into the world of petty crime and the defiantly antisocial society of the *manges* that flourished around the dockyards of Piraeus and the poorer suburbs of Athens, Salonica and the larger towns. The music and songs known as *rebetika* celebrated a different kind of self-sufficiency from the official one.

The *manges* and the urban underclass that sustained them and their songs were never politically organized. But they were the reason that the otherwise surprising item of 'gramophone records' appeared in the list of media to be censored, within weeks of the regime taking power. *Rebetika* were like a red rag to the regime's ideologues. Here was a working class that presented itself as impervious to authority, its own values as superior to those of the state, its practices corrosive of everything that the 'New State' stood for. How was the 'Third Greek Civilization' to be born out of a society that tolerated hashish junkies, criminal behaviour and contempt for the corporate state?

Perhaps most objectionable of all about *rebetika* was the music itself. The favourite instrument of the *manges*, the *bouzouki*, belongs to the same family as the Turkish *saz*. The music of *rebetika* continued to be based on the system of modes, the *makam* system, that characterizes much of the music of the Middle East. It does not sound 'European', still less Western. At a time when the Greek state was more determined than it had been for a hundred years to define itself exclusively as part of western Europe, all such reminders of an 'oriental' past must be blotted out. Probably worse even than the reminder of Turkish rule, the music of *rebetika* kept alive memories of a Greek nation that had been widely dispersed throughout the East, and itself formed part of the Ottoman system. Rapprochement with modern Turkey was one thing – a political form of expediency begun by Venizelos that Metaxas did nothing to disturb. But memories of a past that was specifically Ottoman, and of a Greek nation that had once extended far beyond the reach of the official Greek state, could not be tolerated.

The regime went into action. Musical styles, instruments and vocal techniques regarded as 'Turkish' were cleared from the order books of the recording studios. Composers and performers were harassed, imprisoned, or exiled on islands for various forms of 'antisocial' behaviour. The *bouzouki* itself, identified by this time almost equally with a 'Turkish' past and with the criminality of the underworld that cultivated it, became a symbol of subversion in the eyes of the authorities. Instruments were liable to be seized and smashed, their owners taken in for questioning. This was the time when the younger cousin of the *bouzouki*, the *baglamas*, came into its own – the more easily to be concealed beneath clothing or in a specially designed pocket sewn into an overcoat.

And yet despite these measures, and in marked contrast to all other enemies of the regime, actual or supposed, *rebetika* flourished. Gramophone records – their lyrics 'cleaned up' by censorship – had never been so popular. The greatest songwriter and *bouzouki* player of the interwar generation, Markos Vamvakaris, many years later recalled the summers of the late 1930s when he and a small *rebetika* band set up shop in the blighted shanty-town on the western outskirts of Athens called Votanikos:

> It was pandemonium every night . . . All sorts of people used to come. High society aristocrats as well as *manges* and street kids and they'd rave it up until dawn. The whole crème de la crème of Athens came by . . . The whole of Athens, Piraeus, all the suburbs. They came from Larisa, Tripoli, Salonica, from all over Greece.[30]

The boastful exaggeration is part of the style. But there was truth in it. *Rebetika* were on their way up. However unlikely it may seem, it was during the Metaxas years that this particular expression of Greek identity began to move beyond the underclass that had nurtured it, to enter the mainstream, in due course to be hailed by the painter Giannis Tsarouchis as the 'sole proof of the existence of a modern Greek culture'.[31] The Metaxas dictatorship can hardly take the credit for that. But in a society where every public utterance was controlled, and in which no direct evidence of public attitudes was ever allowed to be collected, the survival of this music and the spread of its appeal through the social classes during those years are testimony to aspects of the Greek character that the regime was never going to tame.

The evidence of *rebetika* gives substance to the verdict of one Greek historian, delivered in the twenty-first century, on the regime and its statist vision: 'For Greeks, unlike the concept of the nation, the state had always been an object of popular derision. Thus, in their time-honoured tradition they merely paid lip-service to this grand design.'[32]

ULTIMATUM

In one respect the Metaxas regime could not have been more different from its Nazi and Fascist counterparts. Mussolini had revealed imperial ambitions overseas in 1935 with his invasion of Abyssinia (modern Ethiopia). In Germany, the goal of expanding the state to create *Lebensraum* (living space) for its citizens at the expense of the 'inferior' peoples of eastern Europe and Asia lay at the heart of Nazi ideology. The Regime of the Fourth of August had nothing militaristic or expansionist about it. Greece had learned its bitter lesson in 1922. Metaxas had been against the war in Anatolia then; nothing that had happened since had inclined him to change his mind. His simple hope, 'for our dear little Greece to be spared', set down in a private letter at the start of one world war, would accompany him to the end of his life at a crucial moment during the second.

The Metaxas regime kept up the system of local defensive alliances that had been brokered by Venizelos, including with Turkey. The greatest headache for the regime, as it would have been for any Greek government during those years, was the threat from the European powers that once again seemed on a collision course that must lead to war. Once Hitler had annexed Austria and part of Czechoslovakia in 1938, it could only be a matter of time before Mussolini would feel the need to flex his own muscles in the Mediterranean and the Balkans.

The only other power that could be a match for Italy in the eastern Mediterranean was Great Britain. On 3 October 1938, just days after the British prime minister, Neville Chamberlain, had declared 'peace for our time' after agreeing to the dismemberment of Czechoslovakia, Metaxas addressed an extraordinary plea to the Foreign Office:

> An alliance with Great Britain is what I want. And why not? We must assume as a plain fact that in the event of European war the use of the Greek islands and Greek ports will be an imperative necessity to the British Fleet and Air Arm. If you cannot have this automatically as an ally, you will be obliged to take it . . .

This was of course what had happened in 1916. Metaxas had lost nothing of the bitterness he and very many Greeks had experienced at that time. Now, his solution was to steal the policy of his then opponent Venizelos: better by far a pre-emptive alliance than the deadly cocktail of partial occupation and civil war.[33]

To his diary Metaxas confided his belief that his offer would be rejected. Recalling the moment a year and a half later, by which time Britain and Germany were at war, but not yet either Italy or Greece, he would speculate, 'Are they now about to offer us an alliance? I shudder. But maybe better if so.'[34] In any case, in 1938 Metaxas's intuition was correct. In Great Britain the climate of appeasement still continued. More pragmatically, if short-sightedly, the Foreign Office calculated that it 'would eventually secure all that Metaxas promised without the obligations of an alliance'.[35] And so the nations stumbled on towards war.

In March 1939 the German army marched into those parts of Czechoslovakia that had not already been annexed by the Third Reich. At the end of the month, the Nazi propaganda minister, Joseph Goebbels, paid his second visit to Greece. After a meeting with Metaxas, Goebbels professed himself satisfied that in the event of war the Greek government would remain neutral and was well disposed towards Germany. Metaxas, for his part, noted telegraphically in his diary, 'Reassurances on both sides.'[36] A week later, on 7 April, Italian troops landed at Durrës on the coast of Albania. Twenty-four hours later they had occupied the entire country. Metaxas was no longer so reassured. A week after that, the governments of Britain and France issued a statement supporting the integrity of Greece and Romania against attack – a declaration well short of a guarantee, and destined to be swept aside by events. Then, on 1 September, Hitler invaded Poland. The Second World War had begun.

The first nine months, which have often been called the 'phoney war', were in the Balkans rather a time of 'phoney' peace. Italy did not join the war until June 1940. By this time most of northern Europe had already fallen to the Nazis. While the Battle of Britain raged in the skies above the English Channel, and then when bombs began to devastate British cities in September, the government of Winston Churchill was in no position to offer much support to Greece, even when it looked increasingly likely that an Italian attack was imminent.

On 15 August, at the height of the annual pilgrimage to the shrine of the Virgin Mary on the island of Tinos, a torpedo fired from a submarine sank the Greek cruiser *Elli*, at anchor outside the harbour. No one doubted that the submarine had been Italian. But the newspapers were not allowed to say so. Metaxas sent an urgent telegram to the British government, asking for help in the event of an attack. A reply came within days from Churchill himself. But there was still no commitment. Metaxas, ever true to his principles, kept all mention of this exchange out of the newspapers, to avoid the risk of provoking further action by Italy.

In the meantime, Metaxas had kept in secret touch with the Germans. He had still not given up hope that Hitler could be prevailed upon to restrain his ally, Mussolini. But the price the Nazis held out to Greece was to join the Axis. This Metaxas could not risk doing – for exactly the same geopolitical reasons that King Constantine had once set out in response to the equivalent demand by the Kaiser. Greece was a maritime power and Great Britain was master of the seas.[37] In the midst of that summer of crisis and uncertainty, Metaxas noted with grim fatalism in his diary:

> If the Germans prevail, *we* will become their slaves. – If the British prevail, we'll become slaves to them! – If neither, Europe will fall apart. It'll fall apart anyway. My God, what despair![38]

Summer ended late in Greece that year. As October drew to a close, the nights were still warm. Athens was full of rumours that the Italians were about to attack from Albania. The government had prepared secret orders to mobilize reservists at a moment's notice. On Friday 25 October there was still no sign of the anticipated invasion. Metaxas went to the opera that evening to hear Puccini's *Madama Butterfly* performed by an Italian company. 'Enthusiastic reception,' he noted in his diary. The next day the Italian ambassador, Emanuele Grazzi, invited the cast and members of the Greek government to his embassy to celebrate. Then on Sunday the Italian news agency claimed that Greek raiders had attacked Italian troops inside Albania.[39]

On the morning of Monday 28 October, Grazzi and Metaxas met again. It was 3 a.m., at the dictator's unassuming home in Kiphisia. Metaxas had to be roused from bed to receive the ambassador. The embarrassed Grazzi had come to deliver an ultimatum. Greece must surrender unspecified strategic positions and allow Italian troops to pass unhindered through the country. Tradition has it that Metaxas answered with a single word: '*Ochi*', the Greek for 'no'. Ever since, the date has been celebrated as a national holiday in Greece, known as 'Ochi Day' in celebration of this act of defiance. In reality, whatever conversation took place would have been conducted in French, the international diplomatic language of the time. What Metaxas actually said was probably most accurately preserved by the first of his ministers to arrive for an urgent cabinet meeting shortly afterwards: '*Donc, Monsieur, c'est la guerre*' ('In that case, sir, it's war').[40]

For the second time in the twentieth century, Greece had been dragged into a European war that would soon engulf almost the entire world. And the never-popular Metaxas, whose entire military and political career had been built on trying to prevent this from happening, overnight became a national hero.

9

Meltdown

1940–1949

The sequel took almost everyone by surprise – and none more so than the Italian dictator. Two weeks before the ultimatum was delivered, Mussolini had outlined to his chiefs of staff his plan to occupy Greece, in the same way that he had previously occupied Albania, virtually unopposed. With German arms triumphant in northern Europe, it was time for the southern component of the Axis to flex its muscles and make conquests of its own. Hitler was not consulted. Victory should be easy.

Instead, the Greek army in Epiros, under the command of General Alexandros Papagos, halted the initial Italian advance into Greece in a matter of days. On 14 November 1940 it was the turn of Greek forces to go on the offensive. The 'Albanian campaign', as it has been called ever afterwards in Greek, was experienced at the time and is still remembered as an 'epic'.

During the winter of 1940–41, Greeks spoke with one voice. They acted and fought as one. Venizelists of lower rank were at last welcomed back into the units they had been forced to leave after the failed coup attempt of 1935. Even now, the spirit of reconciliation did not extend to their superiors. But many of the excluded officers volunteered anyway, and were able to contribute their bravery and expertise in humbler capacities. For once, the overmanning of the officer corps, which had proved such a deadly legacy of the civil war of 1916, may actually have done the country some good. By 10 January 1941, Papagos had secured gains right across the southern part of Albania, stretching some thirty miles into Italian-occupied territory.

It has justifiably been called Greece's 'finest hour', echoing Churchill's much-quoted words in Parliament on the eve of the Battle of

Britain.[1] It had been achieved by the same spirit of unity and self-sacrifice that Britain's wartime leader had called for then. And it had been achieved, just as victory in the Battle of Britain would be achieved, by one country fighting alone for its survival against overwhelming odds. For once, the bitter lesson of 1897, which Metaxas had taken to heart and which had guided his entire career, had been overturned.

Or had it?

The first thing that Metaxas did, that October morning, after he dismissed the Italian ambassador, is recorded telegraphically in his diary: 'Call Palairet and seek help from Britain.' It was not yet dawn when the British Minister arrived. The cabinet had not yet met.[2] From that moment on, all the time that the Greek army was winning its victories in Albania, Metaxas and his government were walking a diplomatic tightrope. As late as January 1941, Metaxas still dared not accept an offer of British reinforcements when it was finally on the table. Hitler would be bound to see their presence as a provocation. And the numbers offered would be nothing like enough to protect Greece against the might of the Third Reich. Greek journalists, throughout that winter, were not allowed to say that their country was fighting against Fascism, 'since we, too, are a fascist state'. Officially, Greece was at war only with 'the armed forces of Italy'.[3] But with pressure increasing from both Britain and Germany, how long could that last?

Metaxas would have been seventy that April. His health had been giving concern for some time. The last entry in his diary is dated 17 January 1941. He died of pneumonia on 29 January, leaving the ever more urgent dilemma unresolved. Sir Michael Palairet, the British Minister, paid a fulsome tribute, in his report to the Foreign Office three days later, to one of 'the great men of Greece and, indeed, of Europe, whose actions and personality have vitally influenced the course of the war'. Palairet believed wholly in the dictator's 'goodwill and friendliness towards Great Britain' and was satisfied that Metaxas at the time of his death had been 'determined to pursue the war, side by side with us, not only against Italy, but also against Germany'.[4]

Metaxas himself saw it differently. In a long diary entry dated less than a month before his death, he railed against the treachery of

Hitler and Mussolini. The Führer and the Duce had ended up betraying their own ideological principles. 'Greece has become since the Fourth of August an anti-communist state, an anti-parliamentary state, a totalitarian state,' he wrote – and these, for Metaxas, were matters for congratulation, not censure. If Hitler and Mussolini had been sincere, he went on:

> they ought to have supported Greece in everything with all their might. They could even have made allowances if short-term interests or necessity, based on its geographical position, brought Greece close to Britain. In fact, the opposite: Greece kept Britain at arm's length – apart from indispensable and in any case necessary friendly relations. Greece has never given or promised any help to Britain.[5]

Metaxas died a fascist, committed to the very ideology whose advance his troops, for the first time anywhere in the world, had turned to flight. In his final months he had given his people the leadership that enabled them to overcome the divisions of a quarter of a century. During those months not much was heard of the 'New State', still less of the 'Third Greek Civilization', to say nothing of the threat of Communism, which had been the excuse for imposing and maintaining the regime in the first place. The painstaking and sometimes obsessive rebuilding of the Greek state and its institutions, which had begun after the catastrophe of 1922, received its final vindication in the united front put up against the Italian invaders between November 1940 and March 1941.

The sudden and total collapse of that state was just around the corner. The cause of the collapse would be Hitler. But the process of dissolution began with the death of Ioannis Metaxas on 29 January 1941.

STATE COLLAPSE

It began at the very top. The Regime of the Fourth of August had no constitutional legitimacy. There was no mechanism for replacing the 'dictator for life' that Metaxas had become. King George was now presented with the first of several opportunities to undo the dictatorial regime at a stroke, and replace it with a broad coalition of political talents and interests. Allowing for the difference that in Greece there was no parliament and no possibility in the circumstances of electing one, this would have followed the example of Churchill's war cabinet that had taken office in Great Britain the previous summer. Instead, the king turned to the director of the National Bank of Greece. Alexandros Koryzis, who had only limited experience of government, became the new prime minister. The rest of the machinery of the regime stayed in place.

The dilemma that had tormented Metaxas during the last weeks of his life would not be resolved until late February. During a visit by the British Foreign Secretary, Anthony Eden, and General Wavell, in command of British forces in the Middle East, it was finally agreed that British troops *would* be sent to Greece. British, Australian and New Zealand units began disembarking at Piraeus at the beginning of March. At the same time, Bulgaria declared for the Axis. German forces immediately began to build up there. Hitler, we now know, had made up his mind as far back as December to invade Greece.

The attack came on 6 April 1941. German divisions simultaneously attacked both Yugoslavia and Greece. The first assault, from Bulgaria, was over in a matter of days. Salonica was occupied on 9 April. A week later the Germans had forced their way through the whole length of Yugoslavia and were pushing into Greece through western Macedonia. This made the British, Australian and New Zealand positions impossible to hold for long. At the same time, the bulk of Greek land forces, which had only recently driven back a renewed assault by the Italians on the Albanian front, suddenly found themselves all but surrounded. Exhausted by almost six months of fighting in the blizzards and sub-zero temperatures of the mountains, few among either officers or men had morale left to face a fresh, and by reputation far more deadly, adversary to their rear. Within days, discipline began to break down. Without proper orders from Athens, local commanders on their own initiative sued for terms.

By this stage, it was a moot point who, in Athens, would have had the authority to issue an order anyway. On the afternoon of 18 April, Orthodox Good Friday, the cabinet met at Command Headquarters in the Grande Bretagne Hotel, with the king presiding. News had already leaked that the government was preparing to be evacuated to the relative safety of Crete. Morale everywhere was collapsing, not least within the cabinet itself. Some members were urging capitulation. The hapless banker Alexandros Koryzis, who by rights should have been chairing the meeting, begged the king to accept his resignation the moment it was over. When the king refused, Koryzis went home and shot himself. Greece had no army and no government. Half the country was already in enemy hands.

A last stand was made by British, Australian and New Zealand troops at Thermopylae, the site of one of the most famous battles of antiquity, between 22 and 25 April. But, just like the action of Leonidas and his Three Hundred in 480 BCE, this was no more than a holding operation. Its purpose was to cover the evacuation of the government and personnel judged by the British to be essential. On 27 April the first armoured columns of the Wehrmacht entered Athens. The swastika was raised on the Acropolis. For most Greeks, the Occupation had begun.

For the second time, with the suicide of Koryzis, King George had the opportunity to create a broadly based administration, even if by this time its effect would have been little more than symbolic. After three chaotic days, when the king took charge himself, the choice of prime minister fell on another banker. Emmanuel Tsouderos would prove to have more staying power than his predecessor. He had other qualifications, too, which would be no less essential now that the government was transferring itself to Crete. This was the homeland of Venizelos, where opposition to Metaxas had always been strongest. Tsouderos was a Cretan by birth and had supported the Venizelists in the past. But with that one concession, the Greek government that fled Athens at the end of April 1941 was still the unreconstructed and not much lamented Fourth of August Regime. Tsouderos would last for almost exactly three years, making him one of the longest continuously serving prime ministers of those turbulent times, but without contesting an election or ever having to win a parliamentary vote of confidence.

The government's sojourn in Crete lasted less than a month. On Tuesday, 20 May the Germans began landing paratroopers at strategic points across the island. Defence was in the hands of New Zealand, Australian and British troops. All available fighting men among the Cretans had been drafted to the Albanian front the previous autumn, and were now being demobbed after the surrender of their commanders to the Germans. Even so, resistance to the invaders by armed Cretan civilians greatly increased their casualties, and would soon lead to brutal reprisals. Meanwhile, King George, his government and the last of their civil servants had to be hustled across the White Mountains to be taken by sea to the safety of Egypt. The Battle of Crete was over in ten days. *Festung Kreta* (Fortress Crete) would remain a German military outpost until the very end of the war.

What was now a government in exile, headed by King George and his prime minister, Tsouderos, slowly made its way, under British protection, via Alexandria and Cape Town to London, only to wind up two years later in the Egyptian capital, Cairo. It would not be until February 1942 that the Regime of the Fourth of August would finally be laid to rest – by which time in most parts of Greece the dissolution of the state would be all but complete.

Greece had been defeated and occupied by the armed forces of Germany alone. But Hitler only ever took a passing interest in his new conquest. Unlike other conquered countries, Greece seems to have been viewed by the Nazis as booty to be plundered and picked clean, rather than as a going concern to be nurtured and maintained in their own interest. This soon became apparent when Hitler handed over control of most of the country to those allies who happened to be most conveniently placed to exercise it: the Bulgarians and the Italians.

Most of western Thrace and all of eastern Macedonia were given to Bulgaria to administer. At once the 'ethnic cleansing' that had been pursued by both sides during the Balkan wars and the First World War resumed. The Germans kept control only of the most strategically sensitive areas: the islands and mainland closest to neutral Turkey, the greater part of Macedonia adjoining Yugoslavia, including Salonica, most of Crete, and a small area around Athens and Piraeus. For all the rest, the Italians would be responsible.

A puppet Greek government was sworn in, headed by Georgios

Tsolakoglou, one of the senior army commanders who had forced the capitulation in Epiros. Real power lay with the plenipotentiaries of the occupying powers and their different, and often competing, agendas. Civil administration soon began to fragment. The Axis powers requisitioned foodstuffs for the military and to supply their own people back home. The yield from the first summer's harvest was much reduced because of the fighting earlier in the year. Then the normal mechanisms for distribution and supply broke down. As often as not, farmers and shepherds refused to hand over their produce. Rations for civilians had to be reduced progressively, until they dipped below subsistence levels. Prices rose and the value of the drachma plummeted. In the first year of the Occupation the price of bread rose from 70 drachmas per unit to 2,350. By 1944 it would reach two million.

Even in the best of times, Greece had never been self-sufficient in cereals. The surpluses of products such as tobacco, currants, citrus fruit and olive oil, which traditionally would be exported to pay for the necessary imports, were now being siphoned off by the occupiers. The British still had naval supremacy and were able to enforce a strict blockade. This was exactly the nightmare that had been foreseen by Metaxas and others, as long ago as 1914, when they insisted that Greece, as a maritime country, could not survive a war in which the other side had command of the sea. Now, the Greeks had no choice. They starved, literally.

During the first winter of the Occupation, as many as forty thousand civilians may have died from starvation in Athens and Piraeus alone. Between 1941 and 1943 the victims of famine are estimated to have reached a quarter of a million, close to 5 per cent of the total population. Conditions were worst in the cities and best in places where people could live on what they produced themselves. It was a sudden and brutal return to the subsistence economy that had been the inheritance of the Ottoman Empire and the Byzantine before it. Athens, Piraeus and Salonica, and many of the larger towns, had grown to sizes that could not be supported without the relatively sophisticated systems of exchange that had now broken down. Eventually, thanks to efforts by the Red Cross, some limited relief would be allowed through the blockade. The first winter was the worst. But throughout the Occupation almost everyone depended for survival on a black market that had largely replaced the legitimate economy. And if the danger of death by starvation to some extent receded, it would soon be replaced by others, as violence took hold all over the country.

DESCENT INTO VIOLENCE

Extreme violence came to Greece with the invaders. This, too, started from the top. By the third year of a brutalizing Occupation its corrosive effects had spread right through Greek society, pitting Greek against Greek. Nothing like it had happened since the Revolution of the 1820s.

Right from the beginning, any overt sign of opposition to the occupying forces could lead to summary imprisonment, torture or execution. Soon mass executions and the destruction of whole villages would become common practice. By the time the Occupation came to an end, 'over a thousand villages had been razed. One million Greeks had seen their homes looted and burned down . . . More than 20,000 civilians had been killed or wounded, shot, hanged or beaten by Wehrmacht troops.'[6] Those numbers exclude the victims of similar actions by the Italians (far less benign in reality than in the fictional portrayal by Louis de Bernières in the best-selling novel *Captain Corelli's Mandolin*) and Bulgarians. They also exclude action by Greeks against other Greeks.

The Occupation's deliberate murder of up to eighty thousand Greek citizens could not even claim the pretext of disobedience or resistance. The only offence of these eighty thousand was to be Jewish. In the spring of 1943 the entire Sephardic population of Salonica was rounded up and deported by train, crammed into goods trucks. 'Almost all were destined for Auschwitz. The records of Auschwitz-Birkenau show that 48,974 Jews arrived there from northern Greece; of these, 37,386 were immediately gassed. Hardly any of the remainder returned home.' Not the least chilling aspect of these numbers is their precision – something that cannot be said of most of the atrocities committed in Greece in the 1940s. Later, the smaller Jewish communities of Athens, the Ionian islands, Ioannina and Crete would suffer the same fate. It has been estimated that overall 'as many as 90 per cent of Greek Jews were killed', one of the highest percentages anywhere in Europe.[7]

The full horror of the Holocaust would not be known until after the war was over. But the culture of violence that had come with the invaders was quick to spread. The first serious plans to organize resistance and retaliate in kind were drawn up in Athens in the autumn of 1941. It would not be long before the centre of operations moved out of the city, and the bitterly fought process of piecemeal liberation of the country began. Greece is after all a country of mountains. Going back several centuries, if not much longer, whenever the central authority was weak, the mountains of the mainland and the hinterland of the larger islands would become a refuge and a breeding ground for brigands, local militias and guerrilla fighters. Although theoretically quite distinct from one another, throughout Greek history the boundaries between these types of activity have often been blurred. In 1821 it had been small-scale, locally based guerrilla action that had liberated the greater part of the country, while the Ottomans had held out in towns and coastal fortresses. The pattern would be repeated throughout the 1940s.

Much of the information that became available about these guerrilla groups immediately after the war, and for a long time afterwards, came from officers of the British Special Operations Executive (SOE) and later the American Office of Strategic Services (OSS). Altogether, some four hundred British and two hundred Americans were dropped by parachute into occupied Greece to work alongside them. Among the British, the figure of C. M. (Christopher Montague) Woodhouse stands out. Known in English as 'Monty' and in Greek as 'Kris', Woodhouse spent more than two years in the mountains of central Greece, latterly as head of the Allied Military Mission to the Greek guerrillas. Like George Finlay more than a century before him, Woodhouse would devote much of the rest of his life to writing the history of the events he had witnessed, and placing them within the longer story of Greece and Greeks in medieval and modern times. Like Finlay, too, Woodhouse developed a deep and sincere love for the Greek people, as well as a sharply critical eye for the foibles and political weaknesses of those who presumed to lead them. Also like

the philhellenes of that earlier time, Woodhouse and his fellow officers played a part in determining the outcome of the struggle that they
witnessed (exactly what part is still contested by historians to this
day). And inevitably, again like the philhellenes but for different reasons, they were at some degree of cross-purposes with those in Greece
whom they were there to help.

From the point of view of SOE, there were very specific wartime
objectives to be met. At first, this was to sabotage German supply
lines to Field Marshal Rommel's troops in North Africa. The destruction of the railway viaduct over the Gorgopotamos ravine, in the
mountains above Lamia, has been much celebrated ever since, though
it came too late to affect the outcome of the North Africa campaign.
That was in November 1942. For the next eight months the objective
was to deceive the Germans and Italians into believing that the new
front to be opened up in Europe would be in Greece. This required a
continuing campaign of sabotage against military targets, and apparently achieved some success. After the Allies in fact invaded Sicily in
July 1943, and Italy capitulated, SOE in Greece was ordered to keep
up the pressure by harassing the occupying forces, while doing its
best to keep the peace among the Greek guerrilla groups until such
time as the Germans withdrew.

The story of SOE, and latterly also of OSS, in Greece has been
told many times, from varying points of view. It is a story of hardi-
ness, bravery, frustration, and often of deep empathy with the sorely
tried Greek people alongside whom the officers worked. But it inevitably skews the reality of what the Greeks were fighting for. This is
not to say, as some have done, that the British were cynically exploiting the Greek Resistance for their own political ends. It was simply
that they had different priorities.

For the Greeks who risked their lives by taking to the mountains,
supply lines to Rommel's forces in North Africa could be of only
the most abstract interest. 'Operation Animals', as the campaign of
deception in 1943 was code-named, would have appealed to them
even less, had they been allowed to know of it, as of course they were
not. What they did know, all too well, was that acts of sabotage, of
the kind that the British were constantly urging on them, would only
lead to mass reprisals against the civilian population. British and

American officers were constantly irked by what they saw as the unwillingness of the guerrilla bands to engage directly with the enemy, and an opportunistic obsession with securing advantage for themselves in the future, when the Occupation would be over. But this was to miss precisely the point of resistance activity.

For those Greeks who participated in it, the overriding purpose of resistance was to extend their group's control over as much territory and as many resources as possible, while avoiding pitched battles, unnecessary casualties or enemy reprisals. In the mountains, between 1942 and 1944, life was a matter of daily survival. 'Liberation' was not, as it would be in many other countries occupied during the Second World War, a future event to be brought about by great armies, by kings and generals. It was happening day by day, inch by inch, in the mountains of what by the summer of 1943 had come to be known as 'Free Greece'.

The first effective moves were made by the Communist Party, the KKE. Many communists held in the country's jails by the Metaxas regime had been set free by the occupying forces when they arrived. After all, at the time Hitler had still been bound to Stalin's Soviet Union by a non-aggression pact. But Nikos Zachariadis, the hardline leader of the party, remained in prison. Zachariadis would spend the greater part of the war in the Dachau concentration camp. In Greece, an interim leadership soon formed. This was the group that in September 1941 established the National Liberation Front, known by its Greek acronym EAM. The organization of EAM was built from the ground up. As its name suggests, it was designed to appeal to a broad base of national solidarity, rather than to supporters of any particular party. But the early success of EAM owed much to the experience gained by communist cadres in underground political activity. Among the leaders of EAM throughout the Occupation were Georgios Siantos, the acting General Secretary in Zachariadis's absence, and Ioannis Ioannidis, with whom he informally shared the leadership of the KKE. Of Siantos, a former tobacco worker, Woodhouse later wrote, 'Ruthless and ambitious though he was, [he] had a simple bonhomie and good humour.'[8]

22. Postcard of 1920 showing the territory of 'Great Greece', according to the terms of the Treaty of Sèvres. Venizelos appears in the top left-hand corner. The inscription reads: 'Greece is destined to live, and will live'. The treaty was never ratified.

23. After the defeat in September 1922 Greek men of military age living in western Anatolia were held in Turkey as prisoners of war. Released in July 1923, they began arriving in Greece, as described by US diplomat Henry Morgenthau (see pp. 235–6).

24. (*above*) Eleftherios Venizelos in 1928, at the start of what was to prove the last stable, elected government in Greece until the 1950s. Oil painting by F. Papoulas, 1928.

25. (*right*) A propaganda photograph of the dictator Ioannis Metaxas (ruled 1936–41), with the title 'Saviour of the Nation'.

26. *Rebetika*: a *bouzouki* band in the 1930s. Musicians such as these were persecuted by the Metaxas regime, but *rebetika* would rise to become one of the best-loved forms of Greek popular culture after the Second World War.

27. Occupation (*left*) and Resistance ('People's Rule' in 'Free Greece') (*right*).

28. (*left*) A burnt mountain village; (*right*) men being rounded up in an Athens neighbourhood (a 'blocco') during the Occupation (see p. 285).

29. Young soldiers of the Democratic Army face defeat at the hands of US-backed government forces in the final phase of the Greek Civil War (1947–9).

30. Melina Mercouri in *Never on a Sunday* (1960). She went on to serve as Minister for Culture in all three socialist governments led by Andreas Papandreou (1981–9, 1993–4).

31. A tank prepares to crush the gate of the Athens Polytechnic in the early hours of 17 November 1973.

ΕΛΛΑΣ

ΖΗΤΩ
Η 21ᴴ ΑΠΡΙΛΙΟΥ 1967

32. Propaganda poster for the regime of the 'Colonels' (1967–74). The caption reads: 'Greece. Long live the 21st of April 1967'.

33. Konstantinos Karamanlis, prime minister 1955–63, 1974–9 and later president, the restorer of Greek democracy in 1974, photographed in 1975.

34. Andreas Papandreou, architect of 'CHANGE' (prime minister 1981–9, 1993–6), photographed in June 1984.

35. The 'modernizer', Kostas Simitis, Greece's longest continuously serving prime minister (1996–2004).

36. The Charilaos Trikoupis Suspension Bridge, connecting northwest Greece with the road network that links Athens with the Peloponnese, opened in 2004.

37. The bronze statue of Archbishop Makarios III (1913–77), the first President of Cyprus, near the Kykkos Monastery in the Troodos mountains.

38. The flag of the 'Turkish Republic of Northern Cyprus' overlooks the Greek-Cypriot sector of divided Nicosia, capital of the Republic of Cyprus.

39. The 'dead zone' that divides the city along the cease-fire line.

40. (*above*) Street art of the post-2010 'crisis': *Poverty is the parent of revolution and crime* by Wild Drawings, Exarcheia, Athens, 2013.

41. (*left*) Alexis Tsipras celebrates his election victory on 25 January 2015 in the 'Propylaea' of the University of Athens. The venue will have been chosen because of its association with student protest since the 1970s. Under the portico Greece's first ruler, 'Otto I', looks down with a matching gesture from a frieze completed shortly after he had lost his throne in 1862.

The aims of the new organization were set out, a year after its founding, in a manifesto signed by the well-known communist intellectual and campaigner for the demotic language Dimitris Glinos. This first manifesto invokes the precedents of Rigas Velestinlis and the Friendly Society that had paved the way for the Revolution of 1821. It calls on all social classes to come together in what it calls a 'national struggle'. A short passage sets out only very broad objectives for what will follow, 'as soon as the People have expelled the foreign conquerors'. These include freedom of speech, of the press and of assembly (all constitutional rights that had been suspended by the Metaxas regime), and elections for a Constituent Assembly.[9]

By the time this manifesto began to circulate, EAM had already created its military offshoot, the Hellenic Popular Liberation Army. Its acronym in Greek, ELAS, sounds the same as the official name of the state, Hellas. From modest beginnings, with two thousand men under arms in February 1943, the size of ELAS grew exponentially, to reach twelve thousand in June. After the Italians capitulated in September of that year, and the Germans took over direct control of the entire country except for the Bulgarian-held northeast, that number doubled again. Captured Italian weapons greatly added to the arsenal available in the mountains. By the time of the German withdrawal in the autumn of 1944, ELAS had an estimated fifty thousand men under its command.

During the years of Occupation, EAM and ELAS together achieved something without precedent in Greek political history. They created a mass movement, independently of the leadership of any one charismatic individual or clearly defined group. Deliberately, the communists who retained control kept in the shadows. Most of those who took up arms with ELAS were not communists. Of those who were, one recruiting officer is reported to have commented, 'I doubt whether some of those knew what communism is.' This is a theme that will surface again and again during those years.[10] On the other hand, EAM and ELAS brought huge political changes to the villages and, latterly, the towns that they liberated. Woodhouse, who thoroughly distrusted their leadership and its motives, saw the effects of these changes at first hand and paid this tribute shortly afterwards:

Having acquired control of almost the whole country, except the principal communications used by the Germans, they had given it things that it had never known before. Communications in the mountains, by wireless, courier, and telephone, have never been so good before or since; even motor roads were mended and used by EAM/ELAS ... The benefits of civilisation and culture trickled into the mountains for the first time. Schools, local government, law-courts and public utilities, which the war had ended, worked again. Theatres, factories, parliamentary assemblies began for the first time.[11]

So far, so rosy. Out of the chaos of Occupation and famine, the apparatus of a functioning state was being recreated in the mountains. People were being empowered who had never been empowered before. This was particularly true of women, who 'were given the vote for the first time in Greece's history, and their help ... enlisted in numerous ways'.[12] For the first time since independence, public notices, announcements and newspapers were written in a language that everyone could understand, demotic Greek. But all this was only one side of the coin. There was another, much darker side.

There is a already a clear hint of this in the manifesto of EAM circulated at the end of 1942. A surprising amount of attention is given there to *internal* enemies. The king and the 'old political parties' are expected targets. More ominous is the warning that *anyone* who 'takes up arms against, or undermines, or frustrates by whatever means the unity of the national-liberation struggle ... is a collaborator with the foreign conquerors, [and consequently, is] voluntarily or involuntarily, a traitor'. A whole paragraph threatens women who enter into sexual relationships with the enemy. Near the end comes the order to 'hunt down and stigmatize all informers, traitors, stool-pigeons, collaborators'. The peroration promises to 'frustrate all the schemes of the barbarian conquerors *and homegrown traitors*'.[13]

At the same time that EAM and ELAS were attracting willing and enthusiastic recruits all over Greece, they were alienating almost as many others. 'Traitors', in the sense of people who willingly supported the ideology and actions of the occupying powers, would have been hard to find in late 1942 – even among the demoralized city police and rural gendarmerie, whom ELAS from the beginning targeted as stooges of the puppet regime that employed them. This language and these tactics ensured that, for all their effective organization, their patriotic appeal and firmness of purpose, EAM and ELAS would never manage to gain a monopoly of resistance activity during the Occupation.

Former military officers and, increasingly, politicians preferred to take advantage of smugglers' routes out of Greece, to wind up, by way of neutral Turkey, in the Middle East. There they took service under the government in exile – and before long would have exported the dissensions of their homeland. For the great majority, who had no opportunity to leave the country, the only alternative to passivity was to 'take to the mountains', as the traditional Greek expression has it. But by no means all who took that route opted to join ELAS. Regional and local loyalties, or the charisma of a leader known to them and their families, often seemed to offer a more reliable sense of solidarity in a dangerous enterprise than the grandiose public pronouncements and intentionally invisible leadership of EAM and ELAS.

Of these groups the most significant were known by the Greek acronyms EDES (National Republican Hellenic League) and EKKA (National and Social Liberation). Both were led by former Venizelist army officers who had been cashiered after the coup attempt of 1935: respectively, the flamboyant Napoleon Zervas and Colonel Dimitrios Psarros, who in particular earned the respect of the British commandos who worked with him. Zervas operated from a power base in Epiros, Psarros in southern Roumeli. There is no reason to doubt that these and many other, smaller organizations, in different parts of the country, were formed with very similar aims to EAM and ELAS, at least as far as the occupying powers were concerned. When the first British commandos arrived in Greece at the end of September 1942 and discovered the existence of competing guerrilla bands in the mountains, they reasonably enough took it upon themselves to try to persuade them to work together in a common cause.

But the leadership of EAM and ELAS had other ideas. The unity of the entire Greek people, urged in the manifesto of EAM and repeated in thousands of proclamations, had nothing to do with consensus, persuasion or cooperation. The occupying forces had already set a benchmark for brutality. ELAS and its security arm, the

Organization for the Protection of Popular Combatants, known by the acronym OPLA (which spells the word for 'weapons' in Greek), were prepared to match them in atrocities. Practices not seen in these mountains since the Revolution returned during the 1940s: summary executions, torture and mutilation both before and after death, the display of severed heads. No group had a monopoly of such horrors, though eyewitnesses and historians down to the present day have often been selective in which ones they choose to report in detail.[14]

EDES had a strength of about four thousand in October 1943. In that month, ELAS went on the offensive against it. Most of its men were either killed or forced to enrol in the ranks of ELAS. A year later, thanks to British support, EDES had recouped its losses and its strength had risen to seven thousand. Membership of EKKA seems never to have topped eight hundred.[15] This organization was twice attacked and dissolved by ELAS during 1943. Many of its members were induced to change allegiance, including its deputy leader, Colonel Evripidis Bakirtzis, who would later briefly become a leading figure in EAM. Then, in defiance of a truce brokered by the British, EKKA was finally attacked and disbanded by a much larger ELAS force in April 1944. Up to a quarter of the organization's members may have been killed on that occasion, with as many again being hunted down in the purge of the surrounding villages that followed. Among the dead, murdered after capture and in some cases also tortured, was its leader, the widely respected Psarros. Even Siantos, the acting General Secretary of the KKE, would concede later that this action had been a propaganda disaster for EAM. Elsewhere in the country, other rival resistance groups were similarly mopped up between mid-1943 and the end of 1944.

Prominent in these acts of extreme violence was a former student of agriculture from Lamia, who had been imprisoned under Metaxas for communist activities, and was now in overall command of guerrilla activities for ELAS. His real name was Athanasios Klaras, but he achieved almost mythical fame and notoriety under the *nom de guerre* of Aris Velouchiotis, meaning 'Ares of Velouchi'. The name combines the ancient Greek god of war with one of the mountain peaks in central Greece that had been the symbolic habitat of the klefts of old, and now, once again, were home to these new guerrilla bands. By all accounts a charismatic leader, bearded and wearing the conspicuous cartridge belt and dagger of the *kapetanios*, or band leader, Aris has been described as softly spoken, a compelling orator – and a 'sadistically violent man'.[16] In 1945, denounced by the communist leadership for refusing to accept the truce that had been signed in February of that year, and surrounded by government forces, Aris preferred to die rather than surrender. The severed heads of Aris and a comrade would be exhibited hanging from a lamp post in Trikala. It was an end, like his deeds, very much in keeping with the heroes celebrated in the traditional songs of the klefts. Aris was not quite forty years old when he died.

It is often supposed by historians that the choice facing the Greek people during the Occupation was between the forces of progress or of reaction.[17] This was certainly how EAM itself and its supporters liked to present it. But what was happening in Greece during those years was far more complex. It was the logic of violence, more often than of political choice, that determined how people behaved under the extreme conditions of the time. In the 1940s, just as during the 1820s, people acted as they did, not for abstract political or even, necessarily, for rational reasons at all, but in order to stay alive and to protect their families and their livelihoods, in conditions that at the time must have appeared set to continue without end. It was the very methods used by ELAS to crush all competitors that drove others to take up arms against it. This in turn ensured that the country would be split among 'at least two political actors who enjoy partial and/or overlapping monopolies of violence' – which is a sociologist's way of defining civil war.[18]

How else to explain a phenomenon that made no sense to outside observers at the time and has embarrassed Greek historians ever since? As ELAS grew in strength towards the end of 1943, so did armed resistance *to the Resistance*. This, too, began with a political initiative in Athens. In April, Ioannis Rallis, an 'old' politician of right-wing and royalist convictions, was induced by the Axis authorities to take charge of the puppet Greek government. He did so on one condition: his government must be allowed to arm and recruit Greek forces to hunt down the communists in the mountains. Recruitment to what would become known as the Security Battalions was slow at first, and relied on coercion. But by the autumn, after the successes of ELAS, not just against the occupiers but against other resistance groups, men began to volunteer for service in bands that might be locally commanded by fellow Greeks but ultimately were under orders from the Nazis. Once the scene of their operations, too, moved out to the mountains, the Security Battalions and other collaborationist militias entered the vicious circle of fighting for local dominance among competing guerrilla groups. This happened all over the country.

Skirmishing and mutual atrocities against civilians were particularly intense in the Peloponnese, where the power of ELAS had previously been unchallenged except by the occupying forces. The total number of collaborationists in arms in early 1944 is estimated to have been about seven thousand, the same number as EDES could field at the same time. By the time of the German withdrawal that autumn, it had risen to a staggering twenty-five to thirty thousand, not far short of the total manpower achieved by ELAS.

It is inconceivable that so many people who had never previously shown the slightest sympathy for Hitler or Mussolini, still less for the brutal occupation their country was enduring, could have been suddenly converted to Nazi ideology at the very time when Italy had capitulated and the armies of the Third Reich were in retreat. What was happening in the Peloponnese and elsewhere was a return to a practice that had been common during the Revolution. Then, armed militias competing for local control had made temporary accommodations with whatever outside forces they could, in order to survive and protect their dependants and their livelihoods. Fear of communism was the key, and was no less easy to whip up than the finger-pointing of EAM/ELAS against 'fascists' and 'traitors'. As one informant put it, a volunteer who had taken part in atrocities committed by the Security Battalions against ELAS members in the southern Peloponnese in 1944, 'We knew they were Communists. But we didn't know what communism was.' In northern Greece, particularly in areas where the scars of religious and ethnic conflict earlier in the century had not yet healed, the dynamics of civil war were even more complex – and have only begun to be disentangled by historians more than half a century later.[19]

During the final year of the Occupation, the same vicious struggle of Greek against Greek was going on in the streets of Athens. A regular event in the poorer neighbourhoods and the shanty-towns that housed the refugees from Asia Minor was the *blocco*:

> The sleeping inhabitants were abruptly woken by the sound of megaphones ordering all males in the neighbourhood to make their way immediately to the main square. Gendarmes and [Security] battalion men began house-to-house searches, with orders to shoot anyone they found hiding. In the cold grey light of early morning, thousands of men sat on the ground, while hooded informers picked out EAM sympathisers . . .[20]

Those picked out would be either shot immediately or taken to the notorious Chaidari prison camp on the outskirts of the city. There they might be tortured, sent to Germany for forced labour or kept in readiness to be executed the next time a reprisal killing was called for. Looting and street fighting between armed gangs loyal to the Rallis government and to ELAS became daily occurrences in the city.

Against this background, EAM succeeded in establishing a Provisional Government in the mountains of 'Free Greece' in March 1944. Styled the Political Committee for National Liberation (PEEA), this included non-communists as well as communists. During the final months of Occupation, Greece had no fewer than three governments: the government in exile, now in Cairo, which was controlled by the British; the puppet government led by Rallis in Athens, controlled by the Germans; and PEEA, controlled by the KKE. The reality was that the country had no government at all. When the Germans left, as they began to do during September, no one knew what would come next. None of the competing Greek organizations, inside and outside the country, could claim a legitimacy that all would accept. The only question was whether any one of them would prove able to command sufficient force to impose its will upon the rest.

The stage was set for violence to breed more violence, until a new actor entered the scene, towards the end of the decade. As 1944 drew to a close, and the end of the Second World War was at last in sight, in Greece there could be no prospect of a resolution any time soon.

THE NEW FAULT LINE

During October 1944 the Germans were in full retreat from Greece. With the exception of a few garrisons still holding out, and now marooned, in Crete and some smaller islands, the last of the occupying forces departed on 4 November. Once again, the fate of Greece was being decided by events far beyond the country's borders. To the north the Red Army was advancing steadily into the Balkans. In the west, British and American forces were making progress through Italy and France. The Third Reich needed to concentrate all its efforts nearer home, before its divisions in Greece were completely cut off. After some particularly horrific destructions of villages and massacres of their inhabitants, the three-and-a-half-year Occupation was over.

It was time for normal political life to take hold once more, and fill the suddenly created vacuum. If only.

Preparations had been going on for some months. The lead had been taken by the British, and channelled through their ambassador to the official Greek government in exile in Cairo, Reginald (Rex) Leeper. It was very much at British insistence that King George was induced first to dismiss his prime minister, Tsouderos, and then to appoint in his place a figure of a very different stamp. Georgios Papandreou had fortuitously arrived in Cairo from occupied Greece in time to take office at the end of April 1944. Papandreou has been described as 'tall, gaunt, imperious in his ways and a brilliant conversationalist', though one, admittedly jaundiced, observer at the time found him a pompous windbag.[21] Papandreou had been one of the few rising stars of the old Liberal Party during the 1920s. More left of centre than Venizelos had ever been, he was at the same time vehemently anti-communist. Leeper and the British authorities in Cairo decided that Papandreou would do.

Under Papandreou's leadership, and overseen at every stage by Leeper, the Greek government in exile had discarded the last vestiges of the Fourth of August regime, to reinvent itself as a 'Government of National Unity'. Under precarious agreements reached in a village outside Beirut in May, and then in September at the Italian town of

Caserta, where the exiled government had temporarily been shunted in the meantime, the Provisional Government of 'Free Greece' effectively merged with it. EAM was beginning to look like a minority party in a wide-ranging coalition. That, at least, seems to have been the intention. But of course EAM had never been a political party in the traditional sense – how could it, given the circumstances of its birth? Together with its armed wing, ELAS, EAM controlled some 90 per cent of occupied Greece. On the other side, Winston Churchill had determined, and the British Foreign Office laid it down, that the only source of legitimacy for a future Greek government lay in the monarchy and the person of King George II. This was blatantly to ignore, as no Greek could be expected to do, the inconvenient fact that the king had been the chief architect and backer of the Metaxas regime. However one looked at it, the auguries for the restoration of a fully functioning, pluralist parliamentary democracy in newly liberated Greece could hardly have been worse. Perhaps the most surprising thing is that EAM agreed to cooperate with Papandreou at all. There were many on both sides who thought it could not last. And events would prove them right.

In the cities the hiatus left by the end of the Occupation passed off peacefully. In Athens there was a brief outpouring of popular rejoicing in the streets. Six whole days would pass between the departure of the Germans on 12 October and the arrival of Papandreou, the Government of National Unity and the six thousand British troops that had been judged necessary to underpin their authority. During that time the atmosphere was already turning brittle. 'I had the feeling it would only need a match for Athens to burst into flames like a can of petrol,' wrote the novelist Giorgos Theotokas in his diary, on the second day.[22] In Salonica, in defiance of an agreement, ELAS columns paraded through the city on 30 October, the first day of liberation. They then handed over without incident to a British peacekeeping force. But the city's mayor was replaced by a 'Municipal Authority' controlled by EAM.

Beyond the cities, wherever EAM and ELAS did not already enjoy full control, the collapse into chaos only intensified. This was particularly the case in the Peloponnese and in parts of Macedonia, where some of the most vicious reprisals and counter-reprisals between ELAS and its local rivals took place in the first months after liberation. In Epiros, Zervas and EDES were for the time being in control. The authority of Papandreou and the government of 'National Unity' barely reached beyond the urban centres of Athens and Piraeus, Salonica and Patras.

Politically, the issue that would soon turn into a lit fuse was how to reconstitute the country's armed forces. In the last months of 1944, the whole of Greece was awash with weapons. But at the time of liberation the owners of these weapons were about evenly divided between those loyal to EAM/ELAS and those opposed to it. The British now found themselves in a distasteful position, not wholly dissimilar from that of the previous occupiers. Most supporters of EAM and ELAS seem to have viewed them, albeit with varying degrees of distrust, as allies and liberators. After all, Great Britain was still fighting a world war shoulder to shoulder with Stalin's Soviet Union. But EDES and the remaining non-communist resistance groups in the north were also relying on the British to protect them from annihilation by ELAS. So, more embarrassingly, did the demoralized city police and rural gendarmerie, and all those who had been armed by the Germans against ELAS and were now being targeted as collaborators. Once again it was the dynamics of the internal division within Greece, rather than political choice, that drew both the British and the Papandreou government to rely on the armed force of some of those who until recently had been acting on the orders of the enemy.

By the end of November 1944, negotiations had reached an impasse. The government had decreed that ELAS must be disbanded, along with all other irregular military formations. A final deadline was set for 10 December. All ranks were to be recruited into a new national army. To ELAS and its supporters it looked as though they were about to be put under the command of monarchists and former collaborators. This, for EAM, ELAS and the Communist Party, would be a step too far.

During the last week of November, ELAS units went on the offensive in parts of the Peloponnese and Macedonia. On 1 December there were even skirmishes on the outskirts of the capital. In Athens, the communist daily *Rizospastis* predicted outright civil war unless the government changed its mind. It was to prove a self-fulfilling prophecy. The next day, Saturday, in the early hours, the six ministers who represented EAM in the Government of National Unity resigned their portfolios. By this time the Communist Party of Greece, which had been outlawed for almost a decade, had moved into one of the buildings on Syntagma Square in the centre of Athens, facing the headquarters of the city police on one corner of the square, and the command HQ of the British in the Grande Bretagne Hotel on another. Photographs show the initials 'KKE' mounted on top of the building against the skyline in letters that must have stood twenty feet high.

The battle lines had now been drawn in the capital. On one side were the communists, the fighters of ELAS, the supporters of EAM and all who sympathized with them, including the great majority of those who had risked their lives to take up arms against the Axis. Against them stood a government that had just lost its paper-thin claim to 'national unity', a British force that would soon prove far too small to defend even the capital, let alone the entire country, one small Greek unit that had been battle-hardened in conventional warfare against the Axis in North Africa and Italy, and a much larger conglomeration of armed groups and individuals tainted, to varying degrees, by the stain of collaboration.

In hindsight it seems extraordinary, given the extent of mutual distrust, that neither side was prepared for what happened next, or even had any serious plan of action. Immediately after the resignation of its ministers from the government, EAM announced a general strike for the next working day, Monday, 4 December, to be preceded by a mass demonstration in Syntagma Square on the Sunday morning. Rather touchingly, in view of what happened later, EAM even filed a request with the authorities for the demonstration to go ahead, in accordance with regulations. At first this was granted. Then within hours the government panicked. Permission was revoked. This was late on Saturday evening, but still in time that news of the change could be featured prominently in all the newspapers next morning – all except *Rizospastis*. The front page of the Communist Party daily made no mention of the ban. Instead, it called on all its readers to gather in Syntagma Square at 11 o'clock. One eyewitness estimated the number of the demonstrators who turned up at sixty thousand.[23]

They converged on the square from several directions. At the entrances their way was blocked by lines of armed police. As a precaution, further lines of police had been drawn up inside the square, in front of Police Headquarters and the Grande Bretagne Hotel. The great majority of those who turned out to demonstrate that day seem to have been women and children. But among them were communist cadres, and some of those were armed. And of course there is no way of knowing what firearms individuals might have brought along with them, in the circumstances of the time. Shortly before 11 o'clock one group of demonstrators, blocked from entering the square, turned aside to lay siege to the house where Papandreou was living. Two grenades were thrown from the crowd, and a guard opened fire, killing one civilian. By this time, there had been scuffles between demonstrators and police at other entrances to the square. It appears that sheer force of numbers pushing from behind overwhelmed the cordons. By 11 o'clock Syntagma Square was full of people, waving Greek and Allied flags, some of them chanting slogans against the government.

Within minutes of the sound of the grenades going off outside Papandreou's house, shooting started in the square itself. The most reliable explanation of what happened suggests that it began with jittery policemen firing from the first-floor windows of their headquarters. Within minutes, shooting was coming from several directions at once. People hit the ground in heaps, to save themselves. By the time the shocked crowds had managed to make their way out of the square, they left behind at least seven dead, and perhaps as many as twenty-two. Given the confusion at the time, it has never been possible to establish the exact number. At least sixty-six were wounded. And this was only the start.

Almost at once, ELAS units began to attack police stations throughout the city, arresting and murdering 'traitors'. At the same time, in those parts of the country that they did not yet control, ELAS units intensified their efforts against their rivals. In Epiros, a renewed assault finally drove out EDES. Zervas and the surviving members of his organization would soon be evacuated by the British to the safety of Corfu. Historians trying to make sense of these events, long afterwards, have disagreed on how far the response by ELAS to the events of Sunday 3 December in Athens was spontaneous or the result of a coordinated strategy.[24] It was both, and neither. The vicious war of the mountains had come to the capital, complete with all its practices of horrific violence that had been handed down from Ottoman times and the Revolution of the 1820s. Here and in the provinces, the ELAS command, no less than the rank and file, was driven by the mentality of revenge and disproportionate reprisal that was the legacy of the Occupation. A calculated bid to seize power would have had to be more discriminating, and might even have succeeded.

It was entirely characteristic that, to begin with, all the violence was Greek on Greek. The leadership of EAM and ELAS showed extreme reluctance to take on the British. This, too, seems to confirm how limited were their objectives – as though the outsiders could be relied upon to sit on the sidelines while the Greeks settled scores among themselves. But here they underestimated the determination of Winston Churchill. He had taken a close personal interest in Greece ever since he had been charmed by Venizelos, in London, back in 1912. The prime minister of Great Britain was not going to be browbeaten by those he called 'miserable Greek banditti', at the very time when the Allies were finally closing in on Nazi Germany, ready for the kill. Another leader might have dismissed events in Greece as a sideshow, not worthy of his attention at such a time. Not so Churchill.

Churchill's orders to General Ronald Scobie, commanding British forces in Greece, on 5 December have become notorious: 'Do not . . . hesitate to act as if you were in a conquered city where a local rebellion is in progress . . . We have to hold and dominate Athens.'[25] The gloves were off. This was the moment when the internal fault line that had burst through the surface to fracture Greek society during the Occupation became fully aligned with the geopolitical split between the communist East and the capitalist West that would divide Europe and the world for the next forty-five years, and become known as the Cold War.

The fighting lasted for a month. The monuments of the Acropolis, which had been spared by the retreating Germans, were effectively held hostage when Scobie's men talked ELAS down from their fortified positions there, only to set up machine-gun positions themselves and dare the insurgents to attack their own heritage. The British had to bring in substantial reinforcements, by air and sea from Italy, and a new commander-in-chief, before they could win the battle. Most accounts agree that it was a close-run thing.

George Seferis, the diplomat and poet whose day job took him the short walk from his home in Plaka to the Foreign Ministry next to Syntagma Square, found himself living on the front line. He wrote in his diary, when the conflict was only four days old: 'As I woke up today I was thinking that idyllic Plaka has become the site of the first battle between the British Empire and Soviet Russia.'[26] During the decades that followed, the 'battle for Athens' would often be presented in this way, as a hot proxy for the Cold War that had not yet begun.

We now know that it was not. The phenomenon that was EAM and ELAS was homegrown. For all the close ideological dependence of the KKE leadership on Moscow, the Greek Resistance had been almost entirely cut off from communication with the Soviet Union throughout the Occupation. When channels had first opened between Moscow and the Provisional Government in the mountains (PEEA), as late as May 1944, it seems that Siantos and his comrades were instructed to cooperate with the British and Papandreou. By that time, soundings between the British and the Soviets had already begun. Soon these would culminate in the so-called 'percentages agreement', drawn up informally between Churchill and Stalin in Moscow on 9 October – just three days before the last German troops evacuated Athens. The agreement was a first stab at the more formal division of the post-war spoils that would emerge when Roosevelt, Churchill and Stalin met together at Yalta in the Crimea four months later. Although it would not become public knowledge until long afterwards, Stalin agreed in October 1944 to allow Great Britain a 90 per cent stake in Greece after the war – in effect in return for a free hand for himself in the rest of the Balkans.

Many commentators have expressed surprise that 'Uncle Joe', who was not otherwise famous for making concessions or for keeping his word, should have done so in this case. But all the evidence indicates that he did. In the summer and early autumn of 1944 no one could tell where the advance of the Red Army would stop. By September,

Romania and Bulgaria had been occupied. Bulgaria now had a communist government. If Stalin had ordered his troops southwards into Greece, they could have been assured of a welcome at least as warm as in countries that only a few years previously had signed up to join the Axis. Instead, as part of the embryonic 'percentages agreement', Churchill demanded the withdrawal of all Bulgarian troops still in Greece. Stalin gave the order at once. It is a little-remembered fact, but this is how the hated Bulgarian occupation of the Greek provinces of eastern Macedonia and western Thrace came to an end, in October 1944.

Soon afterwards, the continued Soviet advance into the rest of the Balkans and eastern Europe would lead to the establishment of the 'Iron Curtain' and become one of the causes of the Cold War, in which Greece was destined to become a front-line state. But for all the hopes of the Greek communists and their many supporters in the country, there was never any serious prospect that Stalin would lend more than token, and ambiguous, support to the embattled communists in Greece. The reason has nothing to do with ideology, and everything to do with geopolitics. Metaxas and the long-dead king he had served during the previous world war would have understood. Stalin chose not to antagonize the British, or later the Americans, over Greece for exactly the same reason that Tsar Nicholas I had chosen not to antagonize the western European powers by supporting the aims of Kolokotronis and the 'Russian party' a hundred years before. Events had shown, again and again, that control over Greece depended on a strong naval presence in the eastern Mediterranean. Except very briefly, during the 1770s, Russia had never been in that position, and certainly was not in 1944. Russia's strategic priorities in the nineteenth and mid-twentieth centuries (and indeed now, with the Soviet Union long gone, in the twenty-first century) have been entirely consistent.

Once EAM and ELAS found themselves proscribed by the British and turned on them, almost two weeks after the start of hostilities, in mid-December 1944, they were on their own. In the long run, unless Stalin were to change his mind, they could only lose. But from now on, the shape of the fault line dividing Greece down the middle would become fixed for as long as the Cold War lasted.

And the division of Europe into mutually antagonistic communist and anti-communist 'blocs' would be mirrored in Greek society for the duration. This would be the legacy of December 1944.

A FIGHT TO THE FINISH

By the third week of December, with further reinforcements arriving from Italy by air and sea, it was clear that the British were gaining the upper hand in Athens. Churchill himself descended like a *deus ex machina*, on a whim flying to Greece with his Foreign Secretary, Anthony Eden, on Christmas Day. Carrying his own pistol, Churchill was driven in a convoy of armoured cars to the centre of Athens the next day. During a tense three days of talks, the basis for a new settlement was hammered out. The politically explosive question of the return of King George II was shelved. In the meantime, a regent was to be appointed, to oversee a referendum on the future of the monarchy. After that, the first parliamentary elections in a decade would be held.

The man chosen to be regent was the Archbishop of Athens and All Greece. Archbishop Damaskinos was in poor health, but he impressed Churchill on their first meeting as 'an enormous tall figure in the robes and high hat of a dignitary of the Greek Church'.[27] Damaskinos had been widely admired for the courage and dignity he had shown during the Occupation. The Papandreou government was already in tatters. Papandreou would have resigned at the beginning of the conflict, but Churchill would have none of it. Now he was allowed to depart.

The choice of interim prime minister fell on a most unexpected figure. This was General Nikolaos Plastiras, the prime mover of one successful military coup (1922) and two failed ones (1933 and 1935). Fleeing for his life after the last of these had brought the long-running 'Schism' once again to the brink of civil war, Plastiras had served since 1942 as the titular head of the republican and anti-communist resistance movement EDES. Since EDES was at that moment being mopped up by ELAS in the mountains of Epiros, the choice of prime minister could hardly have been a more uncompromising statement of intent, though at least no one could have accused Plastiras of being a royalist. It would prove to be the last, brief fling of the old republican right. Even so, the chequered political career of this veteran of all Greece's wars between 1912 and 1922 was not quite over.

By the beginning of January 1945, ELAS had been forced onto the defensive. Even while Churchill had been on his way to Greece, its units were beginning a massive round-up of hostages from the civilian population. As they withdrew from the city over the next two weeks, long columns of starved and beaten men, women and children were forced to stagger along the roads with them. Stragglers were executed. Many were later killed in cold blood. Their bodies would be found, still roped together, tipped into mass graves some weeks later. Up to that time, public opinion in the free world had favoured the insurgents. Churchill had had a hard time justifying his actions in Greece to the House of Commons. But the taking and murder of so many innocent civilians as hostages would turn the tide the other way. It was a desperate measure, and would do irreversible damage to the cause of EAM and ELAS in the court of international opinion. The tactic was yet another reversion to the norms of disproportionate and indiscriminate reprisal that had been handed down from the years of the Occupation, and had even deeper roots in the Ottoman period and the Revolution of the 1820s.

Hostilities ended formally at one minute past midnight on 15 January 1945. The final peace agreement was signed between the representatives of the 'Hellenic Government' and the 'Central Committee of EAM', in the Athens seaside suburb of Varkiza on 12 February. ELAS was to be disbanded after all. Its members were to surrender their weapons. There would be no immunity from prosecution for those accused of common crimes. And although this did not need to be spelt out, the opportunity for EAM to participate in the government of the country had gone for good. Within a year, a referendum was to be held on the monarchy, and elections held for a new Constituent Assembly. These last were the only significant concessions to the losing side, and they only confirmed what Churchill had already set out at the end of December. Not all communists were prepared to accept these terms. Among those who did not was Aris Velouchiotis, soon to be killed in a guerrilla action against government forces. For many on the left, ever since, 'Varkiza' has been remembered, regretted and deplored as an unforgivable act of surrender by the communist leadership at a time when EAM and ELAS still held most of Greece under their control.

The return to political life was slow. Throughout 1945 and into the following year, real political direction came not from unelected and unstable Greek governments but from the British. With peace once again established, however precariously, even more pressing than political and constitutional issues was the need to feed a population that was still living at barely subsistence levels. The country's infrastructure had been wrecked and would take time and investment to rebuild. Hyperinflation during the Occupation had destroyed the currency. Back in November 1944 a 'new drachma' had been introduced, with a conversion rate of fifty billion old drachmas to one new one. This indicates the scale of the problem. It would not begin to be solved until 1946. In the meantime, the black market continued to flourish and the new currency was losing value too. Much-needed emergency measures to provide food were organized by the recently formed United Nations Relief and Rehabilitation Administration, known by the initials UNRRA.

Slowly, during the year that followed the Varkiza agreement, control over the provinces drifted back towards the government. More often than not, the agents of this change were unofficial local militias, the successors to those that had fought against ELAS during the Occupation or had suffered at its hands. These were now tolerated or encouraged by the local representatives of the official state, particularly the rural gendarmerie. Although ELAS itself had been officially disbanded, many of its former members sought protection by regrouping into small-scale bands. Violence and intimidation became the norm once again. But this time, everywhere, the victims were those who had been associated with the wartime resistance that had been led by EAM. It was enough to be related, even distantly, to someone identified as a 'communist', for you to be beaten up, arrested, imprisoned or even killed. In the narrative of the Greek left, the year after Varkiza has always been known as the 'White Terror'. The term has now been uncontroversially adopted by most historians of the period. As usual, precise numbers are hard to come by. But there is no doubting the scale of the persecution.

The British found themselves powerless to stop it. Their forces in Greece were limited and concentrated close to the cities and main towns. The reconstituted political parties that jockeyed for position in the interim government were either pale shadows of their pre-1936 selves (the Liberals and the People's Party, each clinging to a dynastic descendant of its former leader) or new, short-lived splinter groups. By the time the first parliamentary election was held, in the event ahead of the promised referendum on the monarchy, the political ground had become deeply polarized. On one side was the communist left. On the other, an anti-communist right had increasingly coalesced around support for the monarchy as the only guarantee of the established order. The kind of centre-right republicanism that had long been associated with the name of Venizelos became hopelessly squeezed between these two extremes.

The death blow to the moderate, republican legacy of Venizelos, as an alternative to these extremes, was delivered by the return of another political leader who had not been seen in public for ten years. This was Nikos Zachariadis, the Secretary General of the KKE. Zachariadis had been Stalin's personal appointee back in 1931. He had spent most of the previous ten years in prison, latterly in the Dachau concentration camp. It was the British who brought Zachariadis back to Greece, on an RAF transport plane, in May 1945. The KKE was now under new management.

The first Greek parliamentary election in a decade was announced for 31 March 1946. Ten years had passed since the KKE had last been in a position to test its electoral strength. Then, it had come out holding the balance of power. Zachariadis could not have known this, but the next opportunity would not come until 1974. Overruling many in his own party who disagreed with him, and in defiance of an explicit directive from Stalin's foreign minister, Vyacheslav Molotov, the normally obedient and doctrinaire Stalinist Zachariadis ordered a boycott. It was a practice with a long history in Greek politics, and its effects had invariably been disastrous for those who tried it. So it would prove once again.

With the communists (and some minor republican parties) out of it, and conducted under conditions of intimidation, the election of 31 March could only give a very distorted reflection of the true state of public opinion. Victory for the monarchist right was a foregone conclusion. In some ways more revealing than the actual result of the election are indications of what might have been. These suggest that, if there had been no boycott, the combined vote for the communists and republicans would have topped the poll. Certainly the 20 per cent that foreign observers expected the KKE to win, if it had participated, would have marked an all-time high in the party's long history. Supposing that Themistocles Sophoulis, the veteran leader of the Liberals, had been able to form a government with communist support, 'Such a government,' it has been suggested, 'by claiming to represent the wishes of the majority of the people, and by virtue of its composition, would have offered Greece the best opportunity to solve its internal problems.'[28]

But it was not to be. The KKE, under Zachariadis's leadership, and driven into a corner by the continuing 'White Terror', was already stumbling towards the only alternative to the ballot box, if it was to continue to exist at all: armed struggle. On the night before the election, a band of KKE supporters ambushed a police post at the foot of Mount Olympos and killed twelve gendarmes. This event has usually been considered as the start of the third, and bloodiest, round of a three-stage civil war. That the worst was still to come is true. But the reality is that Greece had been in a state of civil war continuously since the summer of 1943. The 'third round' is better understood as the prolonged, and bitter, endgame to a conflict that had begun under the conditions of disintegration brought on by the Axis Occupation.

After March 1946, there were only two political positions left. Either you were a communist or you were not. If you were not, you must be for the king. For many Greeks it must have been an unpalatable choice, to say the least. Thousands would suffer violence, torture or death, through being identified with one side or the other, regardless of what they actually thought or believed. Under conditions of blatant intimidation, the long-promised and long-delayed referendum on the monarchy was held on 1 September, overseen by a government in which monarchists held all the power. The result was a foregone conclusion. Before the month was out, King George II, now aged fifty-six, and as it would turn out with only half a year to live, duly returned to Greece from his second period of exile. He came not as the saviour of his people, and with no prospect, and seemingly with no intention, of uniting them. This unloved, unbending and ultimately egotistical figure was accepted back on his throne as the lesser of two very considerable evils.

By this time, any political will for compromise that there had ever been was long gone. The divisions now ran so deep that neither side had any interest in reconciliation. No less now than during the civil wars of the Revolution, Greece's future direction could only lie on one side or other of the fault line. Reginald Leeper, the British ambassador who had been all but running the Greek government since before the liberation, declared in his final report in February 1946: 'too much blood has been shed and there is too much hatred for the two sides to live together peacefully or for anybody to mediate between them'.[29]

It was far from clear that either side could win. There was nothing for it but to slug it out to the end.

The prime minister after the election of March 1946 was Konstantinos Tsaldaris, nephew of the pre-war leader of the same party that now returned to office, the People's Party. The younger Tsaldaris has been described as 'a small-minded mediocrity'.[30] Under this unpromising (and uncompromising) leadership the 'White Terror' became in effect official government policy. New security legislation permitted arbitrary arrest. Courts martial could hand down sentences of internal exile or even death. The number of political executions by the end of 1946 stood at 116, and would increase significantly during the following years. At the local level, in many parts of the country, and particularly in the Peloponnese, there was as before only a thin line separating the official organs of the state from privately run militias or even outright banditry.

The result was that, while an increasingly authoritarian government was tightening its control over the cities and towns, in the countryside and particularly in the mountains of mainland Greece the chaos of the Occupation returned. Historians minutely scrutinize the utterances and try to probe the motivations of the Communist Party leadership at this time. But it was only gradually, during 1946 and the first months of 1947, that the KKE came to assume control

over all the disparate guerrilla groups that opposed the representatives of the official state. That it could do so at all must have been in
large measure the consequence of actions perpetrated or tolerated by
the government. The remnants of a disbanded ELAS came together
during the last months of 1946, though its successor would never
reach more than half the strength of ELAS at its peak. The formation
of a new Democratic Army of Greece (DSE) was announced in
December. In command was a former ELAS guerrilla leader, Markos
Vapheiadis. A further year would go by before the Communist Party
was ready to revive the Political Committee for National Liberation
(PEEA). This had been the name of the alternative government
established in 'Free Greece' for six months during 1944. Now, with
Vapheiadis as prime minister, it held sway over the mountainous
parts of northern and central Greece – much the same territory as
had been liberated by EAM and ELAS during the Occupation. It
was not until the end of 1947 that the four-year-old civil war became
formalized into a contest between opposing political administrations,
each supported by a regularly constituted army.

The decisive events that would do more than anything else to determine the outcome took place, as so often before in Greek history, far
away – this time in London and in Washington DC. By the beginning
of 1947, the British Labour government that had come to power at
the end of the Second World War had embarked on the process of
disengagement around the world that over the next two decades
would see the transformation of the British Empire into the Commonwealth. The Foreign Secretary, Ernest Bevin, announced that British
forces would be withdrawn from Greece at the end of March. Just
three weeks before that deadline, on 12 March, President Truman in
a famous speech to both houses of Congress announced what has
been known ever since as the 'Truman Doctrine'. For some time the
American government had feared the spread of Soviet Communism
throughout the world. The doctrine stated that massive economic
and military aid from the United States would be made available to
any state that was threatened with a communist takeover. It would be
tried out first in Greece and Turkey. But it was in Greece where the
need was most pressing.

American logistical support for the Greek government began

arriving almost immediately. The Americans did not send any com-bat troops to Greece. This was no Korea or Vietnam – though it has been suggested that the success of the Truman Doctrine in Greece would become the blueprint for both these later interventions.[31] But the support in weapons, money and foodstuffs that came to Greece from the United States during the last years of the 1940s was hugely asymmetrical with the limited aid that could be afforded to the other side by the new communist regimes in Greece's northern neighbours: Albania, Yugoslavia and Bulgaria. All three countries were as impov-erished as Greece. And despite slightly more belligerent rhetoric on the subject, Stalin and the USSR were no more prepared to help their fellow communists in Greece than they had been before. Had the Truman Doctrine been based on a complete miscalculation? Or might Stalin have changed his mind and intervened after all, had it not been for this massive show of American strength?

Even with the dice so heavily loaded in their favour, the Greek gov-ernment and its American backers had their work cut out. At the time when the British handed over their responsibilities to the Americans and the Truman Doctrine swung into action, it seemed to many observers that the guerrillas were 'bound to win'.[32] A year later, it was far from evident that much had changed. The blow-by-blow account of botched campaigns, repeated atrocities and strategic blun-ders on both sides makes depressing reading. Both sides removed large numbers of vulnerable children from combat zones, and sub-jected them to systematic indoctrination, respectively in special camps in government-controlled areas of Greece or in communist Eastern Europe. Much has been written on this practice, particularly as carried out by the communists. Government propaganda presented the insurgents as reviving the traditionally detested Ottoman levy of young children to form the elite janissary corps. But it was successive Greek *governments* that prevented the return of these children from the communist bloc, where most of them would remain until the 1980s.

During the last year of the war, the government forcibly evacuated whole villages in the mountain areas that were within its reach, so as to prevent their menfolk from being recruited or conscripted into the Democratic Army. As many as seven hundred thousand people, or

10 per cent of the total population, may have been displaced in this way. By the end of the conflict, both sides were relying overwhelmingly on unwilling conscripts. The government held thousands of political prisoners under brutal conditions on semi-barren islands. The most notorious of these was Makronisos, just off the east coast of Attica. In these prison camps indoctrination was extended to adults. The practice of extorting recantations under torture, which had begun under the Metaxas regime, reached new heights. Many of those held would not be released until years after the end of the conflict.

By the spring of 1949 the communists had been driven northwards until all their forces were concentrated on two mountain ranges close to the frontiers with Albania and Yugoslavia: Vitsi and Grammos. Vicious fighting at close range, and the use of a new destructive American weapon delivered from the air, napalm, gave the Greek army and air force the upper hand. While the final siege of Grammos was going on, in July, the Yugoslav leader Tito closed his country's frontier with Greece, a consequence of his rift with Stalin. Zachariadis and the last of his comrades withdrew to the safety of communist Albania on the night of 29–30 August. Six weeks later, on 16 October, from its exile behind the 'Iron Curtain', the KKE announced that the armed struggle was over. Sporadic instances of violence continued until January 1950, by which time the Civil War was definitively at an end.

It has been called by Greek historians writing in the twenty-first century a 'completely meaningless war', and one that 'could have been avoided'.[33] It had been far more destructive of lives and property than any previous conflict since the Revolution of the 1820s, including both world wars. According to one estimate, the total population of Greece in 1951 was 11 per cent lower than it would have been after a decade of peace. As many as two hundred thousand Greeks either lost their lives or went into long-term exile. The number of those killed by other Greeks 'is likely to have exceeded 60,000'. The country's infrastructure had barely begun to be rebuilt.[34] The new political and cultural fault line, between Communism and anti-Communism, between 'East' and 'West', as these terms had been newly defined by the Cold War, would continue to divide Greece down the middle for two more generations.

*

What had they been fighting for?

To begin with, the appeal of EAM and the KKE, during the Occupation, had been based on a return to the spirit of 1821. Under the extreme conditions of the 1940s, here was an opportunity to complete the process towards full national self-determination that had been lost in the compromises of state-building under foreign patronage ever since. This was a simple message, and it resonated. The essence of the appeal of EAM, managed with some skill but not necessarily cynically by its communist leadership, was to the integrity of a *nation* that was being dismembered by the Axis. It was not difficult to find other enemies to line up alongside the occupiers in the same camp. *All* foreigners, so the narrative went, ever since independence, had been conspiring to prevent the Greek people from achieving the total freedom that had been their first and only true goal. Now they had the chance to go out and win it for themselves. It was in many ways the message of Theodoros Kolokotronis and the warlords during the 1820s. And just like Kolokotronis and the 'Russian party' during the decade after independence, the leadership of EAM excluded Russia from the list of the Greeks' foreign adversaries.

A famous speech by Aris Velouchiotis, delivered in his home town of Lamia just after the liberation in October 1944, begins, in the speaker's own words, 'like a fairy tale':

> Once upon a time this corner of the earth where we are walking now
> and that we call Hellas was glorious and happy and had a civilization
> that for two and half thousand years continues to be admired by the
> entire world ... We have proved our Hellenicity. It is a fact that our
> country rose up again and was reborn, free once more [in 1821].

'Hellenicity' was a term much beloved by Metaxas and the architects of the 'New State' of the late 1930s. Aris's reassuring 'fairy tale' is the narrative of Greek identity that had been established by Spyridon Zambelios and Konstantinos Paparrigopoulos during the 1850s. No change there. Later, the speech continues: 'Are we going to flay the hides off priests? What would we do that for? We can see for ourselves that thousands of priests today are in the vanguard of our movement.'[35] This was true. Many village priests joined up with the Resistance in the mountains. In Athens, on the first day of liberation,

Giorgos Theotokas watched ELAS parade through the streets, headed by 'priests chanting, "People's rule!"'. A British soldier, during the street fighting in the city two months later, thought there must be some mistake when he saw a sniper on the other side repeatedly making the Orthodox sign of the Cross between shots.[36] This, too, repeated a pattern that went back to the Revolution, when the traditional figure of the 'gunpowder priest' had first gained a place in the popular imagination. In the 1940s many lower-ranking clergy, and a conspicuous few among the bishops, aligned themselves with the revolutionaries among their flocks, just as their predecessors had done during the 1820s, while the highest ranks remained loyal to the status quo.

Something that its opponents have probably never understood, or often have never even been willing to understand, is how deeply the mindset of the great majority of supporters of the Greek left has been infused with a profound, even reverent, sense of their shared identity as Greeks.

True, during the final stage of the conflict, the communist leadership declared itself willing to cede territory to Greece's northern neighbours. It was the price of the logistical support that by this time was keeping the Democratic Army in the field. This had always been the weakest spot in the propaganda armoury of the KKE, going all the way back to the 1920s. Long before these concessions were announced at the beginning of 1949, it had been standard practice for the government to label its opponents as 'EAM-Bulgars', traitors bent on handing back Greek territory, won with great sacrifice during the Balkan wars, to enemies that included now-communist Bulgaria.

These labels had stuck – as they still do, to some extent, today. But neither side possessed a monopoly of patriotism. And the patriotism of both was compromised. The same royalist governments that denounced communist concessions to Yugoslavia and Bulgaria over frontiers were willing to concede much of their own sovereignty first to the British, then to the Americans – again as the price of the firepower needed to defeat their enemies at home. When it came down to it, the side that could field the most powerful outside backer came out on top. But there is no good reason to doubt that most people on *both* sides were fighting for a version of their own Greek identity that they could relate to, one in which they could imagine a place for their own lives and futures.

Some historians have wondered whether the Greek Communist Party, if it had won, would have developed along democratic lines in common with communist parties in Western Europe, or would have established an authoritarian one-party state, on the model of either the Soviet Union or Tito's Yugoslavia.[37] A communist Greece could hardly have remained non-aligned in the late 1940s. So the chances are that the kind of ideal self-determination dreamed of by EAM members in the mountains during the Occupation was never going to happen. The attempt by the Greek left to create a new type of society in the mountains of 'Free Greece' has been hailed, from the vantage point of our own century, as nothing less than an 'undeclared social revolution'.[38] But viewed against the broader sweep of late twentieth-century history, it was perhaps always unrealizable.

The disintegration of the 1940s did not lead to a radically new birth, as the Revolution of the 1820s had done.

10

Uncle Sam's Protégé

1949–1974

The decade of violence and bloodshed was over. A six-year civil war, beginning in 1943, had lasted almost twice as long as the foreign occupation that had triggered it. What followed was a victors' peace. There was to be no accommodation with the losing side. The Communist Party of Greece had been declared an illegal organization at the end of 1947. It would remain banned for the best part of thirty years. Thousands of communist supporters now lived in exile behind the Iron Curtain – many of them concentrated, by the will of the Soviet authorities, in faraway Tashkent. In Greece, those who emerged from prison during the 1950s continued to be subject to surveillance and harassment. Former collaborators with the Nazis found themselves easily rehabilitated, often rewarded with positions of trust and pensions. No such forgiveness would be extended to those who had fought against them, until the 1980s.

Historians today describe Greece during the 1950s as an 'anticommunist state' and 'a client state to the United States', and with good reason.[1] For the first and only time in its history, the nation state that had been created in the nineteenth century out of the dynamics of Great Power politics in Europe now found itself under the direction of a non-European power. It could not be otherwise. The Civil War had been won thanks to American intervention. Once it was over, it was the Americans who held the political reins. After a chaotic start, with no fewer than seven governments and three parliamentary elections in three years, it was American insistence that brought in a new electoral system in 1952, heralding an uninterrupted period of rule by parties of the right until 1963. At the same time a revised constitution gave the vote in national elections to women for the first time. Under the aegis of the United States, Greece joined the NATO alliance, along with Turkey, in October 1951. Both countries would play their part in the next attempt to contain international Communism, sending troops and aircraft to support America and its allies in the Korean peninsula.

The impact of American intervention had a decisive effect on the future shape of the Greek economy. A year after the Truman Doctrine came the Marshall Plan, a four-year programme of massive economic aid to the stricken countries of Europe to help reconstruction after the Second World War. During that period more than one billion dollars were disbursed in aid to Greece, the poorest country in Europe at the time. The sudden influx of American affluence changed the landscape and many aspects of Greek society, just as surely as American weaponry had driven out the communist alternative. In the 1940s the supply of electricity barely reached into the mountains and islands. Three decades later you had to go a long way to come upon a village still unconnected to the network. The long strip of steelworks, oil refineries and shipyards that stretches along the coast of Attica to the west of Athens was developed during this time. Once again, as during the 1930s, attempts were made to turn subsistence agriculture into a profitable business, though with mixed results.

Shipping, which had been a Greek success story since before the Revolution, made a spectacular recovery in the late 1940s and reached new heights thereafter. On shore, the 1950s and 1960s were a boom time for building. Partly reflecting and partly hastening a growing influx of people from villages into the cities, Athens, Piraeus and Salonica grew at a pace and to a size never seen before. Between 1951 and 1971 the population of the capital almost doubled, to reach 2.5 million.[2] This was the era of the *polykatoikia*, the apartment block built of unadorned concrete and typically five or six storeys high. The shape of today's urban landscape was laid down then. Many rural villages that had been depopulated and destroyed during the fighting never fully recovered. Some were abandoned altogether. Once again, large numbers of young male Greeks chose to leave the country to find work abroad. New destinations this time were Australia, Canada and northern Europe, particularly the industrial dynamo of West Germany. At the same time, the foundations of mass tourism were being laid. The growth of cheap air travel, the package holiday and to some extent also the cruise industry began to make Greece accessible to visitors who could never have afforded the journey before. For the first time mass mobility was not all in the one direction.

Several of these initiatives began with the Americans and were filtered through the mechanisms of the Greek state. But the most pervasive effect of American tutelage on the Greek economy seems to have been to unleash a spirit of entrepreneurism that had once flourished in the late eighteenth century, but during the intervening years had often been eclipsed by the centralizing power of the state. In the 1950s and 1960s it was small family businesses that proved to be the engine of growth, especially in construction, tourism and shipping. Between 1950 and 1973 it has been estimated that growth in Greece was 'the highest in the capitalist countries of southern Europe and perhaps in the whole western world', with an increase in Gross Domestic Product that averaged 6.5 per cent per year.[3]

During the first half of the 1950s, the prospects for the Greek state had never looked better. The Americans were the new Bavarians. It had taken them rather longer, but by their intervention they had put an end to a decade of bloodshed, just as the Bavarians had done in 1833. Bringing with them less cultural baggage, but a political agenda dictated by the *Realpolitik* of the Cold War, the Americans opened the way to a new era of modernization.

But it was not to be so simple. Despite all the efforts that had been made during the three decades since the Asia Minor Catastrophe of 1922, the story of the Greek *state* could still never be the whole story. It was time once again for the nation beyond its borders to assert itself – with consequences that at the time were incalculable and have yet to be fully played out, more than half a century later.

THE NATION REDISCOVERED

The defeat in 1922 had all but collapsed the distinction between the Greek state and the wider Greek nation. But not quite. After the end of the Second World War there were still Orthodox Christian, Greek-speaking communities that had been established for centuries in regions of the eastern Mediterranean that remained outside the frontiers of the Greek state. One of these was the southern part of Albania, often in Greek called contentiously 'Northern Epiros'. The political divisions of the Cold War ruled out any adjustment there for the foreseeable future. Another was the Dodecanese, consisting of the twelve islands and surrounding islets in the southeastern corner of the Aegean, lying close to the Turkish mainland. The fortunes of war had ended the Italian occupation of these islands, dating back to 1912, in September 1943. After that they had passed to the Germans, then to the British. Nobody had any serious objection in 1946 to the Dodecanese becoming part of Greece. Even the government of Turkey acquiesced, although previous administrations had resisted Greek expansion so close to the Turkish mainland, and the largest of the islands, Rhodes, had and still does have a significant Turkish minority. The twelve islands duly became united with Greece in March 1947.

That left Cyprus. In the case of 'Northern Epiros' there had been no chance for the people concerned to have a say. In the Dodecanese, there had been no need. With Cyprus, it was different. Cyprus had passed from Ottoman to British administration in 1878 and since 1925 had been governed as a Crown Colony of Great Britain. Out of a population of some six hundred thousand, 80 per cent were Orthodox Christians who spoke the Cypriot dialect of Greek. This was a significantly higher proportion of Orthodox Greek speakers than had existed in many areas that had become part of the Greek state earlier in the century, notably Crete and much of Macedonia, including the city of Salonica, which had by this time become the 'co-capital' of Greece. The Greek Cypriot majority, and many in Greece too, had always assumed that sooner or later the British would allow the island to become part of Greece, as they had once done with the Ionian islands.

This was not a far-fetched proposition. After all, Great Britain had actually offered the island to Greece back in 1915, as a sweetener to the anti-Venizelist government to enter the First World War. Thirty years later, when Archbishop Damaskinos visited London in his capacity as regent, he was urged by the poet and diplomat George Seferis, who was then his private secretary, to add Cyprus to his wish list from the new British Labour government. First responses were not discouraging. Then, in 1947, Britain withdrew from its colonial possessions in the Indian subcontinent, and a month later unilaterally pulled out of Greece, so opening the way to the Truman Doctrine. All the signs were that the old imperial power was in retreat.

Successive governments in Greece had never been keen to push the issue of Cyprus. Britain had been too important an ally to risk alienating by supporting Cypriot claims for *Enosis* – union with Greece. And of all the regions that had seen movements for *Enosis* during the past century, Cyprus was much the farthest away. Although the argument seems not to have been publicly articulated, a unified Greek state that included Cyprus might present formidable logistical problems for its defence. Probably for all these reasons, it had been left to the Greek Cypriots themselves to make the running. When they rebelled in October 1931, the prime minister in Greece had been none other than the former champion of the wider nation, Eleftherios Venizelos. But Venizelos at the time had been preoccupied with managing the fallout from Britain's departure from the gold standard the previous month, and his country's bankruptcy that followed. Despite some agitation in Greece, the Greeks of Cyprus and their grievances had been held at arm's length by the Greek state that so many of them seemed eager to join.

Quite why they were still so eager at the end of the 1940s is an open question. The Cypriots had been in a position to observe from a distance the disintegration of that state and its horrific consequences. They themselves had been fortunate to be spared. Cyprus had never come under attack by the Axis, although Cypriots had volunteered for service with British forces during both world wars. But the fact is that they were eager as never before. What nobody could have foreseen, either in Cyprus or in Greece, at the beginning of the 1950s, was what a vicious lash the dying British Empire still had in its tail.

Political leadership of the majority Greek-speaking community of Cyprus lay with the Orthodox Church. There was no secular alternative, since the British colonial administration had abolished an elected Legislative Council after the disturbances of 1931. Head of the Orthodox Church was the Archbishop of Cyprus. Since the sixteenth century, archbishops had enjoyed the additional title of 'Ethnarch'. This was an elected office from among the island's bishops, with tenure for life. But the Ethnarch, by tradition and long-established practice that had begun under the Ottomans, was more than a spiritual leader. He was expected to act as the spokesman, defender and protector of his flock. It was a legacy of the Ottoman system that political power, responsibility and, incidentally, a great deal of wealth had come to be accumulated by the Church of Cyprus. Successive generations of British colonial rulers, brought up to consider Church and state as separate spheres, had never really got the hang of this. In the new circumstances of the 1950s the consequences would prove explosive.

An unofficial referendum of its members was held by the Church of Cyprus in January 1950. Voting took place in churches and was not secret. But historians accept that the response of 96.5 per cent of eligible votes cast in favour of union with Greece was a fair expression of the popular will. Six months later, the eighty-year-old archbishop and ethnarch, Makarios II, died. In October 1950 his successor was elected 'by a majority claimed to represent 97 per cent of the Greek Cypriot people'.[4] Michael Mouskos, son of Christodoulos, had been born into a family of small-scale farmers and pastoralists in the district of Paphos. Later, on entering the Church, he had given up his family name, as is customary, and taken the monastic name of Makarios, meaning 'blessèd'. As archbishop he became Makarios III. Not quite thirty-seven years old, this third Makarios was one of the youngest to hold the office. And he was not just young. He was a figure of exceptional energy, talent and charisma. During the next two decades Makarios would run rings around British, Greek, Turkish and later Cypriot politicians and diplomats. Makarios remains a towering figure in the political history of the Greek nation during the second half of the twentieth century – indeed literally. At the imposing site of his grave above the Kykkos Monastery in the foothills of the Troodos Mountains, his bronze effigy stands some thirty feet high, still wearing his trademark ecclesiastical robes and enigmatic smile.

The result of the referendum was predictably brushed aside by the British colonial authorities. But the leadership of the Orthodox Church in Cyprus was determined, even before the election of Makarios as archbishop, to maintain momentum and seek support for their cause from outside the island. Their first port of call was Greece. A delegation arrived in Athens in June, bringing with them the bound volumes that held the signatures of the voters in the referendum. Less than a year had passed since the end of the Civil War. The Greek state and its citizens had barely begun to lick the wounds it had inflicted, let alone heal them. And here was a clarion call from beyond their borders that immediately evoked the glory days of 1821 and 1912. Even better (unless you looked too closely at the internal politics of the Greek Cypriots, as most in Greece did not), here was a cause capable of uniting the entire political spectrum: for the right a nationalist struggle along traditional lines, but for the left no less appealing as a stand against imperialism and colonialism. Indeed, as the decade progressed, in Greece it would be the defeated and marginalized left that would most effectively give voice to public opinion in favour of Makarios and *Enosis* for Cyprus.

Throughout that time, the foreign policy of successive Greek governments would be to varying degrees held hostage by an agenda that was set in Nicosia and driven by Makarios. Despite the pragmatic reluctance of government ministers, in Greece the cause of *Enosis* quickly took fire in street demonstrations and in the columns of the press. As early as May 1950, sentiments were being voiced in the Greek parliament that would not have been out of place in the 1840s: the government in Athens had a responsibility to 'the nation as a whole and not just the Greek state in its narrow "politically artificial" borders'. The *nation* came first. And the nation had 'never consisted of the citizens of the Greek Kingdom only'.[5]

It was at the insistence of Makarios that the government led by former Field Marshal Alexandros Papagos made a series of direct appeals to the British to begin negotiations for an orderly transition towards the union of Cyprus with Greece. One of these involved a face-to-face meeting with the Foreign Secretary, Anthony Eden, in 1953. Afterwards, the Greek side considered that Papagos had been gratuitously insulted. The stakes were raised even higher the next year, when a junior minister in the House of Commons went so far as to say that there were certain colonial possessions that for strategic reasons could 'never' be allowed to pass out of British sovereignty. The Conservative government that had come to power in Britain in 1951 had rowed back a long way from the tentative openness shown at first by its Labour predecessor in 1945.

These repeated rebuffs by an ally and former 'protecting power' only served to inflame public opinion in Greece still further. The Athens government was caught in a pincer movement between Makarios on one side and the British on the other. But Makarios and the Cypriot leadership were not content with putting pressure, via the Greek government, on Great Britain. In parallel, and from the beginning, they had determined on a policy of internationalizing their claim for union, through an appeal to the United Nations. Here the grounds were not the century-old appeal to the Grand Idea of uniting the nation, but rather the principle of self-determination for the majority of Cypriots. The practical problem was that only those who already enjoyed self-determination had the right of appeal to that forum. So once again the hard task fell to the government of Greece – first to lobby the Assembly to be allowed to make the case for the Cypriots, and then to make it sufficiently persuasively. The British went to great lengths to prevent the appeal from reaching the Assembly at all. And despite repeated attempts the case was never accepted by the UN.

What the Cypriot leadership was attempting to do was to repeat the successful tactics of the Greek revolutionaries in the 1820s. But in the new conditions of the 1950s, internationalization brought with it new dangers. Historians based in Greece, though not their counterparts in Cyprus, have seen this in hindsight as a fatal mistake: to bring the issue of self-determination before the United Nations would be to open the door to Turkey, which could be expected to intervene to protect the interests of its own minority in Cyprus.[6]

In reality, throughout the first half of the 1950s, this risk was much less than it has come to seem in retrospect. The government of Adnan Menderes and the Democratic Party that had been voted into office in Turkey in 1950 was at first committed to maintaining good relations with Greece. The governments of both countries were keen to participate in the NATO alliance. A new 'treaty of peace and friendship' was signed between them in February 1953. For the Menderes government, as for those of Atatürk and İnönü before it, Cyprus was simply not on the agenda. The territory of the Turkish nation had been defined by the 'National Pact', drawn up at the very beginning of the Turkish national movement, in September 1919. It did not include Cyprus. In the Treaty of Lausanne, in 1923, the Turkish side had abrogated all claims to Cyprus in favour of Great Britain. What would happen if the colonial power were in turn to hand it over to someone else had not been considered at the time. But in the early 1950s the Turkish position was clear and disinterested. The Greek Orthodox leadership in Cyprus and policymakers in Greece could be forgiven for failing to anticipate what happened next. It was not Turkey, the traditional adversary, that first raised the stakes, but Great Britain.

The crunch came in the summer of 1955. Eden's successor as Foreign Secretary, Harold Macmillan, at short notice invited the governments of both Greece and Turkey to send their foreign ministers to London for a 'tripartite conference' on the future of the island. 'The stronger the position the Turks take at the outset [of the conference] the better it will be for us and for them,' wrote Macmillan to his officials shortly before it began. Noting that the purpose of the conference was not to bring agreement, but in effect to 'divide and rule', one British historian has drawn attention to the 'high-risk nature of this gambit, and its not entirely respectable character'. Makarios at the time called it 'crooked'.[7] There were of course no representatives from Cyprus present.

By this time, the tone of Menderes and his foreign minister, Fatin Zorlu, had become markedly more populist. Some in the British Foreign Office were already fearful that the fuse had been lit for an explosion that nobody would be able to control. So it would prove. On 5 September, as the conference was nearing its end, Zorlu seems to have thought that the British were about to yield to the demands of the Greek side. If true, this was a complete misreading of the entire nature and purpose of the conference. In a telephone call to Istanbul from London that evening, the Turkish foreign minister is reported to have said that 'a little activity will be useful'.[8] Next day, a mass demonstration gathered in Taksim Square, in the centre of Istanbul. A tide of violence swept through Beyoğlu, the 'European quarter' of the city, known in Greek as Pera. All the evidence suggests that it was orchestrated, at the beginning at least.

The violence of 6 and 7 September 1955 in Istanbul and other Turkish cities has been called by Greek commentators and historians a 'pogrom'. While the police stood by, some seventy Orthodox churches were looted and set on fire, and Greek businesses and homes were ransacked. In only twenty-four hours ancient hatreds burst through the surface to wreck the rapprochement between Greece and Turkey that went back to 1930 and had so recently been cemented through NATO. The events of those two days would set the seal on Greek–Turkish antagonism that has dominated the relationship between the two countries ever since. The Greek Orthodox community of Istanbul, some hundred thousand strong, had been spared forcible removal under the terms of the Lausanne agreement in 1923. Now began a rapid exodus that within a very few years would reduce it to its present-day level of a couple of thousand.

In order to gain short-term political advantage and keep control of Cyprus for a few years longer, Macmillan and his policy had unleashed the genie of populist anger in the largest and most powerful of Greece's neighbours. It could never again be put it back in its bottle. Six years later Menderes and most of his cabinet, including Zorlu, would be hanged after being ousted in a military coup, in part because of their role in instigating these events. But no subsequent Turkish government, of whatever political colour, military or civilian, has ever yet found it possible or expedient to give ground over Cyprus, more than sixty years later.

By the time the tripartite conference took place, on the island itself an armed struggle had already begun. The guerrilla group that took up arms in April 1955 announced itself as the National Organization of Cypriot Combatants, better known by its acronym in Greek, EOKA. Its leader was a former colonel in the Greek armed forces, Georgios Grivas. Originally from Cyprus, Grivas had fought against the Italians in Albania. Towards the end of the Occupation and for a short time afterwards, he had led a militia known by the Greek initial 'X', pronounced 'Chi', which targeted Greek communists. Far more of a military tactician than a politician, Grivas would evade all efforts by the British security services to hunt him down, just as his political master Makarios equivocated over his support for the armed struggle. While the conflict lasted, Grivas appropriated to himself the name 'Digenis', invoking the quintessential hero of a heroic oral tradition shared throughout the Greek-speaking world. Today one of the main thoroughfares in Nicosia is named Grivas-Digenis Avenue.

In the eyes of the British, EOKA was a terrorist organization. To its supporters its members were freedom fighters engaged in a struggle for national liberation. Sabotage and ambushes targeted the military and the police, the very methods that guerrilla groups had used against the Axis occupiers in Greece during the war. Then, British service personnel had aided and abetted them. Now it was the turn of the British to be targeted as the enemy. At the same time, EOKA meted out exemplary punishment to those perceived to be 'traitors'. It also carried on a subsidiary campaign against members of the Cyprus Communist Party (known by the initials AKEL). These tactics were more reminiscent of the practice of both sides in the Greek Civil War. The EOKA campaign began with a series of explosions and attacks on police stations, more than two hundred of them in the first three months. Soon the British responded by declaring a state of emergency. Under emergency laws anyone caught carrying a weapon would face a mandatory death sentence.

The first executions were carried out under these laws in May 1956. Michael Karaolis, known as Michalakis, was twenty-three at the time of his conviction, Andreas Dimitriou twenty-one. Both were tried by due process, the one for shooting a Greek Cypriot policeman dead in broad daylight in the centre of Nicosia, the other for shooting and wounding an Englishman in Famagusta. But in Greek eyes the trials were flawed because the key witnesses, as well as the prosecutor, were Turkish Cypriots. The executions shocked public opinion throughout Cyprus and Greece. No form of public demonstration was allowed in Cyprus. But in Athens on 9 May news that the men would be executed the next day brought an incensed crowd to Omonoia Square. There they attempted to storm a building that had been cordoned off by armed police. In scenes that must have been alarmingly reminiscent of events in the city's other main square in December 1944, jittery policemen opened fire. Four people were killed and dozens injured.[9]

Afterwards, throughout Greece, towns and squares would be officially renamed after the executed men, names that remain in place today and include the street in front of the building that at the time housed the British Embassy in Athens. EOKA responded immediately by killing two British army corporals it had been holding hostage. These men, who had not harmed anybody, are not commemorated anywhere.

All told, the EOKA struggle cost just over five hundred lives lost, with more than twice that number injured. Over half of these casualties, far outnumbering either British military personnel or members of EOKA, were Greek Cypriot civilians. Compared to other anticolonial struggles of the 1950s and 1960s, the damage was limited.[10] As a military conflict, this one was also inconclusive. As had happened so often before in the history of the Greek nation, the solution would be found far away, this time in New York, Zurich and London.

Before that could happen, the British government further alienated the Greeks of both Cyprus and Greece by the arrest of Archbishop Makarios at Nicosia Airport, in March 1956, as he was preparing to board a plane for talks in Athens. Makarios would not reach his destination for another thirteen months. During that time, the Ethnarch was held a virtual prisoner in an even remoter British island dependency, the Seychelles. When Makarios did finally reach Athens, during Orthodox Holy Week on 17 April 1957, he was treated to a hero's welcome. An American-style motorcade carried him from the airport, with many stops for greetings and speeches from local dignitaries, to the Grande Bretagne Hotel in Syntagma Square. The moment has been aptly called the 'apogee of his entire career'.[11]

While Makarios addressed the crowd with an emotional impromptu address from the balcony overlooking the square, there must have been some in the crowd down below who had stood in the same space to hear Venizelos speak from a similar balcony almost half a century earlier, when he had first arrived from Crete to become prime minister of Greece and lead the country into the triumphs of the Balkan wars. Many more would have known of that occasion from their parents or their history lessons. Could it be that, once again, a spirit of renewal was about to sweep in from the wider nation and clear out the cobwebs and frustrations and petty rivalries that beset the Greek state?

But the times were different, and so was the man. There is no evidence that Makarios ever harboured ambitions to rule in Greece. Venizelos in 1910 had been ready to leave his embattled island behind him and pursue a larger vision, which in time would come to encompass the union of his homeland with Greece. Makarios was in Athens only because the British authorities would not let him go home to Cyprus. Venizelos had been invited to the Greek capital because there had been a vacancy at the top. In 1957 there was no vacancy, even if none of the leaders of the political parties could match Makarios in charisma or (probably) popular following in the country. Possibly Makarios missed an opportunity that might have changed the course of the nation's history. More likely, there was no opportunity.

Whatever the reason, from that moment onwards, the initiative slowly but inexorably began to slide out of Makarios's hands.

By 1957 the international context had changed. The Anglo-French attempt to seize back the Suez Canal, after the Egyptian leader Abdul Gamal Nasser had nationalized it, had ended in disaster the previous November. The 'Suez crisis' was to prove a turning point for the old European colonial powers. In Britain it also ended the political career of Anthony Eden, who had succeeded the ailing Winston Churchill as prime minister the year before, and he resigned in January. The new prime minister was Harold Macmillan, the architect, while he had been Foreign Secretary, of the ill-fated tripartite conference on Cyprus. Political priorities for the British Conservative government were changing too. In the changed climate after Suez, it would no longer be unthinkable to give up Cyprus, provided that Britain could keep its military bases. The Turkish side was now pressing for the island to be partitioned. During 1957 a new possibility began to be canvassed: that Cyprus might instead become an independent state. That way, the two communities might eventually forge for themselves a new national identity as Cypriots.

Just as these ideas were gaining ground in the political arena far away, events in Cyprus took a turn that with hindsight should have been taken as an awful warning. Intercommunal relations in Cyprus had never been marked by the mutual antipathy or outbreaks of reciprocal violence that had been the hallmark of the struggle for *Enosis* in Crete throughout the nineteenth century. Even after the start of its campaign in April 1955, EOKA does not seem to have targeted its victims *as Turks*. On the other hand, since Turkish Cypriots were disproportionately represented in the local security forces, they were increasingly exposed to attack. When a senior Turkish Cypriot officer of the police Special Branch was assassinated in November 1957, the event provoked a long-delayed backlash by the Turkish Cypriot community, aided by the government in Ankara.

This took the form of a new insurgency ('terrorists' or 'freedom fighters', according to perspective). It was called the Turkish Resistance Organization, and known by its initials in Turkish, TMT. The final phase of the EOKA campaign now became a three-way contest, fought throughout 1958. For the first time, the worst of the violence was perpetrated by the two clandestine guerrilla organizations against civilians of the other community. Riots were sparked by Turkish Cypriots in Nicosia in January and June. Victims of the mob were lynched. A convoy of Greek Cypriot prisoners, under British escort, was ambushed in June, and several of the prisoners hacked to death. EOKA now began to strike back against the Turkish Cypriot community. It also used intimidation against its own people, to prevent them moving out of areas where Turkish Cypriots were taking over control. All over Cyprus, houses began to display the national flags of Greece or Turkey – ironically the beginning of a habit that would continue throughout the history of independent Cyprus.

And yet a diplomatic solution *was* found. It came from an unlikely quarter. On the evening of 4 December 1958, on the fringe of a debate in the General Assembly of the United Nations, Zorlu, the Turkish foreign minister, bore down on his Greek counterpart, Evangelos Averof-Tositsa. Why, said Zorlu, should the two of them not sort out their countries' differences over Cyprus? Effectively, this is what happened. The British government was sidelined. So too were Makarios and the Cypriots. Both foreign ministers found they could agree to Cyprus becoming an independent state. That way, Greece would have to give up the idea of *Enosis*, Turkey of partition. Great Britain would give up sovereignty but keep its military bases. All sides would be losers. But it mattered more that none would come out a winner. There are echoes, in this deal, of the way in which Greece itself had won its independence in the early 1830s – except in the outcome.

The details were hastily thrashed out among the representatives of Great Britain, Greece and Turkey at conferences in Zurich in December 1958 and at Lancaster House in London the following February. Makarios was brought in only at the last minute. There came a moment of almost unbearable tension at Lancaster House, when under intense pressure from the Greek and British ministers present, Makarios at first refused to sign a final agreement over which he had

had no say and which he would now be responsible for implementing. The moment passed, and the independent Republic of Cyprus was signed into being on the afternoon of 19 February 1959.

When Makarios landed at Nicosia airport on 1 March, after an absence of almost exactly three years, he greeted the waiting officials and reporters with a single word. It was the word, in the original ancient Greek, supposed to have been spoken by the first Marathon runner when he brought the news to the Athenians of their victory over the Persians in the battle of 490 BCE: 'We have won.' What Makarios privately thought we will never know. He must have known very well that this was no victory. The poet George Seferis, wearing his diplomatic hat, had played a leading part in the negotiations, only to be horrified by the outcome. Foreseeing its likely consequences more accurately than most at the time, Seferis concluded in the privacy of his diary, a year after the agreement had been signed, 'We [Greeks] aren't fit for great things.'[12] It was the saddest of epitaphs for the old Grand Idea that had been buried in the ruins of Smyrna almost forty years before, but whose lingering memory had still not been fully laid to rest.

The Republic of Cyprus formally became an independent member of the British Commonwealth on 16 August 1960. Elaborate constitutional arrangements had been worked out to ensure that power was shared between the two communities. The president would always be a Greek Cypriot, the vice-president a Turkish Cypriot. Lower offices were assigned more or less proportionally (and were the subject of much haggling, both before and afterwards). The republic was to have both Greek and Turkish as its official languages, and a national flag representing the map of the island on a white background above a pair of olive branches, symbolizing peace. Great Britain retained sovereignty in perpetuity over the military bases of Akrotiri and Dhekelia. By an arrangement reminiscent of Greece in the nineteenth century, the independence of the fledgling republic was to be guaranteed by the three powers that had brought it into being: Britain, Greece and Turkey.

With the future of Cyprus seemingly settled, leadership of the Greek nation had been reasserted by the government in Athens. Relations between Greece and Britain had reached an all-time low while the conflict over Cyprus had lasted. But with nothing much at stake thereafter, they would be quickly repaired. America, Greece's new patron, had stood by on the sidelines throughout the conflict, watching events with some degree of bafflement, irritation and, at times, consternation. Once the involvement of Turkey had become clear, the priority for the United States was to minimize disruption to the NATO alliance. This necessarily involved some distancing from Greece. The beginning of popular anti-American sentiment among Greeks, which would peak in the 1980s, has been traced to those years. Not coincidentally, in 1959 the Karamanlis government began to seek a new alignment towards the emerging European Economic Community, the EEC, the forerunner of today's European Union.[13]

In the meantime, during the 1950s and 1960s, creative spirits in Greece were starting to explore rather different ways to be Greek.

DANCING WITH ZORBA

Going to the cinema, in the 1950s, was an inexpensive way to enjoy an evening out. The new favourable conditions for small, family-run businesses combined with the influence of Hollywood to generate a home-grown film industry. In terms of the number of films made per head of population, productivity in Greece would soon grow to rival Hollywood itself. In the cities and larger towns, electricity had now reached most neighbourhoods. By the end of the decade the number of cinemas in Athens and Piraeus seems to have been not far short of five hundred. Vacant building sites were easily converted into open-air cinemas for the summer months. Annual ticket sales more than doubled between 1956 and their peak in 1968, by which time on average Greeks were going to the cinema once a fortnight, the highest rate in Europe. Between 1944 and 1974 more than fifteen hundred films were released.[14]

The role of the Greek state is revealing. At this time there were no state subsidies. The enterprise that proved so productive was entirely private. The subsidized Greek art-cinema of more recent times lay way in the future. Censorship, on the other hand, was strict, and maintained throughout the whole period until 1974. No mention of

Communism, the Civil War, contemporary politics or anything that might offend foreign tourists or investors was permitted. Nothing but respect must be shown to members of the armed forces or the country's ancient monuments. It is sometimes suggested that in this way the state did exercise a controlling function. But in practice this was usually done with a light touch, and a great deal of indifference. If storylines could not be based on books by communist writers, there was no ban on actors or musicians who belonged to the far left. Before 1967 it was rare for the censors to have to intervene. Directors had already internalized the agenda for themselves. Like Hollywood or any other popular art form, Greek cinema of the 1950s and 1960s maintained its own taboos.

Films were made on a minimal budget, until the mid-1960s usually shot in black and white, filmed on suburban or rural locations of a type that would be immediately familiar to most cinemagoers, and aimed at a mass audience – all reasons for them to have been largely ignored by historians until our own century. Greek society was changing very rapidly. The films themselves and their huge popularity were part of those changes. Of course the characters and the storylines that appear in them were not true reflections of everyday life, despite their often recognizable settings. But they did cater to some of the hopes and anxieties of a time when record numbers of people were leaving behind their remote villages, moving to hastily built suburbs and coming to terms with the effects of new-found affluence – whether or not they also shared in it.

Out of this ferment of activity emerged some all-time classics. *Stella*, released in 1955, was only the second film by the young British-educated director from Cyprus, Michael Cacoyannis. It also marked the cinema debut of the future political activist and Minister of Culture, Melina Mercouri. With overtones of classical tragedy and the brutal realities of life in traditional Greek communities, *Stella* adapts the story made famous by Georges Bizet in the opera *Carmen* to a working-class suburb of Athens in the 1950s. Mercouri's character rejects every one of the conventions set by traditional Greek society for female behaviour. She pays the price, as might be expected. Social norms are upheld. But the sheer power of Mercouri's performance forced audiences to recognize in this macho femme fatale that most cherished of all Greek *male* values: heroic defiance in the face of impossible odds.

Soon, Greek films were beginning to be noticed at international festivals. Some of the directors were Greek Americans who already had a foothold in the US industry. It was at Cannes that Mercouri, the star of *Stella*, met the American-born director Jules Dassin, whom she went on to marry. They starred together in *Never on a Sunday*, which Dassin also directed. Very much a 'Greek' film, this was one of the first to be made with English dialogue. It was released in 1960. Dassin plays a young American who on a first visit to Greece is befriended by the Piraeus prostitute Illia, played by Mercouri. Her name is not a real girl's name in Greek, but sounds like the feminine form of the word for 'sun'. He is called Homer. At once he decides that Illia must be a 'symbol' of the quest that has brought him to Greece. Like Professor Higgins in Shaw's *Pygmalion*, Homer takes it upon himself to reform her. Two thousand years ago, he tells her, 'Greece was the greatest country in the whole world'. 'It still is!' retorts Illia. The naiveté of the heart-of-gold good-time girl of Piraeus and the naiveté of the starry-eyed American called Homer (this was long before *The Simpsons*) both raise smiles from a more knowing audience. The reality of what Greece might actually be, or become, in the new decade of the 1960s floats, elusively, somewhere between and beyond the two of them.

Never on a Sunday won the prize for best actress at the Cannes Film Festival. The Oscar for best original song that year went to Manos Hadjidakis, who had composed the soundtrack. This was something else about these Greek films: they guaranteed the popularity of the other great success story of Greek creativity of the time and eventually helped bring it to the attention of an international audience. This was Greek popular music.

Hadjidakis, along with his contemporary Mikis Theodorakis (both of them born in 1925), had been responsible during the previous decade for launching a new style of music that brought to prominence the *bouzouki*, until then the quintessential musical instrument of the urban Greek underworld and the *rebetika* tradition. Based on the characteristic rhythms and some of the tonality of *rebetika*, this 'new wave', as it soon came to be known, also drew on elements of rural

Greek folk music and European and American popular song. The result is an exuberant hybrid, at once easier on Western-trained ears than true *rebetika* or the Middle Eastern modal tradition from which they derive, and melodically as catchy and inventive as nineteenth-century Italian opera.

The twin originators of this movement could not have been more different from one another. But they had one important thing in common. Both were outsiders. Hadjidakis was homosexual at a time when public attitudes to sexuality in Greece were as conservative as they come, Theodorakis a communist who had once been left for dead after a beating during the 'White Terror', and had experienced detention without trial and torture during the Civil War. Both men were poles apart from the 'official' Greek state in the 1950s and 1960s. Perhaps for that reason, ironically, the 'new wave' they introduced into Greek music 'met with *national* acceptance and [was] endorsed by left and right alike'.[15]

All the elements of the new style came together in 1960, when Theodorakis launched his musical setting of eight poems by the communist poet Giannis Ritsos. It was something of a miracle that these songs were allowed to circulate at all. The lyrics came from a poem that Ritsos had published in the communist daily, *Rizospastis*, shortly before the Metaxas dictatorship. They lament the death of a young tobacco worker, shot dead by police during one of the strikes in 1936 that Metaxas had used as his excuse to seize power. The written word was not subject to censorship at this time, but gramophone records were.

More remarkable still was that Theodorakis would soon enter politics as a member of parliament for the United Democratic Left (EDA), the relatively far-left party that was known to be a front for the banned KKE. He would go on to set more poems by Ritsos, including *Romiosyni*, which ever since has been one of his best known and most loved compositions. Ritsos's poem had been written during the 'White Terror', between 1945 and 1947. It celebrates a version of Greek identity throughout history as a never-ending revolutionary struggle against an unforgiving environment and predatory outsiders. Ever since the disc was released in 1966, Greeks of all political stripes and none have sung themselves hoarse to keep up with the thrusting drumbeat and clangorous *bouzouki*, with the words:

> When they clench their fists
> sunshine's a sure thing for the world.[16]

It was not only communist poets whose works became the lyrics of 'new wave' music. George Seferis and Odysseus Elytis may well have been helped towards their respective Nobel Prizes for Literature, the one in 1963, the other in 1979, by the popularity of their poems set to music by Theodorakis. Soon every composer was doing it. Most of the major figures in Greek poetry at the time eagerly and willingly worked with them. Texts that had been written to be intellectually challenging on the page acquired new life, and sometimes quite new meanings, transposed into a musical idiom that was at once new and felt to be deeply rooted in popular traditions that were uniquely Greek: *rebetika* and the even older rhythms and melodies of the mountains and islands.

This remarkable meeting of the popular with 'high' literature reached its apogee in another film directed by Cacoyannis and released in 1964. *Zorba the Greek* is based on the novel written by Nikos Kazantzakis during the Occupation and published shortly afterwards. The film was made in English and uses the catchier title devised for the novel in translation. In this way Kazantzakis's *Life and Opinions of Alexis Zorbas* became a fable about the true identity of the modern Greek – even though the title role was taken by the Mexican-American Anthony Quinn and the other male lead was changed from an overly cerebral Greek intellectual to a gormless Englishman, played by Alan Bates. The film was made on location in Crete with local villagers as extras. Theodorakis composed the music. At the climax of the story, after everything has gone wrong, the earthy, vibrant Zorba is asked humbly by his intellectual 'Boss' to teach him to dance. In the novel, this is a moment of liberation, a short-lived transcendence of the barriers between soul and body, between intellectual deliberation and spontaneous, joyous emotion. In the film, the two characters start off with the slow 'butcher's dance', the *chasapiko* that is one of the staples of *rebetika*, then break into the much faster *chasaposerviko*, which despite its name is a very different dance, this time from the rural tradition. The result, with Theodorakis's pulsing, staccato, unforgettable music, has been known ever since as *syrtaki* – a 'traditional' Greek dance that had never existed before.

Two foreign actors capering in an invented, hybrid dance on a Cretan shore, to music written in a new style for new audiences, both at home and abroad – that is the final image of *Zorba the Greek*. Once again, for good or for ill, the business of being Greek was never going to be a matter for Greeks alone. By 1964 it had entered on an entirely new phase – and one that for once had almost nothing to do with the Greek state or its institutions.

POLITICAL CAR CRASH

Not for the first time in the history of that state, the vitality of its 'bold pioneers' in the creative arts was sadly lacking in the political sphere. The stability of right-wing governments elected since 1952 was beginning to break down ten years later. The governing party, at first known as Greek Rally, morphed after the death of its leader, the former Field Marshal Papagos, into the National Radical Union under Konstantinos Karamanlis, who succeeded him in 1955. In the parliamentary election of 1958 the United Democratic Left (EDA) had overtaken its centrist rivals to become the main opposition party, in part thanks to its strong line against concessions by the government over Cyprus. Then in 1961 that role passed to the recently reorganized party of the centre-left known as the Centre Union.

This was the successor to the party formed by Nikolaos Plastiras, veteran plotter and last true adherent of Venizelism, at the end of the Civil War. Briefly, in its earlier incarnation, Plastiras's party had shared power with the last rump of the old Liberals, led by Venizelos's son Sophocles. Now the leadership had passed to George Papandreou, who had last held office during the chaotic events of 1944. In October 1961 the Centre Union was narrowly defeated at the polls. Papandreou cried foul: the election had been rigged by the so-called 'para-state', a shadowy but not imaginary network of right-wing cronies in the police, the civil service and the armed forces. The actual extent of this interference in the election has never been determined. Probably it had not been enough to determine the outcome. But it did give Papandreou the impetus he needed to declare an 'Unrelenting Struggle' for eventual victory.

The first scent of that victory came two years later. By the summer of 1963 the government of the National Radical Union was struggling. Karamanlis fell out with King Paul, the brother of George II, who had died in 1947, not long after his much-contested return to Greece. The murder of a member of parliament for EDA, Grigorios Lambrakis, in Salonica in May, would provide the most vicious proof yet of the existence of the 'para-state' – and later be brought to worldwide audiences through the 1967 novel Z by Vasilis Vasilikos and the Costa-Gavras film based on it. In the changed political climate, Papandreou's Centre Union came first in the parliamentary election held in November. But its majority was too narrow to enable Papandreou to form a government. So he asked the king for a dissolution. A new election was called for February 1964. This time the Centre Union came home triumphant.

Greece had never before had a government that could be called even very moderately left wing. This one would prove cautious in its approach to radical reform. Under Papandreou, opportunities for education were extended, particularly at university level. The government promoted the demotic form of the language – in the teeth of opposition from diehards who since the Civil War had got used to thinking that only the hated communists used demotic Greek in public. But on the issues that still most divided the nation, Communism and the country's commitment to the NATO alliance, Papandreou was as uncompromising as his predecessors had been. It had been his antipathy to Communism that had recommended Papandreou to the British in 1944. It was no less acceptable to the Americans twenty years later.

As bad luck would have it (and probably it *was* a matter of chance), the arrival in power of the Centre Union coincided with the collapse of constitutional arrangements in Cyprus. At the end of 1963 the intercommunal conflict that had begun during the last year of the EOKA struggle reasserted itself. While the 1964 election campaign was going on in Greece, a peace conference in London was trying to find a solution. Only three weeks after Papandreou's victory, a resolution was passed in New York that would bring United Nations peacemakers to the island to oversee the physical separation of the Greek and Turkish communities. War between Greece and Turkey was only avoided in June 1964 by the intervention of the American president, Lyndon Johnson.

A month after that came a new US plan for Cyprus. The 'Acheson Plan', so called after the former Secretary of State brought in to draft it, proposed to replace the unwieldy Constitution of 1960 and allow the island to be united with Greece after all. The price was to be the lease to Turkey of a military base in Cyprus, proportional with the size of the Turkish Cypriot population. The Turks would also gain sovereignty of the tiny Greek island of Kastellorizo, the remotest from Greece of the Dodecanese. Papandreou might have signed up to this, but Makarios prevented him. If the issue of *Enosis* had not gone away, neither had the tussle for control of the initiative over Greek foreign affairs between Athens and Nicosia. Both would have fateful consequences a decade later.

The other piece of bad luck for the Centre Union government was the death of King Paul from cancer just four weeks into its tenure. The late king had proved a much less divisive figure than his brother. King Paul, who had come to the throne in 1947, had done much during his reign to heal what was still left of the old 'National Schism', at least within the anti-communist camp. His son came to the throne as Constantine II some months short of his twenty-fourth birthday. Greece had not seen so young a sovereign since the early days of King George I, almost exactly a century before. Within months, the young king and his prime minister, who at seventy-six was more than three times his age, were heading for a clash that would prove almost as destructive as the one between the new king's grandfather Constantine and Venizelos half a century before.

On the surface it was about control of the armed forces. Rumours of conspiracies had been coming and going for years. A group of extreme-right officers known by the acronym IDEA (which means the same in Greek as it does in English) had been around since the 1940s. Newly discovered, and far more disturbing to the king, to the right-wing opposition and to the whole anti-communist apparatus of the 'para-state', was a new one called ASPIDA (the acronym means 'shield'). Not only were these left-wing officers plotting to destabilize the armed forces and the state, it was also alleged that among their number was the prime minister's own son.

Andreas Papandreou was at this time in his mid-forties. Not long before, he had given up a promising career as an academic economist in the United States to join his father's government as an adviser. Politically well to the left of the elder Papandreou, it was Andreas, the 'firebrand' (and ever afterwards known in Greece by his first name), who really struck terror into his father's political enemies. In the climate of mutual suspicion that had built up by the summer of 1965, the question of control over the armed forces had become toxic. ASPIDA was probably no more subversive, or perhaps even real, than the Philorthodox Society that had allegedly plotted to oust King Otto in the first years of the Greek kingdom. One American former diplomat, who had been in Athens at the time, later concluded, 'What the ASPIDA officers were trying to do was thwart a rightist military coup against the Papandreou government.'[17]

In July, believing that his position was being undermined by his Minister of Defence, Papandreou sacked him and proposed to take on the portfolio himself. There were plenty of precedents for both actions in Greek parliamentary history. But the king trusted the ousted minister more than he trusted Papandreou. He refused to allow the prime minister to become also Minister of Defence, on the grounds that Andreas Papandreou was under investigation for subversive activity. When Papandreou repeated the (not very successful) tactic of Venizelos exactly fifty years before and offered his resignation, Constantine promptly called his bluff and accepted it. This provoked a constitutional crisis. 'Who governs Greece?' demanded Papandreou. 'The King or the people?'[18]

The king now resorted to the same tactic that in the hands of his uncle George II had opened the way for Metaxas. Once again it would lead to a dictatorship, though this time not immediately. Constantine called on one member of parliament after another to form a government. He was successful on his third attempt, and only after a sufficient number of members from the ruling Centre Union had been induced (it is sometimes alleged bribed) to enter into a coalition with the centre-right opposition to defeat their own party in a vote of confidence. The government of Stephanos Stephanopoulos and the 'apostates', as they were called, took office in September 1965 and held on precariously for fifteen months.

As soon as Papandreou's resignation became known, violence once more spilled out onto the streets of Athens, soon to be dubbed the 'July events'. While the 'apostate' government lasted, life in the cities was continually disrupted by mass demonstrations and politically motivated strikes. The polarization of the Civil War appeared to be returning. The right feared a takeover by the left and the banned communists. The left feared the collapse of the parliamentary system and a right-wing dictatorship. Rumours of an imminent coup d'état flew back and forth. The names of so many plots and potential plotters were bandied about that the one that was actually hatching escaped the notice of everyone – probably even of the American Central Intelligence Agency, which many Greeks have never ceased to believe masterminded it.

After more fractious politicking, a date was finally set for a new parliamentary election: Sunday 28 May 1967. Papandreou's Centre Union party was the favourite to win. A surge in support for the far-left EDA was also a distinct possibility. Parliament was dissolved on 15 April. Three days later a group of middle-ranking army officers met at the house of the most senior among them, Brigadier Stylianos Pattakos. Among their number were Colonel Georgios Papadopoulos and several others who had worked for the Greek secret service. These men had access to the details of a contingency plan that had been drawn up by NATO to secure the country in the event of war with the communist bloc, and known by the codename 'Prometheus'. In the early hours of Friday 21 April, without the knowledge of the king, of the army High Command, or of the Americans whose plan it was, the Prometheus Plan went into action.

Armoured units moved out of their barracks and took up positions throughout the capital. Tanks surrounded the king's country estate at Tatoï on the northern outskirts. Armed soldiers took over the central telephone exchange and the national radio station. Athenians woke up that morning to find the streets empty except for tanks and uniformed soldiers, their telephones dead and the radio blasting out military marches alternating with traditional folk-dance music associated with patriotic anniversaries. Only a few newspapers reached the streets. In those days there were no social media or private radio stations. Television was still in its infancy in Greece, and of course another state monopoly. Most senior politicians who could be found at home were taken into custody. So were officers in the armed forces senior to the plotters, until they had demonstrated their loyalty to the new regime. A round-up of known leftists targeted not just communists but suspected sympathizers and the family members of anyone associated with them. Before long, several thousand would be imprisoned, placed under house arrest, or exiled to the notorious prison islands in the Aegean that were quickly brought back into use for the purpose. The dictatorship of the 'Colonels', also known in Greek by the Spanish term *junta*, had arrived.

STRAPPED IN PLASTER

The first edicts of the new regime sounded all too like a repeat of 1936. Constitutional rights were immediately suspended, including the right of assembly. Strict censorship was imposed, and lists drawn up of forbidden books (including some ancient Greek classics) and forbidden music (anything by the communist Theodorakis, Greece's most popular composer by this time). Long hair on men and miniskirts on girls were prohibited – and this at the height of the 'swinging Sixties'! Everyone was told to go to church. Not even the 'Colonels' could quite repeat the rhetoric of the 'Third Greek Civilization', with its overt echo of the Third Reich. But they came close with the slogan, first heard almost a year after the coup and ubiquitous thereafter: *Hellas of Christian Hellenes*. The leaders (or their backroom ideologues) had benefited from an education more limited than had Metaxas; their rhetoric has been much mocked, both at the time and in retrospect. Here is Papadopoulos, the 'strongman' of the regime, the former colonel who over six years would accumulate the offices of regent (later president), prime minister, defence minister and foreign minister, addressing students of Greece's second university, in Salonica, on 29 March 1968:

We are by inheritance and by tradition the chosen people, which has enlightened mankind with the wonders of the most perfect civilization . . . *Hellenes*, then, according to our racial origin and national conscious-ness, and *Christians* according to the contents of our faith: these make up the diptych that, with its richness of knowledge, traditions, and the facts of history, describes the ideal for us, for the individuals of this country, for the Hellenes of our Nation.

Behold then the ideal, to which we must return. Christian Hellenes we must become once more . . .[19]

The 'Colonels' also followed Metaxas in using economic policy to keep large sections of Greek society compliant. Until 1973 the con-struction boom in cities continued strongly, with easier access for entrepreneurs to capital than before. In 1968 agricultural debts were cancelled, relieving a long-standing source of grievance in rural com-munities. The regime presided over an impressive expansion of the networks of roads, the telephone system and television into parts of the country where they had never reached before. Characteristically, Greece's second TV channel, introduced in 1968, was called the 'Information Service of the Armed Forces'. Along with much-needed development in communications went control over them. For most of its seven years of usurped power, the new dictatorship would prove easily as efficient as the Metaxas machine had been at detecting and forestalling opposition.

But in other ways the two dictatorships were very different. Metaxas had acted in concert with his king. In 1967, King Constan-tine found himself an unwilling accomplice to a coup that had been carried out without his knowledge. Later in the year, when new fears of war with Turkey over Cyprus seemed to have opened up a rift within the armed forces, the king tried to assert himself and over-throw the regime. In the conditions of the 1930s it had been the monarch, not the dictator, to whom the armed services would ult-imately owe their loyalty. Not so in the 1960s. The king's counter-coup, on 13 December 1967, was a dismal failure. King Constantine fled the country, never to return as sovereign. So completely had the old fault line shifted that neither the monarchy itself nor the person of the monarch still roused the passions of earlier years. Throughout the

Greek military in the late 1960s, anti-Communism trumped every other allegiance.

The other great difference lay in the role of the armed forces. In practice, during the seven years that the 'Colonels' ruled, this always meant the army. The much smaller and traditionally elite services, the navy and the air force, were little involved. Unlike any other period in the country's history, these seven years brought the army out of its barracks, onto the streets and into positions of control over every aspect of public life. True, the 'Colonels' and their superior, Brigadier Pattakos, all resigned their commissions early on. But their mentality and their proclamations remained those of the military. A poster campaign all over the country proclaimed 'Long live the Revolution of 21 April 1967'. Huge billboards and fixed metal placards carried the image of an armed soldier in full combat gear, silhouetted against the mythological symbol of the phoenix rising from the fire. The grip of the army was ubiquitous, and everywhere to see. For those who transgressed, or were suspected of transgressing, it could also be brutal.

The regime's own favoured metaphor for what it was doing was drawn from surgery. Papadopoulos himself explained it, during his first appearance before the representatives of the world's press, six days after the coup, with characteristic clumsiness:

> Do not forget, gentlemen, that we find ourselves in front of a patient on the operating table, whom if the surgeon does not strap him down for the duration of surgery and anaesthesia upon the operating table, there is a probability that instead of surgery bringing about the restoration of his health, it will lead to his death.

The more famous metaphor of the plaster cast was an elaboration of this basic idea: 'We have a patient. We have strapped him in plaster. We test him to see whether he can walk without the plaster.'[20] In a short story published in 1970, as part of a collective effort by writers to test, in turn, the limits of changing censorship laws, the novelist Thanasis Valtinos took this metaphor to its absurd and grotesque conclusion. In Valtinos's story, the hapless patient, strapped down, watches in increasing horror as more and more of his body is encased in plaster. Just at the moment when the wet substance is forced into his mouth, shutting him up for ever, he realizes that he has seen the surgeon before. It is the same man who had earlier tripped him up and caused his accident.[21]

In the real world, the years passed, but the patient was never quite ready to be released from the plaster cast. Then, in the summer of 1973, Papadopoulos judged that he could risk a limited experiment. In July a referendum was held on a new republican constitution. In the circumstances, a 'yes' vote was predictable. Even so, a quarter of voters risked prosecution by abstaining. Papadopoulos made some attempt to woo former politicians, but only one responded. On 1 October 1973 the formation of a new government was announced. Papadopoulos was confirmed as president. The sole politician became prime minister, and began to talk of a general election to be held on 10 February. It remained to be seen how far the plaster cast might be eased before then, or whether other reputable politicians would agree to take part.

But Papadopoulos had overreached himself. Visible signs of discontent came from quarters where the dictatorship was already most deeply resented. Relative relaxation brought them to the surface. A mutiny by naval officers was quickly put down in May 1973. But more persistent trouble was emerging in universities. For six years students had been denied the right to elect their own representatives to student unions, traditionally a highly active component of Greek university life. From the start of the year, a series of occupations of faculty buildings by students had begun to bring public attention to the issue. On 4 November many took to the streets in central Athens. More than thirty students were arrested after clashes with police. Scenes such as these had been an almost daily occurrence during the years immediately before the coup. Now, after six years of absence, they had returned. Nine days later students began massing at the Athens Polytechnic.

Those were the *visible* signs. Unseen, but in its effect more deadly for the regime, was reaction among many of the original plotters of the 1967 coup. That was the trouble with taking off the plaster cast. Papadopoulos might or might not deliver what he now seemed to be promising. But from the point of view of those who had never had any intention of handing back power to civilian politicians anyway, the recent signs of unrest were all the proof they needed that the new president had gone too far. Papadopoulos's days in office were already numbered, even while the courtyard and lecture halls of the Polytechnic were filling up with young people chanting 'Bread – Education – Liberty!'

Over three days, beginning on the morning of Wednesday 14 November, the lecture halls and quadrangles of the Athens Polytechnic became the focus for spontaneous mass action. Students from other faculties that had been closed by their governing bodies for fear of trouble all found their way to the Polytechnic. No one was in control – although before long an ad hoc 'Coordinating Committee of Occupation' emerged to maintain a remarkable degree of cohesion and order. At various times during the three days the occupation was swelled by sympathizers who included many school pupils, disaffected workers, self-styled anarchists and, by most accounts, *provocateurs* from both political extremes. By Thursday a crowd estimated at ten thousand had gathered in the wide street outside the wrought-iron railings of the Polytechnic campus and was chanting in support of the students. The next day their number had swelled to anything between double that and a scarcely plausible hundred thousand. Still, after three days, the government sat on its hands.

An extraordinary wave of euphoria and sense of empowerment swept through the young people who had barricaded themselves inside the Polytechnic and their supporters massed outside. Using makeshift equipment scavenged from the occupied laboratories, and their own technical skills, the organizing committee set up a short-wave radio station. From the early hours of Thursday, the call sign 'Polytechnic here' was heard in households all over Athens. The breathless, excited voices of the youthful announcers began to call for political change. Nothing like it had been heard on air for six and a half years. 'Fascism dies tonight' was one of many slogans repeated, along with denunciations of the 'junta' – so named in public for the first time. A manifesto, also broadcast, called for the overthrow of the regime and a return to 'national independence and popular sovereignty'.[22]

For many who later recalled these events, it was a time when everything seemed possible. 'We really thought we had the POWER at this moment,' said one. In the words of another, the future novelist Ioanna Karystiani, who in 2018 would be nominated as a candidate for President of the Republic:

everyone was determined, no matter how mad it seems to you, it was transcendence ... We had taken off, this did not touch us any longer ... Without knowing consciously that history was being written at this moment.[23]

Meanwhile, in the street outside the Polytechnic and in other parts of the city centre the mood was turning ugly. There were several clashes between demonstrators and police during Friday afternoon. Tear gas began to be fired about 5 p.m. An hour later firearms were being issued to police guarding the Ministry of Public Order. Shooting started around 7.30, when some of the crowd forced their way into the building. By 8 p.m. the Chief of the Athens Police had to concede that 'the violence was beyond his control'.[24]

The decision to bring in the army had already been taken – it seems on the authority of Papadopoulos alone. The order to the troops was given shortly after 11 p.m. Violence was continuing in the street outside the Polytechnic and around the Ministry of Public Order a few blocks away. Police marksmen were firing from positions on top of buildings. Victims of bullet wounds were being carried inside the Polytechnic. The student radio began appealing urgently for doctors and medical supplies. Official media claimed that armed 'anarchists' were slaughtering policemen. There were indeed some casualties among the police, but none from firearms.

Between 1 and 2 a.m. on the morning of Saturday 17 November three tanks moved into position facing the outer gate of the Polytechnic grounds. Representatives of the students made a brave and dignified attempt to negotiate an orderly evacuation. There was no question of resistance. Those who stood on the low wall, clinging to the railings that faced the street, and their comrades massed behind them, were waving the blue-and-white national flag and singing the national anthem. The claim that this was a communist insurgency was never going to be credible (even if the most prominent of the students did belong to banned far-left groups). Almost immediately the leading tank began to move slowly forward against the locked double wrought-iron gates. A car that had been parked against them as a barricade was crushed flat, along with the gates and the legs of a girl student. This happened at 3 a.m. The student radio had kept up a running commentary on the violence outside and the movements of the tanks. Now it fell silent.

Marines with fixed bayonets charged through the flattened gates and began forcibly evicting the students. Those leaving were savagely beaten by the waiting police as soon as they reached the street. Many hundreds were arrested. What has remained in popular memory from that night is the image of the tank pushing forward against the gate and the spectacle of the nation's armed forces being turned against its own youth. But it seems that it was the police, not the army, who killed people that night: twenty-four of them, in the streets near the Polytechnic.[25]

Martial law was declared. For several days the army remained on the streets. Sporadic violence continued. It was the turn of the soldiers, mostly snipers on rooftops, to use lethal force. As many as another twenty civilians may have been shot dead between 17 and 20 November. Extraordinarily for a European country in the late twentieth century, it has never proved possible to establish with certainty how many were killed and injured. Families covered up for lost loved ones when they could, for fear of further persecution. In all, by the start of the following week, official figures gave the number of those arrested at almost three thousand. Unofficial estimates come close to three times that number. Many more went into hiding.

Yet for all the drama and horror of those events, it was not the student revolt at the Athens Polytechnic that brought down the regime of Georgios Papadopoulos. On Sunday 25 November, just over a week after the storming of the Polytechnic, the tanks were back on the streets throughout Greece. In a faultlessly executed and bloodless coup, hardliners within the military put into effect the plans they had been laying for several months. Papadopoulos and his fig-leaf civilian government were dismissed. The new figurehead and head of state was a uniformed general whom few had previously heard of, Phaidon Gizikis. His prime minister was an even more obscure figure, and for the sake of appearances a civilian. The Athenian rumour mill quickly established that the real power behind the new junta was one of the original architects of the 1967 coup. A former colonel and latterly brigadier-general, Dimitrios Ioannidis was head of the dreaded Military Police (ESA). Although he held no office in the government, either under Papadopoulos or under Gizikis, it was Ioannidis who now held the reins of power in Greece. Far from being the first dawn of liberation, the student revolt of November 1973 was destined to be buried beneath an even deeper layer of plaster than before.

The 'heroes of the Polytechnic', as they are remembered today in names of streets and squares all over Greece, had achieved precisely nothing by their bravery, optimism and defiance. On the other hand, they would give their name to a 'Polytechnic generation' that in Greece is the equivalent of the 'Generation of May '68' in France. Nothing that has happened in Greek politics since that time makes sense without reference to those days of 1973 and the ways in which they would later become seared into public memory. That is the true legacy of 'the Polytechnic'.

As 1973 gave way to a grim start to 1974, the endgame was still some months off. As had happened so often before, it would be played out in a far corner of the Greek nation – and its victims would not be citizens of the Greek state.

Relations between the governments of Cyprus and Greece had been poisonous since the coup of 1967. Despite surface cordiality, by the summer of 1973 Makarios had already survived two attempts by the Greek junta to have him assassinated. A bomb attempt that narrowly failed to kill Papadopoulos in his car in an Athens suburb in 1968 turned out to have been inspired by maverick supporters of Makarios in Cyprus. While Greece remained encased in 'plaster', with parliament and the democratic process suspended, Makarios went on to win landslide majorities in 1968 and 1973. The tables had been turned on the long-cherished notion of *Enosis*. Cyprus was now the last bastion of democratic freedom in the Greek-speaking world. For as long as the junta lasted, few Greek Cypriots wanted to be united with it.

The junta had other ideas.

The Cypriot National Guard had been established after the disturbances of 1964. It was largely a conscript army, made up of local Greek Cypriots. But its officers were seconded from Greece. In 1971 the elderly Colonel Grivas, the former leader of EOKA in its struggle against the British in the 1950s, returned secretly to Cyprus from Athens. A new clandestine organization began to operate in the island, known as EOKA-B. The National Guard was known to be cooperating with Grivas. Unable to rely on the nominal armed force of his own government, Makarios began recruiting a 'Reserve Corps' made up of loyalists. He also raised the stakes by making overtures to the communist bloc, playing on the non-aligned status of his fledgling republic. In an earlier age this might have been smart politics. But in the conditions of the early 1970s it thoroughly alarmed the American administration of Richard Nixon, and particularly its hawkish Secretary of State, Henry Kissinger. When a supply of arms arrived in Cyprus from communist Czechoslovakia, the two Greek Cypriot armed forces fought a pitched battle to take possession of them. From late 1971 until the summer of 1973 a state of virtual undeclared civil war existed among the Greeks of Cyprus – while the Turkish Cypriots kept to their enclaves and had withdrawn from participation in the island's political life.

All this came to a head in July 1974. Grivas had died in January, and been given a hero's funeral in Athens. Then in June, at a NATO summit, an agreement between the foreign ministers of Greece and Turkey was deliberately torpedoed by the Athens junta, seemingly on the orders of the all-powerful Ioannidis. Three Greek ministers resigned immediately, recognizing that their country was provoking a war it was in a poor position to win. At the beginning of July, Makarios addressed a long letter to the military government in Athens. Soon its contents would be leaked to the newspapers in Cyprus. Insisting that he was 'the elected leader of a large section of Hellenism', Makarios demanded an end to the activities of EOKA-B and the withdrawal of the Greek officers from the National Guard.[26]

The only answer he ever received came on the morning of Monday 15 July. Armoured vehicles of the National Guard moved into strategic positions and began shelling the presidential palace in Nicosia, where Makarios had just arrived. At eleven o'clock, Cyprus state radio, now under control of the military, began to broadcast the news that Makarios was dead. Nikos Sampson, a former EOKA guerrilla fighter with no political experience and with close links to the Greek junta, was named president in his stead.

The Sampson coup was fiercely resisted by Greek Cypriots – a fact that has ever since been overshadowed by subsequent events. But for four days that July, Cyprus was gripped by all-out civil war. It is by no means certain that the junta could have imposed its will on Cyprus, even if there had been no outside intervention. It was Greek Cypriots, the overwhelming majority of them still loyal to their elected president, Makarios, who fought back against the short-lived Sampson regime, and resisted the unilateral declaration of *Enosis* that in the event was never made.

From the point of view of the plotters, everything went wrong that possibly could. Makarios, with great personal courage and the help of devoted associates, escaped alive from the gutted presidential palace. Thanks to his old adversaries, the British, he was flown out of the sovereign base of Akrotiri on an RAF plane and arrived in London two days later. There he found the prime minister of Turkey already lobbying the British government to take a hand in Cyprus. The coup had been a flagrant violation of the treaty guaranteeing the island's independence. Britain, Greece and Turkey were all signatories. It should have been possible for the three NATO allies, with their common patron the United States, to sink their differences in an agreed solution. If that had happened it might even have brought Greece back to civilian rule without bloodshed in Cyprus.

One reason it did not is that the governments of all three allies were deeply insecure at this time. In Britain, the Labour Party led by Harold Wilson had been elected in February but lacked an overall majority and would go to the polls again in October. In Turkey, the newly elected centre-left government of Bülent Ecevit was dependent on an unstable coalition and would prove almost as short-lived. That left the United States. There, the administration had been paralysed for months by the Watergate scandal that would soon put an end to Richard Nixon's presidency. During those weeks the American government was as close to leaderless as it probably ever has been. So it is hardly surprising that no common course of action was agreed in London. Faced with the refusal of British ministers to act, Ecevit determined to intervene unilaterally. Turkey launched an invasion of the north coast of Cyprus by sea and air during the night of 19–20 July 1974. The divided Greek Cypriots stood no chance.

In Greece, it was the moment that the junta seemed to have been waiting for. Within hours Greek state radio announced general mobilization. All reservists throughout the country were called to report to their units. But the Greek armed forces, despite having absorbed the lion's share of government expenditure for seven years, were in no condition to take on an external enemy. All their efforts had been expended on repression at home. The few attempts made by Athens, during the first twenty-four hours of the Turkish invasion, to send reinforcements to Cyprus were half-hearted and ended ignominiously.

At a news conference on 22 July the American Secretary of State, Henry Kissinger, announced that a ceasefire had been brokered in Cyprus. It took effect that afternoon. With little thanks due to the Greek military or the country's leaders, Greece had been saved from the immediate prospect of war. The fate of Cyprus was to be decided by international negotiations, to be held in Geneva over the coming weeks. That only left the junta in Athens, now wholly discredited, to unravel, as it did over the next thirty-six hours. The most senior among the military now sidelined Ioannidis and closeted themselves in the office of President Gizikis to hammer out a face-saving solution. On the afternoon of 23 July it was announced that military rule was at an end. A civilian government would be sworn in the next day. Jubilant crowds thronged every public space. In Syntagma Square in Athens all traffic came to a halt. The square and the surrounding streets filled with people waving the national flag, singing songs by the banned composer Theodorakis, and cheering. Everywhere the emblems of the regime were torn down and trampled.

As darkness fell a new slogan began to swell among the crowd: '*E-e-erchetai*' ('He is coming'). 'He' was Konstantinos Karamanlis, the former leader of the centre-right National Radical Union who had served as prime minister for eight years before going into voluntary exile in Paris. Karamanlis was met by jubilant supporters at Athens airport at 2 a.m. on the morning of 24 July. Much remained to be done before Greece's transition to democracy could be assured. But the rule of the 'Colonels' was over.

It was the people of Cyprus who paid, both Greek Cypriots and Turkish Cypriots. By mid-August two rounds of negotiations in Geneva had failed to produce a political solution. In the United States,

Richard Nixon had resigned on 9 August. Foreign policy was in the hands of Kissinger, to whom the fate of Cyprus was not the highest priority. On 14 August the Turkish army began a new offensive. In three days it advanced to a line that brought some 37 per cent of the island's land area under its control. A second ceasefire was brokered three days later. Centuries of intercommunal living were obliterated, as tens of thousands of Greek Cypriots fled south before the advance of the Turkish army, while Turkish Cypriots abandoned their homes to flee in the opposite direction. One-quarter of the entire population of Cyprus was displaced at this time. Tens of thousands were killed, including twenty thousand 'missing' whose fate remains unknown.

More than forty years later, no peace terms have ever been agreed or a peace treaty signed. The line that has divided Cyprus since August 1974 is not an international frontier. It marks the limit of conquest by the Turkish army that was reached on that August day. Much has been said and written, during those forty-plus years, about the legality of Turkish actions. The simple truth is that international law did justify the *first* offensive, to the extent that its aim might have been the restoration of the status quo before the Sampson coup. Nothing justified the second.[27]

This was the price for the return of democracy to Greece. For Greece itself, July 1974 marked the end of an aberration, but also of an era of bitter division that went all the way back to the early years of the century. The Greek word *metapolitefsi*, meaning 'change of political system', is today applied not just to the moment and its immediate aftermath, but to the whole period of political maturity and prosperity that began in 1974 and would last for more than thirty years.

11

Coming of Age in Europe

1974–2004

Many things would never be the same again after 1974. The role of the national army as a means of internal control came to an end, seemingly for good. It was a role that can be traced back all the way to the Bavarians in the 1830s. Since 1909, army officers had repeatedly taken it upon themselves to make and break governments. Now, the bitter lesson of seven years of military dictatorship and the fiasco of its ending had been learned. The transition from dictatorship to pluralist democracy would call for adroit statesmanship on the part of Karamanlis. Unreconciled elements within the army would have staged another coup given half a chance. Indeed, several plots would be foiled during the first years of transition.

The first parliamentary election in almost exactly ten years was held on 17 November 1974. Only four months had passed since the collapse of the junta. The day had been chosen because it was the first anniversary of the suppression of the student revolt at the Athens Polytechnic. The election was won handsomely by a new political party that had been created almost overnight to supersede the National Radical Union that Karamanlis had led in the 1950s and 1960s. New Democracy was created very much in the image of its leader. Role models for Karamanlis, after a decade of exile in Paris, were General de Gaulle and the Gaullists.

This new centre-right political force was sharply differentiated from its pre-junta incarnation in another way too. Gone were the fierce anti-Communism and the automatic Cold War alignment with the strategic interests of the United States. One of Karamanlis's first acts after his return was to withdraw Greece from the military wing of the NATO alliance. This was a way of channelling public anger against America, which had at the very least tolerated the regime of the 'Colonels' and in many quarters was blamed (and continues to be, to this day) for the disaster in Cyprus. Another of his acts, which would prove politically longer-lasting and more far-reaching, was to renew Greece's application to join the European Economic Community (EEC) as a full member. This had been frozen, on the European side, with the imposition of dictatorship. The process was restarted by the Greek government in June 1975. The move away from the tutelage of the United States towards European institutions, which had begun in the wake of the Cyprus conflict in the 1950s, would be completed over the next fifteen years.

No less significant was the lifting of the ban on the KKE, the Communist Party of Greece, in time for the party to participate in the November election. The ban had been in force since 1947. The last time that the KKE had contested a parliamentary election had been in January 1936. This time it won an increased yet still modest share of the vote, but fewer seats. There was no question, now, of holding the balance of power as the communists had done in 1936. The main opposition party in the new parliament was once again the Centre Union, by this time led by Georgios Mavros, who had been one of the lieutenants of the elder Papandreou in the pre-junta parliament. The Centre Union would soon be eclipsed by another newly formed party, which in 1974 came in only just ahead of the communists but three years later would emerge as the official opposition, and from 1981 would go on to dominate Greek politics for three decades.

This was the Panhellenic Socialist Movement founded and led by Andreas Papandreou, and known by its Greek acronym, PASOK. Back in the 1960s, 'Andreas' – as he has been universally known to friends and foes alike – had instilled terror in government and diplomatic circles with his radical left-wing views. During the junta years, spent mostly in exile, he had become a rallying point for opposition to the dictatorship. In the uncertain climate of 1974, Andreas's moment had not yet arrived. PASOK's founding declaration, dated 3 September that year, announced 'the beginning of a new political Movement' intended to express 'the desires and needs of the ordinary Greek, a Movement that will belong to the peasant, to the worker, to the artisan, to the wage earner, to the employee, to our courageous and enlightened youth'. Its stated aim was to create 'a polity free of foreign control or intervention, a polity free of the control or the influence of the economic oligarchy'.[1] PASOK in its early days combined a populist appeal to the integrity of the nation with an agenda for social reform that had previously been proposed only by the communists. Greece, according to PASOK, should now seek its place on the world stage among the non-aligned nations that sided with neither bloc in the Cold War.

Above all, the new movement was to be *new*. It was not even to be called a 'party'. Its symbol was a dark green half-sun topped by spiky green rays, presumed to be rising, though it could as well have been setting. An early critique by a historian and political scientist, published not long after its rise to power in 1981, would prove correct: 'PASOK is . . . the prodigal son of the Center rather than the illegitimate offspring of the Left.'[2] But in one important respect neither of the two political forces that between them would determine the future shape of the *metapolitefsi* was new at all: both PASOK and New Democracy were the projections of charismatic individual leaders whose careers had been shaped during the pre-junta period.

In the event, *metapolitefsi* came to stand for far more wide-ranging transformations than those to to the political system, drastic though these were. Less than a month after the election, Karamanlis held a referendum on the future of the monarchy on 8 December. In another break with its pre-junta past, this time a centre-right government held aloof from the contest. It was probably the only time in their history when the people of Greece were able freely to express their opinion on the subject. Just under 70 per cent voted for a republic, on a turnout of 77 per cent. A new republican constitution was adopted the following year. Ever since, the official name for the Greek state has been the 'Hellenic Republic'. This is the constitution that remains in force today, subject to some later revisions. A year later, after much deliberation and public discussion, an act of parliament established that demotic Greek was to replace the hybrid *katharevousa* as the official language of education – and therefore, in practice, in most walks of life (exceptions are the Church and the law). This move brought an end to another form of polarization, between rival forms of written Greek, that had become codified in the early twentieth century. During the second half of the 1970s, the divisions that had split Greece along different fault lines for half a century were finally, and rapidly, disappearing.

Another transformation that has come about since 1974 has had an incalculable and continuing effect. This one took place outside the country's borders and beyond the control of the Greek state and its institutions. This was the division of Cyprus by the Turkish army. Ever since 1974, the Republic of Cyprus has had jurisdiction in practice over slightly less than two-thirds of the island's territory. The Constitution of 1960 remains legally in force, with its national flag and both Greek and Turkish as official languages. In theory, and in international law, the government of the Republic of Cyprus retains legitimate authority over all of Cyprus, with the exception of the two British sovereign base areas. But the reality since 1974 has been that the southern part of Cyprus has become a second Greek nation state. This is a situation with few precedents (Germany and Austria come to mind), and it is anybody's guess how it might evolve in future.

Greek Cypriots after 1974, with international support, rebuilt their devastated country and its economy with spectacular success. Relations between the two Greek governments, of Greece and of Cyprus, have been cordial throughout the period. There has been no return to the mutual vendetta between the Greek junta and the democratic Cyprus of Makarios. Instead, successive governments in Greece have loyally stood up for their sister state, both diplomatically and in providing for its defence. But although the Cypriot state shadows the Greek in many things – its national anthem, national holidays, the form of the Greek language used in its education system and bureaucracy – in other ways the period since 1974 has seen the beginning of a divergence both in politics and in culture. The word 'Helladic' has been heard with increasing frequency, not just in Cyprus but to some extent in Greece too, to distinguish the Greek state and its subjects from the Greek institutions and the Greek citizens of the island of Cyprus – a subtle distinction from 'Hellenic', since both peoples regard themselves equally as Hellenes.

For these very good reasons, the story of the Greek nation since 1974 may be predominantly, but never can be only, the story of a single Greek state.

A DECADE OF 'CHANGE'

Andreas Papandreou's Panhellenic Socialist Movement (PASOK) swept to power in an electoral landslide in October 1981, capturing just short of 50 per cent of the popular vote, and close to 60 per cent of seats in parliament. It had been done on the one-word promise of 'CHANGE'. A great many things did change during the rest of the decade, not least among them the governing party itself and its charismatic leader.

It was the first time that Greeks had ever elected an explicitly socialist government. It was also the first time since the early twentieth century (some would say ever) that a change of government had come about entirely through the democratic process, without either violence or the threat of violence, and without interference, whether actual or suspected, by the army, the throne or foreign powers. In that sense 1981 marks a turning point. It would prove to be the first of many orderly changes from one government to the next, a pattern that at the time of writing has not been broken since.

The most radical and far-reaching changes brought about by PASOK were all introduced during its first few years in power. All were domestic, and can broadly be described as social. The most dramatic, and long overdue, was the retrospective recognition of all combatants who had fought against the occupying powers during the Second World War as the 'National Resistance'. For the first time in almost forty years, the role of communists and other supporters of the left in resisting the Axis could be openly and publicly acknowledged. Historians were no longer obliged to step around a taboo topic. Memoirs of those who had taken part began to be published. Novelists, who as a rule had studiously avoided the subject too, now began to mine their own and the collective memory, to begin to come to terms with experiences that until this time had been buried in silence. Veterans of the left were no longer persecuted or marginalized, but became eligible for the pensions that the 'anti-communist state' of the 1950s and 1960s had awarded to former collaborators but not to them. Those who had found refuge in the Soviet bloc during the civil war, and their descendants, were for the first time free to return. The long-delayed process of healing had begun. It would not be completed until shortly after the fall of the second PASOK government in 1989.

Other legislative changes related to family law. Adultery ceased to be a criminal offence. Divorce (never outlawed, as in Catholic countries) could for the first time be obtained by mutual consent, without the obligation to prove adultery as before. Civil marriage was introduced, despite objections from the Church. Women's rights and new standards of gender equality for the first time entered the statute book. Spending on pensions and social welfare went up by almost 50 per cent during PASOK's first four-year term in government. A national health service was created in 1983. New universities and technical colleges sprang up all over Greece. At the same time, the old hierarchy of university governance was shaken up, in part along the lines of the American system that Papandreou had known in his previous life as an economics professor.

PASOK also changed the way that governments were run. Beginning in 1982, at the highest ranks of the civil service tenured professionals were replaced by political appointees. The day-to-day exercise of power became politicized in a way it had not been during earlier periods when governments had been less stable or more extreme, such as the 1930s. Since the early 1980s, commentators have noted the absence of a corps of capable senior civil servants to manage transitions between governments, or indeed to advise on the implementation of policy.[3] The creation of a genuinely mass party, for the first time in Greek history, also had a transformative effect on the traditional system of patronage, one that has come in for trenchant criticism ever since. It was no longer individual members of parliament who were expected to distribute privileges to their voters, but the party to its members. Far from abolishing the inherited system of patrons and clients, often identified with 'corruption', the effect of PASOK's dominance of the political landscape was to reshape it into a state-run institution.

Perhaps the most visible sign of change during the 1980s was the increase in the general standard of living. This was brought about not by growth in the economy, as it had been in the 1950s and 1960s, but by expansion of the state. The role of the state at this time has been called 'parasitical'. The growth in the size of an increasingly politi-cized civil service was only slightly greater during the 1980s, under PASOK, than it had been under New Democracy before it. But the combined effect was that over the two decades until 1991 the number of public servants more than doubled. PASOK policies on welfare and tax have come in for even more excoriating criticism. The traditional 'tax and spend' policy associated with left-of-centre governments, according to one caustic observation, in the Greek case became 'spend and don't tax' – since the taxation system itself became one of the channels through which successive governments (not only PASOK) would seek to 'buy' electoral support.[4]

But if the methods had changed, there was little that was new about attitudes to tax and the state in Greece in the 1980s and 1990s, either on the part of governments or those governed. Kapodistrias at the end of the 1820s or King Otto's Bavarian advisers in the 1830s would have recognized the situation perfectly. Papandreou and PASOK, no less than those early predecessors, were committed to bringing their country into line, at least superficially, with what passed for 'modernization' in the developed world at the time. And superficially, at least, they were remarkably successful, just as their predecessors had been in the 1830s. But the mapping of standards and practices derived from the developed world onto attitudes and behaviours that were deeply ingrained in quite different traditions would once again begin to produce fractures, in the period of *meta-politefsi* just as in the early years of the Greek state. It is often said that these attitudes are the legacy of centuries of Ottoman oppres-sion. The truth is that they arose out of the very particular conditions of the creation of the Greek state itself, which was seen in its earliest years as a cash cow to be milked in lieu of the plunder that had dried up with the departure of the oppressors. It is debatable how far that perception had changed during the last decades of the twentieth century – or indeed has changed today.

Paradoxically, one of the most effective agents of change during the 1980s and beyond, the one that most conspicuously had an impact on living standards and that also affected the entire land-scape of the country, was neither Papandreou nor PASOK but something that they had started out by fiercely opposing. This was

Greece's membership of the European Economic Community (EEC), the precursor of the European Union (EU) of today. Very much thanks to the personal initiative of Karamanlis, going back to his first premiership at the end of the 1950s, and renewed after 1974, Greece became the tenth member in January 1981. Papandreou came to power ten months later. PASOK had from the beginning been viscerally opposed to the EEC. The agenda for 'CHANGE' left no room for dependency on foreign powers, neither the United States (whose influence in Greece would never recover after 1974) nor the emerging European supranational body. But the Greek equivalent of 'Euroscepticism' was a short-lived phenomenon, and it peaked in the election of October 1981.

After four years of being an unwilling partner in the European enterprise, the PASOK government began to discover unexpected advantages of membership during its second term, after being re-elected in 1985. The economy was struggling. Greece, as one of the poorest members, was a net beneficiary, and the benefits exceeded all expectations. In those early days leading up to the completion of the European Single Market in 1992, a large part of the EEC budget was taken up with transfers from the wealthiest states to the poorest. It was a version of PASOK's own policy of income redistribution writ large. Huge sums came to Greece in the form of 'Support Frameworks' and 'Stability Packages', while the Common Agricultural Policy brought unprecedented subsidies to Greek farmers. Not surprisingly, the farmers were grateful. There were votes in EEC membership after all.

And so, almost in spite of itself, PASOK during its second term began to morph into a Western-style social democratic party. From its instinctively Europhobic beginnings it became increasingly wedded to the project of European integration. Thanks to the influx of European funds, in tandem with changing attitudes, lifestyles began to look more Western too. Greek cinema had never recovered the ground it had lost to television after 1968. Now people stayed at home to watch TV – especially after the licensing of the first commercial channels in 1990. The traditional men-only *kapheneion*, where elderly denizens played backgammon, drank coffee and disputed the contents of the daily newspapers, began to be displaced by smart bars where young people of both sexes would congregate. The *taverna* serving locally produced food, with a predictable menu subject to official price control, had increasingly to compete with Western-style restaurants offering international cuisine. The old, somewhat relentless, conventions of Greek hospitality were relaxed. As a foreigner, it became permissible to be entertained to a meal in a public restaurant rather than lavishly at home – though never to pay for it. In the eyes of visitors from Western Europe or North America, Greece was rapidly becoming less 'exotic' and more 'European'. For the majority of Greeks, life was becoming more comfortable than it had ever been.

Before long the change would spread to the physical landscape. Projects born in the late 1980s, and funded by European programmes, would go on to completion during the next decade and a half: among them a network of motorways that has reduced journey times across the mountains of the mainland from a whole day to a few hours, a much-enlarged Metro system and a new airport for Athens, and the spectacular Charilaos Trikoupis Suspension Bridge across the mouth of the Gulf of Corinth, almost three kilometres long, which opened in 2004.

Apart from the move towards European integration, which was unplanned, it was probably in external relations that the promised 'CHANGE' was *least* in evidence. When it came to foreign policy, PASOK has been described as 'a party with a Western mind and a Third World heart'.[5] In its language and symbolic gestures, during its early years, it spoke from its heart. Its actions were usually more pragmatic, and more closely aligned with Western priorities than its heart would acknowledge. For that reason, actual change from the policies of the past was much less than many observers were expecting.

By the time of PASOK's first election victory, the previous government had already rejoined the military wing of the NATO alliance that it had left in 1974 – and for a very good reason. NATO had not been able to prevent the Turkish invasion of Cyprus. But it was only through membership of the military alliance that Greece could hope to maintain its armed forces in a ratio to those of its much larger and better-armed neighbour. And mediation by NATO still looked like the best protection against further conflict with another member of the same alliance. Greece was in a weak position, as much less strategically important in the Cold War than Turkey. And although it was hardly the fault of Greece's post-1974 civilian governments, it was an uncomfortable fact that the war in Cyprus had been started by the Greek junta, with its attempt to topple Makarios and impose *Enosis*, and not by Turkey.

Another factor had entered the equation, to strain relations with Turkey still further. This was the discovery of an oilfield off the northern Greek island of Thasos in late 1973. The international oil crisis caused by the Yom Kippur War that autumn was beginning to bite. With the shortage of oil threatening the entire Western economy, Turkish exploration ships began to prospect beneath the continental shelf in international waters in the Aegean. This was the beginning of an ongoing dispute that has still not been resolved, about the extent of Greek jurisdiction over the Aegean seabed and airspace. Once again, Turkish governments were attempting to revise the terms of their country's founding 'National Pact', in response to conditions that could not have been foreseen at the time when it had been drawn up after the First World War. Greek responses were no less robust under PASOK than they had been under its predecessor. Indeed Papandreou's rhetoric was the more belligerent. When a Turkish survey ship put to sea to prospect for oil in the Aegean in the summer of 1976, Papandreou in opposition notoriously called upon the Karamanlis government to sink it. By the time that PASOK came to power in 1981, no one could plausibly claim any longer that the Greek left was 'soft' on the integrity of the state or lacking in patriotism.

Finally, there was a darker side of life that proved stubbornly resistant to the promised 'CHANGE'. This was domestic terrorism. After 1974 there was a proliferation of tiny splinter groups on the far left that had been formed to oppose the dictatorship. For some of those, the revolutionary potential of the brief student uprising at the Athens Polytechnic in November 1973 became an end in itself. Resistance to the 'Colonels' had seen respectable professors and middle-class students experimenting with home-made bombs. Methods that today would be called 'terrorist' were widely approved among those who resisted the regime, and indeed by some of their foreign supporters. During the years of the junta, little damage had been done. But among a tiny minority the methods of the tight-knit underground cell, bomb attacks and targeted assassinations had a continued appeal after the change to civilian rule. The most notorious, and longest-lasting, of these terrorist groups styled itself 'Revolutionary Organization 17 November' or '17N' for short – in this way appropriating the historic date of the suppression of the Polytechnic uprising. When 17N was finally wound up by the Greek police in 2002, its leader was found to have been a former mathematics student who had been living underground since 1971, and was by then fifty-eight years old.

The campaign by 17N began in 1975, with the murder of the CIA station chief in Athens. At the time this could be seen as the extremist tip of widespread anti-Americanism that had already seen the murder of the US ambassador to Cyprus the year before. Other murders followed, of police officers who had either been involved in repression under the junta or in enforcing public order more recently. Then in 1983, right in the middle of PASOK's first term of office, the group stepped up its activities. Altogether twenty-three people are known to have been its victims, including a prominent newspaper owner, several industrialists, members of parliament, and American, British and Turkish diplomats.

Throughout almost three decades of small-scale but deadly terror, the inability of successive Greek governments to put a stop to it brought many allegations of incompetence, or complicity, or both. The declared ideology of the group has been summed up as 'anti-capitalist, anti-imperialist, anti-statist and anti-totalitarian'.[6] While their apparent ambition to become the spearhead of a mass movement never stood any chance, there has remained a constituency within Greek public opinion that shares these attitudes. Even as recently as November 2017, when the temporary release of one of the ringleaders of 17N on parole provoked international criticism, a group of supporters turned up outside the prison to welcome the event. Although 17N is now a thing of the past, political violence has not disappeared from Greece. The view can be heard even today that targeted terrorism of this sort remains a potential threat. This was one case of 'CHANGE' that PASOK was able to bring about only after it had been in power for the greater part of twenty years.

By the end of the 1980s nothing had changed more radically than the PASOK administration itself. During its second term of office, from 1985 onwards, its largesse led to the growth of a widespread sense of entitlement. At the same time, the cost had proved beyond the means of the state. A loan from the EEC came with stringent conditions attached. For a time these lowered the real value of wages very considerably. Disillusionment with the governing party and its promises set in. The next few years saw a wave of strikes and demonstrations. It soon began to emerge that the sense of entitlement went right through the party organization too, all the way to the top. Cases of fraud and misappropriation of public funds began to become regular news items. When it emerged that a prominent banker and owner of government-supporting media had built his business empire on more than $200 million embezzled from the bank where he had been employed, the scandal reached far beyond Greece. From his temporary refuge in the United States, the accused banker, George Koskotas, made lurid claims about bribes paid to senior members of the government. While the country prepared for a parliamentary election in the summer of 1989, several ministers were forced out or resigned in disgust. Papandreou himself stood accused, and would remain under suspicion until he was acquitted by a narrow majority vote in the Supreme Court in 1992.

The Koskotas scandal was probably the deciding factor with the electorate. But other things came together during 1988 and the first six months of 1989 to doom Papandreou's chances of a third consecutive term in power. A series of revelations about clandestine surveillance by government agencies brought back all too familiar memories of the pre-junta 'para-state'. Then there was 'Andreas' himself. Shortly before the election campaign, Papandreou had undergone surgery in the United Kingdom for a serious heart condition. The possibility of having to find a new leader at short notice paralysed a party that had never learned to function independently of its charismatic chief. The charisma was no longer the same either. Papandreou's affair with Dimitra Liani, an air hostess half his age, had become public knowledge in 1988. As the election campaign gathered momentum, he made clear his intention to divorce his American wife and marry Liani, which he did shortly afterwards. How far this damaged his reputation is hard to tell. It has often been said that traditional-minded male voters identified with the virility projected by the national leader. On the other hand, the divorced Margaret Papandreou had been a champion of the women's movement in Greece. She, their children and their supporters took the divorce badly.

A near-decade of 'CHANGE' ended on 18 June 1989, when New Democracy by a narrow margin took the largest share of the popular vote but did not have enough seats in parliament to form a government.

IDENTITIES IN CONFLICT

By the time that happened, the fortunes of political parties and their leaders in one small Balkan state (or for that matter in even smaller Cyprus) were becoming overshadowed by momentous developments elsewhere. These would prove sufficient to change the geopolitical map of Europe and would irreversibly reshape power relationships across the entire world. In the euphoria of the time it was possible for serious historians in the West to talk of the 'end of history'.

The election that PASOK lost in June 1989 fell on the same day as the second round of voting in Poland that began the peaceful transition from communist to democratic rule. During the next three months, while, one after another, the communist regimes of Eastern Europe collapsed and the 'Iron Curtain' dividing the continent came down, Greece was ruled by an unlikely cohabitation. A coalition of far-left parties, including the once-banned KKE, made common cause with the centre-right New Democracy to outflank PASOK. Such a thing would have been unimaginable at any previous time in the country's history. A second election in the same year, held in November, coincided with the symbolic opening of the Berlin Wall. This time, in Greece, a precariously balanced 'rainbow' coalition held the ring for another three months. It would take a third election, in April 1990, before New Democracy could form a government, with the flimsiest of majorities, that would hold onto power for the next three years.

Most memorable about the three governments that came to power in Greece between 1989 and 1993 was not anything they did, but rather the orderliness of the process by which they came and went. This was the strongest proof yet that democratic institutions had at last become fully embedded in Greek political life. The New

Democracy government was headed by the septuagenarian Konstantinos Mitsotakis, a dynastic descendant of the Venizelos family. While it lasted, the Mitsotakis government brought to bear on Greece a measure of the 'neo-liberal' agenda associated with the US and UK administrations of Ronald Reagan and Margaret Thatcher respectively in the previous decade – and a foretaste of the 'austerity' to come much later.

But these internal political shifts were dwarfed in importance by the fallout from the end of the Cold War. After 1989, Greeks, like everybody else, would have to come to terms with a new political and economic reality. How they did so, and the new strains and renewed anxieties brought about by the adjustment, would become the main story of the Greek nation during the last decade of the century and beyond.

Firstly and most obviously, the new situation brought Greece and Greeks almost unlimited opportunities. For the first time since the 1930s, the Greek state would no longer be cut off from its Balkan hinterland to the north. While every other Balkan state found itself forced into an abrupt transition from a communist command economy to the 'capitalist' system of the West, Greece was the only country in the region already to be fully integrated into that system. Those with an eye to history, and not distracted by 'ancestral voices prophesying war', could see the possibilities for a rejuvenated 'Orthodox commonwealth'. It was like the second half of the eighteenth century all over again. Greeks, their language, and institutions in which they were already deeply embedded were poised to play a transformative role throughout the region, this time founded not just upon a shared religious tradition but on the enlightened self-interest of mature democratic nation states. The prospects had never looked so good for the kind of Balkan civic cooperation dreamed of by Rigas Velestinlis almost exactly two centuries earlier.

To some extent, slowly and modestly, this prospect *has* been realized over the intervening years. Greek firms invest and do business in many of the neighbouring states to the north. This is particularly the case in Romania, where their presence and their visibility intriguingly (and of course within limits) mirror the ascendancy of the Phanariots in the same region during the eighteenth century. The accession of both Romania and Bulgaria to the European Union in 2007 would no doubt have hastened this process further, had it not been for the financial crisis that began shortly afterwards.

But the role played by Greece and Greeks in the economic, political and cultural life of the region since 1989 has been much less than might have been expected. Throughout much of the Balkans, particularly in the early 1990s, the 'ancestral voices' had it. Greece would be spared the shooting wars that tore apart the former Yugoslavia throughout the decade, but not the passions or the fears that fuelled them.

This is because the second consequence of the end of the Cold War was a return to the 'ethnic' rivalries of the late nineteenth and early twentieth centuries and the deeper religious divisions underpinning them. One of those conflicts, which had been frozen during half a century of authoritarian communist rule, was the 'Macedonian Struggle'. This one had peaked during the first decade of the century. It ought to have been laid to rest by the Treaty of Bucharest that ended the Second Balkan War in 1913. Then, the geographical area known as Macedonia had been split among the aspiring nation states of Greece, Serbia and Bulgaria. But inevitably this left behind unfinished business.

The population of 'Slavo-Macedonians' (speakers of a Slavic language who had become subjects of the Greek state after 1912) had become greatly reduced after many of them allied with the communist side in the Greek Civil War of the 1940s. Because it has never been officially recognized, the size of this community in the 1990s and beyond cannot be reliably estimated. Probably many more Greeks in the region speak a Slavic language at home and among themselves than would willingly identify as 'Slavo-Macedonians'. And, despite the suspicions of generations of Greek officialdom, there is no reason to suppose that as a group they are any less loyal to the state than other Greeks. On the other side of the border, the southernmost part of what had previously been Serbia had been constituted, since 1943, as the 'Socialist Republic of Macedonia'. For as long as Yugoslavia remained an integral, federal state, this was purely an internal matter for the Yugoslavs. Then on 8 September 1991 a referendum in the Socialist Republic came out in favour of full independence, following the examples of Slovenia and Croatia a few months earlier. A new 'Republic of Macedonia' applied to the EU and the UN for international recognition.

The reaction in Greece and among Greeks worldwide was visceral and extreme. Outside observers, including representatives of international organizations, foreign ministries and media around the world, have repeatedly found it incomprehensible. What possible threat could the new state be – landlocked, impoverished, with no army to speak of, with a population a fifth the size of that of Greece, and split between a Slavic-speaking majority and a sizeable minority of ethnic Albanians?[7]

Internationally minded Greek commentators at the time, and historians more recently, have been relentless in cataloguing the series of 'errors' on the part of successive Greek governments that followed. Over the next four years Greece would become isolated over the issue. Prospects for a leading role in the redevelopment of the Balkans after Communism seemed to have been needlessly squandered. But this is one of those cases where it is hard to tell whether governments and the educated elite were leading public opinion or being led by it – as was certainly happening elsewhere in the Balkans at this time. In the first months of 1992, huge demonstrations took to the streets in Athens and Salonica. Newspaper editorials were uncompromising. Protests were not confined to Greece. In Australia, Greek and Yugoslav immigrant communities clashed in several cities.[8] As late as 1996, an academic publisher in the United Kingdom pulled out of a contract to publish a serious anthropological study based on fieldwork in northern Greece, for fear of commercial reprisals to its operations in Greece, while the author received death threats.

It was not the *independence* of the republic to their north that raised tempers to such a pitch among Greeks. It was the *name*. The claim by another state to a name that Greeks saw as indissolubly part of their own history and geography (since 'Macedonia' is the name of a region of Greece) was seized upon as an existential threat. In February 1992 the Mitsotakis government boxed itself into a corner by committing itself to the public position that 'no use of the term "Macedonia" in the appellation of the newly independent state would be recognized by Greece'. This was no more than to enshrine as official policy the popular, if unwieldy, slogan that had already gone viral: 'No to the name of Macedonia and its derivatives!'[9] Arrivals at Athens airport were met by ground staff wearing lapel badges that read (in English): 'Macedonia is Greek. Read history!'

At just this time, the veteran Greek archaeologist Manolis Andronikos died. His funeral in Salonica on 1 April 1992 became the occasion for a national outpouring of feeling over the issue. This was because Andronikos, back in 1977, had crowned his career with the discovery of the royal tombs of the ancient Macedonian dynasty and with it the proof that beneath the modern village of Vergina in Greece lay the remains of the long-lost capital city of the ancient kingdom. The partially cremated remains of King Philip of Macedon, the father of Alexander the Great, had been found in one of the tombs. Some archaeologists have been sceptical about these identifications, as archaeologists will. But they had already been widely accepted before 1992. The crowd that followed Andronikos on his last journey could have been grieving for a dead king of their own. The physical presence of Philip II of Macedon, and on incontrovertibly Greek soil, provided the crowd with a tangible link back through the byways of history. Andronikos's discoveries could seem like a comforting, visible proof that 'Macedonia is Greek', whether by that was meant a name or a place or both.[10]

A year later, in 1993, a cumbersome compromise was thrashed out at the United Nations. The new state would be internationally recognized under a name that was explicitly intended to be temporary, pending a more elegant solution. This was 'Former Yugoslav Republic of Macedonia', or FYROM for short. Greece, having previously refused to recognize any name that included 'Macedonia', had reluctantly to agree, as did the government of the new republic, led by Kiro Gligorov, a few months later. The issue then remained deadlocked for twenty-five years, during which time most governments quietly recognized Greece's northern neighbour by the name 'Macedonia'. But not Greece, where the English acronym FYROM remained mandatory. Some Greek politicians would even refuse to allow the full form of the name, as though the acronym had become a word in itself and had nothing to do with the contested 'Macedonia'. In daily speech, and indeed on road signs that direct traffic towards its border, the neighbouring state continued to be known by the name of its capital city, Skopje. In Greek the name 'Macedonia' can only ever be applied to the northern provinces of Greece. And a usage that is now routine in English, on both sides of the Atlantic, is still liable to cause offence to most Greeks. Under the terms of an agreement, signed between the prime ministers of the two countries on the border, not far from the town of Kastoria, on 17 June 2018, and ratified by their respective parliaments early in 2019, a compromise was reached. The 'former Yugoslav republic' is now formally known as the Republic of North Macedonia, or North Macedonia for short.

Back in 1993, Greece's acceptance of the compromise 'FYROM' brought down the New Democracy government. Antonis Samaras, who as foreign minister had taken a strong populist line over the issue, had been dropped from the government the previous year. In response, he set up his own rival political party, called Political Spring, with an explicitly nationalist agenda. It took only two more defections from the ranks of the ruling party to put an end to the government's majority in parliament. PASOK and Papandreou returned to power – but soon decided to follow a policy over the name of the neighbouring state that aligned more closely with the populism of Samaras than with the stance taken by the previous government.

Abandoned, as Papandreou saw it, by its Western allies, Greece took unilateral action in February 1994. A trade embargo against FYROM caused damage to the economy of both countries, and probably helped to foment ethnic tension *within* the fledgling state, which would experience violent confrontations between its Slav majority and Albanian minority in 1995 and again in 2001. The measure did nothing to resolve the issue of the name, not least because most foreign actors were inclined to dismiss it as trivial. With vicious wars still going on between Serbs and Croats, and within Bosnia and Herzegovina, these were bound to be higher priorities for international institutions. The most that could be achieved was an 'interim agreement' between Greece and FYROM in September 1995. According to this, Greece agreed to lift the embargo and to recognize the state under its temporary name, in return for modifications to its constitution and its flag.

These were important concessions. Because even if the international community has always played this down, the early stages of FYROM's pitch for independence had been driven by exactly the same kind of nationalist passions that were in evidence throughout the former Yugoslavia. The original form of the FYROM flag had been based on the motif of the 'sunburst' or 'Vergina star'. Since the late 1970s this emblem has been associated in the public imagination with the tomb of Philip II of Macedon, because it features prominently as a decorative motif among the treasures of Andronikos's excavation. In its earlier version, the constitution of the new republic had referred to a minority of its own 'Macedonian' subjects in Greece. And wild talk of extending that territory to the sea and embracing Salonica, however implausible it might sound, had hardly been conducive to neighbourly relations. If the memoirs of its first leader, Gligorov, later published in Athens, are to be believed, his agenda in the 1990s had been the exact equivalent of the 'Grand Idea' for Greece that had dominated Greek thinking during the later nineteenth century: 'We have already achieved the freedom of one third of Macedonians ... and have not yet addressed the question as to what happens about our brothers in the other dispersed parts of Macedonia.'[11]

But if the crisis was defused in 1995, Greece had lost badly in terms of international prestige and to some extent also in realizing its potential for economic and cultural activity in the Balkans.

Another change that came with the ending of the Cold War has proved even more far-reaching and irreversible. This is inward migration. Throughout its history, the Greek state had always exported surplus population. The dramatic influxes of refugees during the decade of war between 1912 and the early 1920s were the exception. Then, the incomers had all been Orthodox Christians and most of them Greek speakers. Now, with the opening of the northern borders and the relaxation of travel restrictions for citizens of the former Soviet Union, a steady stream of new arrivals began. At first and for some time afterwards, many of these were 'ethnic' Greeks, either from Albania or from the Russian hinterland of the Black Sea. These last were known, often dismissively, as 'Russo-Pontians', who spoke either a different dialect from standard Greek or, as often as not, no

Greek at all. They were the descendants of settlers who had been attracted to Russia in the time of Catherine the Great, two centuries before. Albania had been a closed country, not even aligned with the Soviet Union, under the autocratic rule of its communist leader Enver Hoxha for most of the last half-century. There are tragic tales of families that had been arbitrarily split up at the end of the Second World War coming to terms with painful reunion after more than a generation.[12]

Soon it was not just 'ethnic' Greeks who were arriving over the mountains into northwest Greece. Such was the poverty in post-communist Albania that Greece became overnight a magnet for economic migrants. Nothing like this had ever happened before. Throughout much of the 1990s the largest proportion of immigrants to Greece was made up of Albanians. The immigration service was soon overwhelmed. Very many, perhaps the majority, worked illegally in the country for years. Crime rates rose, especially for various forms of robbery. Press reports and daily discourse routinely placed the blame on 'Albanians', although it has been noticed that the assumption is not borne out by police reports. Soon migrants were arriving from further afield, as well as from other formerly communist states in the Balkans. A report from 1996 mentions Poles, Filipinos, Egyptians and other Africans, and estimated the number of illegal immigrants at between five and seven per cent of the total population.[13] For the first time in its history, Greece in the 1990s was rapidly becoming 'multi-cultural'.

Another development that affected many parts of the world during the same period was the resurgence of religion as a determinant of identity. This was especially visible throughout the Eastern European states that had had a strong Orthodox tradition before the imposition of communist rule. In Greece, an influential group of intellectuals, mostly with a background of involvement in the political left, began to instigate the 'rediscovery of a forgotten but authentic Orthodox tradition'. This movement has been described as not 'a mere religious revival, but a real acquaintance with the spiritual legacy of Greek Orthodox civilization, a civilization clearly differentiated from that of the West'.[14] Known collectively, though never by its adherents, as 'Neo-Orthodoxy', this intellectual current has gone hand in hand with other visible signs of a revival of religious practice. These include increasing church attendance, the funding and building of new Orthodox churches in Greece, Cyprus and in many places further afield, such as Australia. A particularly noticeable sign has been the transformation of the self-governing monastic community of Mount Athos, the Holy Mountain of Orthodoxy, which has seen a remarkable resurgence with a rejuvenated and often highly educated intake of monks in recent decades.[15]

The academic philosopher Christos Giannaras has published a series of books in which he identifies an essentially Byzantine Christian substratum of Greek society and communal life, and seeks to wean fellow Greeks away from what he sees as slavish adoption of ideas and practices emanating from an alien West. In an overtly more political mode, Kostas Zouraris seeks to uncover this Christian and Orthodox 'authentic' Greek way of life in all periods of Greek history. Zouraris is a former communist who at the time of writing holds a portfolio in the government of Alexis Tsipras, representing the minority coalition partner 'Independent Greeks', a small party of the far right. Zouraris has also taken a strident public position on the 'Macedonia' issue, a fact that in itself demonstrates the uneasy co-existence of national with religious identity – since the majority Orthodox population of FYROM logically belongs on the same side of the East/West divide that 'Neo-Orthodoxy' has brought back to prominence.

Although never spilling over into violence as in neighbouring former Yugoslavia, these tensions and these cross-currents of identity were strong in Greece throughout the 1990s and into the new century. Sometimes they manifested themselves in unexpected ways. In the Yugoslav wars, for instance, Greek public opinion generally, and sometimes strongly, aligned with the Serbs. This put the country at odds with opinion almost everywhere in the Western world. The reason is not far to seek. The Serbs share the same Orthodox heritage. Both nations have built their modern identity on an antipathy to the Ottomans who had ruled over them for several hundreds of years. And in pre-Yugoslavia days, Greece had fought alongside Serbia against their common oppressors. (The fact that Serbia at that time had included the territory of FYROM could be conveniently overlooked – that was one of the cross-currents.)

The last of the Yugoslav wars was fought in 1998 and 1999 over the province of Kosovo. There, the Albanian-speaking majority had asserted its independence from a federation that by this time consisted of only Serbia and Montenegro. Unlike most of the previous conflicts, this one brought overt armed intervention from abroad, led by the United States. For three months, from March to June 1999, NATO bombers attacked Serbia. The Greek government, as a member of NATO, was obliged to support the operation officially, but did not take part in it. At the same time a tide of public revulsion took to the streets of Greece's cities. At one point demonstrators broke through police lines to invade the official residence of the British ambassador. As the ambassador later recalled, more serious damage was only averted because the residence's footman, himself a Cretan, shamed the rioters by telling them that the house they were ransacking had belonged to the great Venizelos.[16]

Public reaction against the NATO bombing of Serbia had been stoked by the Archbishop of Athens and All Greece, who had been elected the previous year. Archbishop Christodoulos would do much during his ten-year reign to bring the Church back into the forefront of public life in Greece. Never afraid to court controversy, he was a fiery speaker and could rouse a crowd. Christodoulos was a modernizer in some respects – greatly extending the Church's charitable work and for the first time making systematic use of social media, for instance. He shared with the 'Neo-Orthodox' movement a deep suspicion of globalization and an insistence on the particularity of the Greek Orthodox historical experience. This brought him into conflict with a government that by this time was working hard to consolidate Greece's position within the European Union. In 2000 the PASOK government decided to remove religious affiliation from the identity cards that are compulsory for all Greek citizens, in line with practice elsewhere in the EU. Christodoulos and the bishops once again mobilized public opinion in a series of protests that lasted for almost a year. A petition calling for the restoration of religious data on ID cards gathered more than three million signatures – close to half the adult population of the country.

In the end the government held its ground. The issue petered out and the Church gave up its campaign – but not before the whole question of the relation between Church and state had been thoroughly aired in Greece and its reverberations had been picked up around the world. In the case of the ID cards, it was literally identity that was at stake. People were once again forced to ask themselves, as they had first done probably during the 1830s, when the Autocephalous Church of Greece was created, what is it that defines a Hellene? Is it religion, ethnicity, the ancient heritage (as exemplified in the debacle over the name of FYROM), or participation in the secular institutions of the state?

In the wake of the ending of the Cold War, during the 1990s and beyond, questions and anxieties that are as old as the Greek state itself were finding new forms of expression – but not necessarily answers.

EUROPE'S GOOD CITIZEN

Andreas Papandreou died on 23 June 1996. Six months earlier, as he lay terminally ill in the Onassis Heart Hospital in Athens, his party had elected a very different figure to succeed him as prime minister – and only later, with some reluctance, as party leader. Kostas Simitis had studied law and economics in Germany and in the United Kingdom. Like his predecessor he had worked as an academic before becoming a politician. There the similarities ended. Whereas the larger-than-life personality of 'Andreas' had always roused powerful passions, Simitis was (and is) a quiet, retiring man of unassuming appearance and polite, almost diffident manner. Papandreou's populist rhetoric was always far fiercer than his actions. Simitis, by contrast, set out quietly to transform Greek politics and the standing of his country among its peers.

Simitis has been described, in hindsight, as 'one of the most successful prime ministers in Greek history'.[17] He also served for the longest continuous term, narrowly beating the records set by Karamanlis between 1955 and 1963 and Papandreou between 1981 and 1989. Simitis's programme can be summed up in the one word, frequently used by his supporters and inner circle to this day: 'modernization'. His approach to governing was what would nowadays be called 'technocratic'. He brought new talent into his top team, in the form of high-calibre advisers. Foremost among these was Nikos Themelis, who became director of the prime minister's office in 1996 and loyally served Simitis throughout. Not coincidentally, the indefatigable Themelis also emerged during the same years as a best-selling and much respected novelist, writing historical block-busters that brought to life a more nuanced picture of Greek society during the last decades of Ottoman rule than could be found in offi-cial histories. Academic experts were brought in to advise on such matters as infrastructure, pension reform, IT and administration. Not all of their proposals proved politically possible to implement. Reform to the pension system, which might have pre-empted the much more savage cuts introduced during the 'crisis' period since 2010, was shelved in 2001 in response to political pressure.

It has been said that Simitis's 'technocratic' approach 'never gained the sympathy of the Greek electorate'.[18] But two successive election victories, in 1996 and 2000, proved that he was at least as popular as a party that had been somewhat tarnished by the populism and un-realized promises of the previous decade. It was from within the ranks of PASOK itself that the most systematic opposition to his modern-ization programme came. A populist wing that remained loyal to the ideas and the example of 'Andreas' was a constant threat to the prime minister's authority, and after Simitis's resignation in 2004 would oust the 'modernizers' from its senior ranks. The fact that the imple-mentation of government policies was in the hands of such a small group of trusted advisers has also been identified as a weakness – though one not confined to the Simitis administration alone.[19]

The programme of 'modernization' soon coalesced around two high-profile, overriding objectives. Both were sufficiently eye-catching to mobilize popular support across a wide spectrum that went far beyond party politics. One was to host the 2004 Olympic Games, the other to join the European single currency, the euro. A little over a year after the Simitis government came to power, its bid to the Inter-national Olympic Committee was successful in September 1997. At first cold-shouldered from the euro project, Greece was accepted, more or less at the last minute, into its third stage at the beginning of 2001, and joined the new currency in time for its launch a year later.

These successes were not just emblematic in themselves. Each had knock-on effects on the daily lives of Greeks. The Olympics provided a focal point for an ambitious series of infrastructure projects, not just in and around Athens but at venues all over the country. Despite much carping and scepticism expressed in foreign media over the years leading up to the Games, all of the targets were met, even if often at the last minute. As well as the sporting facilities themselves, most of the large-scale infrastructure projects that had been launched with European finance since the late 1980s were also brought to completion. In Athens the landscaping of a large area of formerly busy and polluting streets at the foot of the Acropolis was carried out to a high standard at the same time. In other cities and towns, public works greatly improved the physical environment. Private enterprise kept pace, with hotels and restaurants all over the country undergoing a facelift, sometimes extensive.

As for entry into the euro, the incentive of membership of the single currency was sufficient to bring about a minor economic miracle in Greece during those years – or so, at least, it appeared at the time. GDP grew strongly between 1994 and 2003. From 1997 until the eve of the financial crisis, in 2007, per capita income grew by an astonishing 33.6 per cent, according to one set of statistics, exceeded during the same period only by Ireland.[20] Standards of living had never been higher.

In its relations with other countries, too, the Simitis government did much to change the way that Greece was seen from abroad, and scored important successes. Joining the euro was only the most visible component of a sustained 'charm offensive' that aimed to bring Greece closer to the heart of the collective European project than it had ever been before or has been since. By the mid-1990s, at home a broadly based consensus had emerged that Greece's future security and prosperity (probably in that order) could best be assured within the architecture of the Maastricht Treaty that had brought the EU into being in 1992. At European Heads of Government meetings, in the European Parliament and throughout other EU institutions, the newly social-democratic PASOK from 1996 onwards began to work at consensus-building with like-minded partners in the capital cities and parliaments of Europe. The Greek Presidency of the EU during the first six months of 2003 was widely praised, and marked the cumulative achievement of the previous years of good citizenship.

Under Simitis's two terms of government, relations in the Balkans greatly improved – even if the issue of the name of 'FYROM' remained unresolved. At least the country was no longer isolated in international fora. With Turkey, relations at first had gone from bad to worse, despite a brief thaw in the late 1980s. In 1996 commandos of both countries landed on two uninhabited islets close to the Turkish coast, known collectively in Greek as Imia and in Turkish as Kardak, and planted their respective national flags. War was only narrowly averted on that occasion, thanks once again to American intervention. A move by the government of Cyprus to purchase ground-to-air missiles from Russia ratcheted tensions even higher. As late as February 1999, well into Simitis's watch, Greece controversially hosted a visit by Abdullah Öcalan, leader of the Kurdistan Workers' Party, or PKK, who was wanted in Turkey as a terrorist. In a dramatic move, Turkish special forces arrested Öcalan as he was leaving the Greek Embassy in Nairobi and flew him back to Turkey for trial. It was a deeply embarrassing moment for Greek diplomacy.

It would also prove to be a turning point. The Öcalan affair cost (if only temporarily) the scalp of the PASOK foreign minister, Theodoros Pangalos, a flamboyant politician whose grandfather had been one of the prime instigators of the 1909 putsch that had brought Venizelos to power, and had then ruled Greece briefly as dictator in the 1920s. Pangalos was replaced by a far more conciliatory figure. Georgios Papandreou also had a famous grandfather. This Papandreou is often known by the diminutive form of his name, Giorgakis, to distinguish him from the elder Georgios Papandreou, who had been prime minister in 1944 and again in the 1960s. Son of Andreas, Georgios Papandreou would go on to become the third prime minister of this political dynasty. Appointed foreign minister by Simitis in 1999, Papandreou brought flexibility and a new approach to the decades-old stand-off with Turkey.

Politically, two closely intertwined issues made dialogue with Turkey at once timely and necessary. Both issues related to the European Union and its ambitions for enlargement to the east. Cyprus was already a candidate for membership, strongly supported by Greece. Turkey, too, had applied as long ago as 1987, but Greek governments until now had exercised their right of veto to block progress, beyond an agreement for Turkey to join the customs union in 1995. At a time when most states throughout the region looked to membership of the EU as their best prospect for the future, there were obvious advantages for both Greece and Turkey if they could settle their differences, at least as far as EU expansion was concerned. Tentative talks began between Papandreou and his Turkish counterpart, İsmail Cem, in June 1999.

Then, in a most unexpected manner, the forces of nature intervened. Early in the morning of 17 August the Turkish city of Ismit was devastated by one of the most severe earthquakes to hit the region in modern times. Half a million Turks were left homeless, with many thousands dead. Damage extended to Turkey's largest city, Istanbul. In the international relief effort that followed, trained disaster recovery units from Greece were among the first to arrive on the scene. The response to human tragedy on such a scale in a neighbouring country was widespread and spontaneous. Three weeks later, the next earthquake to strike the region brought severe damage to the northern suburbs of Athens and panic to the entire city. Damage and loss of life were far less this time. But it was the turn of Turkish relief units to play a conspicuous part in recovering survivors and helping to clear the debris. Relief efforts and public sympathy were now reciprocal.

In national media and public opinion in both countries, as well as in political circles, age-old stereotypes of the feared and despised 'other' were overlaid by images of destruction and loss that could happen to anyone, at any time, in a part of the world where the earth's crust is on the move. 'Earthquake diplomacy', as it quickly became dubbed, gave a new impetus to the efforts of politicians to move beyond the old political antagonisms. The earthquakes, and these responses by their neighbours, brought about a real shift in public opinion in both Greece and Turkey, one that would continue for several years afterwards.[21] In the immediate aftermath of this détente, at the Helsinki summit at the end of 1999, Greece lifted its objection to Turkey becoming a candidate state to join the European Union. Pragmatically Greece had much to gain and nothing to lose by this gesture of solidarity with the rest of the EU. Plenty of other reasons would intervene to stall the beginning of accession talks with Turkey until 2005, and subsequent developments on both sides would combine to make accession a vanishingly remote possibility a decade later. But for Simitis and Papandreou there was a real and lasting prize to be won. This was the full accession of Cyprus.

By 1999, efforts to bring about a formal peace across the 'Green Line' that divided Cyprus had been going on for twenty-five years. Attitudes had become entrenched on both sides. The self-declared Turkish Republic of Northern Cyprus (TRNC) had been established in 1983, but was (and remains today) recognized only by Turkey. Travel between the Republic of Cyprus and the occupied territories (as the TRNC is always called in Greek) had been denied to Cypriots of both communities, although holders of foreign passports could cross at a single checkpoint manned by the United Nations in central Nicosia. How, in these circumstances, was Cyprus to join the European Union, with its *acquis communautaire* and free travel within and among member states?

A breakthrough came in 2002, with the election of Recep Tayyip Erdoğan, leader of the previously banned AKP party in Turkey, as prime minister. Hard though this now seems to believe, the AKP government came to power in 2002 determined to push for full membership of the EU. Erdoğan was therefore – back then – prepared to compromise over Cyprus. Overruling the entrenched position of the veteran leader of the Turkish Cypriot community, Rauf Denktash, the Turkish government opened talks at the United Nations, aimed at reuniting Cyprus. A successful resolution of the Cyprus issue would remove one of the most intractable obstacles to Turkey's own accession.

And so was born the Annan Plan, named after Kofi Annan, Secretary General of the United Nations, in whose name it was drawn up. Five successive drafts between late 2002 and the end of March 2004 were vigorously debated in the EU, the UN, among the 'guarantor powers' of the 1960 Constitution, and within the two communities of Cyprus itself. In its final version, the Annan Plan envisaged a confederation on the model of Switzerland. Every Cypriot would be simultaneously a citizen of the renamed 'United Cyprus Republic' and of one of its two constituent states, a Greek-Cypriot state in the south and a Turkish-Cypriot state in the north. Each state was to have equal constitutional rights, irrespective of their difference in size and population. Those who had lost their homes in 1974 would not have the right to return, but would be entitled to compensation. A new inter-state boundary would increase the size of the Greek-controlled area by some seven per cent, to be implemented over three years. Over a longer period, most but not all foreign troops would be withdrawn.

It was the nearest thing there has ever been to a comprehensive solution to the Cyprus 'problem'. By the time the accession treaty for Cyprus and nine other candidate countries was signed in the ancient Agora of Athens in April 2003, the Annan Plan had gathered behind it a great deal of international momentum and political capital. The governments of both Greece and Turkey were well disposed, a rare alignment. It already enjoyed the backing of both the European Union and the United Nations. EU negotiators could be forgiven for supposing that final terms would be hammered out in time for the accession of the ten countries, which the treaty had fixed for 1 May 2004. Expectations rose even farther when a few weeks after the treaty had been signed in Athens, the Turkish-Cypriot side took the initiative in opening crossing-points between the two zones in Cyprus. Many thousands of Greek Cypriots crossed over, to visit the homes that none of them had seen for almost thirty years, and a whole generation had never seen at all. Elections in the TRNC at the end of the year brought to power a more moderate leader than the veteran Denktash. Public opinion among Turkish Cypriots began to swing behind the Annan Plan.

But, in a phrase that characterizes many such negotiations, 'nothing is agreed until everything is agreed'. Negotiations went to the wire. When the final round failed to come up with agreement on all the terms, the UN Secretary General, Kofi Annan, filled in the blank parts of the text himself. The future of Cyprus was finally to be determined by simultaneous referenda to be held in both communities on 24 April – with just one week to go before the treaty of accession to the EU was due to come into effect. In Greece, Simitis had lost the parliamentary election to New Democracy just a month before. In opposition, PASOK supported the Plan. The new government, headed by Kostas Karamanlis, nephew of the former prime minister and president, declared itself neutral, but was not against. Erdoğan was still pushing strongly for acceptance. Opinion polls in the TRNC showed that a 'yes' vote was very likely there. Clearly, European officials were counting on the popular vote to rubber stamp an agreement that had been made at a higher level. It was a reunited Cyprus that was expected to join the Union a week after the poll. There was no Plan B, to put off accession or renegotiate its terms if the vote were to go the other way.

There was no question, in 2004, of the foreign policy of the Greek state being driven by Nicosia, as had happened half a century earlier. But neither was Athens in a position to direct public opinion in that other sovereign state whose citizens were also part of the Hellenic nation. Left to themselves to govern the Republic of Cyprus in their own way, the Greek Cypriots had had a quarter of a century to establish their own political institutions, based upon the Constitution of 1960. Since 1974, the economy of the Republic of Cyprus had far outstripped the impoverished and isolated north of the island. Its citizens already enjoyed a significantly higher standard of living than in Greece itself. Even if PASOK had still been in power to urge its own diplomatic agenda, Greek Cypriots were masters in what was left to them of their own island. They would make up their own minds.

Presidents of Cyprus are directly elected and enjoy considerable executive power. Tassos Papadopoulos, elected in 2003, was a lawyer who had played a prominent part in the EOKA struggle against British rule in the 1950s. His election campaign had been supported by parties of both left and right that feared concessions being made to Turkey. In the run-up to the referendum on 24 April, Papadopoulos threw the weight of his government against the Annan Plan. His much quoted, succinct declaration in Greek can most accurately be paraphrased, 'I undertook the government of a sovereign state, I will not hand on to my successor a mere statelet.' The Plan was rejected by 72 per cent of Greek Cypriots – a proportion only slightly higher than voted simultaneously to accept it on the opposite side of the 'Green Line'.

For many international observers, probably for most, the Greek Cypriots had thrown away a once-in-a-lifetime opportunity. But at the time, and ever since, the Plan and its shortcomings, from the Greek point of view, have been searchingly exposed.[22] The effect of the double referendum in 2004 has been to perpetuate a division of the island that more than a decade later must surely be irrevocable.

But the Greek-Cypriot Republic of Cyprus did not fare so badly. European negotiators may have assumed that the accession they were negotiating was for the whole of the island, and technically this is indeed the case today. But in practice, since 2004, Greek Cypriots have gained all the benefits of the *acquis communautaire*, whereas the Turkish northern part of Cyprus remains excluded. Just like the creation of Cyprus as an independent state in the first place, this was a consequence that had been foreseen by few and intended by none. Even so, it deserves to be ranked as another success for the PASOK government led by Kostas Simitis, and one that would have been impossible without the diplomatic initiatives and consensus-building of Simitis and his foreign minister, Georgios Papandreou.

The four-year term of the second Simitis government was due to end in April 2004. When the next parliamentary election was called at the beginning of the year, for 7 March, Simitis announced his intention to stand down as party leader. Papandreou was elected in his place. But not even the dynastic name of the leader was enough to revive the fortunes of PASOK at the polls, after eleven years in power. Like so many Greek governments before it, this one had been badly damaged by a series of financial scandals in its closing years. Simitis was not implicated in any wrongdoing, but had been slow to dismiss those who were. So the final achievements of his premiership, the accession of Cyprus to the European Union and the Olympic Games that August, went ahead without their principal architects.

The Athens Olympics were widely described by the world's press as a triumph. For Greeks, wherever in the world they lived, the return of the Games to Athens, where the first modern Olympics had been held in 1896, was a renewal of that century-old vindication for their nation and its place in the modern world. On 13 August 2004 a faultlessly choreographed opening ceremony in the newly built Olympic Stadium at Marousi, outside Athens, presented a living pageant of more than four thousand years of history. Beginning with the stylized marble figurines produced in the Cyclades in the early Bronze Age, it continued through Minoan Crete and the palaces of Mycenae to the arts, athletics and sculpture of the classical period. Alexander the Great appeared in his chariot flanked by spears, reproducing a famous ancient image. Then came the icons of the Byzantine Orthodox Church, and straight afterwards, without any indication of any intervening gap, the heroes of the 1821 Revolution and the 1896 Olympic Games. The twentieth century was represented by the Karagiozis shadow-puppet theatre, a *rebetika* band playing *bouzouki*, and the paintings of Giannis Tsarouchis – the first two of these, at least, deeply rooted in the nation's eastern and Ottoman past. Much of the musical accompaniment was drawn from the old rural traditions of the Greek mountains and islands. Visually, the whole series of tableaux was dominated by the floating figure of a winged angel.

The omissions were as striking as the historical re-enactments themselves. Successive conquerors, from the Romans in antiquity to the Ottomans in the late Middle Ages, were left out of the story completely. It was Greek history as it might have been, compressed into a series of powerfully realized visual images. At least for the three weeks of the Games, the conflicts of identity that had begun to resurface in different forms during recent years could be set aside.

It was a confident, consummate performance, perfectly done. In this way, the *History of the Greek Nation*, first conceived by Konstantinos Paparrigopoulos in the 1850s and 1860s, was distilled down to its barest essentials and packaged for a worldwide audience. Surely, that August evening in 2004, the *modern* nation had at last come of age?

12

Midlife Crisis?

2004–

With the triumph of the Olympics, following the seamless transfer of power a few months earlier from PASOK to its rival New Democracy, and a solution (of sorts) to the thirty-year-old dismemberment of Cyprus, Greece and Greeks in 2004 had everything to look forward to. Membership of the European Union and the common currency, the euro, gave the two Greek states, Greece and Cyprus, the best guarantees that either of them had ever had for their external security and their political and economic stability. The future could only go on getting brighter.

And so, for a time, it appeared.

The new centre-right government in Athens carried little ideological baggage. There was no real programme, no ambitious set of goals to be met, no historic destiny to be fulfilled. After all, Greece had already arrived. The new prime minister chose to be known by the familiar form of his name: Kostas (for Konstantinos) Karamanlis. He brought with him little personal baggage, either, beyond the name of his more famous uncle, at a time when both established parties in a two-party system were led by dynastic descendants of their founders. Karamanlis's governing style has been variously described as informal, relaxed, even (by opponents) as lazy. A certain lassitude, emanating from the top, has been identified as a hallmark of the whole five-year rule of New Democracy that would last until 2009. Reforms begun by the Simitis administration were quietly dropped. The practice of 'buying' votes, for instance by declaring a tax holiday in an election year, which had begun under Andreas Papandreou in the 'populist decade' of the 1980s, now crossed the ideological divide. Allegedly it reached new heights when Karamanlis 'literally spent his way to reelection' in 2007. Even so, a year into New Democracy's second term, in 2008, the economic indicators for Greece looked as good as they had done four years before, with average annual growth of four per cent since the start of the new century.[1]

The signs of trouble to come were not, at first, economic. The worldwide financial crisis had begun in the United States in 2007. It peaked with the collapse of the Lehman Brothers investment bank in September 2008. But neither the Greek state nor Greek banks were exposed directly to the forms of high-wire risk-taking that had brought the world's banking sector to the brink of collapse. The global crisis had passed Greece by – or so, again, it appeared.

And yet, in December 2008, the Greek media were filled with soul-searching, with accusations and counter-accusations, and talk of a 'crisis'. There were several reasons for this, all of them to be found nearer home. Like the 'sub-prime' mortgage crisis in the United States, this one also went back to the summer of the previous year, but was quite unrelated. A series of devastating forest fires in the Peloponnese in August and September had left sixty-eight people dead and destroyed huge areas of woodland. This is a seasonal hazard in the Greek climate and happens every year. No less seasonal are the loudly aired assumptions that most of these fires are started deliberately. The 2007 fires were worse than usual. There was a widespread perception, particularly just after the election in September, that the government was failing to get a grip. The still-unfinished project of a national land registry (begun by Kapodistrias in 1828) focused public attention on allegations that speculators were behind the fires, illegally destroying forests to create opportunities for development.

Then in the autumn of 2008 came the series of headline scandals to which every Greek government seems to become prone after more than three years in office. One involved a bizarre suicide attempt by a senior official of the Ministry of Culture. More serious were revelations about property deals between government ministers and the Vatopedi Monastery on Mount Athos, the self-governing Holy Mountain of Orthodox Christianity. This one forced the resignation of Karamanlis's chief fixer, Theodoros Rousopoulos, at what would prove to be a crucial time, in October 2008. After that, 'the government appeared to drift'.[2]

Ever since the transition to democracy in 1974, there has always been an undercurrent of violent street protest in Greece, and particularly in Athens. Traditionally accepted as part of the legacy of the 'Polytechnic generation', its perpetrators regularly claim to be acting in the spirit of the students who had occupied the Athens Polytechnic in November 1973. By the autumn of 2008, hooded anarchists with petrol bombs were taking to the streets, especially in the Exarcheia district of central Athens, near the National Archaeological Museum. For years nightly battles between balaclava-clad rioters (*koukoulophoroi*) and police had become almost a form of diversion. Ritualized conflicts, with unwritten rules and a tacit understanding of how far they could go, were a kind of bizarre re-enactment of the lives of the irregular militias that had once battled it out in the lawless mountains under Ottoman rule or during the Revolution. The role model of the bandit chief, the outlaw who recognizes no authority but his own, has never entirely gone away.

Then on the night of 6 December 2008 the unwritten rules were broken. That night, in the course of one of these encounters, a school student aged fifteen was shot dead in Exarcheia Square by police. The victim had no connection with the balaclava-wearers. The event caused revulsion throughout the nation, and brought thousands onto the streets. For almost a month the centre of Athens was convulsed by demonstrations, some of them violent. Unusually, the demonstrations spread throughout the country, with almost every town affected. So discredited were the police in the minds of many of the public that law enforcement became all but impossible. Shops were looted and burned, cars overturned and set on fire. Low-level terrorism returned to Athens, with armed attacks on property and police officers.

One historian, writing at the time, accounted for the events as 'a fantasy-driven and incoherent explosion of a society trapped by the whirlwind of an institutional, social and moral crisis' – and this was several months before the first whiff of the far greater 'crisis' waiting just around the corner. The same observer went on to identify its causes as 'the disturbing decay of democratic standards, of rationalism, of mutual respect'. Another, writing some years later, noted the absence of any coherent or identifiable demands on the part of the 'uprising'. Almost more surprising was the total failure of the political left, either to make political capital out of the events or to claim leadership of this 'resistance'.[3] It was a sign that the old fault line that had divided Greeks from the 1940s to the 1980s really had shifted. The new strains were already apparent on the streets of Athens during December 2008. But few could then have predicted where the next cracks would appear, or the nature of the forces that would tear at Greek society during the decade to come.

THE POLITICS OF 'CRISIS'

By April 2009 an uneasy peace had returned to the streets. The Karamanlis government had managed to borrow enough to cover the needs of its budget for the year. But in the economic climate after the global crash the increase in government borrowing could not escape the attention of the European Commission. Eurozone rules on deficits would have to be applied. This would mean cutting back on public spending. It was not an unprecedented situation. The second PASOK government had found itself similarly placed, twenty years earlier. The measures had been unpopular then, and PASOK had lost power in 1989, perhaps in part as a result. But such problems had been contained before. Why should they not be again?

Karamanlis's motivation in calling a parliamentary election for October 2009, two years before the end of his government's second term, has been called into question. Although he fought a vigorous campaign, some thought he was deliberately walking away from a situation that New Democracy could no longer control. It was the same accusation that had been levelled – and then with some justice – against his predecessor Georgios Theotokis almost exactly a century earlier. In 2009, PASOK, led by Georgios Papandreou, far from offering a consensual approach to the country's difficulties, simply denied that there was a problem at all. The good times could continue as before. On 4 October, PASOK won the election with 44 per cent of the vote and 160 seats in the 300-seat parliament. Georgios Papandreou became prime minister.

It fell to the finance minister in the new government, Georgios Papakonstantinou, to break the news to parliament, two weeks after taking office. Although it was couched in the cautious economics-speak of a different age, its import amounted to much the same as the laconic bombshell attributed to Charilaos Trikoupis back in 1893: 'Unfortunately, we are bankrupt.' Jean-Claude Juncker, later to become President of the European Commission, in his capacity as host to the Eurogroup of finance ministers meeting in Luxembourg the next day, responded more laconically still: 'The game is over.'[4] It took a little longer for Papandreou to accept the full scale of the disaster. But by the first months of 2010 the world's media had got hold of the story. Greece was in crisis. And not only Greece. Greece was part of the Eurozone. With European banks and the institutions of the EU still reeling from the slow-burn effects of the financial crash of 2008, the likelihood of a sovereign default by one of its members suddenly threatened the whole project of monetary union, perhaps even the entire political edifice that was the European Union itself. Extraordinary measures were called for.

Much has been written by professional economists about the technical factors that added up to the 'perfect storm' for Greece at the end of 2009 and early 2010. And much remains contentious almost a decade later. Reduced to essentials, the Greek government by April 2010 found itself unable to borrow at affordable rates to service its existing debts. Such things had happened to sovereign states before – not least to Greece itself, in 1843, 1893 and 1932. In the new century it had happened to Argentina in 2001. The classic solution was to default on part of the outstanding debt, devalue the currency and rebuild the national economy from there. It had worked well in Greece in the 1930s. By 2009, it was working well in Argentina. But there was no precedent for a sovereign default by a member of the Eurozone. An economy the size of that of Greece (amounting to no more than two per cent of the economy of the Eurozone) could have been allowed to default without creating more than a ripple in the world's markets. But if a constituent part of the common currency were to default, the consequences would be literally incalculable – because no one had imagined it ever happening. The European institutions suddenly found themselves having to make up the rules as they went along.

It was not just Greece. Other countries on the geographical periphery of Europe were struggling too, under the same pressures that stemmed from the banking collapse of two years before. Governments used taxpayers' money to buy up the debts of banks that had become insolvent and in this way to save their taxpayers from losing their savings. But in the process national treasuries themselves came close to insolvency. What became known as the 'European debt crisis' spawned its own vocabulary of acronyms and metaphors. The at-risk countries were the 'PIGS' (Portugal, Italy, Greece, Spain, later joined by Ireland). The greatest fear was of 'contagion' spreading from one to the other, and then to the heart of the Eurozone itself. The rough-and-ready solution concocted on the hoof was called unofficially a 'bailout' (a benefactor who can afford to do so puts up bail to save his associate from jail) and in the formal jargon of the institutions a 'Memorandum of Understanding', or 'MoU' for short. This last would be translated into Greek as the infamous *Mnimonio*. To make it all work, a new collaboration would be required, so as to spread responsibility among the European Central Bank (ECB), the European Commission (EC) and the US-based International Monetary Fund (IMF). This new, ad hoc conglomeration soon came to be nicknamed, especially in Greece, by another metaphor, the 'Troika'.

Georgios Papandreou formally requested a bailout on 23 April 2010. A Memorandum of Understanding was signed between Greece and the 'Troika' on 2 May. In return for a loan worth 110 billion euros, the PASOK government undertook to implement drastic measures to reduce the country's deficit and restructure its economy along the lines of the more robust economies of northern Europe. It was the beginning of 'austerity'. The government had been elected only six months previously on a promise that all was well and no belt-tightening would be necessary. Three days after the signing of the *Mnimonio* an estimated hundred thousand demonstrators took to the streets of Athens. The protest turned violent. When the crowd set fire to a bank near the city centre, three employees were burned to death. Was the price of saving the euro to be the collapse of public order in Greece, as had last happened in the 1940s?

In the event it was not, or at least it hasn't been so far. But for several years it looked as though it might be. Instead, in Greece, unlike anywhere else where the same measures were applied, it was the economy that collapsed.

*

It soon turned out that the projections contained in the Memorandum had been wildly optimistic. Ninety per cent of the funds disbursed to Greece went not towards relieving the finances of the Greek state, but to service old debts and recapitalize foreign banks, particularly in France and Germany.[5] Over the next four years, personal incomes in Greece were reduced by a third, unemployment rose to 27 per cent and among the young was more than double that. The size of the economy shrank by a quarter. Bank deposits fled abroad. Investment was reduced almost by half. Businesses failed, public services were reduced.

The burden fell most harshly on pensioners and the unemployed. Long queues formed at soup kitchens. Even formerly well-to-do people lost their homes and took to the streets. The number of suicides soared. In a distant echo of the far harsher conditions of the 1940s, many who could no longer make a living in Athens and the larger towns returned to their families' roots in villages that had been steadily depopulated ever since the Second World War. Those with the benefit of higher education, who could contribute to the 'knowledge economy' but had no prospect of finding a job in Greece, took advantage of the EU's right to freedom of movement among member states and settled abroad. It was estimated in 2017 that during the previous seven years half a million graduates had left Greece, equivalent to approximately 10 per cent of the workforce. Tax rates kept rising, with a predictably deflationary effect on the economy.

What had brought Greece to this pass? And why was Greece, alone of the 'PIGS', poisoned rather than cured by the medicine that the European institutions had forced equally on all of them?

There have been many attempts over the last few years to make sense of this conundrum. Most concede that blame lies neither solely with Greece nor solely with the European institutions. Systemic problems at home combined in a toxic way with structural weaknesses in the European project, particularly the systems devised to oversee the single currency without a single fiscal authority for the Eurozone. But beyond that there is little agreement. The world's media, and many serious commentators, have accused the Greeks of being 'profligate' and 'lazy'. Those ill-disposed towards the political project of the European Union for 'ever closer integration', or towards the economic and fiscal ambitions of the single currency, have had a field day as the weaknesses of both have been exposed by the unfolding 'crisis' in Greece.

Inevitably, critics of Greece's socialist experiment have shone the spotlight on specific policies of PASOK, particularly during the 1980s. It is common to cite examples of wastefulness in the public sector, not least in higher education and the health service, and of the failure by governments to collect taxes and of citizens to pay them. Hard evidence from statistics shows that Greeks are not 'lazy' – but the same evidence does underscore how underproductive their labour is.[6] A former PASOK government minister, speaking off the record in 2017, identified the underlying causes of the 'crisis' as 'poor governance, clientelism, weak institutions, lack of competitiveness'. It may be that the headline story of a spectacular boom followed by an even more spectacular crash actually masks quite a different pattern. When GDP growth for Greece is averaged out over the whole period since the start of the international oil crisis in 1973, the underlying rate turns out to have been uniformly flat at no more than one per cent. Perhaps Greece had never, 'really', recovered after that?[7]

It is easy to say, as many now do, that Greece should never have joined the euro. But 'Grexit', a term coined at the time of Greece's second bailout in February 2012, would always have been the 'nuclear option'. Although many predicted that it would happen, there was never sufficient appetite, on the part of either the creditor institutions or successive Greek governments, for either side to be the first to press the button.

By early in 2011 it was becoming clear that, for Greece to avoid a default, a further bailout would be needed, with further austerity measures attached. Violence once again broke out in central Athens at the end of June. Faced with new terms for a second Memorandum, and the threat of more civil unrest in October, a desperate Papandreou announced that he would turn to the electorate. The Greek people would decide in a referendum whether or not to accept the terms or risk default and an exit from the euro. Papandreou announced the referendum on the last day of October. Eleven days later he was gone. Summoned to a crisis meeting with the French president, Nicolas Sarkozy, and the German Chancellor, Angela Merkel, the hapless

Greek prime minister had been told in no uncertain terms that he could not have a referendum. The only thing left for him to do was resign.

That left the way open for a 'technocratic' government to take over. The new administration was supported by a three-party coalition, and headed by a former vice-president of the ECB and former governor of the Bank of Greece, Loukas Papadimos. Unelected, and probably in the climate of the time unelectable, the Papadimos government oversaw the signing of Greece's second bailout on 2 February 2012. That same night Athens once again erupted in violence. But the deed was done. In return for a 'haircut' (another of those metaphors, meaning a partial write-down of Greek sovereign debt) and yet more austerity, Greece signed up for a new loan worth 130 billion euros. The 'haircut' disproportionately hit the country's own banks, with the direct and unintended consequence of spreading the 'contagion' to Cyprus the following year.

With the new deal signed, it was time once more for the electorate to have a say. The main opposition party, New Democracy, was now led by Antonis Samaras – he who had engineered the party's downfall in the 1993 elections, over his hardline stance on the name of Greece's northern neighbour, the 'Former Yugoslav Republic of Macedonia'. Samaras's campaign slogan, 'Let's tear up the *Mnimonio*', repeated the tactic of his rival Papandreou three years before. This time it was only partially successful. The election of 6 May 2012 produced a hung parliament, with no party able to form a government. A second election took place six weeks later. This time, faced with uncompromising threats from European leaders that if Greece were to repudiate the Memorandum it would be thrown out of the euro, enough voters turned to New Democracy to give Samaras a mandate – not to govern outright, but in coalition with what was left of PASOK and one other minor party.

The two elections of 2012 marked another turning point in Greek politics. Ever since 1977, Greece had had a recognizable two-party system. Barring two short-lived coalitions at the end of the 1980s, every government in almost thirty years had been formed by either New Democracy or PASOK. Now, in the May election, the vote for both parties collapsed. Faced with the impasse that followed, enough voters rallied to New Democracy to save the party from oblivion, though Samaras ended up in power with less than 30 per cent of the popular vote. The punishment of PASOK appears to have been terminal, with only 13 per cent of the vote in June 2012, and further to fall three years later. The end of the two-party, relatively centrist consensus was matched by the rise of parties that until now had been on the fringes, to both left and right.

The Coalition of the Radical Left, abbreviated in Greek to SYRIZA, the first syllables of each part of its name, had been formed out of several smaller parties, excluding the traditional Marxist KKE, back in 2004. Between then and 2009, SYRIZA had only just reached the threshold for representation in parliament, with between three and four per cent of the vote. Since 2008 its leader had been the youthful civil engineer and former student activist Alexis Tsipras. Uncompromisingly standing out against austerity and the terms imposed by the 'Troika', SYRIZA overtook PASOK to come second in the election of May 2012, with 17 per cent of the vote. Six weeks later that had risen to just short of 27 per cent, only two percentage points behind the dominant party in the new coalition government. SYRIZA was of course not a candidate to be included in the coalition – it lay too far from the mainstream for that. But a fringe party of the far left had risen from almost nowhere to become the official opposition in parliament.

On the right, a breakaway group from New Democracy contested the 2012 elections as a newly formed party opposed to the Memorandum. Independent Greeks (ANEL) reached 10 per cent of the vote in May, but fell back the following month. More shocking to most shades of opinion in Greece and abroad was the rise of Greece's first and so far only fascist or Neo-Nazi party, Golden Dawn. From infinitesimal beginnings (polling less than one per cent in the first parliamentary election it contested, in 1996), Golden Dawn attracted not far short of half a million votes in each of the two elections in 2012. Unlike other anti-bailout parties, it saw only a tiny drop in its support from the one election to the other, from a peak of seven per cent in May, which it would match again three years later. With its emblem of the 'meander', or 'Greek key pattern', in the colours of the Nazi swastika, which the shape somewhat resembles, Golden Dawn and its members have been associated for many years with violent action, particularly directed against immigrants and anyone well disposed towards them. Their belief in the purity of a Greek bloodline stretching from the militaristic Spartans to today is overtly racist as well as ultra-nationalist. Some of the rhetoric and the symbols favoured by Golden Dawn recall those of the Metaxas dictatorship of the 1930s or the 'Colonels' between 1967 and 1974. But it is worth remembering that neither of those regimes had any roots in a popular movement or political organization, but were imposed from above. The appearance of a grass-roots fascist movement in Greece is largely, if not entirely, a consequence of the 'crisis' and a response to the new conditions since 2010.

With so many voters turning away from the broadly consensual politics of the *metapolitefsi*, once again in Greece the tectonic plates were shifting. Out of the new strains that had first become apparent in the violent street protests at the end of 2008 and then been compounded by the debt crisis, a new political alignment had suddenly emerged. Some commentators have defined the new split as being between those for and against acceptance of the Memoranda. Another sees it as 'ethnocentrism' versus 'Europeanism'.[8] Either way, the new fault line transcends and replaces the traditional face-off between right and left. Its existence can be traced all the way back to the internal conflict during the Revolution of the 1820s, between rival versions of liberty: on the one side an ideal of absolute self-sufficiency, on the other integration into a Western-dominated world order. Once again, Greeks found themselves forced to choose.

In January 2015 the Samaras government was defending a record of enforcing the terms of the second bailout and could point to signs of a fragile recovery as a result. No end to enforced austerity was in sight. Voters had put their trust first in the centre-left (in 2009), then in the centre-right (in 2012). Both had let them down. Now it was the turn of the new boy on the block, Alexis Tsipras, leader of the official opposition, to bang the same drum that first Papandreou and then Samaras had banged before him. This time, under a SYRIZA government, little Greece would stand up to the bullying creditors in the European Union and the IMF. The medicine prescribed by the 'Troika' hadn't worked. So it was time to change the medicine. SYRIZA could deliver that.

Voting in the election of 25 January 2015 was along the new party lines. Pro-bailout parties polled just under 40 per cent, including the rump of a nearly obliterated PASOK. Ranged against the bailouts were SYRIZA, the breakaway right-wing Independent Greeks, Golden Dawn and the Communist Party of Greece, the KKE. The KKE would work with no one else, and no one else could contemplate working with Golden Dawn. Between them, these two extreme anti-bailout parties accounted for some 12 per cent. That left SYRIZA, with 36 per cent of the popular vote and gifted, as the largest party, with a bonus of an extra fifty seats, just two short of an absolute majority in parliament. It was entirely consistent with the new political logic that the far-left SYRIZA should enter a coalition with the far-right (non-fascist) Independent Greeks (ANEL) to give a working majority with 162 seats in the 300-seat parliament. Both parties that formed the new government had been elected on a ticket of national self-sufficiency and resistance to the 'Troika'.

The democratic mandate was fragmented. But it was also clear. It was the turn of the new coalition of formerly 'fringe' political forces to see whether they could succeed where the experienced politicians of the established parties had failed.

The story of what followed is either high tragedy in the ancient Greek manner or farce, depending on your perspective. Either way, the lead role is played by the academic economist and telegenic self-publicist Yanis Varoufakis, who for the best part of six tumultuous months in 2015 served as Greece's Minister of Finance. Varoufakis's highly personal account of these events lifts the lid on the divided loyalties, internal divisions and contradictory behaviour of both sides. The way Varoufakis tells it, he was the plucky champion of the Greek electorate, brought in to do battle with 'Europe's deep establishment', when the dull and corrupt professionals had all failed. He writes of a 'Greek Spring', of a 'rebellion' that was 'ruthlessly suppressed' by the self-defeating obduracy of the European institutions, and betrayed by the leadership of his own party.

Tsipras at the beginning, and Varoufakis throughout, believed that the mandate they had won from the Greek people would be sufficient to force the European institutions to change their policy towards Greek debt. Desirable though that might be, it was never going to be achieved by pressure from the finance minister of one near-bankrupt country of eleven million souls, exerted against the institutions of a political and economic union representing some five hundred million. The riposte of Wolfgang Schäuble, Varoufakis's German counterpart, at a Eurogroup meeting on 11 February 2015 has become notorious: 'Elections cannot be allowed to change economic policy.' But Schäuble, too, was answerable to an electorate – one that was far larger, and not well disposed to those its daily press called 'crooks in the euro family', 'bankrupt Greeks' and other unflattering things.[9]

By the end of June, Greece was once again unable to service its debts. The last instalment of the second Memorandum would not be paid out unless the government signed up to a set of conditions broadly similar to those that had been accepted by its 'technocratic' predecessor in 2012. To do so would have been a complete reversal of everything that the SYRIZA-led coalition stood for. Instead, with only a week's notice, Tsipras announced a referendum, to be held on Sunday 5 July. Voters were to be asked to say 'yes' or 'no' to the conditions laid down by the Eurogroup. On 29 June, the first working day after the announcement of the referendum, the European Central Bank withdrew its liquidity arrangement with the Greek banks. The Greek government and the Bank of Greece had immediately to introduce capital controls, close the banks for several days, and when eventually they reopened impose a strict limit on withdrawals. Most members of SYRIZA, including Tsipras as prime minister, as well as their coalition partners in ANEL and the extreme-right Golden Dawn, campaigned for a 'no' vote.

Against expectations, and under coercion, with the banks closed and the threat that they might not reopen, 61.31 per cent of votes cast were for 'no', on a low turnout (by Greek standards) of 62.5 per cent. The Greek government had been careful to emphasize that the choice was not between staying in the euro or leaving the single currency. This was not a vote for or against 'Europe', although many who favoured a 'yes' vote, both inside and outside Greece, tried to make out that it was. Opinion polls at the time were showing even higher percentages *in favour of* staying in the euro and the EU than voted *against* the specific terms in the referendum. Once again the Greek people had spoken out against austerity, and against the dictates of the European institutions. But they had not voted against the institutions themselves.

The day after the poll, Varoufakis resigned as finance minister. By the end of the week, with support from the pro-bailout opposition, a bill was voted through parliament to go back to the European institutions and seek a third Memorandum. Of all the revelations in Varoufakis's book, the most startling must surely be the reason that he says Tsipras gave, in private, for this 'capitulation': 'He told me that he feared a "Goudi" fate awaited us if we persevered – a reference to the execution of six politicians and military leaders in 1922 . . . [He] then began to insinuate that something like a coup might take place.'[10] If true, was this a remarkable – and uncharacteristic – show of cowardice by an elected prime minister? Or were there still, as Varoufakis at times insinuates, without ever providing the proof, forces at work in the Greek 'deep establishment' that would have been ready, as recently as 2015, to overturn the democratic order, even to threaten the kind of extreme violence that had scarred the country's political life almost a century ago?

On 13 July the heads of government of all those states that make up the Eurozone issued a statement that paved the way for a third Memorandum of Understanding with Greece. Up to 86 billion euros would be made available over the next three years, half to service its debts and the rest to ensure drastic restructuring of the Greek economy. The amount was many times greater than the last tranche of the previous bailout that voters had forgone by voting 'no' in the referendum. But the conditions were even more stringent. More than ever, Greece had become a 'debt colony'. What has been termed 'Europe's symbolic colonization of Greece' had gone one step further.[11] The creditors had made their point, and won their case.

The logic of Greek politics up to this point would lead one to expect that SYRIZA and Tsipras would be punished by the electorate. Theirs had been the most spectacular of the three U-turns by successive Greek governments that had accompanied the acceptance of each *Mnimonio*. This time, the immediate effect was to split the governing party. But Tsipras was able to rely on the votes of opposition MPs. Even so, recognizing that he had lost his mandate, he called a snap election for 20 September. The result again confounded expectations. The splinter group of anti-bailout members of SYRIZA, who were also opposed to continuing membership of the European Union, was wiped out. Their newly formed party failed to reach the minimum threshold for representation in parliament. The state of the parties that resulted was an almost exact re-run of what had happened in January. No party changed its share of the vote by more than two per cent; most, including the largest, SYRIZA and New Democracy, by less than one per cent. The coalition between SYRIZA and ANEL returned to power. And, again confounding expectations in many quarters, it would last for almost a four-year term.

For critics, it was simply incoherent for Tsipras to call a referendum, only to ignore its result and submit to worse terms than had been on offer ten days previously. For the irreconcilable Eurosceptics of the far left, who broke with SYRIZA in August 2015, that U-turn had been a betrayal of the people. Varoufakis has publicly championed this view ever since, although in his case without advocating withdrawal from the European Union. On the opposite side of the argument are those who argue that the first SYRIZA government, and Varoufakis in particular, had 'cost the Greek economy around €100 billion'.[12] Three years later, a third view is beginning to be heard in some quarters: perhaps those hundred billion were what it cost to convince *all* sections of Greek society, finally and beyond all possibility of doubt, that there really was no alternative to the austerity policies imposed by the 'Troika'? Yes, it might have been better to have accepted the medicine sooner. But after three bailouts and three changes of governing party, by the autumn of 2015 there were no other options left on the table. Was this the beginning of the end of the 'crisis'?

LIVING WITH 'CRISIS'

A crisis, literally, is a moment of 'judgement', a turning point. The word itself is yet another legacy of the ancient Greeks to the vocabulary of today's globalized world. But in Greece, and wherever in the rest of the world people talk about Greece, during the last ten years the meaning of 'crisis' has subtly shifted to refer not to a decisive *moment*, but to a *condition*. Part of the nature of that condition, as it has come to be perceived, is that, once in it, nothing changes, or very little. It is a far cry from the normal meaning of the word. For that reason, in this chapter, whenever it applies to the condition of Greece since 2010, 'crisis' appears within inverted commas. In Greece, 'crisis' has become a way of life.

It is a way of life defined almost universally by the effects of sudden impoverishment. No other developed country in modern times has seen its economy shrink by a quarter within five years, incomes and pensions reduced by at least as much, and unemployment persisting at above 25 per cent, rising almost to 60 per cent among the young. Capital controls and restrictions on bank accounts, imposed in July 2015, would not be lifted until September 2018.

While the economic cost is obvious, the effects on society may run deeper and prove more lasting. Greek society had already been changing rapidly, and unevenly, ever since the end of the Cold War. War and failed states in the Middle East, since 2003, have increased the number of displaced people seeking refuge in Europe, many of them travelling via Greece, most dramatically since 2013. Impoverished public institutions and private charities have found themselves responsible for the survival and welfare of unprecedented numbers of migrants arriving on the islands of the eastern Aegean from Turkey – more than a hundred thousand of them, in the first half of 2015, the peak year, alone. The problem was further compounded in 2016, when other states further north closed their borders and began erecting fences to keep migrants out – an option not available to Greece with its hundreds of islands and with its mainland open to the sea on three sides. Many thousands became trapped in a country they had never meant to stay in for more than a few hours. The result was to bring social services in Greece close to breaking point and put further strains on a society already struggling with its own internal 'crisis'.

Another consequence of the new influx is that, for the first time since 1923, Greece once again has a sizeable Muslim population. Historical memories die hard: proposals to build the first mosque in Athens since the end of Ottoman rule have been fiercely contested for years. Although a site was identified and plans approved in 2016, at the time of writing the mosque has still not opened. Other social stresses have increased dramatically too. Street crime and robbery used to be almost unknown in post-war Greece. The years of 'crisis' have changed all that. Muggings take place even in the most well-heeled parts of Athens, where the fewest signs of impoverishment are visible, and on the beautifully designed and still well-maintained Metro. Whole districts of the city's western suburbs, including some close to the centre, have become 'no-go' areas for police and law-abiding citizens, run by people traffickers and drug dealers exploiting the misery of Greeks made homeless by the crisis and migrants without legal status or protection. There are stories of desperate householders turning to the vigilantes of Golden Dawn to protect them and their property, when an overstretched and demoralized police force is unable to do so, even with the connivance of the police themselves.

It is often said that, after the first years, when protesters took to the streets, a climate of despair and resignation set in. Despite the unchannelled currents of violence, fuelled by disillusion and the lack of hope, civil order has not broken down. Greeks have found ways of coping. The traditional family unit is the most important of these. Another is the black economy, based on cash and barter. Many Greeks never did put much trust in banks, and for years their bureaucratic procedures were hardly designed to bring customers through their doors. You don't have to dig too far down into popular memory to find alternative ways of doing business. Those who can, leave and find work abroad. Greeks have been here before. Generations have lived through far worse conditions in the two-hundred-year history of the Greek state. What helps them to survive at such times is a quality that can best be translated as 'endurance' or 'patient resignation'. But if it is the old, traditional ways that enable people to keep going, despite adversity, this is not a very encouraging sign that Greece and Greeks are on the brink of the kind of decisive upswing that might be expected on the far side of a 'crisis'.

That said, there are positives amid the gloom. Nowhere is this more apparent than in the arts and culture. Poetry, traditionally the first recourse for self-expression in the Greek language, has flourished, in new forms, new genres, new environments. Some of Greece's newest poets are immigrants, bilingual in their mother tongue and Greek. All, in different ways, as the editor of a recent anthology in English puts it, bear witness 'to the hard lives being led in Greece and the Balkans today', but at the same time 'offer new ways to imagine what can be radically different realities'.[13] Writers of fiction have continued to widen their horizons, with more and more writers engaging with experiences and situations either far from Greece or involving characters who represent the 'other' in relation to the Greek. Possibly not unconnected with the rise in crime, detective fiction has belatedly come into its own. Several of the best-selling crime novels by Petros Markaris, featuring the dictionary-loving Inspector Haritos, have been translated into English and other languages. His *Crisis Trilogy*, published between 2010 and 2012, gives a characteristically gritty and caustic perspective on daily life during those first years of the 'crisis'.

In other art forms, too, 'an explosion of creativity has been witnessed in Greece during the crisis, particularly in the areas of theatre, film and performance'.[14] Art-cinema films by Giorgos Lanthimos, Alexandros Avranas and others, some of them made in English, have reached international audiences. New compositions and public performances, in the tradition of classical or 'art' music, have blossomed. State-of-the-art cultural venues have opened in Athens since the start of the 'crisis' and now put on impressive programmes: the Onassis Cultural Centre (*Stegi*) in 2010, the Stavros Niarchos Foundation Cultural Centre, housing the new Opera House and National Library, in March 2017. Both of these new ventures are tributes to the one great Greek economic *success* story that goes at least as far back as the eighteenth century, and whose assets have traditionally been held beyond the boundaries of the state: namely shipping. The international art exhibition *Documenta 14* welcomed more than three hundred thousand visitors when it opened for six months in Athens during 2017. Street art in Greece has become elevated from the ugly political scrawls that traditionally deface university campuses to an art form, often exuberant, witty, defiant, inventive.

On the economic and political fronts, some have detected signs of the Memoranda working, or at least of beneficial effects. On paper, at least, the Samaras government had succeeded in generating a primary surplus by the end of 2014, as its successor would once again do in 2018. In the view of at least one Greek economist in 2017, there has been a shift in Greek public attitudes against indebtedness and for 'a reasonable degree of fiscal discipline', matched by the pragmatic turn of the SYRIZA-led coalition after the summer of 2015.[15]

During four and a half years in power, the former fringe party of the 'far left' would morph into something much more like the social-democratic PASOK that it displaced. Far from losing face after the spectacular U-turn of July 2015, Alexis Tsipras went on to consolidate his power within his party. He seems to have achieved this by the exercise of personal authority and charisma, just as every successful Greek prime minister had done before him, all the way back to Ioannis Kolettis in the 1840s. If SYRIZA today has effectively replaced PASOK, Tsipras is the new Andreas Papandreou. A career that started out in the communist left and achieved the highest office by appealing to national-populist ideals of self-sufficiency would soon be tempered by the realities of power, both at home and within Europe.

Some of the strongest of these positives take the form of an *absence* – dire predictions that have not come true, or at least so far. There has been no default or chaotic exit from the euro. There has been no collapse of public order. In Greece, no separatist movements have emerged to threaten the integrity of the state, as has happened elsewhere in Europe in recent decades. There has never been an equivalent to the momentum for independence seen in, for example, the former Czechoslovakia, in Belgium, Spain or the United Kingdom, or even political pressure for greater regional autonomy. Popular movements and uprisings throughout modern Greek history have always been driven by the desire for *unification*. Outside greater Athens, which is home to almost half the country's population, most parts of Greece possess a strong regional identity. But even in Crete, where such sentiments are perhaps most in evidence, no political grouping has yet put forward a serious programme to break away from the Greek state. This is another potential threat that has not, so far, shown any sign of materializing, despite the new strains imposed by the 'crisis'.

The case of that other Greek state, the Republic of Cyprus, is rather different. There, political separation was imposed, in and after 1960, and has tended to be reinforced by geographical distance. The Republic of Cyprus, too, found itself plunged into crisis. But there the similarities end. During 2012, after the second Memorandum had been signed with Greece, the Cypriot financial sector took heavy losses from the write-down of loans to Greek banks. In March 2013 it was the turn of the Cyprus government to risk default and to have to turn to the European institutions for a bailout. Capital controls were imposed and limits placed on the amount that could be withdrawn from banks. These were both measures that would be applied to Greece only later, in 2015. In Cyprus the price demanded for rescue was higher still. The country's second-largest bank was allowed to fail. Depositors in all banks lost up to 10 per cent of their savings. In Cyprus the immediate shock in March and April 2013 was even greater than at the equivalent moments in Greece. It was the Cypriot private sector that bore the brunt. Businesses failed. But retrenchment of the public sector seemed to be contained. Within a few months the limit on bank withdrawals was lifted, and exchange controls two years later.

By the time that in Greece the economy was collapsing again towards its third bailout in the summer of 2015, the Cypriot economy was already out of danger. Once again, as had been proved after the devastation of 1974, the economy of Greek Cyprus was capable of turning itself around in a short time, as has not been the case with Greece. It is another sign of the increasing divergence between the two Greek states, which remain so closely linked in other ways.

But all this is on the surface. The bailouts and the seemingly insoluble problem of Greece's sovereign debt are only one aspect of a 'crisis' that goes deeper. At bottom, once again, it is a crisis of identity.

Under the new pressures of a decade of 'crisis', Greeks in all walks of life, and to some extent irrespective of whether they live in Greece or not, have found themselves forced to take stock, to look again at their history, at the values they grew up with, at their own sense of who they are and where they belong in the world. Once again, official Greece has reaffirmed its alignment with the West, now represented by the institutions of the European Union as much as by the broader culture of all Europe. But once again, this has been narrowly achieved, and at great cost.

Surveys and opinion polls have shown some decline in support among Greek voters for staying within the EU and the euro. But even now there is no evidence that a majority would prefer to leave. Private polling reported in late 2017 showed a drop from 69 per cent wishing to remain at the time of the 2015 referendum to 53 per cent in late

2016. The same populist, nativist trends that have been on the rise in other parts of the world for some years now can also be observed in Greece. The widespread anti-Americanism of the 'Polytechnic generation' has morphed into forms of popular hostility to Germans, perceived as responsible for enforced austerity. Newspaper cartoons have shown the former German finance minister, Wolfgang Schäuble, in Nazi uniform; popular demonstrations have represented the German Chancellor, Angela Merkel, in the role of Hitler.[16] The period of 'crisis' has brought renewed calls in some quarters for payment of reparations by Germany for atrocities committed in Greece during the Second World War and, even more controversially, for repayment of enforced loans extracted by the Reich from the National Bank of Greece during the Occupation. Tensions of this sort seem to have peaked during the 'Greek Spring' of 2015. But they have not entirely gone away.

The most obvious symptom of a populist backlash is the presence of Golden Dawn, seemingly a fixture on the political landscape, with a polling strength of around seven per cent, which is to say within the same range as the Greek Communist Party has enjoyed for the best part of a century. At least Golden Dawn seeks no other alignment than with those it claims as biological ancestors, and especially the militarist, anti-democratic Spartans. At the other end of the political spectrum, there are those on the left for whom the old lure of the Soviet Union, and before that of imperial, Orthodox Russia, still tugs. This was the case with the thirty or so SYRIZA MPs who broke away from the party in protest against the third Memorandum. For them, as well as for Tsipras himself during the 'Greek Spring' of 2015, a serious alternative to 'ever closer integration' in Europe lay in reviving the old dream of closer ties to Russia.

That this was not just a fantasy is shown by the official visits paid to Moscow and St Petersburg by more than one member of the first SYRIZA government, including Tsipras himself in April 2015. At the end of 2013, when tensions were at their height over Ukraine and Russia's annexation of Crimea, advisers to President Putin had even imagined a role for Greece, Cyprus and Turkey within the emerging Eurasian Union, which is the current Russian president's way of restoring something of the old Russian empire. In a speech in December 2014, Putin had claimed 'a special relationship with Greece because of our religious affinity'.[17] In return, one of Tsipras's first actions after his election victory a month later was to oppose EU sanctions against Russia over its actions in Ukraine.

In parallel with Varoufakis's high-wire negotiations in Brussels, Washington and the capitals of Europe, other members of the same government were trying to negotiate an alternative loan from Russia. If that had been offered, it might just have provided the leverage needed to bring concessions from the 'Troika', or at least the possibility of a slightly softer landing if Greece were to be ejected from the euro. But President Putin's interest in Greece seems to be no greater than that of any of his predecessors since Catherine the Great. It is said that it was on the night of the referendum that Tsipras learned finally that Putin had turned down his government's request for a loan – a possible further reason for the U-turn that followed.[18]

There remains a strong strand in Greek public opinion, going most of the way to the top, that still identifies either with the Orthodox Christian or the Soviet communist tradition with which it intriguingly overlaps historically. The passing notion, in the Kremlin, of a 'Eurasian' Greece, or Cyprus for that matter, might have seemed far-fetched in 2013. But there could yet come a time when it might not. And in the case of Cyprus, although no state loans have been involved, the recovery since 2013 has been aided by private investment from Russia on a scale that Western observers find troubling. Today, restaurants in Nicosia print their menus with a page in Russian, as well as in Greek and English. Arrivals at Larnaca International Airport are greeted with glitzy advertisements for real estate written entirely in Russian. High-profile Russian 'oligarchs' have been awarded citizenship of the Republic of Cyprus, and therefore of the European Union. When in March 2018 the majority of NATO and EU countries expelled Russian diplomats in response to the use of a banned Russian nerve agent in the United Kingdom, no one should have been surprised that Greece and Cyprus were not among their number.

So far, most of these responses to the 'crisis' have involved various degrees of either introspection or retrospection – whether falling back on resources or strategies that have worked in the past, or turning wistfully towards avenues not taken. But there is one aspect of the 'crisis' that crops up again and again. This one, too, needs metaphors to express itself. Greece since 2010 has become a 'testing ground', a 'laboratory', or is itself the subject of experiment: a 'guinea pig' or laboratory animal. Most chilling of all these metaphors is that of the 'canary in the coalmine'. The purpose of the caged bird down the mine was to give warning of poisonous gases that human senses could not detect. If the canary died, the miners had time to escape before being overcome. It is in that sense that Greece has been tested by the European institutions and the IMF. The very survival of the institutions, and of the global financial system that they in turn shore up, was at risk from the financial crisis of 2008. Following the logic of the metaphor, Greece was the small, weak songbird whose life could be sacrificed for the greater good.

These metaphors and their constant reiteration are not very flattering to Greeks – who nonetheless repeat them as often as anyone else. Their only effect is to reinforce a sense of victimhood that can be traced back through Greek popular culture for hundreds of years. A better metaphor is that of the pioneer.

The pioneer originally was a foot soldier sent ahead of the main force to prepare the way for the rest. In that sense, the pioneer is not totally unlike the canary. But there is a difference. The pioneer, even if he is acting under orders, still has human agency. He may end up losing life or limb to protect his comrades. But he can also use his ingenuity to find the safe path and guide them. It was in that sense, surely, that the novelist Giorgos Theotokas, writing in 1929, in the aftermath of a much greater national disaster, called for 'bold pioneers' to carry forward a programme of cultural renewal by reaching out to the rest of Europe.

And this is where the 'crisis' and the years that will follow it must surely present opportunities, alongside the more obvious threats. Greece was the first country to be bailed out by a 'Memorandum', devised by a 'Troika' that had been brought into existence expressly for that purpose. Greece is the only country to have gone through the process three times. The strength of Greek institutions and the endurance of the Greek people have been tested severely, but they have come through the test. Europe, the euro and the Eurozone are the stronger for that. And they have the Greeks to thank, for taking the risks of the pioneer to make it possible.

Two hundred years ago, during the 1820s, Greeks were the pioneers who first mapped out the route that would lead from the old Europe of great empires to the Europe of nation states that we know today. No one should take it for granted that Greece and Greeks in future will always align with the values, traditions and politics that we tend to lump together and call 'Western'. Geography, and to some extent also history, may pull the other way. But as they prepare to celebrate the two-hundredth birthday of the Greek nation state in 2021, Greeks can take pride in an achievement that by its very nature, and from the very beginning, has been won not through isolation, but in partnership, every difficult step of the way, with other Europeans. It could not be otherwise. Because 'Greece', however understood, or misunderstood, has always been part of the modern identity of Europe too.

Notes

INTRODUCTION: THE NATION AND
ITS ANCESTORS

1. Giorgos Seferis, Δοκιμές [*Essays*], vol. 3, ed. D. Daskalopoulos (Athens: Ikaros, 1992), 167 (original in French).
2. Speech by Melina Mercouri to the Oxford Union, 12 June 1986 (original emphasis) <http://www.parthenon.newmentor.net/speech.htm> (accessed 27 February 2018).
3. Loukia Droulia, 'Towards modern Greek consciousness', *The Historical Review / La Revue Historique* (Institute for Neohellenic Research, Athens) 1 (2004), 51–67 (see p. 51). For the original Greek text see the website of the Hellenic Parliament.
4. Kostis Palamas, Άπαντα [*Complete Works*], 17 vols (Athens: Biris, n.d.), vol. 6, 279.
5. Patrick Leigh Fermor, *Roumeli: Travels in Northern Greece* (London: John Murray, 1966), 96–101, 106–13; Michael Herzfeld, *Ours Once More: Folklore, Ideology and the Making of Modern Greece* (Austin, TX: University of Texas Press, 1982), 18–21.
6. Samuel Huntington, *The Clash of Civilizations and the Remaking of the World Order* (London: Simon and Schuster, 2002; first published 1996), 162.
7. Stathis Kalyvas, *Modern Greece: What Everyone Needs to Know* (Oxford: Oxford University Press, 2015), 34.
8. David Brewer, *Greece: The Hidden Centuries. Turkish Rule from the Fall of Constantinople to Greek Independence* (London: I. B. Tauris, 2010).
9. Steven Runciman, *A History of the Crusades*, 3 vols (Harmondsworth: Penguin, 1971; first published 1951–4), vol. 3, 130.

1. EAST MEETS WEST?

1. Lucien Frary, *Russia and the Making of Modern Greek Identity, 1821–1844* (Oxford: Oxford University Press, 2015), 20–27.

2. Paschalis Kitromilides, *An Orthodox Commonwealth: Symbolic Legacies and Cultural Encounters in Southeastern Europe* (Aldershot: Variorum, 2007), ix–xv.

3. On science: Paschalis Kitromilides, *Enlightenment and Revolution: The Making of Modern Greece* (Cambridge, MA: Harvard University Press, 2013), 52, 365 n. 108, 366 n. 111; Efthymios Nicolaidis, 'The Greek Enlightenment, the Orthodox Church and modern science', in Paschalis Kitromilides (ed.), *Enlightenment and Religion in the Orthodox World* (Oxford: Voltaire Foundation, 2016), 49–62. On anticlericalism see Kitromilides, *Enlightenment and Revolution*, 250–59.

4. Nicolas Mavrocordatos, *Les Loisirs de Philothée* [parallel Greek and French texts], trans. Jacques Bouchard (Athens and Montreal: Les Presses de l'Université de Montréal, 1989).

5. Daniel Philippidis and Grigorios Konstantas, *Γεωγραφία νεωτερική. Περί της Ελλάδος* [*Modern Geography: On Greece*], ed. with introduction by Aikaterini Koumarianou (Athens: Ermis, 1970), editor's introduction (18–19, 28, 30–1) and text (37, 38, 44–51).

6. Peter Mackridge, *Language and National Identity in Greece, 1766–1976* (Oxford: Oxford University Press, 2009), 80–83.

7. Gelina Harlaftis and Sophia Laiou, 'Ottoman state policy in Mediterranean trade and shipping, c. 1780–1820: The rise of the Greek-owned Ottoman merchant fleet', in Mark Mazower (ed.), *Networks of Power in Modern Greece: Essays in Honour of John Campbell* (London: Hurst, 2008), 1–44 (see 9–15). The authors do not indicate whether the characterization 'Greek' is their own (presumably inferred from recognizably Greek names) or already to be found in their sources.

8. Harlaftis and Laiou, 'Ottoman state policy', 17.

9. David Constantine, *In the Footsteps of the Gods: Travellers to Greece and the Quest for the Hellenic Ideal* (London: I. B. Tauris, 2011), 52.

10. Johann Hermann von Riedesel, *Remarques d'un voyageur moderne au Levant* (Amsterdam, 1773); Henry Miller, *The Colossus of Maroussi* (San Francisco, CA: Colt, 1941); Lawrence Durrell, *Prospero's Cell* (London: Faber and Faber, 1945).

11. Matthew Bell, 'The Greek body beautiful and the origins of European Romanticism', in Ian Jenkins (ed.), *Defining Beauty: The Body in Ancient Greek Art* (London: British Museum, 2015), 40–49 (42–3 quoted).

12. J. J. Winckelmann, *History of the Art of Antiquity*, trans. H. F. Mallgrave (Los Angeles, CA: Getty, 2006; first published in German, 1764), 187.

13. P. A. Guys, *A Sentimental Journey through Greece* (Dublin: Milliken, 1773; first published in French, 1771), vol. 1, iv; Nasia Giakovaki, *Ευρώπη μέσω Ελλάδας. Μια καμπή στην ευρωπαϊκή αυτοσυνείδηση, 17ος–18ος αιώνας [Europe via Greece: A Turning Point in European Consciousness, 17th–18th Centuries]* (Athens: Estia, 2006), 26–7, 448.

14. Giakovaki, *Ευρώπη [Europe]*, and (quite independently) Paul Stock, *The Shelley–Byron Circle and the Idea of Europe* (Basingstoke: Palgrave Macmillan, 2010), 9–11, 175–97.

15. Iosipos Moisiodax, *Θεωρία της γεωγραφίας [Theory of Geography]* (Vienna, 1781), x; Stratos Myrogiannis, *The Emergence of a Greek Identity (1700–1821)* (Newcastle upon Tyne: Cambridge Scholars, 2012), 92.

16. John Campbell, *Honour, Family, and Patronage: A Study of Institutions and Moral Values in a Greek Mountain Community* (Oxford: Oxford University Press, 1974; first published 1964), v (quoted), 318–19, 353–6.

17. I am indebted to the anthropologist Maria Couroucli for this insight.

18. E. Legrand, *Bibliothèque grecque vulgaire* (Paris: Maisonneuve, 1881), vol. 3, 312, based on the earliest extant text, published in 1784.

19. V. Laourdas (ed.), *Μπάρμπα-Παντζελιού. Το τραγούδι του Δασκαλογιάννη [Barba-Pantzelios: The Song of Daskalogiannis]* (Heraklion, Crete: Marmel, 1947), lines 8–9, 12, 754–8 (quoted), 989–94.

20. Anton Jeannaraki (ed.), *Άσματα κρητικά [Cretan Songs]* (Leipzig: Brockhaus, 1876), 142; reprinted in Giorgos Ioannou (ed.), *Τα δημοτικά μας τραγούδια [Our Folk Songs]* (Athens: Tachydromos, 1966), 30. Variants on the theme can be found in almost every anthology of Greek folk songs.

21. Alexis Politis (ed.), *Το δημοτικό τραγούδι. κλέφτικα [Folk Songs: Kleftic]* (Athens: Ermis, 1973), 2–3.

22. Claude Fauriel, *Chants populaires de la Grèce moderne*, 2 vols (Paris: Dondey-Dupré, 1824–5), vol. 2, 340.

23. I. Th. Kakridis, *Οι αρχαίοι Έλληνες στη νεοελληνική λαϊκή παράδοση [The Ancient Greeks in the Modern Greek Popular Tradition]* (Athens: Cultural Foundation of the National Bank [MIET], 1997; first published in German, 1966), 39.

2. A SEED IS SOWN

1. Panagiotis Chiotis, *Σειράς ιστορικών απομνημονευμάτων, τόμ. Γ'* [*Historical Memoirs Series, vol. 3*] (Corfu: Government Printing House, 1863), 573 (quoted), 584, 586; J.-P. Bellaire, *Précis des opérations générales de la Division française du Levant* (Paris, 1805), 11.

2. Christine Philliou, *Biography of an Empire: Governing Ottomans in an Age of Revolution* (Berkeley, CA: University of California Press, 2011), 49–51.

3. Rigas Velestinlis, *Νέα πολιτική διοίκησις των κατοίκων της Ρούμελης, της Μικράς Ασίας, των Μεσογείων Νήσων και της Βλαχομπογδανίας*, ed. P. M. Kitromilides (vol. 5 in the series *Ρήγα Βελεστινλή. Άπαντα τα σωζόμενα* [*Rigas Velestinlis: Complete Surviving Works*]) (Athens: Hellenic Parliament, 2000), with introduction, commentary and appendices, including the French text of the 1793 constitution. Hereafter: 'Rigas'. Substantial excerpts in English translation can be found in Richard Clogg (ed. and trans.), *The Movement for Greek Independence, 1770–1821: A Collection of Documents* (London: Macmillan, 1976), 149–63.

4. Rigas, 48 (Constitution, article 7); 33 (Preface); 45 (Constitution, articles 1–2).

5. Rigas, 35, 119.

6. Rigas, 46–7 (Constitution, article 4); 67 (Constitution, article 109).

7. Rigas, 44 (Rights of Man, article 35); 70–71.

8. Rigas, 33–5 (Preface); 73–7 ('Thourios' ['War song']).

9. Adamantios Korais, *Άπαντα τα πρωτότυπα έργα, τόμ. Α'* [*Complete Original Works, Vol. 1*], ed. G. Valetas (Athens: Dorikos, 1964), 40. Hereafter: Korais, *Complete*.

10. Cited in Korais, *Complete*, 44–5; Clogg (ed. and trans.), *Movement*, 56–64.

11. Korais, *Complete*, 54, 56–7.

12. Korais, *Complete*, 1 ('Autobiography', 1829).

13. See further Stratos Myrogiannis, *The Emergence of a Greek Identity (1700–1821)* (Newcastle upon Tyne: Cambridge Scholars, 2012), 142–50.

14. Korais, *Complete*, 65–6 ('Martial trumpet-call', 1801).

15. Korais, *Complete*, 853 ('Improvised thoughts I').

16. *Mémoire sur l'état actuel de la civilisation dans la Grèce, par Coray* [Korais] (Paris, 1803), photographic reprint, National Foundation for Neohellenic Research, Athens (1983). For an English translation see Adamantios Koraes, 'Report on the present state of civilization in Greece', in E. Kedourie (ed.), *Nationalism in Asia and Africa* (London: Weidenfeld and Nicolson, 1971), 153–88.

17. *Mémoire*, 1; Koraes, 'Report', 153.

18. *Mémoire*, 33, 37, 52; Koraes, 'Report', 169, 172, 179.

19. *Mémoire*, 33, 37, 52, 63, 65; Koraes, 'Report', 180, 183–4, 186, 186 (quoted).

20. Korais, *Complete*, 8, 9 ('Autobiography', 1829).

21. Ανωνύμου του Έλληνος, *Ελληνική νομαρχία, ήτοι λόγος περί ελευθερίας* [Anonymous the Hellene, *Hellenic Nomarchy, or Discourse on Liberty*], ed. G. Valetas (Athens: Vivlioekdotiki, 1957; originally published in 1806). Hereafter: 'Anonymous'. For a translated excerpt see Clogg (ed. and trans.), *Movement*, 106–17.

22. Anonymous, 52, 82–3 (quoted), 218.

23. Anonymous, 197, 200, 202, 205, 217, 219.

24. Anonymous, 78–82 (81 quoted), 210–17.

25. Anonymous, 205–7, see also 136 and 217.

26. Anonymous, 150–4, 163–82 (163 quoted), 201, 204 (quoted).

27. Kostas Kostis, *History's Spoiled Children: The Formation of the Modern Greek State*, trans. Jacob Moe (London: Hurst, 2018; Greek original published in 2013), 41.

28. Lord Byron, *Complete Poetical Works*, ed. Jerome McGann, 7 vols (Oxford: Clarendon Press, 1980–93), vol. 1, 330–2.

29. Henry Holland, *Travels in the Ionian Isles, Albania, Thessaly, Macedonia, &c. during the Years 1812–1813* (London: Longman, 1815), 530–31.

30. The fullest early accounts are Ioannis Philemon, *Δοκίμιον ιστορικόν περί της Φιλικής Εταιρίας* [*Historical Essay on the Friendly Society*] (Nafplion, 1834) [hereafter: Philemon, *Friendly*], and the 'Memoirs of Emmanouil Xanthos' (1845), translated in Clogg (ed. and trans.), *Movement*, 182–200. See also K. Svolopoulos, 'Η σύσταση της Φιλικής Εταιρείας. Μια επαναπροσέγγιση' ['The establishment of the Friendly Society: A reappraisal'], *Ta Istorika* 35 (2001), 283–98.

31. Philemon, *Friendly*, 155 (quoted), 172, 173.

32. Kostis, *History's Spoiled Children*, 49–51.

33. Philemon, *Friendly*, 128. Compare the famous saying of Massimo d'Azeglio, *after* the achievement of Italian independence, 'L'Italia è fatta. Restano da fare gli italiani' ['Italy has been made. Now it remains to make Italians'].

34. Vasilis Kremmydas, *Η ελληνική επανάσταση του 1821. Τεκμήρια, αναψηλαφήσεις, ερμηνείες* [*The Greek Revolution of 1821: Documents, Investigations, Interpretations*] (Athens: Gutenberg, 2016), 38–9, 49–53, 58.

3. BORN IN BLOOD

1. Kostas Kostis, *History's Spoiled Children: The Formation of the Modern Greek State*, trans. Jacob Moe (London: Hurst, 2018; Greek original published in 2013), 59; Thomas Gallant, *The Edinburgh History of the Greeks, 1768 to 1913* (Edinburgh: Edinburgh University Press, 2015), 117; Thomas Gallant, *Modern Greece: From the War of Independence to the Present*, 2nd edn (London: Bloomsbury, 2016), 119.

2. Spyridon Trikoupis, Ιστορία της Ελληνικής Επαναστάσεως [*History of the Greek Revolution*], 4 vols (London, 1853-7), vol. 1, 9, echoed in 2016 by Vasilis Kremmydas, Η ελληνική επανάσταση του 1821. Τεκμήρια, αναψηλαφήσεις, ερμηνείες [*The Greek Revolution of 1821: Documents, Investigations, Interpretations*] (Athens: Gutenberg, 2016), 99.

3. George Finlay, *History of the Greek Revolution*, 2 vols (Edinburgh: Blackwood, 1861), vol. 1, 283; see also vol. 1, 119, 177-8, 195; vol. 2, 194, 381.

4. Mavrokordatos to Dimitrios Ypsilantis, 27 October [= 8 November] 1821, first published in Ioannis Philemon, Δοκίμιον ιστορικόν περί της Ελληνικής Επαναστάσεως [*Historical Essay concerning the Greek Revolution*], 4 vols (Athens: Karyofyllis, 1859-61), vol. 4, 513-14.

5. Finlay, *History*, vol. 1, 299.

6. Petros Pizanias (ed.), *The Greek Revolution of 1821: A European Event* (Istanbul: Isis Press, 2011; Greek original published 2009).

7. Pizanias (ed.), *Greek Revolution*, 64.

8. Finlay, *History*, vol. 2, 81.

9. Christos Evangelatos, Ιστορία του Μεσολογγίου [*History of Missolonghi*] (Athens: Govostis, 2007), 377; Thomas Gordon, *History of the Greek Revolution*, 2 vols (Edinburgh: Blackwood, 1832), vol. 2, 265, 260; Finlay, *History*, vol. 2, 105; see also vol. 2, 111.

10. Gordon, *History*, vol. 1, 183. The Greek text, presumably the original, given by Trikoupis (Ιστορία [*History*], vol. 1, 368-9) does not include the final sentence quoted.

11. Lord Byron, *Don Juan*, canto 10, lines 135-6.

12. Roderick Beaton, *Byron's War: Romantic Rebellion, Greek Revolution* (Cambridge: Cambridge University Press, 2013), 152-3, citing James Hamilton Browne, 'Narrative of a visit, in 1823, to the seat of war in Greece', *Blackwood's Edinburgh Magazine*, vol. 36, no. 226 (September 1834), 404.

13. Gordon, *History*, vol. 2, 283-4.

14. Gordon, *History*, vol. 2, 278-9.

15. Hüseyin Şükrü Ilıcak, 'A radical rethinking of empire: Ottoman state and society during the Greek War of Independence (1821–1826)' (PhD dissertation, Harvard University, 2011), 169, 193, 196, 257–60.

16. Gary Bass, *Freedom's Battle: The Origins of Humanitarian Intervention* (New York: Vintage, 2009), 92–7; William St Clair, *That Greece Might Still Be Free: The Philhellenes in the War of Independence* (Cambridge: Open Book, 2008; first published 1972), 274–6.

17. Lucien Frary, *Russia and the Making of Modern Greek Identity, 1821–1844* (Oxford: Oxford University Press, 2015), 44, 53.

18. Douglas Dakin, *The Greek Struggle for Independence, 1821–1833* (London: Batsford, 1973), 273.

19. Ministry of Foreign Affairs of Greece, Service of Historical Archives, *The Foundation of the Modern Greek State: Major Treaties and Conventions (1830–1947)*, ed. Ph. Constantopoulou (Athens: Kastaniotis, 1999), 30 (in French). Facsimile of the original in J. M. Wagstaff (ed.), *Greece: Ethnicity and Sovereignty, 1820–1994. Atlas and Documents* (Archive Editions [Cambridge: Cambridge University Press], 2002), 141–5.

20. Finlay, *History*, vol. 2, 199, 209, 217, 218, 220, 227.

21. Kremmydas, *Επανάσταση [Revolution]*, 198–9.

22. Peter Bien, *Nikos Kazantzakis: Politics of the Spirit*, vol. 2 (Princeton, NJ: Princeton University Press, 2007), 197–223; Adamantios Korais, Ἄπαντα τα πρωτότυπα έργα, τόμ. Aʹ [*Complete Original Works, Vol. 1*], ed. G. Valetas (Athens: Dorikos, 1964), 802 (Καποδιστριακοί διάλογοι Εʹ [*Capodistrian Dialogues, no. 5*], dated 30 October 1831); C. M. Woodhouse, *Capodistria: The Founder of Greek Independence* (London: Oxford University Press, 1973), 502–3.

23. Finlay, *History*, vol. 2, 275–6.

4. FIRST STEPS

1. George Finlay, *History of the Greek Revolution*, 2 vols (Edinburgh: Blackwood, 1861), vol. 2, 290–93; Panagiotis Soutsos, Ο Λέανδρος [*Leander*], ed. A. Samouil (Athens: Nefeli, 1996; first published Nafplio, 1834), 130.

2. Leonard Bower and Gordon Bolitho, *Otho I, King of Greece: A Biography* (London: Selwyn and Blount, 1939), 72; Thomas Gallant, *The Edinburgh History of the Greeks, 1768 to 1913* (Edinburgh: Edinburgh University Press, 2015), 110.

3. Alexis Politis, *Ρομαντικά χρόνια. Ιδεολογίες και νοοτροπίες στην Ελλάδα του 1830–1880* [*Romantic Years: Ideologies and Mentalities in Greece, 1830–1880*] (Athens: Mnimon, 1993), 108.

4. Leo von Klenze, speaking on the Acropolis in 1833, cited in Yannis Hamilakis, *The Nation and its Ruins: Antiquity, Archaeology, and National Imagination in Greece* (Oxford: Oxford University Press, 2007), 61, 89.

5. Roderick Beaton, *An Introduction to Modern Greek Literature*, 2nd ed. (Oxford: Clarendon Press, 1999), 307–8; Peter Mackridge, *Language and National Identity in Greece, 1766–1976* (Oxford: Oxford University Press, 2009), 182–4.

6. Athina Kakouri, *1821. Η αρχή που δεν ολοκληρώθηκε* (Athens: Patakis, 2013).

7. John Koliopoulos and Thanos Veremis, *Greece: The Modern Sequel, from 1821 to the Present* (London: Hurst, 2002), 229.

8. Soutsos, *Λέανδρος* [*Leander*], 101; Elli Skopetea, *Το «πρότυπο βασίλειο» και η Μεγάλη Ιδέα. Όψεις του εθνικού προβλήματος στην Ελλάδα (1830–1880)* [*The 'Model Kingdom' and the Grand Idea: Aspects of the National Problem in Greece (1830–1880)*] (Athens: Polytypo, 1988), 274.

9. John Petropulos, *Politics and Statecraft in the Kingdom of Greece, 1833–1843* (Princeton, NJ: Princeton University Press, 1968), 445.

10. *Η της τρίτης Σεπτεμβρίου εν Αθήναις Εθνική Συνέλευσις. Πρακτικά* [*The '3 September' National Assembly in Athens: Proceedings*] (Athens, 1844; photographic reprint, Athens and Komotini: A. N. Sakkoulas, 1993), 190–4 (190 quoted).

11. James Emerson, *The History of Modern Greece, from its Conquest by the Romans B.C. 146, to the Present Time* (London: Colburn & Bentley, 1830); Johann Wilhelm Zinkeisen, *Geschichte Griechenlands vom Anfange geschictlicher Kunde bis auf unsere Tage* (Leipzig: Barth, 1832); George Finlay, *A History of Greece: From its Conquest by the Romans to the Present Time*, 7 vols (Oxford: Clarendon Press, 1877; originally published between 1844 and 1861).

12. Spyridon Zambelios, *Άσματα δημοτικά της Ελλάδος* [*Folk Songs of Greece*] (Corfu: Ermis, 1852), 5–7 (5 quoted).

13. G. Babiniotis, *Λεξικό της νέας ελληνικής γλώσσας* [*Dictionary of the Modern Greek Language*], 2nd edn (Athens: Centre for Lexicography, 2002).

14. Zambelios, *Άσματα δημοτικά* [*Folk Songs*], 20, 63–5, 23.

15. Konstantinos Paparrigopoulos, *Ιστορία του ελληνικού έθνους* [*History of the Greek Nation*] (Athens: Koromilas, 1853), 1 (original emphasis).

16. Paschalis Kitromilides, 'On the intellectual content of Greek nationalism: Paparrigopoulos, Byzantium and the Great Idea', in David Ricks

and Paul Magdalino (eds), *Byzantium and the Modern Greek Identity* (Aldershot: Ashgate, 1998), 25–33 (28 quoted).

17. Dolphus Whitten, 'The Don Pacifico affair', *The Historian* 48/2 (1986), 255–67 (260 quoted).

18. Robert Holland and Diana Markides, *The British and the Hellenes: Struggles for Mastery in the Eastern Mediterranean 1850–1960* (Oxford: Oxford University Press, 2006), 60, citing a letter of 4 November 1862.

19. Skopetea, *Το «πρότυπο βασίλειο»* [*The 'Model Kingdom'*], 240–41, 235.

20. Finlay, *History*, vol. 2, 382.

21. Skopetea, *Το «πρότυπο βασίλειο»* [*The 'Model Kingdom'*], 162.

5. IDEALS AND SORROWS OF YOUTH

1. George Finlay, *A History of Greece: From its Conquest by the Romans to the Present Time*, 7 vols (Oxford: Clarendon Press, 1877), vol. 7, 281.

2. Eleutherios Prevelakis, *British Policy towards the Change of Dynasty in Greece* (Athens: n.p., 1953), 167–8; facsimile treaties in J. M. Wagstaff (ed.), *Greece: Ethnicity and Sovereignty, 1820–1994. Atlas and Documents* (Archive Editions, [Cambridge: Cambridge University Press], 2002), 178–90. The Greek title, proposed by the National Assembly in 1863 and in use for more than a century after that, is Βασιλεύς των Ελλήνων. The official translation was emended from *Roi des Grecs* to *Roi des Hellènes*.

3. Walter Christmas, *King George of Greece* (New York: McBride, Nast, 1914); Aristea Papanikolaou-Kristensen (ed. and trans.), «Φίλτατε ...». *Επιστολές από την Ελλάδα 1897–1913* [*"Dear ...": Letters from Greece 1897–1913*] (Athens: Ermis, 2006).

4. Konstantinos Svolopoulos, 'Η εξωτερική πολιτική του Χαριλάου Τρικούπη. Διαχρονική θεώρηση' ['The foreign policy of Charilaos Trikoupis: A diachronic perspective'], in Kaiti Aroni-Tsichli and Lydia Tricha (eds), *Ο Χαρίλαος Τρικούπης και η εποχή του* [*Charilaos Trikoupis and his Times*] (Athens: Papazisis, 2000), 28.

5. Mark Mazower, *The Balkans* (London: Weidenfeld and Nicolson, 2000), 1–4.

6. Gerasimos Augustinos, *The Greeks of Asia Minor* (Kent, OH: Kent State University Press, 1992), 199.

7. Konstantinos Svolopoulos, *Κωνσταντινούπολη 1856–1908. Η ακμή του Ελληνισμού* [*Constantinople 1856–1908: The High Point of Hellenism*] (Athens: Ekdotiki Athinon, 1994), 37–8.

8. George Vassiadis, *The* Syllogos *Movement of Constantinople and Ottoman Greek Education, 1861–1923* (Athens: Centre for Asia Minor Studies, 2007), 55–6.

9. Alexis Politis, *Ρομαντικά χρόνια. Ιδεολογίες και νοοτροπίες στην Ελλάδα του 1830–1880* [*Romantic Years: Ideologies and Mentalities in Greece, 1830–1880*] (Athens: Mnimon, 1993), 103–4, quoting in Greek translation Georges Perrot, *Souvenirs d'un voyage en Asie Mineure* (Paris, 1864), 11.

10. Hasan Kayalı, 'Elections and the electoral process in the Ottoman Empire, 1876–1919', *International Journal of Middle East Studies* 27/3 (1995), 265–86 (see 266–7); Alexandros Alexandris, 'Οι Έλληνες στην υπηρεσία της Οθωμανικής αυτοκρατορίας 1850–1922' ['Greeks in the service of the Ottoman Empire 1850–1922'], *Δελτίον της Ιστορικής και Εθνολογικής Εταιρείας της Ελλάδος* [*Bulletin of the Historical and Ethnological Society of Greece*] 23 (1980), 378–9, citing a letter from the representatives of Pera to Lord Salisbury, December 1876.

11. See Thomas Gallant, *The Edinburgh History of the Greeks, 1768 to 1913* (Edinburgh: Edinburgh University Press, 2015), 170–71, for a compilation of competing census data from the period; see Mark Mazower, *Salonica: City of Ghosts* (London: HarperCollins, 2004), 269, for what are probably the most accurate figures.

12. Augustinos, *Greeks*, 241, cf. 197, citing in translation letters from the Educational Society of Raidestos to the Hellenic Literary Association of Constantinople, dated 1871 and 1872.

13. Vasilis Gounaris, *Τα Βαλκάνια των Ελλήνων. Από το Διαφωτισμό έως τον Α΄ Παγκόσμιο Πόλεμο* [*The Balkans of the Greeks: From the Enlightenment to the First World War*] (Thessaloniki: Epikentro, 2007), 403–4.

14. Mazower, *Salonica*, 245.

15. Kostas Kostis, *History's Spoiled Children: The Formation of the Modern Greek State*, trans. Jacob Moe (London: Hurst, 2018; Greek original published in 2013), 207, citing a speech to parliament in 1894.

16. Andrew Mango, *Atatürk* (London: John Murray, 1999), 42–3.

17. Kostis, *History's Spoiled Children*, 230–33.

6. MILITARY SERVICE

1. Gerasimos Augustinos, *Consciousness and History: Nationalist Critics of Greek Society, 1897–1914* (New York: Columbia University Press/East European Quarterly, 1977), 26, quoting (in translation) Neoklis Kazazis in *Ellinismos* 1 (1899), 7–8 (emphasis added).

2. Ion Dragoumis, *Ελληνικός πολιτισμός* [*Hellenic Civilization*] [1913], in *Έργα* [*Works*], 2 vols (Athens: n.p., 1927), vol. 2, 180.

3. Eleni Bastéa, *The Creation of Modern Athens: Planning the Myth* (Cambridge: Cambridge University Press, 2000), 194, and figs 73, 77, 78, 85.

4. Thomas Gallant, *The Edinburgh History of the Greeks, 1768 to 1913* (Edinburgh: Edinburgh University Press, 2015), 215–16.

5. S. Victor Papacosma, *The Military in Greek Politics: The 1909 Coup d'État* (Kent, OH: Kent State University Press, 1977), 170.

6. Maria Anastasopoulou, *Η συνετή απόστολος της γυναικείας χειραφεσίας: Καλλιρρόη Παρρέν* [*The Discreet Apostle of Female Emancipation: Callirhoe Parren*] Athens: Σύλλογος προς Διάδοσιν Ωφελίμων Βιβλίων [Association for the Dissemination of Useful Books], 2012); Gallant, *Edinburgh History*, 303–4.

7. Georgios Skliros, *Το κοινωνικόν μας ζήτημα* [*Our Social Question*] (Athens: Konstantinidis, 1907); Gallant, *Edinburgh History*, 302.

8. George Margaritis, 'The nation and the individual: Social aspects of life and death in Greece (1896–1911)', in Philip Carabott (ed.), *Greek Society in the Making, 1863–1913: Realities, Symbols and Visions* (Aldershot: Ashgate, 1997), 87–98 (97 quoted).

9. Pericles Giannopoulos, *Άπαντα* [*Complete Works*], vol. 1, ed. D. Lazogiorgos-Ellinikos (Athens, n.p., 1963), 191, 162.

10. Dragoumis, *Ελληνικός πολιτισμός* [*Hellenic Civilization*], 234; Augustinos, *Consciousness*, 114–15.

11. Douglas Dakin, *The Unification of Greece, 1770–1923* (London: Benn, 1972), 155; Kostas Kostis, *History's Spoiled Children: The Formation of the Modern Greek State*, trans. Jacob Moe (London: Hurst, 2018; Greek original published in 2013), 222, 236–7; Alexis Dimaras, 'Modernisation and reaction in Greek education during the Venizelos era', in Paschalis Kitromilides (ed.), *Eleftherios Venizelos: The Trials of Statesmanship* (Edinburgh: Edinburgh University Press, 2006), 319–45 (see 321, 339 n. 8).

12. Cited in Dimitris Livanios, ' "Conquering the souls": Nationalism and Greek guerrilla warfare in Ottoman Macedonia, 1904–1908', *Byzantine and Modern Greek Studies* 23 (1999), 195–221 (see 196).

13. John Koliopoulos, *Brigands with a Cause: Brigandage and Irredentism in Modern Greece 1821–1912* (Oxford: Clarendon Press, 1987), 215, 222–7, 234.

14. Vasilis Gounaris, *Τα Βαλκάνια των Ελλήνων. Από το Διαφωτισμό έως τον Α΄ Παγκόσμιο Πόλεμο* [*The Balkans of the Greeks: From the Enlightenment to the First World War*] (Thessaloniki: Epikentro, 2007), 411.

15. Mark Mazower, *Salonica: City of Ghosts* (London: HarperCollins, 2004), 275, citing in translation A. Sarrou, *La Jeune Turquie et la Révolution* (Paris: Berger-Levrault, 1912), 25.

16. Konstantinos Svolopoulos, *Κωνσταντινούπολη 1856–1908. Η ακμή του Ελληνισμού* [*Constantinople 1856–1908: The High Point of Hellenism*] (Athens: Ekdotiki Athinon, 1994), 98, citing Ioannis Gryparis to the Ministry of Foreign Affairs, Athens, 30 July 1908.

17. Eleftherios Venizelos, cited in translation in Michael Llewellyn Smith, 'Venizelos' diplomacy, 1910–23: From Balkan alliance to Greek–Turkish settlement', in Kitromilides (ed.), *Venizelos*, 140; Ion Dragoumis, *Ο ελληνισμός μου και οι Έλληνες (1903–1909)* [*My Hellenism and the Greeks (1903–1909)*], in *Έργα* [*Works*], vol. 2, 144.

18. Svolopoulos, *Κωνσταντινούπολη* [*Constantinople*], 23, citing Greek representatives in the Ottoman parliament, shortly after its reconstitution.

19. Maria Mandamadiotou, *The Greek Orthodox Community of Mytilene: Between the Ottoman Empire and the Greek State, 1876–1912* (Bern: Peter Lang, 2013).

20. Cited in Svolopoulos, *Κωνσταντινούπολη* [*Constantinople*], 79.

21. Papacosma, *Military*, 42, 49.

22. Robert Holland and Diana Markides, *The British and the Hellenes: Struggles for Mastery in the Eastern Mediterranean 1850–1960* (Oxford: Oxford University Press, 2006), 143, citing a Foreign Office memorandum of 17 June 1909.

23. Translated text in Papacosma, *Military*, 190–6.

24. Papacosma, *Military*, 115–20, citing J. B. Bourchier in *The Times*, 13 January 1910.

25. Giorgos Mavrogordatos, *1915. Ο Εθνικός Διχασμός* [*1915: The National Schism*] (Athens: Patakis, 2015), 28; Dakin, *Unification*, 186.

26. Alexis Dimaras, *Η μεταρρύθμιση που δεν έγινε* [*The Reform that Never Was*], 3 vols (Athens: Ermis, 1974), vol. 2, 75–7.

27. Sean McMeekin, *The Ottoman Endgame: War, Revolution and the Making of the Modern Middle East, 1908–1923* (London: Allen Lane, 2015), xv–xviii, 62–5.

28. McMeekin, *Endgame*, 68–9.

29. Michael Llewellyn Smith, *Ionian Vision: Greece in Asia Minor, 1919–1922* (London: Hurst, 1998; first published 1973), 17–20 (18 quoted).

30. Athina Kakouri, *Τα δύο βήτα* [*The Two Vs*] (Athens: Kapon, 2016), 84.

31. Richard Hall, *The Balkan Wars, 1912–1913: Prelude to the First World War* (London: Routledge, 2002), 107–23.

7. THE SELF DIVIDED

1. Cited in translation in Mark Mazower, *Salonica: City of Ghosts* (London: HarperCollins, 2004), 295.

2. George Leon, *Greece and the Great Powers, 1914–1917* (Thessaloniki: Institute for Balkan Studies, 1974), 29, citing a diplomatic telegram of 7 August 1914.

3. Cited in Leon, *Greece*, 145.

4. Despoina Papadimitriou, 'Ο εθνικισμός στο βενιζελικό και αντιβενιζελικό τύπο και η εσωτερική διαμάχη 1914–1917' ['Nationalism in the Venizelist and anti-Venizelist press and the internal conflict, 1914–1917'], in *Συμπόσιο για τον Ελευθέριο Βενιζέλο, Πρακτικά 1986* [*Symposium on Eleftherios Venizelos, Proceedings 1986*] (Athens: ELIA and Benaki Museum, 1988), 96.

5. Leon, *Greece*, 218, citing a German diplomatic telegram of 2 September 1915.

6. Giorgos Mavrogordatos, *1915. Ο Εθνικός Διχασμός* [*1915: The National Schism*] (Athens: Patakis, 2015), 84.

7. Mavrogordatos, *1915*, 93, 217.

8. Mavrogordatos, *1915*, 271, citing the diary of Penelope Delta.

9. Mavrogordatos, *1915*, 89, 99.

10. Mavrogordatos, *1915*, 226–7, 274–5, quoting newspapers of the period.

11. Cited in Michael Llewellyn Smith, *Ionian Vision: Greece in Asia Minor, 1919–1922* (London: Hurst, 1998; first published 1973), 67, 140.

12. Llewellyn Smith, *Ionian Vision*, 146; Mavrogordatos, *1915*, 134, citing Gounaris's speech on 25 October 1920.

13. Mavrogordatos, *1915*, 168–9 (citing a newspaper of 15 August 1920), 171–4.

14. Llewellyn Smith, *Ionian Vision*, 166.

15. Mavrogordatos, *1915*, 142–3, 154.

16. Llewellyn Smith, *Ionian Vision*, 224.

17. Sean McMeekin, *The Ottoman Endgame: War, Revolution and the Making of the Modern Middle East, 1908–1923* (London: Allen Lane, 2015), 456.

18. Mavrogordatos, *1915*, 228–30.

19. McMeekin, *Endgame*, 483–4.

20. Mavrogordatos, *1915*, 150–5, 314–18, and George Mavrogordatos, *Μετά το 1922. Η παράταση του διχασμού* [*After 1922: The Extension of the Schism*] (Athens: Patakis, 2017).

21. Compare Llewellyn Smith, *Ionian Vision*, 134, citing Venizelos to Lloyd George, 5 October 1920, with p. 203, citing Metaxas's diary for 11 April 1921. On defensibility, see the views of Metaxas as early as 1915 and Toynbee in 1921–2, both summarized in Llewellyn Smith, *Ionian Vision*, 48–51, 55, 109–10; on economic isolation from the hinterland, Llewellyn Smith, *Ionian Vision*, 73 n., citing the view of an American analyst in 1918; Mavrogordatos, *1915*, 121–5.

22. For instances see Llewellyn Smith, *Ionian Vision*, 117, 124, 131.

23. Andrew Mango, *Atatürk* (London: John Murray, 1999), 316–17; Halidé Edib, *The Turkish Ordeal* (London: John Murray, 1928), 284–310.

24. Douglas Dakin, *The Unification of Greece, 1770–1923* (London: Benn, 1972), 237.

25. Ioannis Metaxas, *Το προσωπικό του ημερολόγιο* [*His Private Diary*], 4 vols (Athens, 1951–64), vol. 2, 314 (emphasis added); Athina Kakouri, *Τα δύο βήτα* [*The Two Vs*] (Athens: Kapon, 2016), 150.

26. Text reproduced in full in Dimitri Pentzopoulos, *The Balkan Exchange of Minorities and its Impact on Greece* (Paris and The Hague: Mouton, 1962; reprinted with a new preface by Michael Llewellyn Smith, London: Hurst, 2002), 257–63, and Renée Hirschon (ed.), *Crossing the Aegean: An Appraisal of the 1923 Compulsory Population Exchange between Greece and Turkey* (Oxford: Berghahn, 2003), 282–7.

8. STARTING OVER

1. Kostas Kostis, *History's Spoiled Children: The Formation of the Modern Greek State*, trans. Jacob Moe (London: Hurst, 2018; Greek original published in 2013), 264, 291.

2. Stathis Kalyvas, *Modern Greece: What Everyone Needs to Know* (Oxford: Oxford University Press, 2015), 76, 79.

3. Dimitri Pentzopoulos, *The Balkan Exchange of Minorities and its Impact on Greece* (Paris and The Hague: Mouton, 1962; reprinted with a new preface by Michael Llewellyn Smith, London: Hurst, 2002), 96–100. For the number of Muslims covered by the Convention see p. 69. See also Renée Hirschon (ed.), *Crossing the Aegean: An Appraisal of the 1923 Compulsory Population Exchange between Greece and Turkey* (Oxford: Berghahn, 2003), esp. 3–37.

4. Pantelis Prevelakis, *Το χρονικό μιας πολιτείας* [*The Chronicle of a Town*] (Athens: Estia, 1976; first published 1938), 85. See also Sophia Koufopoulou, 'Muslim Cretans in Turkey: The reformulation of ethnic identity in an Aegean community', in Hirschon (ed.), *Crossing*, 209–33;

Bruce Clark, *Twice a Stranger: Greece, Turkey and the Minorities they Expelled* (London: Granta, 2006), 184–7.

5. Henry Morgenthau, *I Was Sent to Athens* (New York: Doubleday, Doran and Co., 1929), 101; Pentzopoulos, *Balkan Exchange*, 96.

6. Vasso Stelaku, 'Space, place and identity: Memory and religion in two Cappadocian Greek settlements', in Hirschon (ed.), *Crossing*, 188.

7. John Koliopoulos and Thanos Veremis, *Greece: The Modern Sequel, from 1821 to the Present* (London: Hurst, 2002), 112.

8. On Jews, see K. E. Fleming, *Greece: A Jewish History* (Princeton, NJ: Princeton University Press, 2008), 91–109; Mark Mazower, *Salonica: City of Ghosts* (London: HarperCollins, 2004), 402–20. On other groups see Giorgos Margaritis, *Ανεπιθύμητοι συμπατριώτες. Στοιχεία για την καταστροφή των μειονοτήτων στην Ελλάδα* [*Undesirable Compatriots: Evidence for the Destruction of Minorities in Greece*] (Athens: Vivliorama, 2005); Elisabeth Kontogeorgi, *Population Exchange in Greek Macedonia* (Oxford: Oxford University Press, 2006).

9. Giorgos Theotokas, *Argo*, 2 vols (Athens: Estia, [1933, 1936]), vol. 1, 57–8.

10. Giorgos Theotokas, *Ελεύθερο πνεύμα* [*Free Spirit*], ed. K. Th. Dimaras (Athens: Ermis, 1973; first published 1929), 70.

11. George Seferis, *Complete Poems*, translated, edited and with an introduction by Edmund Keeley and Philip Sherrard (London: Anvil, 1995), 41.

12. Theotokas, *Argo*, vol. 2, 107.

13. George Mavrogordatos, *Stillborn Republic: Social Coalitions and Party Strategies in Greece, 1922–1936* (Berkeley, CA: University of California Press, 1983), 36–7.

14. Mavrogordatos, *Stillborn*, 41.

15. Mark Mazower, *Greece and the Inter-War Economic Crisis* (Oxford: Clarendon Press, 1991), 278.

16. Mavrogordatos, *Stillborn*, 47–8.

17. John Campbell and Philip Sherrard, *Modern Greece* (London: Benn, 1968), 154.

18. John Koliopoulos, *Greece and the British Connection, 1935–1941* (Oxford: Clarendon Press, 1977), 18, citing a Foreign Office telegram of 13 May 1935.

19. Koliopoulos, *British Connection*, 98, citing a Foreign Office memorandum of 12 October 1938.

20. Ioannis Stefanidis, 'Reconstructing Greece as a European state: Venizelos' last premiership, 1928–32', in Paschalis Kitromilides (ed.), *Eleftherios Venizelos: The Trials of Statesmanship* (Edinburgh: Edinburgh University Press, 2006), 193–233 (see 208–9).

21. Mazower, *Economic Crisis*, 276 (citing Emmanuel Tsouderos, Governor of the Bank of Greece) and 301, 285 (citing Sydney Waterlow to Foreign Office, January 1935, original emphasis).

22. Mazower, *Economic Crisis*, 292, citing Waterlow to Foreign Office, 8 April 1936.

23. Marina Petrakis, *The Metaxas Myth: Dictatorship and Propaganda in Greece* (London: I. B. Tauris, 2006), 206 n. 100, citing Palairet to Foreign Office, 21 August 1939.

24. *Εφημερίς της Κυβερνήσεως* [*Government Gazette*], 31 August 1936, cited in translation in Petrakis, *Metaxas Myth*, 9; original available online.

25. Constantine Sarantis, 'The ideology and character of the Metaxas regime', in Robin Higham and Thanos Veremis (eds), *Aspects of Greece, 1936–40: The Metaxas Dictatorship* (Athens: Hellenic Foundation for Defense and Foreign Policy, 1993), 151, citing (in translation) speeches of May and November 1937; Jon Kofas, *Authoritarianism in Greece: The Metaxas Regime* (East European Monographs, Boulder, CO, distributed by Columbia University Press, New York, 1983), 100 (quoted), citing a translation sent by Waterlow to Foreign Office, 30 October 1936. The original Greek is not included in Ioannis Metaxas, *Λόγοι και σκέψεις, 1936–1941* [*Speeches and Thoughts, 1936–1941*], 2 vols (Athens: Ikaros, 1969).

26. Koliopoulos, *British Connection*, 79, citing a state paper signed by Metaxas, quoted in translation in a British Legation despatch dated 2 June 1938.

27. Sarantis, 'Ideology', 154, citing (in translation) a speech by Metaxas in 1939.

28. *Τέσσαρα χρόνια διακυβερνήσεως Ι. Μεταξά* [*Four Years of Government I. Metaxas*], 4 vols (Athens, [1940]), vol. 2, 213; Petrakis, *Metaxas Myth*, 34–5, 209–10 n. 28.

29. Metaxas, *Λόγοι* [*Speeches*], vol. 2, 124 (speech by Metaxas on 8 August 1939); Petrakis, *Metaxas Myth*, 63.

30. Markos Vamvakaris, *Αυτοβιογραφία* [*Autobiography*], ed. Angela Kail (Athens, 1973), 175, 187. A translation of this work by Noonie Minogue is available from Greeklines, London.

31. Stathis Gauntlett, *Ρεμπέτικο τραγούδι. Συμβολή στην επιστημονική προσέγγιση* [*Rebetiko Song: Contribution to a Scholarly Approach*] (Athens: Eikostos Protos, 2001), 68.

32. Thanos Veremis, '1922: Political continuations and realignments in the Greek state', in Hirschon (ed.), *Crossing*, 53–62 (60 quoted).

33. Koliopoulos, *British Connection*, 89, citing Waterlow to Foreign Office, 3 October 1938.

34. Ioannis Metaxas, *Το προσωπικό του ημερολόγιο* [*His Private Diary*], 4 vols (Athens, 1951–64), vol. 4, 311 (20 October 1938), vol. 4, 460 (2 April 1940).

35. Koliopoulos, *British Connection*, 91.

36. Mogens Pelt, 'The establishment and development of the Metaxas dictatorship in the context of Fascism and Nazism, 1936–41', *Totalitarian Movements and Political Religions* 2/3 (2001), 143–72 (164 quoted); Metaxas, *Ημερολόγιο* [*Diary*], vol. 4, 362 (1 April 1939).

37. Pelt, 'Establishment', 165–6, citing German diplomatic documents of June and July 1940.

38. Metaxas, *Ημερολόγιο* [*Diary*], vol. 4, 484 (14 July 1940).

39. Metaxas, *Ημερολόγιο* [*Diary*], vol. 4, 512–15.

40. Metaxas, *Ημερολόγιο* [*Diary*], vol. 4, 747.

9. MELTDOWN

1. John Koliopoulos, *Greece and the British Connection, 1935–1941* (Oxford: Clarendon Press, 1977), 213; C. M. Woodhouse, *Modern Greece: A Short History*, 5th edn, revised (London: Faber 4 Faber, 1991; first edition 1968), 236.

2. Ioannis Metaxas, *Το ποσωπικό του ημερολόγιο* [*His Private Diary*], 4 vols (Athens, 1951–64), vol. 4, 516.

3. Giorgos Seferis, *Χειρόγραφο Σεπ.'41* [*Manuscript Sept. '41*] (Athens: Ikaros, 1972), 51–3.

4. Koliopoulos, *British Connection*, 220, citing Palairet to Foreign Office, 1 February 1941.

5. Metaxas, *Ημερολόγιο* [*Diary*], vol. 4, 552–4 (553 quoted) (2 January 1941).

6. Mark Mazower, *Inside Hitler's Greece: The Experience of Occupation, 1941–44* (New Haven, CT, and London: Yale University Press, 1993), 173, 155.

7. Mazower, *Inside Hitler's Greece*, 244, 256.

8. C. M. Woodhouse, *The Struggle for Greece, 1941–1949* (London: Hart-Davis, 1976; reprinted with an introduction by Richard Clogg: Hurst, 2002), 14.

9. Dimitris Glinos, *Τι είναι και τι θέλει το Εθνικό Απελευθερωτικό Μέτωπο* [*What the National Liberation Front is and what it Wants*] (Athens: Rigas, 1944; reprinted by Estia, n.d.), 39, 41.

10. Mazower, *Inside Hitler's Greece*, 311.

11. C. M. Woodhouse, *The Apple of Discord: A Survey of Recent Greek Politics in their International Setting* (London: Hutchinson, 1948),

146-7. David Brewer (*Greece: The Decade of War. Occupation, Resistance and Civil War* [London: I. B. Tauris, 2016], 86) is sceptical, and notes that Woodhouse's later account (*Struggle*, 62-3) is 'more guarded'. But by the time the later account was written Cold War attitudes had hardened. In 1948, Woodhouse was recording what he had seen and the impression it had made on him at the time.

12. Mazower, *Inside Hitler's Greece*, 279.

13. Glinos, *Τι είναι* [*What . . .*], 60, 61, 62-3 (emphasis added).

14. For example, Mazower (*Inside Hitler's Greece*, 155-261) devotes a great deal of space to atrocities committed by the occupying forces, whose dynamics and motivation he examines closely, but gives no specific instances of extreme violence by EAM/ELAS, though he accepts that they happened. André Gerolymatos, on the other hand, repeats contemporary reports of murders and mutilations by ELAS and the KKE (*An International Civil War: Greece, 1943-1949* [New Haven, CT, and London: Yale University Press], 2016, 88-9, 108, 162, 164, 222-6), but is silent on the achievements of 'people's rule' in the mountains and does not so much as mention Mazower's classic study.

15. David Close, *The Origins of the Greek Civil War* (London: Longman, 1995), 94.

16. Mazower, *Inside Hitler's Greece*, 125-7; cf. Woodhouse, *Struggle*, 3-5, 63.

17. See, for example, Thanasis Sfikas, *Πόλεμος και ειρήνη στη στρατηγική του ΚΚΕ, 1945-1949* [*War and Peace in the Strategy of the KKE, 1945-1949*] (Athens: Philistor, 2001), 15, 20.

18. Stathis Kalyvas, *The Logic of Violence in Civil War* (Cambridge: Cambridge University Press, 2006), 31.

19. The source for the remark quoted is presented as a work of fiction: Thanasis Valtinos, *Orthokostá* (Athens: Agra, 1994), 114, and English translation by Jane Assimakopoulos and Stavros Deligiorgis (London and New Haven, CT: Yale University Press, 2016), 85. The novel consists of detailed oral testimonies closely based on real events. See also the foreword to the English edition by Stathis Kalyvas. On northern Greece, see, for example, John Koliopoulos, *Plundered Loyalties: Axis Occupation and Civil Strife in Greek West Macedonia, 1941-1949* (London: Hurst, 1999; first published in Greek, 1994-5).

20. Mazower, *Inside Hitler's Greece*, 342.

21. Procopis Papastratis, *British Policy towards Greece during the Second World War, 1941-1944* (Cambridge: Cambridge University Press, 1984), 57; Roderick Beaton, *George Seferis: Waiting for the Angel. A Biography* (New Haven, CT, and London: Yale University Press, 2003), 235-6.

22. Giorgos Theotokas, Τετράδια ημερολογίου, 1939–1953 [Diary Notebooks, 1939–1953], ed. Dimitris Tziovas (Athens: Estia, [1987]), 509 (13 October 1944); Mazower, Inside Hitler's Greece, 362.

23. John Iatrides, Revolt in Athens: The Greek Communist 'Second Round', 1944–1945 (Princeton, NJ: Princeton University Press, 1972), 192.

24. Mazower, Inside Hitler's Greece, 368; Close, Origins, 137.

25. Winston Churchill, The Second World War, vol. 6: Triumph and Tragedy (London: Cassell, 1954), 97, 289.

26. Giorgos Seferis, entry for 7 December 1944 in his Μέρες Δ΄ [Diary, vol. 4] (Athens: Ikaros, 1977), 374; Beaton, Seferis, 252.

27. Churchill, Triumph, 271.

28. Haris Vlavianos, Greece, 1941–49: From Resistance to Civil War (Basingstoke: Macmillan, 1992), 257.

29. Close, Origins, 159, citing Leeper to Foreign Office, 22 February 1946.

30. Close, Origins, 190.

31. Spyridon Plakoudas, The Greek Civil War: Strategy, Counterinsurgency and the Monarchy (London: I. B. Tauris, 2017), 120.

32. G. M. Alexander, The Prelude to the Truman Doctrine: British Policy in Greece, 1944–1947 (Oxford: Clarendon Press, 1982), 251.

33. Kostas Kostis, History's Spoiled Children: The Formation of the Modern Greek State, trans. Jacob Moe (London: Hurst, 2018; Greek original published in 2013), 324; John Koliopoulos and Thanos Veremis, Greece: The Modern Sequel, from 1821 to the Present (London: Hurst, 2002), 98.

34. David Close, 'Introduction', in David Close (ed.), The Greek Civil War, 1943–1950: Studies of Polarization (London: Routledge, 1993), 7–11; for the fullest figures available for 1946–9, see Giorgos Margaritis, Ιστορία του ελληνικού εμφυλίου πολέμου [History of the Greek Civil War], 2 vols (Athens: Vivliorama, 2000), vol. 1, 50–51.

35. Panos Lagdas, Άρης Βελουχιώτης [Aris Velouchiotis], 2 vols (Athens: Kypseli, 1964), vol. 2, 461, 466; Woodhouse, Struggle, 4–6.

36. Theotokas, Τετράδια [Diary], 507; Mazower, Inside Hitler's Greece, 314; Seferis, Μέρες Δ΄ [Diary, vol. 4], 381–2.

37. Close, Origins, 131; Heinz Richter, British Intervention in Greece: From Varkiza to Civil War, trans. Marion Sarafis (London: Merlin, 1985), x; John Hondros, Occupation and Resistance: The Greek Agony, 1941–44 (New York: Pella, 1983), 234; John Iatrides, 'Greece at the crossroads, 1944–1950', in John Iatrides and Linda Wrigley (eds), Greece at the Crossroads: The Civil War and its Legacy (Philadelphia, PA: Pennsylvania University Press, 1995), 12–13.

38. Antonis Liakos, 'Greece', in Peter Furtado (ed.), *Histories of Nations: How their Identities were Forged*, 2nd edn (London: Thames and Hudson, 2017), 39-46 (45 quoted).

10. UNCLE SAM'S PROTÉGÉ

1. Kostas Kostis, *History's Spoiled Children: The Formation of the Modern Greek State*, trans. Jacob Moe (London: Hurst, 2018; Greek original published in 2013), 331; Thomas Gallant, *Modern Greece: From the War of Independence to the Present*, 2nd edn (London: Bloomsbury, 2016), 255.

2. Kostis, *History's Spoiled Children*, 351.

3. David Close, *Greece since 1945: Politics, Economy and Society* (London: Longman, 2002), 52, 48.

4. Stanley Mayes, *Makarios: A Biography* (London: Macmillan, 1981), 39.

5. Ioannis Stefanidis, *Stirring the Greek Nation: Political Culture, Irredentism and Anti-Americanism in Post-War Greece, 1945-1967* (Aldershot: Ashgate, 2007), 81, citing parliamentary debates of May 1950.

6. Stefanidis, *Stirring*, 77-8; Evanthis Hatzivassiliou, *Britain and the International Status of Cyprus, 1955-59* (Minneapolis, MN: University of Minnesota, *Modern Greek Studies Yearbook* supplement, 1997), 14; Kostis, *History's Spoiled Children*, 341; Stavros Panteli, *A New History of Cyprus: From the Earliest Times to the Present Day* (London and The Hague: EastWest, 1984), 248-55.

7. Robert Holland, *Britain and the Revolt in Cyprus, 1954-1959* (Oxford: Clarendon Press, 1998), 69 (citing Macmillan to Foreign Office, 16 July 1955), 65; Hatzivassiliou, *Britain*, 32, citing Makarios.

8. Holland, *Britain*, 76.

9. Holland, *Britain*, 89-91, 127-31; Stefanidis, *Stirring*, 105.

10. David French, *Fighting EOKA: The British Counter-Insurgency Campaign on Cyprus, 1955-1959* (Oxford: Oxford University Press, 2015), 307.

11. Holland, *Britain*, 184-5.

12. Roderick Beaton, *George Seferis: Waiting for the Angel. A Biography* (New Haven, CT, and London: Yale University Press, 2003), 358, citing Seferis's diary for 29 February 1960.

13. Stefanidis, *Stirring*, 80, 174-6; James Edward Miller, *The United States and the Making of Modern Greece: History and Power, 1950-1974* (Chapel Hill, NC: University of North Carolina Press, 2009), 56-65; Susannah Verney, 'Greece and the European Community', in Kevin

Featherstone and Dimitrios Katsoudas (eds), *Political Change in Greece: Before and After the Colonels* (London: Croom Helm, 1987), 253–70.

14. Vrasidas Karalis, *A History of Greek Cinema* (New York and London: Continuum, 2012), 79–80; Achilleas Hadjikyriacou, *Masculinity and Gender in Greek Cinema, 1949–1967* (London: Bloomsbury Academic, 2013), 66–7; Maria Stassinopoulou, 'Reality bites: A feature film history of Greece, 1950–1963' (Vienna: University of Vienna, Habilitationsschrift, 2000), 3.

15. Dimitris Papanikolaou, *Singing Poets: Literature and Popular Music in France and Greece* (London: Legenda, 2007), 84 (emphasis added).

16. Giannis Ritsos, Ποιήματα [*Poems*], vol. 2 (Athens: Kedros, 1989–90), 59–72.

17. Stan Draenos, *Andreas Papandreou: The Making of a Greek Democrat and Political Maverick* (London: I. B. Tauris, 2012), 133, citing the testimony of Robert Keeley.

18. Kostis, *History's Spoiled Children*, 356.

19. G. Papadopoulos, Το Πιστεύω μας [*Our Creed*], 7 vols (Athens, 1968–72), vol. 2, 80 (original emphases).

20. Papadopoulos, Πιστεύω [*Creed*], vol. 1, 11, vol. 2, 171; Karen van Dyck, *Kassandra and the Censors: Greek Poetry since 1967* (Ithaca, NY: Cornell University Press, 1998), 16–17.

21. Thanasis Valtinos, 'The plaster cast', trans. Theodora Vasils, in Willis Barnstone (ed.), *Eighteen Texts: Writings by Contemporary Greek Authors* (Cambridge, MA: Harvard University Press, 1972), 153–9 (Greek original published 1970).

22. Kostis Kornetis, *Children of the Dictatorship: Student Resistance, Cultural Politics, and the 'Long 1960s' in Greece* (New York and Oxford: Berghahn, 2013), 269–70.

23. Kornetis, *Children*, 255, 270.

24. C. M. Woodhouse, *The Rise and Fall of the Greek Colonels* (London: Granada, 1985), 134.

25. Kornetis, *Children*, 273–80.

26. Woodhouse, *Rise and Fall*, 151–2.

27. James Ker-Lindsay, *The Cyprus Problem: What Everyone Needs to Know* (Oxford: Oxford University Press, 2011), 44–6.

11. COMING OF AGE IN EUROPE

1. Michalis Spourdalakis, *The Rise of the Greek Socialist Party* (London: Routledge, 1988), 289–90.

2. George Mavrogordatos, *Rise of the Green Sun: The Greek Election of 1981* (London: King's College London, Centre of Contemporary Greek Studies, 1983), 9, 55 (quoted).

3. Kevin Featherstone and Dimitris Papadimitriou, *Prime Ministers in Greece: The Paradox of Power* (Oxford: Oxford University Press, 2015), 16, 45, 90, 217.

4. David Close, *Greece since 1945: Politics, Economy and Society* (London: Longman, 2002), 161–2, 178–82; Stathis Kalyvas, *Modern Greece: What Everyone Needs to Know* (Oxford: Oxford University Press, 2015), 140–42, citing an unpublished manuscript by Gerassimos Moschonas.

5. Theodore Couloumbis, 'PASOK's foreign policies, 1981–89: Continuity or change?', in Richard Clogg (ed.), *Greece, 1981–89: The Populist Decade* (Basingstoke: Macmillan, 1993), 120.

6. George Kassimeris, *Europe's Last Red Terrorists: The Revolutionary Organization 17 November* (London: Hurst, 2001), 206.

7. See, for example, Misha Glenny, *The Balkans, 1804–1999* (London: Granta, 1999), 656.

8. Loring Danforth, *The Macedonian Conflict: Ethnic Nationalism in a Transnational World* (Princeton, NJ: Princeton University Press, 1997), 202–12.

9. Thanos Veremis, *A Modern History of the Balkans: Nationalism and Identity in Southeast Europe* (London: I. B. Tauris, 2017), 143, 145–6.

10. Yannis Hamilakis, *The Nation and its Ruins: Antiquity, Archaeology, and National Imagination in Greece* (Oxford: Oxford University Press, 2007), 125–34.

11. Cited in Veremis, *Modern History*, 151–2.

12. See, for example, Sotiris Dimitriou, *May Your Name Be Blessed*, trans. Leo Marshall (University of Birmingham, 2000).

13. Close, *Greece*, 197; Thomas Gallant, *Modern Greece: From the War of Independence to the Present*, 2nd edn (London: Bloomsbury, 2016), 303.

14. Vasilios Makrides, 'Byzantium in contemporary Greece: The Neo-Orthodox current of ideas', in David Ricks and Paul Magdalino (eds), *Byzantium and the Modern Greek Identity* (Aldershot: Ashgate, 1998), 142.

15. Graham Speake, *Mount Athos: Renewal in Paradise* (New Haven, CT: Yale University Press, 2002).

16. Michael Llewellyn Smith, *Athens: A Cultural and Literary History* (Oxford: Signal, 2004), 207.

17. Kostas Kostis, *History's Spoiled Children: The Formation of the Modern Greek State*, trans. Jacob Moe (London: Hurst, 2018; Greek original published in 2013), 384.

18. Kostis, *History's Spoiled Children*, 383–4, 386.

19. Featherstone and Papadimitriou, *Prime Ministers*, 1, 165, 203.

20. Gallant, *Modern Greece*, 306–7; Miranda Xafa, 'Back from the brink: How to end Greece's seemingly interminable crisis', in Spyros Economides (ed.), *Greece: Modernisation and Europe 20 Years On* (London: London School of Economics, Hellenic Observatory, 2017), 46–53 (see 47–8).

21. Dimitrios Theodossopoulos, 'Politics of friendship, worldviews of mistrust: The Greek-Turkish rapprochement in local conversation', in D. Theodossopoulos (ed.), *When Greeks Think about Turks: The View from Anthropology* (Abingdon: Routledge, 2007), 193–210.

22. See, for example, James Ker-Lindsay, *The Cyprus Problem: What Everyone Needs to Know* (Oxford: Oxford University Press, 2011), 68–74, and the critiques of the Annan Plan in Andrekos Varnava and Hubert Faustmann (eds), *Reunifying Cyprus: The Annan Plan and Beyond* (London: I. B. Tauris, 2009).

12. MIDLIFE CRISIS?

1. Stathis Kalyvas, *Modern Greece: What Everyone Needs to Know* (Oxford: Oxford University Press, 2015), 153, 156.

2. Kevin Featherstone and Dimitris Papadimitriou, *Prime Ministers in Greece: The Paradox of Power* (Oxford: Oxford University Press, 2015), 189.

3. Giannis Voulgaris, *Η μοιραία πενταετία. Η πολιτική της αδράνειας, 2004–2009* [*The Fateful Five Years: The Politics of Inaction, 2004–2009*] (Athens: Polis, 2011), 311 (10 January 2009); Kostas Kostis, *History's Spoiled Children: The Formation of the Modern Greek State*, trans. Jacob Moe (London: Hurst, 2018; Greek original published in 2013), 388–9.

4. George Papaconstantinou, *Game Over: The Inside Story of the Greek Crisis* (English edition privately published, 2016), 30–40 (37 quoted).

5. Loukas Tsoukalis, *In Defence of Europe: Can the European Project be Saved?* (Oxford: Oxford University Press, 2016), 89.

6. Kalyvas, *Modern Greece*, 163.

7. For the period 1974–2000, see David Close, *Greece since 1945: Politics, Economy and Society* (London: Longman, 2002), 168–70; for 1999–2015, Miranda Xafa, 'Back from the brink: How to end Greece's seemingly interminable crisis', in Spyros Economides (ed.), *Greece: Modernisation and Europe 20 Years On* (London: London School of Economics, Hellenic Observatory, 2017), 46–53.

8. Kostis, *History's Spoiled Children*, 416; Dimitris Tziovas (ed.), *Greece in Crisis: The Cultural Politics of Austerity* (London: I. B. Tauris, 2017), 26.

9. Yanis Varoufakis, *Adults in the Room: My Battle with Europe's Deep Establishment* (London: Bodley Head, 2017), 237 (quoted); Johanna Hanink, *The Classical Debt: Greek Antiquity in an Era of Austerity* (Cambridge, MA: Harvard University Press, 2017), 200, 223, citing headlines in the German press from 2010.

10. Varoufakis, *Adults*, 469.

11. Varoufakis, *Adults*, 48; Hanink, *Classical Debt*, 219.

12. Varoufakis, *Adults*, 474.

13. Karen van Dyck (ed.), *Austerity Measures: The New Greek Poetry* (London: Penguin, 2016), xviii.

14. Tziovas (ed.), *Greece in Crisis*, 4.

15. George Pagoulatos, 'From project modernisation to forced adjustment: two decades of incomplete reforms (1996–2016)', in Spyros Economides (ed.), *Greece: Modernisation and Europe 20 Years On* (London: London School of Economics, Hellenic Observatory, 2017), 37–45 (44 quoted).

16. Tziovas (ed.), *Greece in Crisis*, 30; see also Hanink, *Classical Debt*, 255–7.

17. Denis Vovchenko, *Containing Balkan Nationalism: Imperial Russia and Ottoman Christians, 1856–1914* (Oxford: Oxford University Press, 2016), 329.

18. Kostis, *History's Spoiled Children*, 421.

Sources and Further Reading

GREEK HISTORY AND CULTURE SINCE THE EIGHTEENTH CENTURY

Beaton, Roderick, *An Introduction to Modern Greek Literature*, 2nd edn (Oxford: Clarendon Press, 1999)

Beaton, Roderick and David Ricks (eds), *The Making of Modern Greece: Nationalism, Romanticism, and the Uses of the Past (1797–1896)* (Farnham: Ashgate, 2009)

Campbell, John and Philip Sherrard, *Modern Greece* (London: Benn, 1968)

Clogg, Richard, *A Concise History of Greece*, 3rd edn (Cambridge: Cambridge University Press, 2013)

Dakin, Douglas, *The Unification of Greece, 1770–1923* (London: Benn, 1972)

Fleming, K. E., *Greece: A Jewish History* (Princeton, NJ: Princeton University Press, 2008)

Gallant, Thomas, *Modern Greece: From the War of Independence to the Present*, 2nd edn (London: Bloomsbury, 2016)

Gallant, Thomas, *The Edinburgh History of the Greeks, 1768 to 1913* (Edinburgh: Edinburgh University Press, 2015)

Hamilakis, Yannis, *The Nation and its Ruins: Antiquity, Archaeology, and National Imagination in Greece* (Oxford: Oxford University Press, 2007)

Holland, Robert and Diana Markides, *The British and the Hellenes: Struggles for Mastery in the Eastern Mediterranean 1850–1960* (Oxford: Oxford University Press, 2006)

Kalyvas, Stathis, *Modern Greece: What Everyone Needs to Know* (Oxford: Oxford University Press, 2015)

Koliopoulos, John, *Brigands with a Cause: Brigandage and Irredentism in Modern Greece 1821–1912* (Oxford: Clarendon Press, 1987)

Koliopoulos, John and Thanos Veremis, *Greece: The Modern Sequel, from 1821 to the Present* (London: Hurst, 2002)

Koliopoulos, John and Thanos Veremis, *Modern Greece: A History since 1821* (Hoboken, NY: Wiley, 2009)

Kostis, Kostas, *History's Spoiled Children: The Formation of the Modern Greek State*, trans. Jacob Moe (London: Hurst, 2018; Greek original published in 2013)

Mackridge, Peter, *Language and National Identity in Greece, 1766–1976* (Oxford: Oxford University Press, 2009)

Mazower, Mark, *The Balkans* (London: Weidenfeld and Nicolson, 2000)

Veremis, Thanos, *A Modern History of the Balkans: Nationalism and Identity in Southeast Europe* (London: I. B. Tauris, 2017)

Veremis, Thanos, *The Military in Greek Politics: From Independence to Democracy* (London: Hurst, 1997)

Wagstaff, J. M. (ed.), *Greece: Ethnicity and Sovereignty, 1820–1994. Atlas and Documents* (Archive Editions, [Cambridge: Cambridge University Press], 2002)

Woodhouse, C. M., *Modern Greece: A Short History*, 5th edn, revised (London: Faber & Faber, 1991; first edition 1968)

1. EAST MEETS WEST?

Crossing Borders: People, Ideas, Goods on the Move

Frary, Lucien, *Russia and the Making of Modern Greek Identity, 1821–1844* (Oxford: Oxford University Press, 2015)

Greene, Molly, *The Edinburgh History of the Greeks, 1453–1768: The Ottoman Empire* (Edinburgh: Edinburgh University Press, 2015)

Kitromilides, Paschalis, *Enlightenment and Revolution: The Making of Modern Greece* (Cambridge, MA: Harvard University Press, 2013)

Kitromilides, Paschalis (ed.), *Enlightenment and Religion in the Orthodox World* (Oxford: Voltaire Foundation, 2016)

Myrogiannis, Stratos, *The Emergence of a Greek Identity (1700–1821)* (Newcastle upon Tyne: Cambridge Scholars, 2012)

Philliou, Christine, *Biography of an Empire: Governing Ottomans in an Age of Revolution* (Berkeley, CA: University of California Press, 2011)

Travellers in an Antique Land

Constantine, David, *In the Footsteps of the Gods: Travellers to Greece and the Quest for the Hellenic Ideal* (London: I. B. Tauris, 2011)

Eisner, Robert, *Travelers to an Antique Land* (Ann Arbor, MI: University of Michigan Press, 1991)

Pollard, Lucy, *The Quest for Classical Greece: Early Modern Travel to the Greek World* (London: I. B. Tauris, 2015)

Spencer, Terence, *Fair Greece Sad Relic: Literary Philhellenism from Shakespeare to Byron* (London: Weidenfeld and Nicolson, 1954)

Peasants, Fishermen, Farmers, Monks

Alexander, John, *Brigandage and Public Order in the Morea 1685–1806* (Athens: n.p., 1985)

Beaton, Roderick, *Folk Poetry of Modern Greece* (Cambridge: Cambridge University Press, 1980; reprinted 2004)

Campbell, John, *Honour, Family, and Patronage: A Study of Institutions and Moral Values in a Greek Mountain Community* (Oxford: Oxford University Press, 1974; first published 1964)

Herzfeld, Michael, *Ours Once More: Folklore, Ideology, and the Making of Modern Greece* (Austin, TX: University of Texas Press, 1982; reprinted New York: Pella, 1986)

Roudometof, Victor, 'From *Rum millet* to Greek nation: Enlightenment, secularization, and national identity in Ottoman Balkan society, 1453–1821', *Journal of Modern Greek Studies* 16 (1998), 11–48

2. A SEED IS SOWN

A World in Turmoil

Alexander, John, *Brigandage and Public Order in the Morea 1685–1806* (Athens: n.p., 1985)

Fleming, K. E., *The Muslim Bonaparte: Diplomacy and Orientalism in Ali Pasha's Greece* (Princeton: Princeton University Press, 1999)

Jelavich, Charles and Barbara, *The Establishment of the Balkan National States, 1804–1920* (Seattle, WA: University of Washington Press, 1977)

Philliou, Christine, *Biography of an Empire: Governing Ottomans in an Age of Revolution* (Berkeley, CA: University of California Press, 2011)

Pratt, Michael, *Britain's Greek Empire: Reflections on the Ionian Islands from the Fall of Byzantium* (London: Collings, 1978)

Vucinich, Wayne S. (ed.), *The First Serbian Uprising, 1804–1813* (Boulder, CO: Brooklyn College Press, 1982)

Revolutionary Ideas

Clogg, Richard (ed. and trans.), *The Movement for Greek Independence, 1770–1821: A Collection of Documents* (London: Macmillan, 1976)

Dascalakis, A., *Rhigas Velestinlis: la Révolution française et les préludes de l'Indépendance hellénique* (Paris, n.p., 1937)

Kitromilides, Paschalis, *Enlightenment and Revolution: The Making of Modern Greece* (Cambridge, MA: Harvard University Press, 2013)

Kitromilides, Paschalis, 'From republican patriotism to national sentiment: A reading of *Hellenic Nomarchy*', *European Journal of Political Theory* 5 (2006), 50–60

Kitromilides, Paschalis (ed.), *Adamantios Korais and the European Enlightenment* (Oxford: Voltaire Foundation, 2010)

López Villalba, María, 'Balkanizing the French Revolution: Rhigas's *New Political Constitution*', in Dimitris Tziovas (ed.), *Greece and the Balkans: Identities, Perceptions and Cultural Encounters since the Enlightenment* (Aldershot: Ashgate, 2003), 141–54

Myrogiannis, Stratos, *The Emergence of a Greek Identity (1700–1821)* (Newcastle upon Tyne: Cambridge Scholars, 2012)

Woodhouse, C. M., *Rhigas Velestinlis: The Proto-Martyr of the Greek Revolution* (Limni, Evia: Denise Harvey, 1995)

Something Growing in the Dark

Angelomatis-Tsougarakis, Helen, *The Eve of the Greek Revival: British Travellers' Perceptions of Early Nineteenth-Century Greece* (London: Routledge, 1990)

Xanthos, E., 'Memoirs of Emmanouil Xanthos' (1845), translated in Richard Clogg (ed. and trans.), *The Movement for Greek Independence, 1770–1821: A Collection of Documents* (London: Macmillan, 1976), 182–200

3. BORN IN BLOOD

Abney-Hastings, Maurice, *Commander of the Karteria* (Bloomington, IN: AuthorHouse, 2011)

Barau, Denys, *La Cause des Grecs. Une histoire du mouvement philhellène (1821–1829)* (Paris: Honoré Champion, 2009)

Bass, Gary, *Freedom's Battle: The Origins of Humanitarian Intervention* (New York: Vintage, 2009)

Brewer, David, *The Flame of Freedom: The Greek War of Independence, 1821–1833* (London: John Murray, 2001)

Dakin, Douglas, *The Greek Struggle for Independence, 1821–1833* (London: Batsford, 1973)

Finlay, George, *History of the Greek Revolution*, 2 vols (Edinburgh: Blackwood, 1861)

Gordon, Thomas, *History of the Greek Revolution*, 2 vols (Edinburgh: Blackwood, 1832)

Ilıcak, Hüseyin Şükrü, 'A radical rethinking of empire: Ottoman state and society during the Greek War of Independence (1821–1826)' (PhD dissertation, Harvard University, 2011)

Koukkou, Helen, *Ioannis A. Kapodistrias: The European Diplomat and Statesman of the 19th Century. Roxandra S. Stourdza: A Famous Woman of her Time. A Historical Biography*, trans. E. Ghikas (Athens: Society for the Study of Greek History, 2001)

Pizanias, Petros (ed.), *The Greek Revolution of 1821: A European Event* (Istanbul: Isis Press, 2011; Greek original published 2009)

Rodogno, Davide, *Against Massacre: Humanitarian Interventions in the Ottoman Empire, 1815–1914* (Princeton, NJ: Princeton University Press, 2012)

St Clair, William, *That Greece Might Still Be Free: The Philhellenes in the War of Independence* (Cambridge: Open Book, 2008; first published 1972)

Woodhouse, C. M., *Capodistria: The Founder of Greek Independence* (London: Oxford University Press, 1973)

Woodhouse, C. M., *The Battle of Navarino* (London: Hodder and Stoughton, 1965)

4. FIRST STEPS

Bastéa, Eleni, *The Creation of Modern Athens: Planning the Myth* (Cambridge: Cambridge University Press, 2000)

Frazee, Charles, *The Orthodox Church and Independent Greece, 1821–1852* (Cambridge: Cambridge University Press, 1969)

Koubourlis, Ioannis, *La Formation de l'histoire nationale grecque. L'Apport de Spyridon Zambélios (1815–1881)* (Athens: Institut de Recherches Néo-Helléniques, 2005)

Petropulos, John, *Politics and Statecraft in the Kingdom of Greece, 1833–1843* (Princeton, NJ: Princeton University Press, 1968)

Politis, Alexis, *Ρομαντικά χρόνια. Ιδεολογίες και νοοτροπίες στην Ελλάδα του 1830–1880* [*Romantic Years: Ideologies and Mentalities in Greece, 1830–1880*] (Athens: Mnimon, 1993)

Skopetea, Elli, *Το «πρότυπο βασίλειο» και η Μεγάλη Ιδέα. Όψεις του εθνικού προβλήματος στην Ελλάδα (1830–1880)* [*The 'Model Kingdom' and the Grand Idea: Aspects of the National Problem in Greece (1830–1880)*] (Athens: Polytypo, 1988)

5. IDEALS AND SORROWS OF YOUTH

The Politics of Expansion

Carabott, Philip (ed.), *Greek Society in the Making, 1863–1913: Realities, Symbols and Visions* (Aldershot: Ashgate, 1997)

Christmas, Walter, *King George of Greece* (New York: McBride, Nast, 1914)

Finlay, George, *A History of Greece: From its Conquest by the Romans to the Present Time*, vol. 7 (Oxford: Clarendon Press, 1877)

Jenkins, Romilly, *The Dilessi Murders* (London: Longmans, Green, 1961)

Prevelakis, Eleutherios, *British Policy towards the Change of Dynasty in Greece* (Athens: n.p., 1953)

Skopetea, Elli, *Το «πρότυπο βασίλειο» και η Μεγάλη Ιδέα. Όψεις του εθνικού προβλήματος στην Ελλάδα (1830–1880)* [*The 'Model Kingdom' and the Grand Idea: Aspects of the National Problem in Greece (1830–1880)*] (Athens: Polytypo, 1988)

Vovchenko, Denis, *Containing Balkan Nationalism: Imperial Russia and Ottoman Christians, 1856–1914* (Oxford: Oxford University Press, 2016)

The Nation and its Limits

Augustinos, Gerasimos, *The Greeks of Asia Minor* (Kent, OH: Kent State University Press, 1992)

Clogg, Richard (ed.), *The Greek Diaspora in the Twentieth Century* (Basingstoke: Macmillan, 1999)

Detorakis, Theocharis, *History of Crete*, trans. John Davis (Heraklion, Crete: n.p., 1994)

Doumanis, Nicholas, *Before the Nation: Muslim–Christian Coexistence and its Destruction in Late-Ottoman Anatolia* (Oxford: Oxford University Press, 2012)

Gondicas, Dimitri and Charles Issawi (eds), *Ottoman Greeks in the Age of Nationalism* (Princeton, NJ: Darwin Press, 1999)

Hill, George, *A History of Cyprus*, vol. 4 (Cambridge: Cambridge University Press, 1952)

Mazower, Mark, *Salonica: City of Ghosts* (London: HarperCollins, 2004)

Şenışık, Pinar, *The Transformation of Ottoman Crete: Revolts, Politics and Identity in the Late Nineteenth Century* (London: I. B. Tauris, 2011)

Vassiadis, George, *The* Syllogos *Movement of Constantinople and Ottoman Greek Education, 1861–1923* (Athens: Centre for Asia Minor Studies, 2007)

Triumph and Disaster

Ashmead Bartlett, E., *The Battlefields of Thessaly* (London: John Murray, 1897)

Kitroeff, Alexander, *Wrestling with the Ancients: Modern Greek Identity and the Olympics* (New York: Greekworks.com, 2004)

Levandis, John, *The Greek Foreign Debt and the Great Powers, 1821–1898* (New York: Columbia University Press, 1944)

Llewellyn Smith, Michael, *Olympics in Athens 1896* (London: Profile, 2004)

6. MILITARY SERVICE
Doldrums at Home

Augustinos, Gerasimos, *Consciousness and History: Nationalist Critics of Greek Society, 1897–1914* (New York: Columbia University Press/*East European Quarterly*, 1977)

Gauntlett, Stathis, *Rebetika, carmina Graeciae recentioris* [in English] (Athens: Denise Harvey, 1985)

Action Abroad

Dakin, Douglas, *The Greek Struggle in Macedonia, 1897–1913* (Thessaloniki: Institute of Balkan Studies, 1966)

Karakasidou, Anastasia, *Fields of Wheat, Hills of Blood: Passages to Nationhood in Greek Macedonia, 1870–1990* (Chicago, IL: University of Chicago Press, 1997)

Mandamadiotou, Maria, *The Greek Orthodox Community of Mytilene: Between the Ottoman Empire and the Greek State, 1876–1912* (Bern: Peter Lang, 2013)

Mazower, Mark, *Salonica: City of Ghosts* (London: HarperCollins, 2004)

Veremis, Thanos, 'The Hellenic Kingdom and the Ottoman Greeks: The experiment of the "Society of Constantinople"', in Dimitri Gondicas and Charles Issawi (eds), *Ottoman Greeks in the Age of Nationalism* (Princeton, NJ: Darwin Press, 1999), 181–91

Yosmaoğlu, İpek, *Blood Ties: Religion, Violence, and the Politics of Nationhood in Ottoman Macedonia, 1878–1908* (Ithaca, NY: Cornell University Press, 2014)

Called to Arms

Kitromilides, Paschalis (ed.), *Eleftherios Venizelos: The Trials of Statesmanship* (Edinburgh: Edinburgh University Press, 2006)

Papacosma, S. Victor, *The Military in Greek Politics: The 1909 Coup d'État* (Kent, OH: Kent State University Press, 1977)

Into Battle

Hall, Richard, *The Balkan Wars, 1912–1913: Prelude to the First World War* (London: Routledge, 2002)

McMeekin, Sean, *The Ottoman Endgame: War, Revolution and the Making of the Modern Middle East, 1908–1923* (London: Allen Lane, 2015)

7. THE SELF DIVIDED

Housepian Dobkin, Marjorie, *Smyrna 1922: The Destruction of a City* (London: Faber, 1972)

Leon, George, *Greece and the Great Powers, 1914–1917* (Thessaloniki: Institute for Balkan Studies, 1974)

Llewellyn Smith, Michael, *Ionian Vision: Greece in Asia Minor, 1919–1922* (London: Hurst, 1998; first published 1973)

Mackenzie, Compton, *Greek Memories* (London: Biteback, 2011; first published 1932)

Mango, Andrew, *Atatürk* (London: John Murray, 1999)

Mavrogordatos, Giorgos, *1915. Ο Εθνικός Διχασμός* [*1915: The National Schism*] (Athens: Patakis, 2015)

Milton, Giles, *Paradise Lost: Smyrna 1922. The Destruction of Islam's City of Tolerance* (London: Sceptre, 2008)

Pentzopoulos, Dimitri, *The Balkan Exchange of Minorities and its Impact on Greece* (Paris and The Hague: Mouton, 1962; reprinted with a new preface by Michael Llewellyn Smith, London: Hurst, 2002)

Petsalis-Diomidis, N., *Greece at the Paris Peace Conference (1919)* (Thessaloniki: Institute for Balkan Studies, 1978)

Toynbee, Arnold, *The Western Question in Greece and Turkey: A Study in the Contact of Civilisations* (London: Constable, 1922)

8. STARTING OVER
Recovery and Renewal

Clark, Bruce, *Twice a Stranger: Greece, Turkey and the Minorities they Expelled* (London: Granta, 2006)

Hirschon, Renée (ed.), *Crossing the Aegean: An Appraisal of the 1923 Compulsory Population Exchange between Greece and Turkey* (Oxford: Berghahn, 2003)

Lytra, Vally (ed.), *When Greeks and Turks Meet: Interdisciplinary Perspectives on the Relationship since 1923* (Farnham: Ashgate, 2014)

Pentzopoulos, Dimitri, *The Balkan Exchange of Minorities and its Impact on Greece* (Paris and The Hague: Mouton, 1962; reprinted with a new preface by Michael Llewellyn Smith, London: Hurst, 2002)

Tziovas, Dimitris (ed.), *Greek Modernism and Beyond* (Lanham, MD, and New York: Rowman & Littlefield, 1997)

Politicians and Generals

Mavrogordatos, George, *Stillborn Republic: Social Coalitions and Party Strategies in Greece, 1922–1936* (Berkeley, CA: University of California Press, 1983)

Mazower, Mark, *Greece and the Inter-War Economic Crisis* (Oxford: Clarendon Press, 1991)

The Fault Line Shifts – Ultimatum

Butterworth, Katharine and Sara Schneider (eds), *Rebetika: Songs from the Old Greek Underworld* (Athens: Aiora, 2014; first published 1974)

Gauntlett, Stathis, *Rebetika, carmina Graeciae recentioris* [in English] (Athens: Denise Harvey, 1985)

Higham, Robin and Thanos Veremis (eds), *Aspects of Greece, 1936–40: The Metaxas Dictatorship* (Athens: Hellenic Foundation for Defense and Foreign Policy, 1993)

Joachim, Joachim, *Ioannis Metaxas: The Formative Years, 1871–1922* (Mannheim: Bibliopolis, 2000)

Kenna, Margaret, *The Social Organisation of Exile: Greek Political Detainees in the 1930s* (Amsterdam: Harwood, 2001)

Kofas, Jon, *Authoritarianism in Greece: The Metaxas Regime* (East European Monographs, Boulder, CO, distributed by Columbia University Press, New York, 1983)

Koliopoulos, John, *Greece and the British Connection, 1935–1941* (Oxford: Clarendon Press, 1977)

Pelt, Mogens, *Tobacco, Arms and Politics: Greece and Germany from World Crisis to World War 1929–41* (Copenhagen: Museum Tusculanum Press, 1998)

Petrakis, Marina, *The Metaxas Myth: Dictatorship and Propaganda in Greece* (London: I. B. Tauris, 2006)

Petropoulos, Elias, *Songs of the Greek Underworld: The Rebetika Tradition*, trans. Ed Emery (London: Saqi, 2000)

Vatikiotis, P. J., *Popular Autocracy in Greece, 1936–41* (London: Frank Cass, 1998)

9. MELTDOWN

Alexander, G. M., *The Prelude to the Truman Doctrine: British Policy in Greece, 1944–1947* (Oxford: Clarendon Press, 1982)

Baerentzen, Lars, 'The demonstration in Syntagma Square on Sunday the 3rd of December, 1944', *Scandinavian Studies in Modern Greek* 2 (1978), 3–52

Baerentzen, Lars, John Iatrides and Ole Smith (eds), *Studies in the History of the Greek Civil War, 1945–1949* (Copenhagen: Museum Tusculanum Press, 1987)

Beevor, Antony, *Crete: The Battle and the Resistance* (London: John Murray, 1991; Penguin, 1992)

Brewer, David, *Greece: The Decade of War. Occupation, Resistance and Civil War* (London: I. B. Tauris, 2016)

Carabott, Philip and Thanasis Sfikas (eds), *The Greek Civil War: Essays on a Conflict of Exceptionalism and Silences* (Aldershot: Ashgate, 2004)

Clogg, Richard (ed.), *Greece 1940–1949: Occupation, Resistance, Civil War. A Documentary History* (Basingstoke: Palgrave Macmillan, 2002)

Close, David, *The Origins of the Greek Civil War* (London: Longman, 1995)

Close, David (ed.), *The Greek Civil War, 1943–1950: Studies of Polarization* (London: Routledge, 1993)

Danforth, Loring and Riki van Boeschoten, *Children of the Greek Civil War: Refugees and the Politics of Memory* (Chicago, IL: University of Chicago Press, 2012)

Delis, Panagiotis, 'The British intervention in Greece: The battle of Athens, December 1944', *Journal of Modern Greek Studies* 35 (2017), 211–37

Gerolymatos, André, *An International Civil War: Greece, 1943–1949* (New Haven, CT, and London: Yale University Press, 2016)

Hart, Janet, *New Voices in the Nation: Women and the Greek Resistance, 1941–1964* (Ithaca, NY: Cornell University Press, 1996)

Hatzipateras, Kostas and Maria Fafaliou (eds), Μαρτυρίες 41–44. Η Αθήνα της Κατοχής [*Testimonies 1941–1944: Athens under Occupation*], 2 vols (Athens: Kedros, 2002)

Higham, Robin, *Diary of a Disaster: British Aid to Greece, 1940–1941* (Lexington, KY: University Press of Kentucky, 1986)

Hionidou, Violetta, *Famine and Death in Occupied Greece, 1941–1944* (Cambridge: Cambridge University Press, 2006)

Hondros, John, *Occupation and Resistance: The Greek Agony, 1941–44* (New York: Pella, 1983)

Iatrides, John, *Revolt in Athens: The Greek Communist 'Second Round', 1944–1945* (Princeton, NJ: Princeton University Press, 1972)

Iatrides, John (ed.), *Greece in the 1940s: A Nation in Crisis* (Hanover, NH, and London: University Press of New England, 1981)

Iatrides, John and Linda Wrigley (eds), *Greece at the Crossroads: The Civil War and its Legacy* (Philadelphia, PA: Pennsylvania University Press, 1995)

Kalyvas, Stathis, 'Red Terror: Leftist violence during the Occupation', in Mark Mazower (ed.), *After the War was Over: Reconstructing the Family, Nation, and State in Greece, 1943–1960* (Princeton, NJ: Princeton University Press, 2000), 142–83

Kalyvas, Stathis, *The Logic of Violence in Civil War* (Cambridge: Cambridge University Press, 2006)

Koliopoulos, John, *Greece and the British Connection, 1935–1941* (Oxford: Clarendon Press, 1977)

Kousoulas, D. George, *Revolution and Defeat: The Story of the Greek Communist Party* (Oxford: Oxford University Press, 1965)

Mazower, Mark, *Inside Hitler's Greece: The Experience of Occupation, 1941–44* (New Haven, CT, and London: Yale University Press, 1993)

Papastratis, Procopis, *British Policy towards Greece during the Second World War, 1941–1944* (Cambridge: Cambridge University Press, 1984)

Plakoudas, Spyridon, *The Greek Civil War: Strategy, Counterinsurgency and the Monarchy* (London: I. B. Tauris, 2017)

Richter, Heinz, *British Intervention in Greece: From Varkiza to Civil War*, trans. Marion Sarafis (London: Merlin, 1985)

Vlavianos, Haris, *Greece, 1941–49: From Resistance to Civil War* (Basingstoke: Macmillan, 1992)

Woodhouse, C. M., *The Apple of Discord: A Survey of Recent Greek Politics in their International Setting* (London: Hutchinson, 1948)

Woodhouse, C. M., *The Struggle for Greece, 1941–1949* (London: Hart-Davis, 1976; reprinted with an introduction by Richard Clogg: Hurst, 2002)

10. UNCLE SAM'S PROTÉGÉ

Close, David, *Greece since 1945: Politics, Economy and Society* (London: Longman, 2002)

McNeill, William, *The Metamorphosis of Greece since World War II* (Oxford: Blackwell, 1978)

Mazower, Mark (ed.), *After the War was Over: Reconstructing the Family, Nation, and State in Greece, 1943–1960* (Princeton, NJ: Princeton University Press, 2000)

Miller, James Edward, *The United States and the Making of Modern Greece: History and Power, 1950–1974* (Chapel Hill, NC: University of North Carolina Press, 2009)

The Nation Rediscovered

French, David, *Fighting EOKA: The British Counter-Insurgency Campaign on Cyprus, 1955–1959* (Oxford: Oxford University Press, 2015)

Hatzivassiliou, Evanthis, *Britain and the International Status of Cyprus, 1955–59* (Minneapolis, MN: University of Minnesota, *Modern Greek Studies Yearbook* supplement, 1997)

Holland, Robert, *Britain and the Revolt in Cyprus, 1954–1959* (Oxford: Clarendon Press, 1998)

Mayes, Stanley, *Makarios: A Biography* (London: Macmillan, 1981)

Stefanidis, Ioannis, *Stirring the Greek Nation: Political Culture, Irredentism and Anti-Americanism in Post-War Greece, 1945–1967* (Aldershot: Ashgate, 2007)

Vryonis, Speros, *The Mechanism of Catastrophe: The Turkish Pogrom of September 6–7, 1955, and the Destruction of the Greek Community of Istanbul* (New York: Greekworks.com, 2005)

Dancing with Zorba

Hadjikyriacou, Achilleas, *Masculinity and Gender in Greek Cinema, 1949–1967* (London: Bloomsbury Academic, 2013)

Karalis, Vrasidas, *A History of Greek Cinema* (New York and London: Continuum, 2012)

Papanikolaou, Dimitris, *Singing Poets: Literature and Popular Music in France and Greece* (London: Legenda, 2007)

Stassinopoulou, Maria, 'Reality bites: A feature film history of Greece, 1950–1963' (Vienna: University of Vienna, Habilitationsschrift, 2000)

Political Car Crash – Strapped in Plaster

Draenos, Stan, *Andreas Papandreou: The Making of a Greek Democrat and Political Maverick* (London: I. B. Tauris, 2012)

Featherstone, Kevin and Dimitrios Katsoudas (eds), *Political Change in Greece: Before and After the Colonels* (London: Croom Helm, 1987)

Ker-Lindsay, James, *The Cyprus Problem: What Everyone Needs to Know* (Oxford: Oxford University Press, 2011)

Kornetis, Kostis, *Children of the Dictatorship: Student Resistance, Cultural Politics, and the 'Long 1960s' in Greece* (New York and Oxford: Berghahn, 2013)

van Dyck, Karen, *Kassandra and the Censors: Greek Poetry since 1967* (Ithaca, NY: Cornell University Press, 1998)

Woodhouse, C. M., *Karamanlis: The Restorer of Greek Democracy* (Oxford: Clarendon Press, 1982)

Woodhouse, C. M., *The Rise and Fall of the Greek Colonels* (London: Granada, 1985)

11. COMING OF AGE IN EUROPE

Clogg, Richard, *Parties and Elections in Greece: The Search for Legitimacy* (London: Hurst, 1987)

Clogg, Richard (ed.), *Greece, 1981–89: The Populist Decade* (Basingstoke: Macmillan, 1993)

Close, David, *Greece since 1945: Politics, Economy and Society* (London: Longman, 2002)

Danforth, Loring, *The Macedonian Conflict: Ethnic Nationalism in a Transnational World* (Princeton, NJ: Princeton University Press, 1997)

Featherstone, Kevin and Dimitris Papadimitriou, *Prime Ministers in Greece: The Paradox of Power* (Oxford: Oxford University Press, 2015)

Giannaras, Chrestos, *Orthodoxy and the West: Hellenic Self-Identity in the Modern Age*, trans. P. Chamberas and N. Russell (Brookline, MA: Holy Cross Orthodox Press, 2006)

Kassimeris, George, *Europe's Last Red Terrorists: The Revolutionary Organization 17 November* (London: Hurst, 2001)

Kassimeris, George, *Inside Greek Terrorism* (London: Hurst, 2013)

Makrides, Vasilios, 'Byzantium in contemporary Greece: The Neo-Orthodox current of ideas', in David Ricks and Paul Magdalino (eds), *Byzantium and the Modern Greek Identity* (Aldershot: Ashgate, 1998), 141–53

Mavrogordatos, George, *Rise of the Green Sun: The Greek Election of 1981* (London: King's College London, Centre of Contemporary Greek Studies, 1983)

Roudometof, Victor and Vasilios Makrides (eds), *Orthodox Christianity in 21st Century Greece* (Farnham: Ashgate, 2010)

Spourdalakis, Michalis, *The Rise of the Greek Socialist Party* (London: Routledge, 1988)

Varnava, Andrekos and Hubert Faustmann (eds), *Reunifying Cyprus: The Annan Plan and Beyond* (London: I. B. Tauris, 2009)

Veremis, Thanos, *Greeks and Turks in War and Peace* (Athens: Athens News, 2007)

Woodhouse, C. M., *Karamanlis: The Restorer of Greek Democracy* (Oxford: Clarendon Press, 1982)

12. MIDLIFE CRISIS?

The Politics of 'Crisis'

Economides, Spyros (ed.), *Greece: Modernisation and Europe 20 Years On* (London: London School of Economics, Hellenic Observatory, 2017)

Karyotis, Georgios and Roman Gerodimos, *The Politics of Extreme Austerity: Greece in the Eurozone Crisis* (Basingstoke: Palgrave Macmillan, 2015)

Mitsopoulos, Michael and Theodore Pelagidis, *Understanding the Crisis in Greece: From Boom to Bust* (Basingstoke: Palgrave Macmillan, 2012)

Ovenden, Kevin, *Syriza: Inside the Labyrinth* (London: Pluto, 2015)

Papaconstantinou, George, *Game Over: The Inside Story of the Greek Crisis* (English edition privately published, 2016)

Triandafyllidou, Anna, Ruby Gropas and Hara Kouki (eds), *The Greek Crisis and European Modernity* (Basingstoke: Palgrave Macmillan, 2013)

Tsoukalis, Loukas, *In Defence of Europe: Can the European Project be Saved?* (Oxford: Oxford University Press, 2016)

Tzogopoulos, George, *The Greek Crisis in the Media: Stereotyping in the International Press* (Farnham: Ashgate, 2013)

Varoufakis, Yanis, *Adults in the Room: My Battle with Europe's Deep Establishment* (London: Bodley Head, 2017)

Vasilopoulou, Sofia and Daphne Halikiopoulou, *The Golden Dawn's 'National Solution': Explaining the Rise of the Far Right in Greece* (New York: Palgrave Macmillan, 2015)

Verney, Susannah, 'Waking the "sleeping giant" or expressing domestic dissent? Mainstreaming Euroscepticism in crisis-stricken Greece', *International Political Science Review* 36/3 (2015), 279–95

Living with 'Crisis'

Chiotis, Theodoros (ed. and trans.), *Futures: Poetry of the Greek Crisis* (London: Penned in the Margins, 2016)

Douzinas, Costas, *Philosophy and Resistance in the Crisis: Greece and the Future of Europe* (Cambridge: Polity, 2013)

Hamilakis, Yannis, 'Some debts can never be repaid: The archaeo-politics of the crisis', *Journal of Modern Greek Studies* 34 (2016), 227–64

Hanink, Johanna, *The Classical Debt: Greek Antiquity in an Era of Austerity* (Cambridge, MA: Harvard University Press, 2017)

Knight, Daniel, *History, Time and Economic Crisis in Central Greece* (Basingstoke: Palgrave Macmillan, 2015)

Lemos, Natasha and Eleni Yannakakis (eds), *Critical Times, Critical Thoughts: Contemporary Greek Writers Discuss Facts and Fiction* (Newcastle upon Tyne: Cambridge Scholars, 2015)

Pine, Richard, *Greece through Irish Eyes* (Dublin: Liffey Press, 2015)

Tziovas, Dimitris, 'From junta to crisis: Modernization, consumerism and cultural dualisms in Greece', *Byzantine and Modern Greek Studies* 41 (2017), 278–99

Tziovas, Dimitris (ed.), *Greece in Crisis: The Cultural Politics of Austerity* (London: I. B. Tauris, 2017)

van Dyck, Karen (ed.), *Austerity Measures: The New Greek Poetry* (London: Penguin, 2016)

Acknowledgements

Many people have helped to bring this book to its final form. Institutions have played no small part as well. Heartfelt thanks are due to all of them. Among the latter the largest share goes to King's College London, my institutional base for almost all of my professional career, and to colleagues in the former Department of Byzantine and Modern Greek Studies, in the thriving Department of Classics and the Centre for Hellenic Studies. A book such as this cannot be written without extensive use of libraries – the 'laboratories' of the Humanities, as many of us like to think of them. The Maughan Library at King's College London boasts the largest collection in Great Britain of Greek publications and of books and periodicals dedicated to Greece and the Greek world from the last two centuries and more, housed in the Burrows collection and the Foyle Special Collections Library. I cannot begin to estimate the hours and days spent working through these rich holdings, and I am particularly grateful to Teresa Elmes, Library Liaison Manager, and Katie Sambrook, Head of Special Collections, for all their personal support during the writing of this book, and indeed for far longer.

The other institution to which I owe a special debt is the British School at Athens, an institute for advanced research supported by the British Academy. I have been associated with the British School since I first went there as a postgraduate student in the 1970s. Its friendly hostel and the garden it shares with the American School of Classical Studies (truly an oasis in the heart of the modern city) provide a home from home for visiting scholars from all over the world. It was always a pleasure to go back there, while I was working on this book, to make use of the excellent and comfortable library (open all hours if you are fortunate enough to be resident) and to have a base for forays to other essential resources in Greece. Foremost among these is the Gennadius Library (the premier collection in the world for the subjects covered by this book, and just across the road from the British School). The libraries, resources and staff of several universities and research institutes in Greece and Cyprus have contributed too: among them the National and Kapodistrian University of Athens, the Aristotle University of Thessaloniki, the University of Crete, the National Hellenic Research Foundation (Athens) and the University of Cyprus.

When it comes to personal debts, those incurred in the research and preparation for this book are far too numerous to name, and often came about unwittingly. A chance remark in conversation or a student's question in a seminar can often have a resonance, long afterwards, that neither party might have recognized at the time. Not everyone who has contributed to the perspective on Greek history and culture developed in this book will necessarily find themselves in agreement with what I have written. On occasion, where the later chapters are concerned, I have had the privilege of speaking to participants in the story under 'Chatham House rules', which respect the privacy of such conversations.

The book in its final form, which I am proud to see published under the Penguin imprint, owes everything to the enthusiasm of my agent, Felicity Bryan, and of Simon Winder, commissioning editor at Allen Lane. Both seized upon my project at an early stage and have been unstinting, ever since, in their support, encouragement and advice. I have been particularly fortunate to have had eagle-eyed readers of earlier versions of my text: Simon Winder, himself a prolific writer of history books; Haris Vlavianos, who combines a day job as Professor of History at the American College of Greece with a public role as one of his country's foremost poets; and my son Mike, who (unlike me) studied History for his first degree. Richard Mason brought to the task of copy-editing the final typescript an exemplary blend of tact, sensitivity to the style and subject matter of the book, and attention to detail. My thanks go also to Cecilia Mackay for much-needed professional help with the images. Needless to say, all remaining flaws, as well as the selection and interpretation of facts and opinions, are my own responsibility.

Roderick Beaton
King's College London
August 2018

Index

Author's note: as promised on p. xvii, I have added to Greek proper names the acute accent that shows the position of the strees when pronounced. Where the names listed below are anglicized equivalents, no stress mark is shown.

ALLEN LANE
an imprint of
PENGUIN BOOKS

Also Published

Stuart Russell, *Human Compatible: AI and the Problem of Control*

Serhii Plokhy, *Forgotten Bastards of the Eastern Front: An Untold Story of World War II*

Dominic Sandbrook, *Who Dares Wins: Britain, 1979-1982*

Charles Moore, *Margaret Thatcher: The Authorized Biography, Volume Three: Herself Alone*

Thomas Penn, *The Brothers York: An English Tragedy*

David Abulafia, *The Boundless Sea: A Human History of the Oceans*

Anthony Aguirre, *Cosmological Koans: A Journey to the Heart of Physics*

Orlando Figes, *The Europeans: Three Lives and the Making of a Cosmopolitan Culture*

Naomi Klein, *On Fire: The Burning Case for a Green New Deal*

Anne Boyer, *The Undying: A Meditation on Modern Illness*

Benjamin Moser, *Sontag: Her Life*

Daniel Markovits, *The Meritocracy Trap*

Malcolm Gladwell, *Talking to Strangers: What We Should Know about the People We Don't Know*

Peter Hennessy, *Winds of Change: Britain in the Early Sixties*

John Sellars, *Lessons in Stoicism: What Ancient Philosophers Teach Us about How to Live*

Brendan Simms, *Hitler: Only the World Was Enough*

Hassan Damluji, *The Responsible Globalist: What Citizens of the World Can Learn from Nationalism*

Peter Gatrell, *The Unsettling of Europe: The Great Migration, 1945 to the Present*

Justin Marozzi, *Islamic Empires: Fifteen Cities that Define a Civilization*

Bruce Hood, *Possessed: Why We Want More Than We Need*

Susan Neiman, *Learning from the Germans: Confronting Race and the Memory of Evil*

Donald D. Hoffman, *The Case Against Reality: How Evolution Hid the Truth from Our Eyes*

Frank Close, *Trinity: The Treachery and Pursuit of the Most Dangerous Spy in History*

Richard M. Eaton, *India in the Persianate Age: 1000-1765*

Janet L. Nelson, *King and Emperor: A New Life of Charlemagne*

Philip Mansel, *King of the World: The Life of Louis XIV*

Donald Sassoon, *The Anxious Triumph: A Global History of Capitalism, 1860-1914*

Elliot Ackerman, *Places and Names: On War, Revolution and Returning*

Jonathan Aldred, *Licence to be Bad: How Economics Corrupted Us*

Johny Pitts, *Afropean: Notes from Black Europe*

Walt Odets, *Out of the Shadows: Reimagining Gay Men's Lives*

James Lovelock, *Novacene: The Coming Age of Hyperintelligence*

Mark B. Smith, *The Russia Anxiety: And How History Can Resolve It*

Stella Tillyard, *George IV: King in Waiting*

Jonathan Rée, *Witcraft: The Invention of Philosophy in English*

Jared Diamond, *Upheaval: How Nations Cope with Crisis and Change*

Emma Dabiri, *Don't Touch My Hair*

Srecko Horvat, *Poetry from the Future: Why a Global Liberation Movement Is Our Civilisation's Last Chance*

Paul Mason, *Clear Bright Future: A Radical Defence of the Human Being*

Remo H. Largo, *The Right Life: Human Individuality and its role in our development, health and happiness*

Joseph Stiglitz, *People, Power and Profits: Progressive Capitalism for an Age of Discontent*

David Brooks, *The Second Mountain*

Roberto Calasso, *The Unnamable Present*

Lee Smolin, *Einstein's Unfinished Revolution: The Search for What Lies Beyond the Quantum*

Clare Carlisle, *Philosopher of the Heart: The Restless Life of Søren Kierkegaard*

Nicci Gerrard, *What Dementia Teaches Us About Love*

Edward O. Wilson, *Genesis: On the Deep Origin of Societies*

John Barton, *A History of the Bible: The Book and its Faiths*

Carolyn Forché, *What You Have Heard is True: A Memoir of Witness and Resistance*

Elizabeth-Jane Burnett, *The Grassling*

Kate Brown, *Manual for Survival: A Chernobyl Guide to the Future*

Roderick Beaton, *Greece: Biography of a Modern Nation*

Matt Parker, *Humble Pi: A Comedy of Maths Errors*

Ruchir Sharma, *Democracy on the Road*

David Wallace-Wells, *The Uninhabitable Earth: A Story of the Future*

Randolph M. Nesse, *Good Reasons for Bad Feelings: Insights from the Frontier of Evolutionary Psychiatry*

Anand Giridharadas, *Winners Take All: The Elite Charade of Changing the World*

Richard Bassett, *Last Days in Old Europe: Triste '79, Vienna '85, Prague '89*

Paul Davies, *The Demon in the Machine: How Hidden Webs of Information Are Finally Solving the Mystery of Life*

Toby Green, *A Fistful of Shells: West Africa from the Rise of the Slave Trade to the Age of Revolution*

Paul Dolan, *Happy Ever After: Escaping the Myth of The Perfect Life*

Sunil Amrith, *Unruly Waters: How Mountain Rivers and Monsoons Have Shaped South Asia's History*

Christopher Harding, *Japan Story: In Search of a Nation, 1850 to the Present*

Timothy Day, *I Saw Eternity the Other Night: King's College, Cambridge, and an English Singing Style*

Richard Abels, *Aethelred the Unready: The Failed King*

Eric Kaufmann, *Whiteshift: Populism, Immigration and the Future of White Majorities*

Alan Greenspan and Adrian Wooldridge, *Capitalism in America: A History*

Philip Hensher, *The Penguin Book of the Contemporary British Short Story*

Paul Collier, *The Future of Capitalism: Facing the New Anxieties*

Andrew Roberts, *Churchill: Walking With Destiny*

Tim Flannery, *Europe: A Natural History*

T. M. Devine, *The Scottish Clearances: A History of the Dispossessed, 1600-1900*

Robert Plomin, *Blueprint: How DNA Makes Us Who We Are*

Michael Lewis, *The Fifth Risk: Undoing Democracy*

Diarmaid MacCulloch, *Thomas Cromwell: A Life*

Ramachandra Guha, *Gandhi: 1914-1948*

Slavoj Žižek, *Like a Thief in Broad Daylight: Power in the Era of Post-Humanity*

Neil MacGregor, *Living with the Gods: On Beliefs and Peoples*

Peter Biskind, *The Sky is Falling: How Vampires, Zombies, Androids and Superheroes Made America Great for Extremism*

Robert Skidelsky, *Money and Government: A Challenge to Mainstream Economics*

Helen Parr, *Our Boys: The Story of a Paratrooper*

David Gilmour, *The British in India: Three Centuries of Ambition and Experience*

Jonathan Haidt and Greg Lukianoff, *The Coddling of the American Mind: How Good Intentions and Bad Ideas are Setting up a Generation for Failure*

Ian Kershaw, *Roller-Coaster: Europe, 1950-2017*

Adam Tooze, *Crashed: How a Decade of Financial Crises Changed the World*

Edmund King, *Henry I: The Father of His People*

Lilia M. Schwarcz and Heloisa M. Starling, *Brazil: A Biography*

Jesse Norman, *Adam Smith: What He Thought, and Why it Matters*

Philip Augur, *The Bank that Lived a Little: Barclays in the Age of the Very Free Market*

Christopher Andrew, *The Secret World: A History of Intelligence*

David Edgerton, *The Rise and Fall of the British Nation: A Twentieth-Century History*

Julian Jackson, *A Certain Idea of France: The Life of Charles de Gaulle*

Owen Hatherley, *Trans-Europe Express*

Richard Wilkinson and Kate Pickett, *The Inner Level: How More Equal Societies Reduce Stress, Restore Sanity and Improve Everyone's Wellbeing*

Paul Kildea, *Chopin's Piano: A Journey Through Romanticism*

Seymour M. Hersh, *Reporter: A Memoir*

Michael Pollan, *How to Change Your Mind: The New Science of Psychedelics*

David Christian, *Origin Story: A Big History of Everything*

Judea Pearl and Dana Mackenzie, *The Book of Why: The New Science of Cause and Effect*

David Graeber, *Bullshit Jobs: A Theory*

Serhii Plokhy, *Chernobyl: History of a Tragedy*

Michael McFaul, *From Cold War to Hot Peace: The Inside Story of Russia and America*

Paul Broks, *The Darker the Night, the Brighter the Stars: A Neuropsychologist's Odyssey*

Lawrence Wright, *God Save Texas: A Journey into the Future of America*

John Gray, *Seven Types of Atheism*

Carlo Rovelli, *The Order of Time*

Mariana Mazzucato, *The Value of Everything: Making and Taking in the Global Economy*

Richard Vinen, *The Long '68: Radical Protest and Its Enemies*

Kishore Mahbubani, *Has the West Lost It?: A Provocation*

John Lewis Gaddis, *On Grand Strategy*

Richard Overy, *The Birth of the RAF, 1918: The World's First Air Force*

Francis Pryor, *Paths to the Past: Encounters with Britain's Hidden Landscapes*

Helen Castor, *Elizabeth I: A Study in Insecurity*

Ken Robinson and Lou Aronica, *You, Your Child and School*

Leonard Mlodinow, *Elastic: Flexible Thinking in a Constantly Changing World*

Nick Chater, *The Mind is Flat: The Illusion of Mental Depth and The Improvised Mind*

Michio Kaku, *The Future of Humanity: Terraforming Mars, Interstellar Travel, Immortality, and Our Destiny Beyond*

Thomas Asbridge, *Richard I: The Crusader King*

Richard Sennett, *Building and Dwelling: Ethics for the City*

Nassim Nicholas Taleb, *Skin in the Game: Hidden Asymmetries in Daily Life*

Steven Pinker, *Enlightenment Now: The Case for Reason, Science, Humanism and Progress*

Steve Coll, *Directorate S: The C.I.A. and America's Secret Wars in Afghanistan, 2001 - 2006*